Decolonizing the Landscape

SERIES EDITORS

Gordon Collier   Bénédicte Ledent   Geoffrey Davis
(Giessen)   (Liège)   (Aachen)

CO-FOUNDING EDITOR
†Hena Maes–Jelinek

Decolonizing the Landscape
Indigenous Cultures in Australia

Edited by
Beate Neumeier and Kay Schaffer

Amsterdam - New York, NY 2014

Cover Image
Lin Onus, *Arafura Swamp* (1990).
© Lin Onus Estate/Licensed by Viscopy, 2013.

The paper on which this book is printed meets the requirements of "ISO 9706:1994, Information and documentation - Paper for documents - Requirements for permanence".

ISBN: 978-90-420-3794-6
E-Book ISBN: 978-94-012-1042-3
© Editions Rodopi B.V., Amsterdam – New York, NY 2014
Printed in The Netherlands

Table of Contents

List of Illustrations — vii

Introduction
BEATE NEUMEIER AND KAY SCHAFFER — ix

SHARING ACROSS BOUNDARIES

From Drill to Dance
KIM SCOTT — 3

The Great Tradition: Translating Durrudiya's Songs
STEPHEN MUECKE — 23

Aboriginal Families, Knowledge, and the Archives: A Case Study
ANNA HAEBICH — 37

Decolonizing Methodology in an Arnhem Land Garden
MICHAEL CHRISTIE — 57

The 'Cultural Design' of Western Desert Art
ELEONORE WILDBURGER — 71

ETHICAL AND OTHER ENCOUNTERS

Modernism, Antipòdernism, and Australian Aboriginality
IAN HENDERSON — 89

Material Resonance: Knowing Before Meaning
BILL ASHCROFT — 107

Waiting at the Border: White Filmmaking on the Ground of Aboriginal Sovereignty
LISA SLATER — 129

Wounded Spaces/Geographies of Connectivity:
Stephen Muecke's *No Road (bitumen all the way)*,
Margaret Somerville's *Body/Landscape Journals*,
and Katrina Schlunke's *Bluff Rock: Autobiography of a Massacre*
KAY SCHAFFER   149

Recovering the Past: Entangled Histories
in Kim Scott's *That Deadman Dance*
SUE KOSSEW   169

READING TRANSFORMATIONS

The Geopolitical Underground: Alexis
Wright's *Carpentaria*, Mining, and the Sacred
PHILIP MEAD   185

Identity and the Re-Assertion of Aboriginal Knowledge
in Sam Watson's *The Kadaitcha Sung*
HEINZ ANTOR   207

Gallows Humour and Stereotyping in the Nyungar Writer
Alf Taylor's Short Fiction: A White Cross-Racial Reading
ANNE BREWSTER   233

"And in my dreaming I can let go of the spirits
of the past": Gothicizing the Common Law
in Richard Frankland's *No Way to Forget*
KATRIN ALTHANS   255

Performative Lives – Transformative Practices: Wesley Enoch
and Deborah Mailman, *The 7 Stages of Grieving*, and Richard
Frankland, *Conversations with the Dead*
BEATE NEUMEIER   275

Notes on Contributors   293

List of Illustrations

FIGURE 1:
Galliput (Gyallipert), Map of Native Encampment
(drawing, quill and ink, February 1833). 5

FIGURE 2:
Helen Kunoth Ngwarai, *Bush Honey Dreaming* (1998;
synthetic polymer paint on canvas 80x62 cm); private
collection. © The artist. 77

FIGURE 3:
Blueprint (modified) courtesy of Christine Nicholls. 78

FIGURE 4:
The hermeneutic spiral. (Bill Ashcroft.) 116

FIGURE 5.
Lin Onus, *Road to Redfern* (1988; synthetic polymer paint
on canvas, 60x120cm). © Lin Onus Estate, licensed by
Viscopy 2013. 122

Introduction

THIS VOLUME GREW OUT OF A JOINT INTEREST in Australian studies by colleagues in the English Department at the University of Cologne. It profited from the implementation of an Australian Studies programme and the establishment of the Dr R. Marika Guest Chair for Australian Studies in 2009, funded by the DAAD and the University of Cologne and supported by the Australian Embassy. These initiatives provided the basis for a series of cross-disciplinary research and teaching collaborations, conferences and workshops in literary, linguistic, and cultural studies among scholars in the English department at Cologne and Australian partner institutions. The essays assembled in this volume are based on papers given in several lecture series and as part of the international conference on "Indigenous Knowledge: Issues of Cultural Transfer and Transformation" (July 2011) organized by the editors.

One of the central concerns recurring throughout this collection is the question of how to probe the limitations of Anglo-European knowledge-systems so as to lay the groundwork for entering into a true dialogue with Indigenous writers and critics. The multitude of creative texts, performance practices, and artworks produced by Indigenous writers and artists calls upon Anglo-European academic readers, viewers, and critics to acknowledge the impact of Australia's colonial past as a violent history of oppression, to engage with alternative ways of knowing, and to adapt counter-strategies of resistance which do not cultivate the comforting position of redemptive empathy and identification, but which, rather, enforce a process of self-questioning and un-settlement, calling for a renewed ethical response. This process has its pitfalls and works differently for different readers, viewers, and critics, given their own different embeddedness in histories of cultural and national trauma and the complex processes of healing. The essays assembled here trace the faultlines between and connections across those histories and geographies while respecting their differences.

The contributions to this volume address a plethora of creative works by Indigenous writers, poets, playwrights, filmmakers, and painters, including Wesley Enoch, Richard Frankland, Lionel Fogarty, Romaine Moreton, Helen Kunoth Ngwarai, Lin Onus, Kim Scott, Alf Taylor, Sam Watson, and Alexis Wright, as well as Durrudiya song cycles and works by Western Desert artists. They also take up works by non-Indigenous writers and filmmakers who actively engage in questioning their complicity with the past in order to enter into an ethical dialogue with the Other. These include texts and films by Stephen Muecke, Katrina Schlunke, Margaret Somerville, and Jeni Thornley. The geographical reach, language groups, and kinship lines represented in the essays stretch from Broome in the far north to Albany in the southwest of Western Australia (home respectively to Ngumbal, Djaberdjaber, and Noongar peoples), through the Central Desert, along the Cape York Peninsula (Yolngu lands), and Gulf of Carpentaria in Far North Queensland, to places of Koori displacement in central and southwest Victoria (the Gunditjmara), central and coastal New South Wales, and Tasmania (Palawa country). Such a diversity of kinship ties and language groups and the varied histories of Indigenous land ownership and dispossession across the vast continent foreground the necessity to recognize and respect the cultural differences, spatial diversity, and historical atemporalities of Indigenous lives, while inviting critics to communicate responsibly across those differences, as is emphasized in Kim Scott's opening essay. The complexity of these creative works by Indigenous writers and artists from different parts of Australia transcends categorical boundaries. It calls for a less compartmentalizing definition of literature and the arts and highlights the processual aspect of creative activity, which encompasses poetry, fiction, life writing, film, performance, music, dance, and painting. The readings follow the invitation of Indigenous writers and artists to enter into dialogue with their works, exploring strategies of resistance to appropriation, and acknowledging and respecting differences, a challenge taken up in diverse ways by Heinz Antor, Bill Ashcroft, Katrin Althans, Anne Brewster, Philip Mead, Beate Neumeier, and Eleonore Wildburger.

The need for a non-appropriating approach to enable such dialogue is expressed variously in the essays of this volume: Bill Ashcroft calls for openness and releasement; Lisa Slater uses the metaphor of waiting at the border; Kay Schaffer and Beate Neumeier study processes of unravelling and unsettlement, drawing on and questioning theoretical concepts across different disciplines, from philosophical, ethnographic, psychoanalytical, feminist, and postcolonial studies. In some of the essays, the necessary self-questioning of the non-Indigenous reader/author/critic is connected to a discussion of the possibilities and limitations of attempts at 'becoming other' in creative texts by non-Indigenous writers and artists, as referenced in essays by Kay Schaffer and Lisa Slater, while other essays, such as those of Anne Brewster and Beate Neumeier, focus on the white recipient's perspective on Indigenous works, and still others, like that of Sue Kossew, discuss recovery narratives by Indigenous writers, notably Kim Scott's *That Deadman Dance*, which attempt to escape the unremitting victim orientation that attends narratives of first encounter. These approaches are complemented by a number of essays that explore white misreadings of Indigenous cultures, including a critique of the organizational knowledge-frames of former and contemporary governmental endeavours, as discussed by Anna Haebich and Michael Christie, as well as the limitations of and blind spots in Anglo-European thought, literary understanding, and canonization, differently addressed by Ian Henderson and Stephen Muecke, and aesthetic categorization, a concern that motivates the essay by Eleonore Wildburger.

The essays assembled here share an interest in exploring questions of how to communicate across boundaries, how to engage in an ethical encounter, how to turn the inevitability of misreading into a productively transformative process. A relatively new insistence on relationality, connectivity, and processuality is evident in many of these essays as well as the creative work of Indigenous writers and artists challenging received categorizations and knowledge-frames. The grouping of the essays into three parts is thus not designed to draw lines between them or interfere with their dialogic interrelatedness but, rather, to highlight interrelated issues circulating among them.

Sharing Across Boundaries

In the opening essay, Kim Scott addresses the importance of "a controlled sharing" of Aboriginal tradition(s) across cultural boundaries. Scott describes a workshop in which he participated along with members of his extended kinship family in the Albany Noongar community in the southwest of Western Australia. He emphasizes the inseparability of language and creativity in the production of knowledge involving the reclaiming of ancestral creation stories. In contradistinction to limited Anglo-European notions of a "literary tradition," Scott redefines Indigenous literary activity, recognizing pre-colonial and ongoing Indigenous literary traditions, including different forms of creative inscription, of which the printed story on paper is only one component. Consequently, the creative process of the workshop involved different media and formats for a "controlled" publication of stories and material in print, on CD, and on DVD. Scott's essay foregrounds the possibility of "empowerment through [...] a controlled giving" in a cross-fertilizing process of individual and community-based literary and creative activities, including the transformation of a military drill into an Aboriginal dance, which Scott evokes so powerfully in his novel *That Deadman Dance*, and which is taken up subsequently in Sue Kossew's essay.

Stephen Muecke engages with the argument for a necessary redefinition of Anglo-European notions of Australian literature and literary traditions, arguing for an embracing of the great Indigenous traditions, in contradistinction to F.R. Leavis' project of defining "the great tradition" (1948). Drawing on an oral tradition of poetry (evident in the work of Paddy Roe in the north of Western Australia) as well as on "the grand tradition of ethnography," Muecke accentuates the importance of rethinking the notion of literature, not in terms of "a storehouse" based upon generic classifications and boundaries, but in terms of a continuous process of transformation and translation, emphasizing that "the poetics does not reside in the forms of language, in a unitary language that can be lost, but in the techniques and abilities to change things."

Anna Haebich engages with another form of knowledge: namely, the governmental archives which collect, organize, and manage information about Aboriginal families. These archives are of vital importance, as Aboriginal people are obliged to draw on them in formal procedures to prove identity, make Native Title claims, and seek compensation in Stolen Generations and Stolen Wages campaigns, as well as for family reunions. In her essay, Haebich unfolds a case study of the West Australian archive known as the DIA files (Department of Indigenous Affairs) and its impact on the report for the Royal Commission into Aboriginal Deaths in Custody and for the Bringing Them Home Report, stressing the necesssity of an "archival turn" -- from the archive as an instrument of "controlling and monitoring" Aboriginal lives to an instrument participating in a healing process, based on a sharing controlled by Aboriginal communities. Although these archival records have been despised as reductive reminders of the struggle against white authority in the colonial past, Haebich argues that "in the long term, repositories could be created and developed into Aboriginal-controlled 'healing centres' of history, culture, and language." Not only are these documents, oral history archives, genealogies, and histories of Indigenous child removal testament to the impact of governmental policies and practices on families, but they also reveal the knowledge, experience, and skills of those who had been stolen yet managed to survive and even return to their communities, as well as the work of community elders and traditional healers.

Michael Christie continues this exploration of knowledge practices, positing the usefulness of a "decolonizing methodology" for social-science researchers involved with Indigenous communities. His essay focuses on a project (proposed by an international group) to establish a Yolŋu community garden in East Arnhem in the Northern Territory. The project received support from the government and involved academic researchers like himself as government consultants as well as Yolŋu consultants as mediators in the negotiations with the community. Drawing on the work of the feminist moral philosopher Kathryn Pyne Addelson, Christie analyses the contrast between bureaucratic governmental assumptions based upon fixed technical categories and the Yolŋu community's social and moral approach to the garden in terms of a "network of accountabilities to people, places and stories" which necessitated a complex set of negotiations and understanding of Indigenous relations of care and responsibility. The essay studies the difficulties experienced by the consultants in acknowledging and negotiating these differences with the Yolŋu, tracing the project's eventual failure. Christie's experience underscores the need for a decolonization of Western methodology if government and academic mediators are ever able to negotiate projects successfully, taking account of Indigenous knowledges and relations to people, place, and story.

Eleonore Wildburger's essay takes up the issue of Western knowledge practices and sharing across boundaries by looking at Indigenous Western Desert Art. She calls for a re-thinking of Western art categories which are based upon a misleading separation between Indigenous cultural embeddedness and Western aesthetic criteria. Wildburger proposes a new art category that takes into account the diversity and specificity of non-Western art production. Through her analysis of the dot painting *Bush Honey Dreaming* (1998) by the Anmatyerre artist Helen Kunoth Ngwarai from the Aboriginal homeland of Utopia in the Northern Territory, Wildburger illustrates her alternative concept of the "cultural design" of the painting, which acknowledges the interrelationship between ceremonial designs and performances and Indigenous Law. Such an approach might be the starting point for viewing Indigenous Australian art through a non-appropriating lens, leading to a more nuanced understanding of Indigenous art and enhancing the dialogue across cultures.

Ethical and Other Encounters

The ethical implications of a Western framing and knowledge-systems are the central theme of a number of essays which explore Anglo-European constructions of Indigenous Otherness and attempt to transcend their limitations. Thus, Ian Henderson's exploration of modernism, antipòdernism, and Australian Aboriginality engages with the central, but seldom acknowledged, place of Australian Aboriginality in the work of Émile Durkheim, James Frazer, and Sigmund Freud, all of whom made extensive use of Francis Gillen's and Baldwin Spencer's work on the Arrernte desert people, notably *The Native Tribes of Central Australia* (1899). He argues that European constructions of Australian Aboriginality played a decisive role in the development of Anglo-European modernism in contrast to an alternative modernism in Australia, for which Henderson coins the deliberately unattractive label 'antipòdernism'. Antipòdernism refers to the entanglement of white settler visions of progress and degeneration that flourished in modern Australia. Drawing on the work of Miles Franklin, Katharine Susannah Prichard, D.H. Lawrence, A.D. Hope, and Christina Stead, Henderson not only shows how Australian Aboriginality, albeit erroneously figured, is there at the birth of the modern, but also explains the development of antipòdernism in Australia in terms of an anti-modernist sentiment which embraced technological progress but rejected modernist aesthetic experimentation, underpinned by materialist theories of the human subject.

While Ian Henderson's essay acknowledges the decisive impact of Aboriginality in the production and circulation of a specifically framed knowledge at a specific historical moment in Western history, it is the increasing dissatisfaction with and criticism of the limitations of Western knowledge-frames in contemporary creative practices and criticism that is the starting point for analysis in the essays by Bill Ashcroft, Kay Schaffer, Sue Kossew, and Lisa Slater.

Bill Ashcroft's contribution, "Material Resonance: Knowing before Meaning," is based upon the observation that there are ways of experiencing, responding to, and 'understanding' the world apart from structures of meaning: that is, apart from the kind of interpretation that can be fixed in language. He takes the fact that these moments can be glimpsed in art, music, and literature as an important discovery for the concept of presence. Ashcroft turns to the space between languages, to the non-semantic and pre-linguistic aspects of literature, or the beyond and before interpretation, to raise epistemological and ontological questions and engage in approaches to literature that enhance intersubjective contact and mutual change for readers and critics. Drawing on a multiplicity of theoretical and philosophical sources – from Bakhtin and T.S. Eliot to Gadamer, Benjamin and Gumbrecht, from Wittgenstein to Heidegger, and referencing a number of non-Indigenous and Indigenous literary texts – from the writing of David Malouf and Les Murray, to the poetry of Romaine Moreton and Lionel Fogarty, the novels of Kim Scott and Alexis Wright, and the art of Lin Onus – Ashcroft explores the resonance between the 'presence effects' and the 'meaning effects' in Aboriginal literature, poetry, and art, highlighting the ways in which an openness to Otherness can enhance true dialogue – beyond meaning and before interpretation – and enable non-Indigenous readers and viewers to apprehend the true wonder of Indigenous knowledge.

Ashcroft's call for an openness to Otherness as a necessary precondition for an ethical encounter, or what he calls a "true dialogue," resonates with what Lisa Slater describes as "waiting at the border" in her investigation into white documentary filmmaking. Taking up Irene Watson's contention that Aboriginal people have never relinquished their sovereignties, Slater argues that settler Australians need to test the (im)possibility of recognizing Aboriginal sovereignty and law in order to take responsibility for creating an anticolonial future. Her essay focuses on Jeni Thornley's film *Island Home Country* (2008), which contrasts the white documentary filmmaker's fond memories of growing up in Tasmania with the colonial violence of the past and continued non-recognition of Indigeneous sovereignty. This juxtaposition sets up the filmmaker's unsettling confrontation with her own "possessive whiteness" – her blindness to and complicity with neo-colonialism. Drawing on Chris Healey's injunction to remember our own forgetting, *Forgetting Aborigines* (2008), as well as on Rosalyn Diprose's concept of *Corporeal Generosity* (2002), Slater traces Thornley's ethical encounter with sovereign Palawa protocols in the course of her filmmaking as a model of how an unsettling experience of exposing oneself to questioning can occur, without taking shelter in sympathy, anxiety or resentment.

Kay Schaffer's essay "Wounded Spaces/Landscapes of Connectivity" turns to three texts written by white Australians that either attempt to explore

Indigenous relationships to land or address the legacies of white settler violence, seeking new ways of belonging to country and new connections with peoples and landscapes. The texts incude Steven Muecke's *No Road (bitumen all the way)* (1997), Margaret Somerville's *Body/Landscape Journals* (1999), and Katrina Schlunke's *Bluff Rock* (2004). Weaving together autobiographical material with postcolonial and postmodern theory, ethnography, spatial history, cultural geography, ecological ethics, and decolonizing critique, these texts and their narrators seek ways to speak across cultures – attempting to traverse a contested ground of knowledges, cosmologies, and modes of being – in order to forge an ethics of being together. In the first two narratives, the non-Indigenous authors look to Aboriginal cultures in order to find ways to be other than what one is. The third, Katrina Schlunke's *Bluff Rock*, returns 'home', to the place of her childhood, to mine the landscape for traces of its violent, and all but silenced, colonial past. Schaffer reads the text as a critical engagement with whiteness, a writing practice of decolonization that registers dis-ease in its complicity with the past and its dissatisfactions with the present. Schaffer argues that Katrina Schlunke's *Bluff Rock* establishes, however tentatively, the beginning of an ethical connection that opens up "new geographies of connectivity."

Sue Kossew addresses another attempt to recover the past in her exploration of the Noongar writer Kim Scott's *That Deadman Dance*. Kossew notes that many writers, both Indigenous and non-Indigenous, underscore the violence, trauma, and legacy of dispossession in their historical revisioning of the past and, in particular, of early contact encounters. Kim Scott, however, excavates a shared history of cultural contact, which, he insists, was mutually transformative. The utopian potential of his first encounter narrative allows for the possibility of an other history, a further unravelling of the past in which Indigenous agency, risk-taking, and trust in heritage prevail. Instead of highlighting the clashes of cultures (at first contact and in the present day) that have been the hallmark of much Australian writing, Scott's novel projects a more conciliatory version of encounter. Scott, like Lynette Russell in her study of Aboriginal whalers and sealers, *Roving Mariners* (2012), recovers the agency of Indigenous people in the early phases of the colonial process of cultural contact and exchange. However, the complexity of recovery is underlined by the way the novel both celebrates Indigenous survival and draws attention to the acts of betrayal that contributed to its destruction.

Reading Transformations

The third section of essays brings together a number of readings of creative works by Indigenous writers, playwrights, and filmmakers. All of the essays share the concerns discussed so far: namely, with ways of performing cultural translations across boundaries and the ethical and political issues involved. The authors inevitably question their own position in the reading and reception processes in relation to the demands of an "ethical encounter." The writers of papers in this section, like those of the middle section, not only trace the transformative power of the works they explore but also question their own implication in the transformative processes they engage in.

Philip Mead focuses on Alexis Wright's award-winning novel *Carpentaria*. Exploring its geopolitical underground, he traces the conjunction of Christian eschatology and the Aboriginal dreaming of the Gulf country as two cultural master-narratives, both informing volatile historical events and human lifeworlds, one of settlement, the other of displacement, as they combine and clash, generating the trajectory of the novel. Foregrounding this clash in terms of the incompatibility between the pragmatic interests of the mining industry and the sacredness of Aboriginal burial grounds, Mead reads this "hybridly Indigenous-postmodern" text as an engagement with a "radical critique of the culture of literature in Australia." His analysis thus underscores the interconnectedness of Wright's text with the debates addressed in the essays of the first section of this volume, as the novel highlights "urgent questions about the realm of literary knowledge, about the functions and institutions of critical discourse, about the relations of power between a metropolitan, global critical theory and a peripheral, postnational literary work."

Like Alexis Wright's *Carpentaria*, Sam Watson's novel *The Kadaitcha Sung* opens with contrasting cultural narratives, as the juxtaposition of "an Aboriginal creation story with the biblical book of Genesis and thus challenges the latter's authority and its claims as a white master-narrative" connected to colonial history. Heinz Antor turns to notions of identity and the reassertion of Aboriginal knowledge in Sam Watson's *The Kadaitcha Sung*, tracing the novel's ambivalences in connection with its "strategic essentialism," according to which an Indigenous, organic, socially responsible, and caring way of existence is challengingly pitted against white culture, which is characterized as mindlessly hedonistic, self-centred, and potentially destructive. While Antor's reading of Sam Watson's novel focuses on the text's strategies of resistance to an appropriating white readership in a re-assertion of Aboriginal knowledge and identity, Brewster's essay reflects on the effects of a specific positioning of the white reader in texts by Indigenous writers in the process of undoing racist stereotypes and challenging the legacies of colonization of land and peoples.

Anne Brewster focuses on Aboriginal humour, speculating on how this world-view draws her, as a white reader, into relations of proximity with Aboriginality and, as a result, bodily and cognitively estranges her from whiteness. Her analysis centres on a white cross-racial reading of what she calls "gallows humour and stereotyping" found in the Nyoongar writer Alf Taylor's short fiction. Drawing on concepts of the social nature of humour and on Freud's concept of the joke, Brewster reads gallows humour in Taylor's *Long Time Now* (2001) as a strategy of Indigenous resistance to the colonizing culture, which affirms intra-group bonding and at the same time works cross-racially to critique racialized violence. Focusing on Taylor's use of the stereotype of the drunken Aborigine, for example, Brewster demonstrates how Taylor links the role of white violence to the introduction of alcohol and the historical production of Indigenous degradation, thus liberating Indigenous subjectivity from stereotyping and making whiteness the object of satire. According to Brewster's reading, this strategy creates a renewed awareness of relationality as the white gaze doubles back on itself.

The final essays explore Richard Frankland's cinematographic and dramatic work on Aboriginal deaths in custody. Katrin Althans, like Anne Brewster, studies an Indigenous appropriation of a Western genre, in her case the literary gothic. She traces Frankland's crititique of Anglo-European constructs of law and literature in Australia. Althans argues that Franklin, in his film *No Way to Forget* and playscript *Conversations with the Dead*, reads against the grain of Australian law and literature, highlighting the destructive role of Australian common law in denying and silencing Aboriginal Law. In legal terms, the films enact a reversal of traditional gothic binaries of victim and villain, and depict an ongoing trauma which haunts in the shape of never-to-be-exorcized ghosts. Franklin's take on the gothic as a fictional form, here transformed into a gothic road movie, fades when compared to the gothic reality of Aboriginal life and death. By transforming the gothic mode into a subversive tool in the service of decolonization, Frankland challenges the master-discourses of both law and the gothic tradition, rewriting them into what Althans terms an "Aboriginal gothic," in which viewers cannot escape the gothic reality of Aboriginal deaths in custody.

Beate Neumeier's essay focuses on Richard Frankland's play *Conversations with the Dead* and on Wesley Enoch's and Deborah Mailman's play *The*

7 Stages of Grieving, in a continuation of the discussions about questions of an ethical encounter and a controlled sharing across cultural boundaries. The essay looks at life writing for the stage in terms of Indigenous performance practices that thematize the trauma of Australian (post)colonial history, as these performances engage in a transformative process which positions different audiences differently. The two plays explore questions about the potentialities and limitations of a relational ethics using different strategies of resistance to appropriating empathy and identification, enforcing an unsettling, discomforting recognition of the non-Indigenous spectator's own entanglement in an ongoing decolonizing endeavour as a necessary starting point for an ethical encounter.

As editors, we would like to thank all our contributors for engaging in the dialogue outlined here, which has produced so many resonances between different essays. The conference which served as the book's starting point as well as the time-consuming preparation of the manuscripts for print was managed by the Cologne team, Laura von Czarnowsky, Friederike Danebrock, Victoria Herche, Johanna Schorn, and Sarah Youssef. We would like to thank all of them for their extraordinary organizational skills, diligence, and untiring work before, during, and after the conference, as well as for their impressive skills in the editing process, corresponding with contributors, proof-reading, and checking sources. Our particular thanks go to Victoria Herche, who worked most closely with the guest chair, and whose skills as coordinator and mediator were invaluable for the finalization of the manuscript.

The collaborative efforts in establishing an Australian Studies programme in the University of Cologne English department, substantiated by the Australian Studies guest chair and accompanied by lecture series, workshops, and conferences in the area of Australian Studies, would not have been possible without the German Academic Exchange Service (DAAD), the University of Cologne, and the Australian Embassy in Berlin. We would like to thank all of these sponsors for their generous material and immaterial support.

Last but not least, we would like to express our gratitude to Cross/Cultures for accepting this volume. Our particular thanks go to Gordon Collier for his invaluable guidance and patience. Without his meticulous critical reading of the manuscripts the volume would not have materialized.

COLOGNE/ADELAIDE, SUMMER 2013

Sharing Across Boundaries

From Drill to Dance

Kim Scott

BEING DESCRIBED AS 'the first Indigenous writer to win the Miles Franklin Award twice', and 'the first (Australian) Indigenous writer to win a Commonwealth Writers' Prize' made me uncomfortable.

Now, such a slyly boastful beginning might seem a way for me to brag of my talent or luck, or even to claim special privileges and insights in the context of a discussion such as 'Indigenous Knowledge: Issues of Cultural Transfer and Transformation'.

Or you even might be thinking that I am about to discuss my identity-crisis, since I carry something of the "privilege of whiteness"[1] and am consequently often required to justify identifying myself as an Australian Aboriginal person or, more specifically, a Nyungar (the people and culture Indigenous to south-west Australia). In fact, a popular Australian newspaper columnist included me in his list of people, under the headline "Hip to be Black," who were supposedly exploiting their Aboriginal ancestry to enhance career opportunities.[2] But no, even this doesn't explain my discomfort when being praised.

My discomfort – in terms of literary achievement and the shared history of Australia – comes from sharing, at least in part, the 'postcolonial angst' of those who, displaced linguistically if not geographically, write in the colonizer's tongue, for an audience of which their own people are a tiny minority

---

[1] Aileen Moreton–Robinson, *Whiteness in Constructions of Australian Nationhood: Indigenes, Immigrants and Governmentality* (Canberra: Aboriginal Studies Press, 2004).

[2] Andrew Bolt, "It's So Hip to be Black," *Herald Sun* (25 April 2009), http://www.abc.net.au/mediawatch/transcripts/1109_heraldsun09.pdf (accessed 20 March 2012).

and thus for an audience that is effectively "the conquerors of one's people."[3] Eduardo Galeano's words are apt: "Let us mistrust applause. At times we are congratulated by those who consider us innocuous."[4]

It may be my own prickly defensiveness, but phrases like 'the first Indigenous writer to…' seem to imply a hierarchy, and a perhaps unconscious condescension, as if suggesting that one of 'them' has finally managed to reach 'our' level. Literary achievement is thus seen as a measure of assimilation, and of disconnection from an Indigenous heritage. In other words, of failure and defeat.

By way of contrast, in this essay I want to show classical Nyungar culture's propensity for literature and suggest ways that a Nyungar heritage might inform contemporary literary work. I will also explore the possibility of an Australian literature being 'grafted' onto the strong, nurturing roots of one part of Aboriginal Australia's storytelling traditions. I believe that the 'first' literary achievement referred to at the opening of this essay should really have happened long ago. That it did not is a function of Australia's 'shared history'.

For the purposes of my argument, I will use the definition of writing – that essential element of literature – espoused at the 1983 inaugural National Aboriginal Writers Conference held in my home city of Perth, Western Australia. The anthology derived from that conference includes letters, graphics, oral testimony, songs, political addresses, and extracts from plays and musicals, and its foreword states:

> In a broader sense, writing is definable as any sort of meaningful inscription, and in the case of Aboriginal Australia this would include sand paintings and drawings… body markings, paintings as well as engravings on bark or stone.[5]

In fact, I will also use examples from an oral tradition embedded in a culture which, although not privileging reading and writing, nevertheless created the propensity for great visual acuity and the meaningful interpretation of tiny

---

[3] Mudrooroo Narogin, *Writing from the Fringe: A Study of Modern Aboriginal Literature* (Melbourne: Hyland House, 1990): 148.

[4] Eduardo Galeano, "In Defence of the Word," in *The Graywolf Annual Five: Multicultural Literacy*, ed. Rick Simonson & Scott Walker (Saint Paul MN: Graywolf, 1988): 116.

[5] Jack Davis, Stephen Muecke, Mudrooroo Narogin & Adam Shoemaker, *Paperbark: A Collection of Black Australian Writings* (St Lucia: U of Queensland P, 1990): 3.

markings. I thus make the activity of 'tracking' a metaphor for reading, if not writing. A nineteenth-century account by Bishop Salvado of an encounter with a group of young Nyungar people reveals the aptness of the metaphor. The Bishop drew the letters of the Spanish alphabet in the sand, uttering each sound as he did so. His journal tells us that his new companions readily reproduced his markings and then, casually confirming their expertise, their mirror images.[6]

Another example of literacy 'readiness' is a pen-and-ink drawing produced in 1833 – the very first years of the colonization of this part of the world – by a Nyungar person, Galliput:

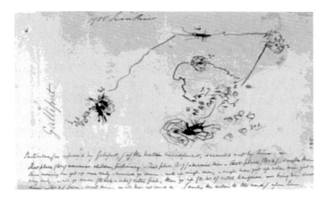

FIGURE 1: Galliput (Gyallipert), Map of Native Encampment (drawing, quill and ink, February 1833).[7]

---

[6] Rosendo Salvado, *The Salvado Memoirs: Historical Memoirs of Australia and Particularly of the Benedictine Mission of New Norcia and of the Habits and Customs of the Australian Natives*, tr. Edward James Stormon (*Memorias historicas sobre la Australia y particularmente acerca la mision Benedictina de Nueva Nursia y los usos y costumbres de los salvajes*, 1851; Perth: U of Western Australia P, 1977).

[7] Lois Tilbrook, *Nyungar Tradition: Glimpses of Aborigines of South-Western Australia 1829–1914* (Perth: U of Western Australia P, 1983): 11 (archive.aiatsis.gov.au/m0022954.pdf). Swan River Papers, Public Record Office London, comp. Alice J. Mayes (Battye Library of West Australian History), vol. 15, Morgan to Hay. The accompanying handwritten text reads: "Particulars, (as expressed by Galliput) of the Native encampment, scrawl'd out by him.—That place (No. 1) womanar, children, pickninny.—That place (No. 7)—married men—that place (No. 2) single Men—Some morning sun get up vera early—married go down—call up single men,—single men get up when sun get up very early—all go down (to No. 6 a lake) catch fish, then go up

Galliput was more than ready to adopt new technologies in the interests of storytelling and communication. An even more sophisticated example of appropriation – in terms of control, experimentation, and 'language play' – is provided by a colonial diarist's observation of an Aboriginal guide telling his community of the 'expedition' from which he has just returned:

> [Nakina had] treasured up in his memory a detailed recollection of the various incidents and scenery, arranged in the form of a Diary, where each day was designated by some leading distinctive mark, in place of numerals.[8]

Nakina was curious about the diarist's habits – the collecting of plant specimens, the habit of pressing flowers into a book – and must also have engaged with the diarist about the nature of his writing because his public 'recitation' of their journey clearly incorporated some of the structural characteristics of that ubiquitious literary form of the time, the expedition journal.

In *Writing Never Arrives Naked*, Penny van Toorn claims that "the cultures of reading and writing introduced to Australia […] became entangled with the oldest living Indigenous cultures in the world."[9] Van Toorn argues that Aboriginal people didn't necessarily see writing or books as foreign, irrelevant or evil, but were intrigued, and considered them as curiosities to be assimilated into their own traditions. Nakina's account of the expedition may be an exemplary instance of new media being incorporated into oral and performance culture, and the existence of what van Toorn calls "entangled objects."

There are numerous examples of cultural forms becoming entangled in this sort of way. According to another diarist, the Nyungar Mokare interrupted his conversation with a group of soldiers and sang out as his brother entered the room, "Oh where have you been all the day, Billy Boy, Billy Boy."[10] Mokare's version of the Scottish air demanded attention, and still does. For one thing, it

---

(to No. 5) catch Kangaroo—bring him down dare—(No. 3) fire—roast him—all Men set round so—(suiting the action to the word) upon ham."

[8] Alexander Collie, "Anecdotes and Remarks relative to the Aborigines at King George's Sound," (1834), in *Nyungar – the People: Aboriginal Customs in the Southwest of Australia*, ed. Neville Green (Perth, WA: Creative Research, 1979): 56.

[9] Penny van Toorn, *Writing Never Arrives Naked: Early Aboriginal Cultures of Writing in Australia* (Canberra: Aboriginal Studies Press, 2006): 3.

[10] John Mulvaney & Neville Green. *Commandment of Solitude: The Journals of Captain Collet Barker 1828–1831* (Carlton, Victoria: Melbourne UP/Miegunyah Press, 1992): 281.

serves as a functional statement. Secondly, Mokare uses it to demonstrate to his companions – the soldiers – that he is learning their language and songs (and, by implication, their own failure to learn his). His action also accords with his own Nyungar tradition, in which you 'know' people by their sound. Mokare's 'sampling' and re-contextualizing of the song is a witty and 'postmodern' performance.

The incorporation of new media into an existing tradition is also evident in the following nineteenth-century Nyungar song:

> Ngayn Ngan demangar
> (my old people)
> Kitjiny Miyal
> (Spearing eyes)
> Boorniny warabiny
> (trees-ing/cutting bad-becoming)
> Kin-joor-town
> (King George Town).[11]

I have used contemporary orthography for the Nyungar texts, above and below, and so it is more accurate to say that they are derived, rather than taken directly, from the archive. However, the item of interest is the last word, a version of a colonial place-name more usually rendered as King George Town. Thus we have a quite rare example of colonial experience contained within a Nyungar cultural frame. Another song of approximately the same era begins in English:

> Captain on a cruel sea,
> Captain on a cruel sea,
> Captain on a cruel sea.[12]

At a later point the text apparently describes the captain's view through his telescope of women dancing on the shore. Such a 'point-of-view exercise' is a remarkable contrast to colonial Australian literature's tendency to denigrate Indigenous subjects as inferior and 'other'.

The willingness of historical Nyungar individuals to play with the language of strangers is notable, as is their linguistic ability. The founder of the Western Australian colony was startled on his first exploratory river trip in

---

[11] Daisy Bates, *Papers 1907–1940*, microfiche, MN 1406, ACC. 6193A and ACC. 1212A (Perth, WA: Battye Library).

[12] Daisy Bates, *Papers 1907–1940*.

Nyungar country to hear Nyungar people on the riverbank calling out to him in English,[13] a language they'd picked up from other maritime explorers. Later in the nineteenth century, the Australian author Henry Lawson met a Nyungar who, although clad only in a possum-skin garment, spoke French fluently.[14]

All this language fluency, all this skill in language play and cross-cultural communication, suggests at least a propensity for literary activity. Such historical examples of 'entanglement' partly inspired my novel *That Deadman Dance*, particularly the transformation of a military drill into an Aboriginal dance. Such acts, it seems to me, indicate considerable confidence and self-assurance, and, drafting that novel, I asked myself: 'What sort of novel would Aboriginal characters in the earliest years of colonization have written? What sort of historical novel might they have *wanted* to write? What sort of novel should a descendant of such people write?'

The confidence and curiosity of these early Nyungar individuals may seem curiously apolitical and naive. Were they mistaken? I think the very nature of my questions indicate that colonial history has prevented such attitudes and knowledge from being fully transferred.

There are considerable pressures on contemporary Indigenous writers not only to be political – which is inevitable – but to be *overtly* and intentionally political, and to supply 'ammunition for the cause'.

The Australian inaugural National Aboriginal Writers' Conference in 1983 from which I quoted earlier was apparently in no doubt about this issue:

> Aboriginal literature [...] has not yet succumbed to the rhetorical ploy of saying that 'politics gets in the way of literature'. It asserts the contrary: literature is one of the ways of getting political things done.[15]

Yet the examples I have given from early history indicate an approach quite distant from the use of literature as an instrument to achieve certain political ends. Of course, those early Nyungar were in a very different position in

---

[13] Neville Green, "Aborigines and White Settlers in the Nineteenth Century," in *A New History of Western Australia*, ed. C.T. Stannage (Nedlands, WA: U of Western Australia P, 1981): 77.

[14] Henry Lawson, "The golden nineties" (1899), in *First Impressions: Albany: Travellers' Tales 1791–1901*, compiled by Douglas R.G. Sellick (Perth, WA: Western Australian Museum, 1997): 189–205.

[15] Davis, Muecke, Narogin & Shoemaker, *Paperbark*, 2.

terms of power from those who followed. Within fifty years of first contact only something like twenty percent of the original Nyungar population remained, and these were subject to oppressive legislation.[16] No wonder political imperatives came to dominate. Some examples from the writing of Bessie Flower demonstrate something of this shift. Bessie Flower, a Nyungar woman, was raised and educated in her ancestral country by a well-meaning missionary, before being sent to teach at a mission in another state of Australia. Soon after her departure she wrote:

> The second officer came to us and was talking about Albany. He said they considered it a great banishment to be sent there, that nothing grew but rocks and stones and I said that added to the beauty of the place. He laughed and said a good deal more [...]. I did not answer rudely though, dear Missie ....[17]

A much later example of her writing suggests something of the experience she came to endure, and her growing politicization:

> I will not say much on his style of calling us niggers ... I know the way niggers have been treated in America [...] we will [...] go on our way, trying what is in our power to bring up our children [...] it comes hard on the children and myself wandering about without a home, & I feel it the more as I had a good home when I was young, & then to be tossed about in old age.[18]

Another Nyungar person, 'Norn' or 'Tommy King', dictated a petition on Proclamation Day near the end of the nineteenth century:

> We would humbly remind Your Excellency that in the year 1829, all this country belonged to my tribe [...] but [...] her Most Gracious Majesty the Queen was pleased to take it from us. Since that time we have been gradually deprived of our hunting grounds and nearly all our kangaroos have been killed by the white man, and we are now in extreme poverty and a deplorable condition [...] we would humbly ask your Excellency to give us something that we may rejoice.[19]

---

[16] See Anna Haebich, *For Their Own Good* (Nedlands: U of Western Australia P, 1988).

[17] Penny van Toorn, *Writing Never Arrives Naked*, 187.

[18] *Writing Never Arrives Naked*, 192.

[19] Kyan Gadac, "Noongar Resistance on the South Coast," *Kiangardarup* (4 May 2008), www.kiangardarup.blogspot.com (accessed March 2012).

There are many examples that could be used to demonstrate Nyungar writers necessarily using language as an instrument or tool, and as part of the overwhelming political struggle against oppression that continues to the present day. Certainly a great many Aboriginal writers would probably agree that literature is one way, among others, of 'getting things done'. The poet and playwright Jack Davis was a key figure in the expansion of the number of Aboriginal writers, and opened up space into which other writers could grow. Jack Davis was also important, but not alone, in reintroducing Nyungar language to the 'mainstream' of Western Australian literature; an admittedly small and isolated arena.

Nyungar language could be very important to south-western Australia's literary tradition, and perhaps beyond that. The earliest examples of a 'nascent' Nyungar literary tradition I offer in this essay occurred within the frame of Nyungar language and demonstrate a confidence and preparedness to appropriate and play with new forms that is, arguably, quite rare in more contemporary work, where most writers write in English, and where 'resistance' is foregrounded. Arguably, the contemporary social context is one in which the empirical realities of Indigenous experience have reduced the possibilities of expression of Indigenous identity, and created a sense of self and culture that is reactive and trapped within parameters established by colonization: don't live long, don't be employed, don't earn a good income, don't venture beyond your own community – don't achieve. Older stories, rooted in the language of pre-colonial experience rather than oppression, may offer quite different messages and a less 'reactive' and 'resistant' sense of identity.

By definition, Indigenous languages are a link to a pre-colonial heritage, and in this instance to those members of a culture about whom I asked, 'What sort of novel would they have written?' It is possible that Indigenous language itself might answer such questions.

Consider that a language – especially one which is relatively 'pure' and carries very little evidence of the influence of other languages – can "represent the distillation of the thoughts and communication of a people over their entire history."[20] In Australia, the history of Aboriginal people is that of those who first created human society in their part of the world,[21] and such narratives of place are of obvious significance.

---

[20] David Crystal, *Language Death* (Cambridge: Cambridge UP, 2000): 38.

[21] Jared Diamond, *Guns, Germs and Steel* (New York: W.W. Norton, 1997): 321.

Objectively, Nyungar language is likely to carry attitudes and perspectives otherwise unknown. Certainly, many speakers of Indigenous languages argue that those languages are the only means of articulating traditional knowledge, and that 'Dreamtime stories in English are nothing; it's gotta be in language'. They further argue that certain kinds of traditional knowledge, perhaps even aspects of a world-view, may be 'embedded' in the characteristics of traditional languages, and that a reduction in the transmission of traditional languages seems to correspond to a reduction in "the transmission of at least certain types of traditional knowledge."[22]

However, Nyungar is an endangered language, and many would argue that its use merely as a source of 'insight' for literature in English or indeed of perspectives unknown to wider society is of very limited value unless it also contributes in some way to the revival and continued survival of the language itself and – most especially – the well-being of the community descended from its first speakers. I certainly take that position, which may require further explanation.

There are three interconnected reasons why an Indigenous novelist may feel obliged to do more than simply research Nyungar language as preparation for a novel even if, on an individual level, that research is part of a consolidation and reclamation of an aspect of one's own heritage.

First, there is the fact that it is an endangered language in the context of a history of dispossession and disempowerment of its speakers. Secondly, a sense of 'ownership' of Nyungar language is very important to the individual and collective identity of Nyungar people. Thirdly – bearing in mind my initial comments on that 'postcolonial angst' – the audience for any novel will be predominantly non-Nyungar and so, in effect, writing in language (if with an educative function) means taking it from one group to give to another.

Why is the language endangered? Colonialization has been a process of destruction and denigration of Nyungar culture and has functioned to disadvantage Nyungar people and discourage pride in Nyungar heritage and identity.

In this context, working with an endangered ancestral language seems a very important part of 'literary activity' for an Indigenous novelist, but also suggests a shift in how we might define literary activity and, indeed, tradition.

---

[22] John Henderson & David Nash, *Culture and Heritage: Indigenous Languages* (Rockhampton, Queensland: Central Queensland University Publishing Unit, 1997): 29.

Working with an endangered language can become in itself a story of recovery. And 'rebuilding' language and connections between its people and country is also a crucial part of 'rebuilding' spirit and getting communities "back to a point where we are no longer just victims of a system that sets out to destroy us."[23]

Sound language-based programmes need to include consideration of why the language has become endangered, argues Lesley Jolley, and the very existence of such a programme can, of itself, be positive:

> Language loss, language retention, and the possibility of language revitalisation, then, can be emblematic of the whole history of colonial dispossession, Aboriginal persistence and a self-assertive and self-determined Aboriginal future.[24]

This is not 'heritage' as museum pieces, but more in line with what the Aboriginal and Torres Strait Islander Board of the Australia Council states as part of its mission to help Indigenous communities "claim, control and enhance" their heritages. I argue that Nyungar language needs to be returned to, and consolidated in, home communities before being shared with the non-Indigenous community. This is particularly so when, as appears to be increasingly the case, the importance of that language and what it represents is, after a long history of denigration, commercially valued. There's a strong argument that people are further disempowered when their cultural heritage – especially ancestral knowledge partially lost to a significant proportion of a "community of descendants" – is accessible to them only by means of commercial transactions and then on a supposedly 'equal' footing with members of a community which has, at least historically, been their oppressors.[25] The above is about language revival; it is even more pertinent when applied to the recovery and re-animation of ancient stories told in that language.

The consolidation of language and story in home communities in ways that strengthen and create opportunities for community members to profitably

---

[23] Jeanie Bell, "Linguistic Continuity in Colonized Country," in *Language in Native Title*, ed. John Henderson & David Nash (Canberra: Aboriginal Studies Press, 2002): 47.

[24] Lesley Jolley, *Waving a Tattered Banner? Aboriginal Language Revitalisation* (Brisbane: Aboriginal and Torres Strait Islander Studies Unit, University of Queensland, 1995): 4.

[25] See Kim Scott, "An Island Home," in *Just Words: Australian Authors Writing for Justice*, ed. Bernadette Brennan (St Lucia: U of Queensland P, 2008): 158.

share revitalized, ancestral knowledge with increasingly wider, concentric circles of people can be an important part of community development and, importantly, help build something other than drawing upon the experience of oppression. And it is that 'experience other than oppression' which informs the examples of Nyungar strength and creativity that I quoted earliest in this essay.

So, as part of my discussion of what I must, admittedly, only call a nascent Nyungar literary tradition I now propose to discuss a particular project that is a response to language endangerment, and which is itself an example of literary activity expressing political action in a specific, and non-polemical, fashion.

First, allow me to briefly discuss a range of responses to language endangerment. It is usually agreed that what is most needed are programmes of language maintenance, usually involving language education.

In *Culture and Heritage: Indigenous Languages*, Henderson and Nash examine a range of activities which indicate "language health," some of which are responses to language endangerment and include language documentation and linguistic studies, language-education programmes, and community language programmes. Their own focus is on "institutional or formal activities" which, although they leave a "paper trail [...] vary enormously in their effectiveness."[26] Disturbingly, their discussion of language education in schools concludes that "experience from a range of places is that if the children do not speak the language, there is probably very little a school can do to get them to speak it fluently."[27] Furthermore,

> the expectation that children might start speaking or writing a language fluently and in a traditional form as the result of a language revitalization program is one of the unrealistic expectations that are sometimes found in indigenous communities.[28]

---

[26] Henderson & Nash, *Culture and Heritage: Indigenous Languages*, 13.

[27] Deborah Hartmann & John Henderson, *Aboriginal Languages in Education* (Alice Springs, Northern Territory: IAD Press, 1994): 8.

[28] Patrick McConvell & Graham McKay, "Aboriginal and Torres Strait Islander language maintenance intervention activities," paper presented to Workshop on Language Shift and Maintenance in the Asia–Pacific Region (Melbourne: Australian Linguistic Institute, Latrobe University, 1994): 11.

In fact, learning "an Australian Aboriginal language is hard work for someone raised in English [...] much harder work than picking up Spanish, and quite a job to expect of whole communities of people."[29]

The problems associated with 'reviving' a language include the status and clout of the dominant language, the need to get community support for language education in schools and to balance and integrate dialects, and, of course, how to deal with the extent and reasons for such loss.

The project of which I will speak is not a language-revival programme as such, nor is it a formal activity associated with an institution. It is about reclaiming ancestral 'creation' stories, and consolidating them in a home community of descendants in ways intended to empower members of that community by means of a controlled sharing of those stories. It is about developing a repertoire of stories to share across cultural boundaries.

Some years ago I helped assemble a group of people descended from some Nyungar men who had spoken to the American linguist Gerhardt Laves in Albany – King George Town – in 1931. They told him stories in Nyungar language, and he recorded them by means of the International Phonetic Alphabet (IPA).

The group of descendants wanted to return the material to its community in a meaningful way. It is one thing to say archival material must be returned to its community, but what does that mean? Where do you store or archive it? Often a poorly funded Aboriginal Centre is the venue, even though it will usually have inadequate storage conditions and no one responsible for cataloguing, ensuring access, and facilitating engagement with the material. Furthermore, some families connected to the archival material may feel marginalized by the group managing such a centre. Is the local public library a better choice? A university?

How do you 'share' stories written in a linguist's alphabet that very few can read, and which appears to show a difference between the way Nyungar was spoken in 1931 and how it is today? Yes, we had identified "senior contact people," but what if they did not want to share the material, other than with a very limited group of people? One may argue that the material is 'owned' by a community of descendants, but what if that community has a strong tendency, for all sorts of reasons, to fracture into smaller groups?

---

[29] John McWhorter, *The Power of Babel: A Natural History of Language* (New York: HarperPerennial, 2003): 270.

Laves' version of the International Phonetic Alphabet was hard to read, and apparently idiosyncratic. There was no punctuation, and often no translations. I studied the current alphabet and, based upon that and recordings I had made of Nyungar speakers, attempted to read aloud some of the Bob Roberts stories to Lomas Roberts, a Nyungar elder and biological nephew to three of Laves' Nyungar informants and who had called all the informants "Uncle" when he was a child.

Lomas Roberts recognized words and phrases, and had heard parts of some of the stories. He was befuddled by some of the texts, and said some of the language didn't sound right. Of course, both the linguist and I made mistakes, but there did seem to have been changes in Nyungar language in the seventy-plus years since they'd been written down. When I mentioned the differing pronunciation of one particular word – Laves had written it to represent a slightly different sound to what is common today – Lomas Roberts's older sister Hazel Brown said, "Yes, we used to say it like that."

Sometimes Lomas Roberts alerted me to mistakes in Laves' translation. Often, he was reminded of stories. So, in this way we gathered more information than either archives or oral history alone would have been able to offer.

It was intense and demanding work, although we were only skimming the texts for an idea of what might be 'sensitive', and it was exciting to hear these stories of people who had passed away long ago. I began to realize how it might be a sort of 'value-adding' exercise to bring archives and elders together. It was difficult to make the time to do this, and more often than not there were people coming and going, and uninterrupted time was rare. When we read the stories aloud together, young and old people in the house moved a little closer. They were attracted by the sound, the vocabulary and – when they stayed a little longer – the stories themselves. We thought more people should hear them.

How?

Who first?

The texts were very difficult, hard to share. The sounds didn't quite match the way most Nyungar was spoken today. Some of the information contradicted what Nyungar people today might say. Returning the stories to community meant finding a way to share them. Under the heading "The Future: Using Laves' Field Notes," the Laves protocol says:

> We recognise a pressing need for materials and activities to be developed to assist in language revitalisation [… and] look forward to

appropriate stories being published for the family and community members to read.[30]

Those of us who remained of the original group took it as a starting point, and planned a process leading to publication which

- contributed to the return of archival language material to its home community;
- helped people engage with that material, and consolidated Nyungar language in its home community;
- created opportunity for members of that community to increasingly participate in sharing their heritage of language and story – first, within their own community, and then, with an increasingly wider audience; and
- trialled a process for achieving the above.

The main thrust of the ideas at our first meeting was that we needed to develop a few of the 'safer' stories through a series of 'workshops' designed to involve an increasing number of people, familiarize them with the material, and create opportunities for sharing them with an increasingly wider community. We intended to develop picture books, because that gave opportunities for people to engage with the stories, and skills with which to help share them.

Three workshops were held, to which the Reference Group invited people with whom they wished to share some of the stories.

At the first workshop, a package of printed copies of all the stories of their ancestors was handed to each of the people named in the protocol as "key people." Nearly everyone in the room was crying at one stage; a measure of the emotional intensity behind what's normally given to words like 'ownership' and 'rights', and 'reclaiming a heritage'. People said it was good to gather around the stories of our old people, rather than at a funeral.

Over the next two days we worked with four stories chosen earlier by members of the Reference Group and myself. The stories had been written on large sheets of paper, using Laves's IPA script, contemporary Nyungar spelling, and some of Laves's translation notes, and we read them aloud, together,

---

[30] John Henderson, Hannah McGlade, Kim Scott & Denise Smith-Ali, "A Protocol for Laves' 1931 Noongar Field Notes" (MS; Nedlands, WA: Linguistics Department, University of Western Australia, 2006): 22.

stumbling. We recorded our discussion of pronunciation, semantics, and cultural references.

The number of descendants/elders in the immediate circle varied between seven and thirteen, although a greater number of people observed from elsewhere in the room, and people left and arrived at different points. There were probably never more than about sixty people present at any one time, never fewer than about twenty.

At the end of the weekend, we'd agreed to try and develop three of the stories for publication, with some other workshops to help further consolidate and share them.

The three stories were redrafted using Laves's original notes, the weekend's recordings, and other archival language material from the south coast.

Some months later we invited people to participate in a second workshop led by an experienced children's book illustrator. This promoted more engagement with the stories, and offered opportunities for relevant people to be involved in sharing them with a wider audience.

The third workshop was held at the 'Noongar Centre' in Albany with an exhibition of the artwork produced in the second workshop, photographs from all the workshops so far, and a 'reading' of each of the stories. We handed out fifty packages, each containing three picture books of three stories and a CD of them being read aloud in Nyungar language, to the people in the Reference Group and individuals who represented most if not all of the key families in the Albany Nyungar community (we also handed out a few to people not living in Albany, but who represented families connected to the material). Our intention was to return the stories in a meaningful way, to increase a sense of community ownership, and to help individuals gain employment in schools and elsewhere through familiarity with the stories and the process of their creation.

A fourth workshop developed a one-hour "performance package" featuring the stories and the process of their creation, which later toured selected schools in Albany and Perth and was, in a couple of instances, presented at community events. The presentation consisted of a repertoire of language pieces: an introduction in Nyungar language, the three stories, and one or two songs. The team of presenters varied slightly as individuals felt ready to take on greater roles, and included elders.

A fifth event involved filming elders returning to geographical sites connected with the stories and sharing at the same time their social histories of the region. Edited DVDs of this material were distributed at a later community gathering.

This may seem a long departure from my discussion of a nascent Nyungar literary tradition, and the potential for grafting a regional 'literature' onto Indigenous traditions. My point is that the production of printed stories on paper is only one component of a broader storytelling tradition, and that literary activity in the sense of working with one's endangered Indigenous language in the manner I have described above includes attention to the manner of composition, and of the 'telling'.

Earlier, I mentioned what must be termed moral imperatives for returning and consolidating Indigenous language in its home community, and the process I have described uses language and story to develop a different relationship between Aboriginal and non-Aboriginal people. In saying this, I take it as given that Aboriginal people are, by and large, relatively disadvantaged and marginalized in Australian society. Our experience in presenting at schools and public events (see workshop four above) is that Nyungar people are – unusually – at the centre of the social event, and in relatively empowered positions. It is a paradox: empowerment through giving. It is however, a *controlled* giving, aligned with community development and the creation of opportunities to remain near the centre of ever-widening circles of audiences. It is a quite unusual power-relationship for most Australian Aboriginal people to experience. Thus, I think both the transfer and the transformation that occur via our workshop process are worthy of interest in a number of ways.

The first set of workshops in the above process began in early 2007 and culminated in the launch of two books in late 2011: *Mamang* and *Noongar Mambara Bakitj*.

What is being transferred – passed on – in these publications derived from the stories of ancestors? Well, the protagonists

- trust their heritage;
- take risks;
- travel alone and far from their communities; and
- return to their home communities enriched and better able to contribute to its welfare.

These pre-colonial narratives are directly relevant to the contemporary world, perhaps more so than contemporary ones grounded in the experience of oppression.

At an earlier point in this essay I wondered if 'traditional' narratives might offer alternative models, perhaps more useful than contemporary ones characterized by oppression. The above list of characteristics suggests that this is the case, and it certainly accords with sentiments expressed elsewhere in Aboriginal Australia:

> Noel Pearson talks about this philosophy of orbiting – being armed with a first-class education but going back to your community [...]. I want kids to see it as possible to be indigenous and (transiting) between both worlds.[31]

In this essay I have suggested the propensity for a specific Indigenous heritage (Nyungar) to move into literary activity – literary activity that can include community-based consolidation of language and story, and collective composition of narratives inspired by texts indirectly left by ancestors that are then shared in ever-widening concentric circles. There is a community-development and obvious political dimension to this, although quite different from the use of literary skills as overt polemical weapons.

I began by referring to the success of my recent more orthodox literary work – a novel – and to the 'postcolonial angst' an Indigenous writer might experience. It is my thesis that a 'dual focus' of literary activity – on the one side, individual work that allows for ambivalence, nuance, and 'interiority' that the novel form enables; on the other, community-based work that facilitates the consolidation and enhancement of a storytelling heritage – is one way of meeting pressing political imperatives. This strategy also enables the more orthodox literary work to be used to illuminate other stories that are less accessible, and to bring other people into the spotlight to be, paradoxically, empowered by the shift in power-relationships created by the storytelling situation. It is my experience that there is an element of social healing in such processes, and even the looming possibility that a relatively juvenile and shimmering nation-state might anchor itself to its continent more securely through such processes and stories.

I also know I could not have written my last novel, *That Deadman Dance*, without the concurrent workshop process I have outlined, because I would not have had the confidence to have an Aboriginal protagonist demonstrating, by

---

[31] Patricia Karvelas, "World stage for young leader Tania Major," *Australian* (1 November 2009), http://www.theaustralian.com.au/news/world-stage-for-young-leader/story-e6frg6oo-1111117915763 (accessed 20 March 2012).

his non-polemical approach to visitors from another culture, his assured and confident sovereignty. The novel – and my efforts to do justice to pre-colonial ancestors – was partly inspired by an account of a twentieth-century Nyungar dance derived from a military drill that had been performed on the beaches of my home town some three decades before colonization. I thought it was a very impressive thing to appropriate the shrill assertion of a military drill and turn it into a dance; such confidence, such creativity, such a transformation in the transfer.

WORKS CITED

Aboriginal Legal Service of Western Australia. *Telling Our Story: A report by the Aboriginal Legal Service of Western Australia on the removal of Aboriginal Children from their families in Western Australia* (Perth, WA: The Service, 1995).

Bates, Daisy. *Papers 1907–1940,* microfiche, MN 1406, ACC. 6193A and ACC. 1212A (Perth, WA: Battye Library).

Bell, Jeanie. "Linguistic Continuity in Colonized Country," in *Language in Native Title,* ed. John Henderson & David Nash (Canberra: Aboriginal Studies Press, 2002): 43–52.

Bolt, Andrew. "It's So Hip to be Black," *Herald Sun* (25 April 2009), http://www.abc.net.au/mediawatch/transcripts/1109_heraldsun09.pdf (accessed 20 March 2012).

Collie, Alexander. "Anecdotes and Remarks relative to the Aborigines at King George's Sound," in *Nyungar – the People: Aboriginal Customs in the Southwest of Australia,* ed. Neville Green (Perth, WA: Creative Research, 1979): 56–97. Originally in *Perth Gazette and Western Australian Journal,* 5 and 12 July 1834.

Crystal, David. *Language Death* (Cambridge: Cambridge UP, 2000).

Davis, Jack, Stephen Muecke, Mudrooroo Narogin & Adam Shoemaker. *Paperbark: A Collection of Black Australian Writings* (St Lucia: U of Queensland P, 1990).

Diamond, Jared. *Guns, Germs and Steel* (New York: W.W. Norton, 1997).

Gadac, Kyan. "Noongar Resistance on the South Coast," *Kiangardarup* (4 May 2008), www.kiangardarup.blogspot.com (accessed March 2012). [Petition, 1890.]

Galeano, Eduardo. "In Defence of the Word," in *The Graywolf Annual Five: Multicultural Literacy,* ed. Rick Simonson & Scott Walker (Saint Paul MN: Graywolf, 1988): 113–25.

Green, Neville. "Aborigines and White Settlers in the Nineteenth Century," in *A New History of Western Australia,* ed. C.T. Stannage (Nedlands, WA: U of Western Australia P, 1981): 72–123.

——. *Aborigines of the Albany Region 1821–1898: The Bicentennial Dictionary of Western Australians* (Nedlands, WA: U of Western Australia P, 1989).

——. *Nyungar – the People; Aboriginal Customs in the Southwest of Australia* (Perth, WA: Creative Research, 1979).

Haebich, Anna. *For Their Own Good* (Nedlands: U of Western Australia P, 1988).

Hartmann, Deborah, & John Henderson. *Aboriginal Languages in Education* (Alice Springs, Northern Territory: IAD Press, 1994).

Henderson, John, & David Nash. *Culture and Heritage: Indigenous Languages* (Rockhampton, Queensland: Central Queensland University Publishing Unit, 1997).

——, Hannah McGlade, Kim Scott & Denise Smith–Ali. "A Protocol for Laves' 1931 Noongar Field Notes" (MS; Nedlands, WA: Linguistics Department, University of Western Australia, 2006).

Jolley, Lesley. *Waving a Tattered Banner? Aboriginal Language Revitalisation* (Brisbane: Aboriginal and Torres Strait Islander Studies Unit, University of Queensland, 1995).

Karvelas, Patricia. "World stage for young leader Tania Major," *Australian* (1 November 2009), http://www.theaustralian.com.au/news/world-stage-for-young-leader/story-e6frg600-1111117915763 (accessed 20 March 2012).

Lawson, Henry. "The golden nineties" (1899), in *First Impressions: Albany: Travellers' Tales 1791–1901*, compiled by Douglas R.G. Sellick (Perth, WA: Western Australian Museum, 1997): 189–205.

McConvell, Patrick, & Graham McKay. "Aboriginal and Torres Strait Islander language maintenance intervention activities," paper presented to Workshop on Language Shift and Maintenance in the Asia–Pacific Region (Melbourne: Australian Linguistic Institute, Latrobe University, 1994).

McWhorter, John. *The Power of Babel*: *A Natural History of Language* (New York: HarperPerennial, 2003).

Moreton–Robinson, Aileen. *Whiteness in Constructions of Australian Nationhood: Indigenes, Immigrants and Governmentality* (Canberra: Aboriginal Studies Press, 2004).

Mulvaney, John, & Neville Green. *Commandment of Solitude: The Journals of Captain Collet Barker 1828–1831* (Carlton, Victoria: Melbourne UP/Miegunyah Press, 1992).

Narogin, Mudrooroo. *Writing from the Fringe: A Study of Modern Aboriginal Literature* (Melbourne: Hyland House, 1990).

Salvado, Rosendo. *The Salvado Memoirs: Historical Memoirs of Australia and Particularly of the Benedictine Mission of New Norcia and of the Habits and Customs of the Australian Natives*, tr. Edward James Stormon (*Memorias historicas sobre la Australia y particularmente acerca la mision Benedictina de Nueva Nursia y los usos y costumbres de los salvajes*, 1851; Perth: U of Western Australia P, 1977).

Scott, Kim. "An Island Home," in *Just Words: Australian Authors Writing for Justice*, ed. Bernadette Brennan (St Lucia: U of Queensland P, 2008): 152–61.

Tilbrook, Lois. *Nyungar Tradition: Glimpses of Aborigines of South-Western Australia 1829–1914* (Perth: U of Western Australia P, 1983).

Van Toorn, Penny. *Writing Never Arrives Naked: Early Aboriginal Cultures of Writing in Australia* (Canberra: Aboriginal Studies Press, 2006).

The Great Tradition
Translating Durrudiya's Songs

STEPHEN MUECKE

> I'm saying that the domain of poetry includes both oral and written forms, that poetry goes back to a pre-literate situation and would survive a post-literate situation, that human speech is a near-endless source of poetic forms, that there has *always* been more oral than written poetry, & that we can no longer pretend to a knowledge of poetry if we deny its oral dimension.[1]

L ET US CONSIDER THE CONSEQUENCES of 'graphocentrism' (the fetishization of the written word) and of 'technocentrism' (the fetishization of the machine) in the history of world literature. It is precisely these two key and successive developments in the technology of language and its distribution that have supposedly placed European modernity in a leading position ever since the Enlightenment. The first, writing, defeated the frailty of human memory, and the second, printing, gave power to those ideas chosen for reproduction. While both statements are no doubt true, it is also the case that speech has not disappeared, and that our most valued ideas are still those transmitted via a more embodied proximity, through the affinities of family and friends.

In fact, it is the *process of translation* from spoken forms to written, and then the subsequent distribution, that gives the ideas their power. This process of translation is really hard work, and it contains all sorts of mysteries. It is far from being a simple matter of transposing form or content from the medium

---

[1] Jerome Rothenberg, *Pre-Faces & Other Writings* (New York: New Directions, 1981): 11.

of the spoken word to the written or printed one. The process begins with someone noticing something strange going on, then struggling to put this event into words. If there is nothing strange, and no labour of expression, then there is no point to the events of language at all. Language would be as unexpressive as breathing – unchanging and not moving anything it encounters.

You will notice that I am not saying that speech has priority over writing, because it came first in an evolutionary sense, or still comes first in an ontogenetic or naturalist one. Jacques Derrida has been here already. I am saying that processes of translation – complex mediations of languages, things, and people – give certain ideas priority. Take the case of the Gutenberg revolution and the printing of the Bible. Certainly, the writing down of the Gospels was important for the spreading of the Word, certainly the appearance of the Bible in nearly every household was equally important. But these words still have to be read out in sermons on Sundays, repeated in schools, whispered at prayer-time, sworn on in courts of law, and fought over in religious wars. These are all processes of translation in the sense of Bruno Latour, and they require embodied human effort. Christian ideas got lucky, to the extent that humans were prepared to cherish them, labour over them, fight over them – and print them. I will elaborate a little on Latour and translation later.

But first, let us take our discussion to Australia. There's a fair degree of consensus, I reckon, about what constitutes Australian literature, among the writers, publishers, academics, and critics: Australian literature is in English, and it is written.

The upheaval that was brought about in Australian archaeology and in history, when those fields engaged with data from before colonization, has not really touched the shape of our literary culture. The discovery of Mungo Lady in 1969 suddenly transformed the scale of Australian history; Australian deep history now went back 40,000 or 60,000 years, and this became a catch-cry for Indigenous politics and then for what was to become known as the cultural renaissance. This was not news for Indigenous peoples, but it made this ancient history public in a dramatic way, coupled with the kind of validation that science can bring. In the process, the concept of Indigenous sovereignty was strengthened.

In history, only a few years later, a new set of archives was being uncovered and Aboriginal histories proliferated. These were often written by, or in collaboration with, Indigenous people, and they had a quite new perspective, one that came from 'the other side of the frontier'.[2]

A bit later, in the visual arts, the Papunya phenomenon had a revolutionary effect on representations of the Australian landscape. The global art market agreed: this movement originating in central Australia became the most significant thing to happen in Australian visual arts at the end of the twentieth century. The whitefella landscape artists must have felt a little marginalized after the considerable success of the previous generation of figures like Fred Williams, John Olsen, and Sir Sidney Nolan. Perhaps the success of the 'dot' paintings was because, being abstractly visual, they could be so easily misinterpreted. The translation of this visual language onto canvas, and removed from any ceremonial context, with only a cursory synopsis of the 'story' or associated 'dreaming' attached, made them easy to sell into all sorts of markets, facilitated also, no doubt, by an implicit primitivist contextualizing.

No such luck for the literary arts that are the subject of my discussion. How much work has to be done by a linguist–poet knowledgeable in Arrernte, Pintupi, Worora or Wik-Munkan to translate a song cycle into English: word by word, concept by concept. Problems of rhythm, figures of speech, cultural codings. They are also produced by quite different concepts of creativity and authorship, which I have described elsewhere.[3]

These are the same songs that the painters seated around a canvas sing as they work. The cultural bedrock is the same. At this very spot the tradition is being transformed in two directions, at least two. From the fingers the paint descends onto the canvas and produces art commodities; from the lips the whispered words die on the breeze. There is no one there to translate them, except maybe the kids with their guitars.

This, then, is the tragedy and the missed opportunity for Australian literature. It could have – it still could – draw much more strongly on the Indigenous traditions. But to do so it has to subject itself to the humbling experience of comparing itself to the Great Tradition, as I am calling it, or, rather, great traditions, that are not re-inventing themselves every thirty years, as Ivor

---

[2] Henry Reynolds, *The Other Side of the Frontier* (Kensington: New South Wales UP, 1981). This was a key first text, followed by numerous other volumes in the new field of Aboriginal history.

[3] See also Stephen Muecke, *Textual Spaces: Aboriginality and Cultural Studies* (Kensington: U of New South Wales P, 1992)

Indyk puts it, as he was reported musing on the 'idealism' of his yearning "for a European notion of a literary community":

> The culture [of Australian literature] is only 200 years old, not even that. There has been wave after wave of migration, so in a sense the culture reinvents itself every 30 years and is still in the process of formation. That's a fascinating thing to watch and to be part of.[4]

Indyk, the editor and publisher of Alexis Wright, is a great supporter of Indigenous literature, but here he defaults to the conventional model of what 'Australian literature' is: literature written in English drawing on the anglophone heritage, but renewed by waves of different kinds of traditions: non-English-speaking migrants are registered here:

> I really like that sense that everything is provisional, and conditional, and you can't be sure of its origins, or what traditions it's bringing with it or how it should be read. For an interpreter that's really exciting.[5]

I want to suggest that the Indigenous traditions in Australian literature are not just one of these "strange accents" (as he says) coming along to renew the mainstream. This was not the case with the Papunya revolution in central Australia which raged through the art scene with the enormous levelling energy of a bush-fire. This culture was reborn with the momentum of millennia of traditions behind it. Despite fifty to a hundred years of whitefellas predicting the demise of Indigenous cultures, these magnificent paintings burst through in massive abundance like desert flowers after rain. They had always been there.

So, we wonder if it is still much too early to speak of the demise of Indigenous poetics. True, languages are disappearing. Many have been lost. But, bearing in mind what I was saying about the poetics being carried by the work

---

[4] Indyk, quoted in Miriam Cosic, "Incandescent Ivor Indyk turns down the heat," *The Australian* (26 February 2011), http://www.theaustralian.com.au/news/arts/incandescent-indyk-turns-down-the-heat/story-e6frg8n6-1226012001145 (accessed 20 March 2012). Further:

> You don't know where the contributions are going to come from, you have to exercise all your critical faculties to distinguish what's genuinely interesting and new from what's not, and the really interesting work may well come in a strange accent.

[5] Indyk, quoted in Cosic, "Incandescent Ivor Indyk turns down the heat."

of the process of translation, then the poetics does not reside in the *forms* of language, in a unitary language that can be lost, but in the techniques and abilities to change things. That is my understanding of tradition and how it works. A tradition is not a storehouse. A tradition is an understanding of how to transform things, it is a style with the momentum of a collectivity. So the tradition could, and would already, be leaving that language that might be disappearing. I am saying this partly because of the power of resurgence that we observed with the desert-painting movement of the 1970s. It had power not because it stuck to its pure forms in ground and body painting, but because it changed in a movement to new materials: acrylic paint and canvas.

Let's now take a little trip to a small community in north-west Australia, a place people in the 'settled' areas like to call 'remote Australia'. Mowanjum had a population of about three hundred when I went there first in the 1970s. It is eight kms out of Derby (4,000 people). Mowanjum has a missionary background, with people from Worora, Ngarinyin, and Wunumbul tribal groups from the Mitchell plateau and King George Sound areas to the North.

If you enter the term 'Mowanjum' on the Austlit. database, it produces thirty-three authors or organizations, and twenty-nine works, most of them Indigenous,. Four of these twenty-nine have more than five works each:

- Barunga, Albert b. 1912 d. 1977 (13 works by)
- Woolagoodjah, Sam b. ca.1905 d. 1979 (7 works by)
- Utemorrah, Daisy b. Feb 1922 d. 1994 (81 works by)
- Umbagai, Elkin b. 19 Feb 1921 d. 24 Jan 1980 (17 works by).

One of the most prominent men was David Mowaljarlai, who for some reason doesn't appear on this initial list. A search under his name produces seventeen works by him. I only get sixty works, and I've been writing every day for thirty years or so. Newtown, where I live, gets a hundred entries as a key word, and, as an inner-city Sydney suburb with a population of 13,000, it has forty-three times the number of potential writers compared to Mowanjum, and one of the highest numbers of people with PhDs in the country. If the Newtown writers, with all their PhDs, were as prolific as the Mowanjum writers, the bookshops would be overflowing with their work. My point is that the Mowanjum traditions are much richer in terms of longevity (up to 50,000 years) and denser (number of literary producers). The settler literary traditions are scant, but they dominate because the alphabet and the printed word say they should. Yet they are derivative, because they come from Europe, they haven't yet engaged with the country in the way that the Indigenous traditions always have. Listen to David Mowaljarlai on the word of God:

> We showed you that sharp hill over there, that's Malara. It's a kangaroo stomach. It fell out of the kangaroo and now it's a mountain. People say it's a joke, how can it come into a big mountain? People laugh, how can it be a kangaroo stomach, eh?
> I told one missionary, "Do you believe that God made those Ten Commandments? You take it seriously?"
> "Yes."
> "What is the mountain called where God gave those Ten Commandments to Moses?" He said the name of it.
> "And is it important?"
> "No, it is not important."
> "How come it is not important, wherever it was in Christian land?" And then he tells me, "God gave the *Law Tablets* to Moses, that is important. The mountain is not important."
> How come? He has never been there, but he read about it in the Bible and he takes that more seriously. I don't think the Christian missionaries take the Old Testament very seriously. "Too much law and too little salvation," I told him.[6]

It is the 'Law Tablets' that are important, the writing down of the Law, and this writing makes the literature disengaged from places, makes it mobile and potentially imperial. The Ten Commandments have certainly gone a long way around the world.

There is another curious side issue, a slight diversion, that contributes to this argument, and it concerns the place of ethnographic writing in Australia. Marcia Langton has spoken of the "grand tradition of ethnography in Australia, that has produced, arguably, the most important literature in our history."[7] Her use of the phrase 'grand tradition' alerted me to my theme once again. She presumably means R.H. Mathews, Norman Tindale, Phyllis Kaberry, T.G.H. Strehlow, W.E.H. Stanner, A.P. Elkin, Donald Thompson, right

---

[6] Jutta Malnic & David Mowaljarlai, *Yorro Yorro: Everything Standing Up Alive: Spirit of the Kimberley* (Broome, WA: Magabala, 1993): 83.

[7] Marcia Langton, "Certainty and Uncertainty: Aboriginal Studies as the Fulcrum of National Self-Consciousness," in *First Peoples: Second Chance*, ed. Terry Smith (Canberra: Australian Academy of the Humanities, 1999): 39. Quoted in Stephen Muecke, *Ancient & Modern: Time, Culture, and Indigenous Philosophy* (Kensington: New South Wales UP, 2005): 9.

through to Deborah Bird Rose today. It is a literature, but it is excluded for generic reasons from the literary canon, which is, of course, dominated by fiction. Remember how F.R. Leavis, a pioneer in the invention of the discipline of English literature, first defined the 'Great Tradition' in 1948, a tradition which he was creating as he wrote:

> The great English novelists are Jane Austen, George Eliot, Henry James and Joseph Conrad. [...] They are all distinguished by a vital capacity for experience, a kind of reverent openness before life, and a marked moral intensity.[8]

In 1948, for political reasons, the study of English literature was being forged as a discipline against the dominance of the Germanic philological tradition in Oxford and Cambridge.[9] It was thus a nationalist project. So I will have to be careful about just what kind of counter-nationalism I might be positing with an Indigenous Great Tradition. Nevertheless, what Marcia Langton calls the "grand tradition of ethnography in Australia"[10] is endorsed by her because it engages with what it finds in Indigenous Australia, all that surprising reality in the traditions that have networked the most intimately with the geographical spaces that define where we live. The ethnographers have talked to the people who know these places. And they do the hard work of translation, of words, concepts, and structural patterns. One of the most famous of these ethnographic writers was Ted Strehlow, whose *Songs of Central Australia* was a monument to translation of Arrernte traditions, something he could do because of his multilingual skills. The results were imperfect, they always will be, but nonetheless some very important aspects of central Australian poetics burst through into his texts.

---

[8] F.R. Leavis, *The Great Tradition* (1948; Harmondsworth: Peregrine, 1962): 17.

[9] Terry Eagleton, *Literary Theory: An Introduction* (1983; Minneapolis: U of Minnesota P, 1996): 160–61.

[10] Marcia Langton, "'The fire that is the centre of each family': Landscapes of the Ancients," in *Visions of Future Landscapes: Proceedings of the Australian Academy of Science 1999, Fenner Conference on the Environment, 2–5 May 1999, Canberra*, ed. Ann Hamblin, foreword by Peter O'Brian (Kingston, ACT: Bureau of Rural Sciences, 2000): 172.

Lilyin Songs from Cape Leveque

In order to add something a little original to this material, I want to go to the producer of Indigenous oral literature with whom I worked, Paddy Roe, who lived in Broome, just up the road from the Mowanjum mob we looked at earlier (he has eighteen works on Austlit.). Here I want to take the opportunity to reproduce and translate some songs that he, in turn, was reproducing and translating in June/July 1985. I said before that translation is quite a mystery. And I want to elaborate briefly on two senses of the word. The first is sociolinguistic, and here I call on the help of Naoki Sakai. Paddy Roe sang some songs which were composed by a Ngumbal woman some years before, and then helped me render them in English. Paddy spoke a few traditional languages from around Broome, plus Broome English. I never got the impression, when he was talking about languages, that they were clearly delineated from one another. Rather, they were 'bordering' on one another all the time.[11] There was no one doing the nation-building work of separating languages off from one another, standardizing and unifying them. Naoki Sakai rather cleverly shows that the unity of language is in fact schematic, an effort of the imagination. No one ever experiences a language in all its unity, but what we do experience all the time are acts of translation. So, as he says, 'translation is anterior to the organic unity of language and [...] this unity is posited through the specific representation of translation" (71). We conventionally represent translation as bridging two languages, as a 'communication model of equivalence and exchange', but that is not what it is, it is a "form of political labour to create continuity at the elusive point of discontinuity in the social" (72). Paddy Roe was creating continuity within the political grouping of the people called 'goolarbooloo'. This is not a 'tribe', since it is composed of different land-holding groups speaking different languages. It is a kind of political confederacy unified by significant ceremonies and responsibility for sites up the coast from south of Broome to One Arm Point. Now, what happens when I join Paddy Roe and we translate into English? The political labour is now across another social discontinuity: Aboriginal regionality can now link to a putative Australian nation, and the songs could now impinge upon what we think is the representation of the national literature.

Now, the second sense of translation, as I indicated before, is the Latourian one. Here translation can be heterogeneous and cross different registers of

---

[11] Naoki Sakai, "How do we count a language? Translation and discontinuity," *Translation Studies* 2.1 (2009): 83. Further page references are in the main text.

reality; it is not just from word to word. Objects can be transformed and translated, too. So, the most important relation in my work with Paddy Roe was not necessarily human-to-human. It was great that I met him and everything, but our relationships were always multiple and mediated in a multiple fashion. Our European-derived theories tend to privilege encounters between humans (the intersubjective) and encounters between humans and the so-called 'world': the subject–object relation. But what if the most important thing in our camp was my Sony cassette tape-recorder? This is not just a helper for the inevitably more important human relationships, some "transparent intermediary," as Graham Harman glosses Latour's thought:

> not some sycophantic eunuch fanning its [human] masters with palm leaves, but always does new work of its own to shape the translation of forces from one point of reality to the next.[12]

The tape-recorder created the capacity for me, and now us, to listen carefully. Listening carefully took the form of me, back at my desk, employing headphones and a stop–start replay device with a foot-pedal, while my fingers were creating a text on a typewriter. In the process, this whole human-technical assemblage engendered a new style of writing.

So the aim is not to *reduce* the number of mediators – for instance, with a narrow humanist view – but to marvel at how many there are, and to pay attention to their multiple effects. And the chain of mediations keeps going on; it doesn't start with some unique human inspiration nor stop at the other end of an imaginary line, with some output, like publication.

In 1985, then, the Sony tape-recorder listened to some songs by Dorothea [durrudiya]. The material is "half Ngumbal," Paddy Roe said, Dorothea herself being a 'half-caste woman', but she "could talk language" and "died in [the] Native Hospital when it was still new," so that would be about the 1960s.[13] The Ngumbal country incorporates a place called James Price Point, which is currently under threat of having a huge liquified natural gas factory built there. Paddy Roe's grandson is engaged in trying to stop this industrialization. I mention this political dimension because Paddy Roe could foresee at that time that whitefellas would try to take over the country he was entrusted to protect. It was the Djaberdjaber and Ngumbal peoples who had passed this country into the hands of Paddy and his daughters. What Paddy Roe was

---

[12] Graham Harman, *Prince of Networks: Bruno Latour and Metaphysics* (Melbourne: re.press, 2009): 15.

[13] Stephen Muecke, field notebook, June–July 1985.

doing in getting me to record these songs was to document his knowledge of the country and its language. So that is a brief translation of the political context; now to the songs:

Lilyin Song, Dorothea talking, in the voice of the *Karrkida* (*chicken hawk song*):

Mingalagan	ngaya	gudibirr	ngumarla
Follow me	I am	rubbish, long feathers	wing
marrgin	karra	buru	narraga
hungry	—	time	dry wood/make a tune

Dandji- ma ngalama   nimbirri-birri djin-ngi minyi

Dance/when I was walking/dancing   rolling head from side to side / full of grasshoppers

Djarlil djarlil dja:rlil   barna nawadja
All tree/bush   ??

Follow me, with my tail feathers all askew
Hungry, time for supper, the wood is dry
I dance as I go, my head rolls east and west, plenty of grasshoppers
And bushes all around…

Part II

nilirrin djirri djinggi   ngayu   marda   gigninya
gets them in his beak, (alongside of me) holds them in claw, nibbles

ganbardja   balgarr ilinyi ngayu   mirranngul
never can catch me any more   be prepared

nanggandjarri djin wandi marda
when I sit down by and by

wanga bula djanu buru
next time come follow me, you'll get more grasshoppers

ngangunda gunda manangarr[14]
Sorry you get no tucker

I can hold them in my beak and claw, right close, and nibble
I'm too quick for you, you're not ready
when I sit down by and by
I'll say, 'Next time come follow me, you'll get more grasshopper.'
Really sorry you missed out!

---

[14] *Manangarr* is an expression used for 'break my heart'.

This is followed by another *lilyin* song in the voice of a little boy 'Moses' [Nurdugun] from Carnot Bay. This is a song composed in the *wirralburru* season, in April, when there are the last storms before the long dry.

> Moses addresses the clouds:
>
> Lighting will come to you as you fly away
> Lightning will come to you, flash, lightning
> Everywhere it sparks off the clouds, rips and holes.
> Goodbye my country.

And the third song I recorded that day is in the voice of a ship's cat, on a pearling boat called *Salvador* [*djalbadjur*], operating out of Beagle Bay. The boat was made in Beagle Bay by Nyul Nyul workers. Dorothea, the creator of the song, was a diver on that boat, "no gardiya" [whitefellas], says Paddy Roe, "only naked divers, picking up two or four shells at a time."[15]

> The cat is called *ngimbicat*, and he is 'growling', telling Captain Augustine off:
>
> Keep that fire away, it's too hot, I can't eat the rice, it can wait.
> This cutter is sailing in today.
> Plates and cups rattling, I grab a knife,
> Got the saucepan, but just can't get it out.
> I would if I could, but now it's a mess.

You see what I mean about the hard work of translation? Let me introduce another aspect of context. *Lilyin* songs are fun; people laugh as they sing them and listen to them. There is always going to be some kind of double meaning going on, otherwise no humour. So that is why, in the first song about the chickenhawk, bearing in mind that it is a woman's song, I risk eroticizing the translation: "Follow me, with my tail feathers all askew."

Just to reinforce the idea that translation is not always about reducing the number of mediations or, indeed, 'facilitating the transfer of meaning', consider the following from Andreas Lommel, remembering fieldwork in the Kimberley in 1938:

> They, of course, taught the corroboree to others still roaming in the bush. I even met some Worora men months later in Broome who taught the corroboree for a fee to others who did not understand their language – this did not matter.

---

[15] Stephen Muecke, field notebook, June–July 1985.

> The poet made his songs in the language of his tribe, but, for rhythm and sentimental reasons, he changed the language so that some of his songs could not be translated.[16]

Now, of course, *lilyin* songs are not the only literary genre in that part of the country. There is an oral narrative poetics, here illustrated by the master-storyteller Paddy Roe:

> just about towards morning -
> just about towards morning -
> *tjipeee* they hear-im -
> he's coming they can hear-im -
> somewhere here - (Laugh)
> they hear-im he's comin' back -
> so they get ready these two bloke -
> (Soft) these two bloke get ready
>
> just about towards morning -
> just about towards morning -
> *tjipeee* they hear-im -
> he's coming they can hear-im -
> somewhere here - (Laugh)
> they hear-im he's comin' back -
> so they get ready these two bloke -
> (Soft) these two bloke get ready.

The mode of transcription brings out the patterns of repetition and elaboration. It is an exciting moment in the story; Paddy is slowing the pace before a moment of climax. He does this with the full repetition of two lines (each line is a breath group), plus two instances of chiasmus or cross-parallelism, plus a mimetic moment (the imitation of the call of the giant eagle *djaringgalong*), plus a moment of deixis, "somewhere here –" reinforced with a laugh. As Stuart Cooke notes, "the story never stops moving, but Roe is still able to change his speed":

> The change of pace exerts a potent gathering power: overlapping and repeating phrases in such a way slows the story considerably, and draws the listener/reader closer with a seductive rhythm.[17]

---

[16] Andreas Lommel & David Mowaljarlai, "Shamanism in North-West Australia," *Oceania* 64.4 (June 1994): 281.

[17] Stuart Cooke, *Speaking the Earth's Languages: A Theory for Australian–Chilean Postcolonial Poetics* (Cross/Cultures 159; Amsterdam & New York: Rodopi, 2013): 204.

⌘   *The Great Tradition*   35

Miriam Sultan, in her work on *Carpentaria*, notes the same overlapping technique:

> End of paragraph:
> Other things touched him too, and the madness went on and on…
> Beginning of following paragraph:
> On and on the floodwaters raced…[18]

This supports, I hope, the argument that the work of Alexis Wright and Kim Scott, among others, assures continuity, not between the ancient and the modern, as if the break were always there to reassure whitefellas that their moment of intervention should always be marked, that real history began in 1788, but simply that there is continuity in the Great Tradition. I have suggested that this comes not so much via preservation of forms or contents as through, for instance, the force of numbers: there was and is a lot of stuff out there. Dorothea could have had her book of song-poetry if a researcher had got to her; Butcher Joe would have had his, if the ethnomusicologist Ray Keogh had lived to publish his songs, his *nurlu* that he had recorded so lovingly and meticulously. Forces run through traditions, vitalizing them. "Everything stands up alive brand new," as David Mowaljarlai says.[19] It is an a-modern, non-periodizing vision of literary formations that follows the traces of energy across forms and through materials that are brought together sometimes fortuitously. A song-poem might find new life as a written text, sure, but it might fail in the translation. An archive might join forces with a narrative style and a visual cinematic language and the result is Rolf de Heer's *Ten Canoes* (2006). These forms and materials coexist; they are not lined up on a time-line of technological improvement, such that the printed word must always confirm while displacing the spoken, and so on.

I want to thank you for bringing me here to hear me speak, and to transmit and translate the words of those Kimberley people to whom I owe so much. I could have just emailed the text, but you wanted me here to hear me speak; why is that?

---

[18] Miriam Sultan, "Don't read, better to listen: Oral and Written literatures in Alexis Wright's *Carpentaria*" (Honours thesis, University of New South Wales, 2011): 45.

[19] Malnic & Mowaljarlai, *Yorro Yorro: Everything Standing Up Alive.*

Works Cited

Cooke, Stuart. *Speaking the Earth's Languages: A Theory for Australian–Chilean Postcolonial Poetics* (Cross/Cultures 159; Amsterdam & New York: Rodopi, 2013).

Cosik, Miriam. "Incandescent Ivor Indyk turns down the heat," *The Australian* (26 February 2011), http://www.theaustralian.com.au/news/arts/incandescent-indyk-turns-down-the-heat/story-e6frg8n6-1226012001145 (accessed 20 March 2012).

De Heer, Rolf, & Peter Djigirr. *Ten Canoes* (Memento Films, Fandango Australia; Australia, 2006; 90 min.).

Eagleton, Terry. *Literary Theory: An Inroduction*, (1983; Minneapolis: U of Minnesota P, 1996).

Harman, Graham. *Prince of Networks: Bruno Latour and Metaphysics* (Anamnesis; Melbourne: re.press, 2009).

Langton, Marcia. "Certainty and Uncertainty: Aboriginal Studies as the Fulcrum of National Self-Consciousness," in *First Peoples: Second Chance*, ed. Terry Smith (Canberra: Australian Academy of the Humanities, 1999): 23–45.

——. "'The fire that is the centre of each family': Landscapes of the Ancients," in *Visions of Future Landscapes: Proceedings of the Australian Academy of Science 1999, Fenner Conference on the Environment, 2–5 May 1999, Canberra*, ed. Ann Hamblin, foreword by Peter O'Brian (Kingston, ACT: Bureau of Rural Sciences, 2000): 169–78.

Leavis, F.R. *The Great Tradition* (1948; Harmondsworth: Peregrine, 1962).

Lommel, Andreas, & David Mowaljarlai. "Shamanism in Northwest Australia," *Oceania* 64.4 (June 1994): 277–87.

Malnic, Jutta, & David Mowaljarlai. *Yorro Yorro: Everything Standing Up Alive: Spirit of the Kimberley* (Broome, WA: Magabala, 1993).

Muecke, Stephen. *Ancient & Modern: Time, Culture, and Indigenous Philosophy* (Kensington: New South Wales UP, 2005).

——. *Textual Spaces: Aboriginality and Cultural Studies* (Sydney: U of New South Wales P, 1992).

Reynolds, Henry. *The Other Side of the Frontier* (Kensington: New South Wales UP, 1981).

Rothenberg, Jerome. *Pre-Faces & Other Writings* (New York: New Directions, 1981).

Sakai, Naoki. "How do we count a language? Translation and discontinuity," *Translation Studies* 2.1 (2009): 71–88.

Aboriginal Families, Knowledge, and the Archives: A Case Study

ANNA HAEBICH

P ROFESSOR MICK DODSON has written that as "the fulcrum and the map of indigenous law and power" Aboriginal kinship and family structures have been the target of "the unilateral seizure of power and the uninvited encroachment of the state."[1] As an Indigenous minority within the Western state, Aboriginal families experienced "constant structural conflict" (2). Subjected to "systematic violation" (2) through direct and indirect state intervention, they have been denied the right to "live according to their culture and to transmit that culture" (4) and to preserve their knowledge and educate their children "'in conformity with their own convictions'" (2). British invasion and colonization during the nineteenth century took Aboriginal lands by force, decimated communities, and undermined the foundations of their cultures. The consequent erosion of kinship structures and knowledge transmission continued during the twentieth century through direct government attacks on the Aboriginal family: children were forcibly taken and reared in institutions to become menial servants, never to return to their homes; assimilation policies in the 1950s and 1960s sought to truncate extended families into nuclear units living the 'Australian way of life' within the Australian nation. Aboriginal extended families survived despite this onslaught due to their vital role in providing economic and emotional support

---

[1] Mick Dodson, "The Rights of Indigenous Peoples in the International Year of the Family," *Family Matters* 37 (1994): 3, 2; repr. in *Australian Institute of Family Studies*, http://www.aifs.gov.au/institute/pubs/fm1/fm37md.html (accessed 20 March 2012). Further page references are in the main text.

and security in a punitive racist environment and as a site of Aboriginal agency, resistance, and survival.

In the bureaucratic apparatus set up to govern Aboriginal populations, the model of the patriarchal settler family provided a vital classifying unit and tool of management in the record systems built up in most states and territories last century. Many Aboriginal family surnames today can be traced back to early record keepers who replaced personal and kinship names with patronymic surnames (often derived from employers or place of residence) and in this way tracked and ordered groups of people related by kinship and place.[2] Most families adopted these names as their own. New surnames given to children removed from their families also endured. These surnames provided the basis for organizing thousands of records containing vast amounts of information about the families and their members assembled over the decades. Governments organized and managed this knowledge to suit their own purposes in executing their responsibilities and duties to Aboriginal families and in controlling and monitoring their activities. By appropriating and taking authority over this knowledge, they further eroded the authority of the family. Until recent decades, few Aboriginal families even knew of the existence of these records.

What is striking about the archives is the degree of totalitarian control, overt racism, and absence of accountability they evince concerning the history of past treatment of Aboriginal people. One can, then, express little wonder at the actions of governments in Queensland and Western Australia to quarantine and destroy files and even threaten to take legal action against researchers.[3] But what is the value of this information, produced through a Western bureaucratic system of knowledge-creation, for Aboriginal families today? Governments continue to validate the records, and Aboriginal people are obliged to draw on them in formal procedures to prove Aboriginal identity, to make claims for native title, and to seek compensation for Stolen

---

[2] Sally Marie Babidge, "Family affairs: an historical anthropology of state practice and Aboriginal agency in a rural town" (doctoral dissertation, James Cook University, 2004): 104–105.

[3] Lauren Marsh & Steve Kinnane, "Ghost Files: The Missing Files of the Department of Indigenous Affairs Archives," *Journal of Studies in Western Australian History* 23 (2003): 115–16, *West Australian* newspaper (18 July 1981), and Ros Kidd, "Indigenous Archival Records at risk," in *Australian Indigenous Knowledge and Libraries*, ed. Martin Nakata & Marcia Langton (Canberra, Australian Academic and Research Libraries, 2005): 156–59.

Generations and Stolen Wages and for family reunions. Yet Aboriginal researchers warn against the inherent biases and contradictions of these records. Steve Kinnane and Lauren Marsh[4] note their "inherent subjectivity [...] these archives speak from the voice of a European." For Lynette Russell, the Western and Aboriginal knowledge systems are "incommensurable ontologies"; nevertheless, she argues that "communication and decision-making" between Aboriginal people and archivists may enable Aboriginal researchers to reclaim the information as their own.[5] In doing so, she draws on J.M. Flavier's position that "Indigenous information systems are dynamic, and are continually influenced by internal creativity and experimentation as well as by contact with external systems."[6]

In his Loris Williams Memorial Lecture at the 2011 Australian Society of Archivists Symposium, Professor Martin Nakata endorsed the view that it is vital to "re-contextualize the record" to ensure readings from an Indigenous viewpoint.[7] An example is Russell's documentation of her "conflicted relationship" with the medical files concerning her great-grandmother, but, too, how the family transformed and embraced the painful details as a profound understanding of her life experience.[8] In his family biography *Shadow Lines*, Kinnane demonstrates the creative use of the files "in Aboriginal hands" as he weaves together family memory and government records to re-create the life of his grandmother, Jessie Argyle. He describes the files as "double-edged": while they enabled him to reconstruct the story of her life, it would have been "preferable" if the files and "the culture that created them also did not exist."[9]

---

[4] Marsh & Kinnane, "Ghost Files," 111.

[5] Lynette Russell, "Indigenous Knowledge and Archives: Accessing Hidden History and Understandings," in *Australian Indigenous Knowledge and Libraries*, ed. Martin Nakata & Marcia Langton (Canberra, Australian Academic and Research Libraries, 2005): 167, 162.

[6] Juan M. Flavier, Antonio de Jesús, Conrado S. Navarro & D. Michael Warren, "The regional program for the promotion of Indigenous knowledge in Asia," in *The Cultural Dimension of Development: Indigenous Knowledge Systems*, ed. D. Michael Warren, L. Jan Slikkerveer & David Brokensha (London: Intermediate Technology, 1995): 479.

[7] Cited in Brenda Gifford, "Conference report on Archiving the Iconic – Australian Society of Archivists Symposium 20th October 2011" (MS).

[8] For further details, see Russell, "Indigenous Knowledge and Archives," 162–64.

[9] Steve Kinnane, *Shadow Lines* (Fremantle, WA: Fremantle Arts Centre Press, 2003): 127.

In a poignant scene of a visit with his mother to his grandmother's first employer, Kinnane describes how he deliberately placed her personal file on the table for all to see. But, as memories were shared over cups of tea and cake, the file remained unopened and untouched, the silent reminder of the many painful stories in her life.[10]

In 2005, Professors Marcia Langton and Nakata stated that under international human rights covenants Aboriginal people have the right to know and access the files and to "claim, restore and continue their knowledge and cultural heritage."[11] Indigenous claims have intensified since Australia's ratification of the 2007 Declaration on the Rights of Indigenous Peoples. The Aboriginal and Torres Strait Islander Social Justice Commissioner Mick Gooda, at the 2010 *Archives and Indigenous Human Rights Interdisciplinary Workshop: Archives and Indigenous Human Rights*,[12] described the Declaration as a "pathway for law and policy reform," with its covenants based on principles of self-determination, participation in decision-making, free prior and informed consent, and cultural rights. Gooda called for a "resettling of relationships" between Aboriginal people and the archives through a process described by Langton and Nakita as being "about dialogue, conversation, education, and working through things together [...] [and] providing the opportunity and means for Indigenous people to be part of what they determine should be done."[13]

Governing Families Through the Files: A Case Study

This essay further explores the nature of these records through a case-study of the West Australian archive known as the DIA files (Department of Indigenous Affairs). The archive covers the period from the passing of the 1905 Aborigines Act to the 1972 Aboriginal Affairs Planning Authority Act, which

---

[10] Kinnane, *Shadow Lines*, 138–39.

[11] Martin Nakata & Marcia Langton, "Introduction" to *Australian Indigenous Knowledge and Libraries*, ed. Martin Nakata & Marcia Langton (Canberra, Australian Academic and Research Libraries, 2005): 4.

[12] Mick Gooda, "Towards an Understanding of the Archival and Recordkeeping Implications of Australian and International Human Rights for Indigenous Australians," in *Interdisciplinary Workshop: Archives and Indigenous Human Rights* (Melbourne: Australian Human Rights Commission, 2010): 2–8.

[13] Langton & Nakata, "Introduction," 5.

brought an end to the discriminatory legislative regime. The case-study addresses the archive as an artefact of history and documents its provenance: how the records were collected, organized and used over time; how they shaped the lives of Aboriginal people; the politics surrounding the opening up of the archives to researchers; and recent initiatives to protect Aboriginal rights over such records. The case study follows the example of Ann Stoler[14] in her study of Dutch colonial archives by addressing the records as "active, generative substances with histories, as documents with itineraries of their own." The intended outcome is the beginning of what Nicholas Dirks calls "a biography of the archive."[15]

My relationship with the DIA archive spans a period of over thirty years and includes intensive periods of research for my doctorate, three major books and numerous articles. For much of this time I was scouring the archives for material to construct narratives about how the state managed and governed Aboriginal people in Western Australia. To this I added details about the impact on Aboriginal people that I gleaned from reading against the bureaucratic grain of the archive and listening to Aboriginal voices captured in the documents and collecting oral histories from families. Along the way I observed the changing status of the archives and the new uses of its files. I forged relationships with the archivists and other researchers. I did research in similar archives around Australia and found difference and sameness. My own interests became more reflective, influenced by the broader 'archival turn' furthered by Jacques Derrida in *Archive Fever*[16] from 'archive-as-source to archive-as-subject'. The turn encouraged a 'blurring' of approaches from cultural studies and critical history in studies of what Stoler describes as "the broader social life of an archive, what might be called 'ethnography in an archival mode'."[17]

The DIA archive is a tangible artefact of the State's power over Aboriginal families. The sense of control and oppression of Aboriginal bodies and minds is overwhelming. There is no escaping the tumult of family and personal information contained in its pages. Marsh and Kinnane describe the records as

---

[14] Ann Laura Stoler, *Along the Archival Grain: Epistemic Anxieties and Colonial Common Sense* (Princeton NJ: Princeton UP, 2009): 1.

[15] Quoted in Stoler, *Along the Archival Grain*, 48.

[16] Jacques Derrida, *Archive Fever: A Freudian Impression* (Chicago: U of Chicago P, 1995).

[17] Stoler, *Along the Archival Grain*, 44–45.

"archives of a repressive regime" that were deliberately forged to meet the needs of "an autocratic administration."[18] They draw comparisons with the "repressive archives" of the East German Secret Police (Stasi) about their civilian populations.[19] Eric Ketelaar likens the archive to the "record-prison" of Stasi "womb-to-tomb" surveillance.[20]

The DIA archive is unique among West Australian archival collections in terms of the degree of racism, power, and control. Its records demonstrate the totalitarian powers exercised over Aboriginal people and the lack of accountability in terms of control, surveillance, services provided, and punishments meted out. Racism and discrimination are legalized and institutionalized in its files. Racial classifications based on descent, culture, and associations categorize people as 'Aboriginal native', 'half-caste' or 'quarter-caste' and administrators deciding on which classification applied left a trail of fractional calculations across the files. Classification was a life sentence with serious implications for Aboriginal families. Some family members were assigned to different categories so that, under the terms of the 1905 Act, they could no longer live together. Responsibility lay with the family to prove that categories did not apply to their particular case. Exemptions of people who had attained a suitable degree of 'civilization' were rarely granted and could be revoked at any time.

Duties of care outlined in the 1905 Aborigines Act determined the subjects of files in the archive. In practice this meant neglectful treatment and meagre fare of rations; medicine, and shelter for the destitute, care and education for children; and protection in the work place and, for women, from sexual abuse. Families were refused access to mainstream state and federal welfare services and benefit payments until the reforms of the 1950s and 1960s. The 1905 Act also contained punitive controls over Aboriginal people: who they could associate with; where they could live and work; their earnings and personal property; family life; women's choice of marriage partners and sexual contacts; and parents' right to guardianship of their children. They could be removed to

---

[18] Marsh & Kinnane, "Ghost Files," 114.

[19] "Ghost Files," 112.

[20] Arthur R. Miller, *The Assault on Privacy: Computers, Databanks, and Dossiers* (Ann Arbor: U of Michigan P, 1971), quoted by Thomas S. McCoy, "Surveillance, Privacy and Power: Information Trumps Knowledge," *Communications* 16 (1991): 33–47, here 35.Quoted in Eric Ketelaar, "Archival Temples, Archival Prisons: Modes of Power and Protection," *Archival Science* 2 (2002): 228.

institutions and detained indefinitely or imprisoned under the 1905 Act for drinking alcohol or entering prohibited areas, and could be punished in a myriad of ways for resisting or speaking out against their oppressive treatment.

The files created prior to the 1950s are also unique in being the product of an idiosyncratic ad-hoc administrative process with failings that raise serious doubts about their reliability and accuracy as well as about the breaching of rights to privacy of Aboriginal families. This system operated from a small, centralized head office in Perth with honorary protectors acting on the local level who were mainly police officers but also employers and missionaries. Police officers who were untrained and had many other duties were mainly responsible for collecting information on local Aboriginal families. That this was often inaccurate and unreliable has been verified by families today. It was also the case that private family and personal information travelled back and forth between police officers and the Aborigines Department and this could find its way into police files as well. While the ill-defined chain of command often manifested itself in punitive action, it could also provide opportunities for evasive action – for example, when sympathetic police officers failed to carry out orders to remove Aboriginal children from their families.

The records of the DIA archive were created by various departments.[21] The departments administered the 1905 Aborigines Act and its amending Acts,[22] which were all fully repealed in 1972. They acted in accord with policies that shifted from protectionism in 1905 to biological absorption in the 1930s, assimilation in the 1950s, and self-management in the early 1970s. New policies and laws together with the intentions of new departmental heads (termed Chief Protectors of Aborigines) and changing historical contexts shaped the archive and its shifts in pace and rhythms, referred to by Stoler as "uneven densities" of "archival preoccupations."[23] Other vital documentation includes Annual Reports, Royal Commissions and inquiries, parliamentary

---

[21] The Aborigines Department, which was amalgamated at various times between 1905 and 1936 with the Departments of Aborigines and Fisheries, the Chief Secretary, and the North West; the Department of Native Affairs (1936–55); and the Department of Native Welfare (1956–72).

[22] In the years 1911, 1936, 1944, 1954, and 1964.

[23] Stoler, *Along the Archival Grain*, 35.

debates and papers, and press reports and files of departments of the police and of health.[24]

The first period of the emerging archive from 1905 to 1915 saw the establishment of a loose system of administrative files concerned with implementing the new 1905 Act. Their subject titles bear testimony to the wide scope of the departments new duties – missions, removals of half-caste children, children's homes, rations, blankets, and medical care, Lock Hospitals on Dorre and Bernier Islands, employment on licenced premises, girls in domestic service, circulars to local protectors explaining their new duties, marriage to non-Aboriginal men, cohabitation, legal advice, requests for exemption, ill-treatment of women, prohibited areas, and expulsion of Aboriginal children from state schools. The file covers list the department name, file subject-title, number, and year, and action taken, such as movement of the file within and outside the department. Most files were hand-written, with pages with comments in side columns and references to families and family members scattered through them.

In 1915, a far more active period of the archive began under the watch of the new Chief Protector of Aborigines, A.O. Neville (1915–40). He invigorated the department with his determined application of the Act, attention to efficiency and economy, expansion of departmental institutions, and tours of inspection around the state. On his watch, he accelerated forcible removals of children, training of young people, employment controls and expansion of native settlements in the south. However, Neville's enduring legacy was the record system that he built up from this time. He began by creating a central card series register that assigned to files a number and year and recorded their movement around departments and combinations with any other files. This improved access to data generally and permitted more professional planning as well as supervision of duties of local protectors. With a limited budget, Neville used the records to monitor the issue of rations, blankets, and clothing, the collection of fees for employment agreements and permits, and earnings placed in trust accounts. There were also records about gun licences, exemption applications, and data on convictions, breaches of the Act, deaths and marriages, and the native settlement scheme. Standardized circulars were

---

[24] For a summary listing of these records and the DIA archive, see Damien Hassan, "Records Relating to Aboriginal People and the Administration of Aboriginal Affairs held by the State Records Office of Western Australia," *Journal of Studies in Western Australian History* 22 (2001): 169–76.

issued to protectors and their returns on population size and conditions were filed for use in Annual Reports. Activity quickened over the period and in the Depression years the size and number of files began to swell with admissions of unemployed families to the Moore River Native Settlement, press clippings of public discussion about the Aboriginal 'problem', and new solutions and reporting on the Moseley Royal Commission investigating Aboriginal conditions in the state in 1934.

The major expansion of the archive into a vast collection occurred between 1926 and 1959, when over 27,000 files were created. This has been documented by Marsh and Kinnane and the following discussion draws on their research.[25] The 1915 Series index is the key to these records, providing subject-title and often family names for personal, staff, and administrative files and details tracking their travels through the system. From 1920 onwards, Neville initiated personal files to control and manage individuals and their families that would make up 15,400 or 54 percent of all files created between 1926 and 1959. The average annual population for the same period was 15,000, suggesting the level of scrutiny of individuals around the state. Information, once recorded, was used to control and manage their lives and determine the outcome of all decisions made on their behalf. Over the same period, 10,787 administrative files were created. They vary from short files about specific bureaucratic actions to monoliths of two or three inches thick covering the history of town camps and resident families over decades. During the period, 854 staff files were created, including staff at head office but principally superintendents of settlements and missions, medical practitioners, nurses, and teaching assistants, along with increases during the 1950s with the appointment of field staff. However, staffing levels were always modest and the number of these files suggests the rapid turnover outside of head office.

Personal files demonstrate the department's invasive actions in micromanaging individuals and families. Steve Kinnane allows us to survey the personal file of his grandmother, Jessie Smith (née Argyle) between 1923 and 1936 and the "neat phrases and minimally constructed sentences" that he combined with family memories to construct her life story.[26] When we meet Jessie in 1923 she is around eighteen years of age, she has left the Swan Native Half-Caste Mission where she was sent from the Kimberley when she

---

[25] Marsh & Kinnane, "Ghost Files," 120–25.
[26] State Records Office of Western Australia files 312/1926 and 346/1931 and personal card no 646.

was five years old and given the name Jessie Argyle. She is working as a domestic servant in the country. Her wages and conditions, the employer's permit and fee to hire her and travel were all organized by the department on her behalf, along with payment of her wages into a bank account operated by its officers. They arrange her transport to Perth Hospital for medical treatment and then accommodation in Perth in between jobs. When Jessie starts a relationship with a young Aboriginal man, the department calls in the police. In 1924, after Jessie refuses to settle down or to work for lower wages, she is banished to the Moore River Native Settlement, where she spends long hours sewing garments for no pay at all. The settlement is virtually a prison and living there is a serious health risk: Kinnane records that during the eleven months Jessie was there twenty-four people died out of a population of around a hundred.[27] In 1927, when Jessie is aged twenty-five, her employer is still paying half of her wages to the department and she has to request its officers to buy clothes on her behalf. In 1929 a new file indicates growing personal problems: a stand-up fight with another girl, ejection from accommodation in Perth run by Nurse Mulvale for the department, and Jessie is seriously ill. However, while surveillance of her activities is close, there are many things the department does not know about her life at this time, in particular her serious relationship with Steve's future grandfather – a white man, Edward Smith, who works for the *West Australian* newspaper. In 1930, Jessie informs Chief Protector Neville of her intention to marry and permission is granted under section 42 of the 1905 Aborigines Act. But the surveillance continues, this time over visits by Jessie's 'half-caste' girlfriends to her home, and Smith is informed that, since he is a white man, this is prohibited under Section 21b of the 1905 Act. Neville calls on the Commissioner of Police to stop the girls' visits and threatens to charge Smith over an Aboriginal youth lodging with the couple. Here the file ends.

In 1948, the records underwent a further major shift following the appointment of Stanley G. Middleton as Commissioner for Native Affairs to administer the new policy of assimilation and implement a field system of regional patrol officers who were directly responsible to him. A major goal of the new policy of assimilation was to create model nuclear Aboriginal families living the 'Australian way of life' in the growing suburbs of Perth and country towns around the state. The record system was decentralized, with files being copied and housed in regional offices. Also, as mainstream services were

---

[27] Kinnane, *Shadow Lines*, 183.

opened to Aboriginal families there was more cross-referencing of files between departments. The Department for Community Welfare began its own files for Aboriginal wards now under its care, and child removals and case files dealing with families were created.

Marsh and Kinnane also document the destruction of many of the records, dating from 1938 and escalating during the 1950s. Some were recklessly burned in office incinerators, prompting the authors to again draw comparisons with Stasi agents hastily shredding incriminating documents from their extensive archive. Using the entries in the series card register, Marsh and Kinnane calculated the percentages of files destroyed: 55 percent of administrative files, 21 percent of personal files, and 71 percent of staff files. They also trace the gradual realization of the historic value of West Australia's archival records with the appointment of a State Archivist in 1945, the depositing of archive records in the J.S. Battye Library of West Australian History and State Archives from 1956 onwards, and the appointment of a Records Committee in 1958 to oversee disposal schedules for departments. In 1961, the Committee approved the Department of Native Welfare disposal schedule, which still permitted the destruction of valuable material. It was not until the 1990s that there were calls for a moratorium on the destruction of these invaluable records.

1972 was a pivotal year in the history of the archive, when the Department of Native Welfare was dismantled and its duties divided between two new departments, the Aboriginal Affairs Planning Authority (AAPA) and the Department for Community Welfare (DCW). The former assumed responsibility for policy and services to Aboriginal people and the new areas of Aboriginal land, sites of significance, and cultural heritage. The DCW took over the care and placement of Aboriginal children in the welfare sector and family and community support. The archive was split up in the division: files still in use were transferred to the appropriate departments, while other historical files were housed in the Battye Library, to be managed by the State Archivist but still under the control of the AAPA and the DCW.

The records were not fated to gather dust on the shelves of the Library annexes where I first encountered them in the 1970s. Instead, they took on a new lease of life as invaluable sources in the new field of Aboriginal history and then as the centre of controversy in conflicts between the government and

Aboriginal leaders and researchers.[28] The 1970s was a time of growing tension over Aboriginal issues. Historians were exposing past injustices documented in the records, and Aboriginal activists on the National Aboriginal Consultative Committee (re-formed as the National Aboriginal Conference in 1976) used their work to further their attacks on the conservative Court Liberal government. This escalated in 1976 when the Laverton Royal Commission, investigating clashes between police and Aboriginal people at Laverton and Skull Creek in December 1974 and January 1975, found that police officers could not justify arrests made and had invented some parts of their accounts. Then, in the late 1970s, came the Noonkanbah dispute in the Kimberley region and the Aboriginal struggle publicized nationally and internationally that succeeded in stopping mining on the disputed sacred land.

The Court government, on high alert to avoid any further embarrassment over Aboriginal issues, acted quickly to protect its own. In 1980, the Police Department placed an embargo on researchers using its records and lodged a complaint with the State Archivist over their use in documenting the actions of an ancestor of a serving senior police officer then in charge of Police Community Relations and the Police Library. The culprit was the historian Andrew Gill, in a 1977 article.[29] Then, in November, Mr Bill Hassell, the Chief Secretary, Minister for Police and Traffic, and Minister for Community Welfare, placed a blanket restriction on the use of Department of Community Welfare files as well, following a reported breach of classified material. Hassell was known as an arch-conservative who was unsympathetic to Aboriginal issues. By mid-1981 both departments had devised systems where researchers were required to make written applications to use identified records and to provide proof of identity, reasons for requesting the files, and names of three referees. They also appointed researchers, and, in the case of the DCW, a lawyer to read through the files and declare them to be 'restricted' or 'open' for use by researchers. They were the only government departments in Western Australia to take such action.

Speaking to the *West Australian* newspaper in mid-1981, the Acting Minister Mr Ray Young claimed that it was "normal practice" to restrict files that could cause embarrassment to individuals or families and sensitive papers that

---

[28] Historians included Bob Reece, Peter Biskup, Andrew Gill, Mary–Anne Jebb, Lois Tilbrook, Neville Green, Su–Jane Hunt, Anna Haebich, and Cathy Clement.

[29] Andrew Gill, "Aborigines, Settlers and Police in the Kimberleys, 1887–1905," *Journal of Studies in Western Australian History* 1 (June 1977): 1–8.

were contrary to public interest on security or other grounds.[30] He warned that researchers "breaking promises not to disclose classified information could be prosecuted." Aboriginal leaders had a different view of this. The Executive Officer of the Aboriginal Legal Service, Rob Riley, claimed that access would be restricted to researchers viewed favourably by the Minister. The Deputy Chair of the Australian Institute of Aboriginal Studies, Ken Colbung, opposed the embargo on historical files and ministerial control over the information. The State Archivist, Margaret Medcalfe, recommended that the files be screened for personal content. She noted the conflict between the upsurge of research and increasing concern about privacy and worried that the files would be used for "other than pure research."

The archives also acquired growing significance for Aboriginal families and communities, who by now were well aware of their existence. For many, there was a passionate interest in learning from the files about their family history and how their people had been treated in the past. Some were obliged to turn to them for evidence to meet official requirements for proof of their Aboriginal identity and family background. For example, proof of Aboriginal identity for official purposes is based on self-identification as an Aboriginal person, acceptance by the Aboriginal community, and evidence of Aboriginal descent. For members of the Stolen Generations and their descendants and organizations assisting them, these government records may contain the only documentation to establish their Aboriginality for these official purposes and to reunite with their families. In 2010, when the West Australian government introduced the Redress programme offering limited monetary compensation for the Stolen Generations, many applicants were obliged to turn to the files to prove they were removed and had suffered hardship in institutions and employment. Government officers used the same records to check the reliability of their claims. The government's offer in 2012 of compensation of $2,000 for Stolen Wages lost when wages of Aboriginal workers were deposited in department accounts similarly required applicants to provide proof of their work history and statements of wages deposited on their behalf. Once again the government records were the only place where most could hope to find this information.

The archive also became a vital area of research for native-title claimants after the 1992 Mabo decision of the High Court of Australia paved the way for Aboriginal people to seek to have their native title recognized under

---

[30] *West Australian* (18 July 1981).

Australian law. To do so, they need to demonstrate their family history and connection to their land, heritage, and culture. Native-title claims require extensive research by government and claimant representatives seeking either to dispute or prove descent, and connection to country and, once again, the archive is a vital source of this information and in some areas becomes the core of a claim. It is also the case that these official documents and departmental records generally take precedence over family accounts of their own history.

With growing awareness of the records, Aboriginal leaders began to lobby for greater community access and control of the archive, and during the 1990s two national government inquiries focused attention on their vital significance for Aboriginal families. In his report for the Royal Commission into Aboriginal Deaths in Custody in 1991, Pat Dodson, the Aboriginal Commissioner for Western Australia, addressed the tragic impact of the official breaking up families, noting that of the ninety-nine people whose cases were examined by the Royal Commission forty-three had been separated from their families in childhood. Dodson called on governments to help rebuild Aboriginal families, reinstate pride in family experiences, and foster a stronger sense of identity and interaction within family networks. Vital to this process was access to all government archival records pertaining to family and community and the development of research capacity and resources to create family histories and understanding of the past and to re-establish links with family members removed under past policies of the government.[31]

In the *Bringing Them Home Report* (1997) of the National Inquiry into the Separation of Aboriginal and Torres Strait Islander Children from Their Families, Commissioners Sir Ronald Wilson, President of the Human Rights and Equal Opportunity Commission, and Mick Dodson, the Aboriginal and Torres Strait Islander Social Justice Commissioner, went much further in their conclusions. They acknowledged the profoundly tragic impact of the history of the Stolen Generations on Aboriginal families, a policy that had "jeopardized their very survival [and] impoverished their capacity to control and direct their future development."[32] Government responsibility to return re-

---

[31] Pat Dodson, in *National Report of the Royal Commission into Aboriginal Deaths in Custody*, vol. 2: 78.

[32] Human Rights and Equal Opportunity Commission, *Bringing Them Home: Report of the National Inquiry into the Separation of Aboriginal and Torres Strait*

cords of this history of genocidal government policies identified by the Commissioners as "gross violations of human rights" to families and communities went far beyond any "standard justifications."[33] The knowledge was vital for their survival as Indigenous peoples and for their recovery from these violations. Free and open access was their fundamental right. The extensive review conducted by the Inquiry into existing archival services and procedures found them to be sadly lacking in most jurisdictions, and the report recommendations proposed the adoption of a human-rights framework for archives, based on self-determination, non-discrimination, and cultural renewal.

In her evidence to the inquiry, the Indigenous-heritage activist Henrietta Fourmile provided a compelling human-rights argument for Aboriginal ownership and control of the records and for them to be rehoused in "Aboriginal cultural facilities comparable to those available to non-Aboriginal Australians."[34] Restitution of the records would bring back to families vital information for retelling and passing on history and to restore the benefits of this cultural heritage and stimulate memories of cultural knowledge and history. This would break the cycle of non-Aboriginal specialists interpreting and disseminating Aboriginal knowledge. An informed community of Aboriginal specialists in culture, history, and teaching would create a strong sense of power and destiny. Fourmile concluded that for the revitalization and resurgence of Aboriginal culture and to "contribute our culture to the world heritage on our own terms, then we must once again be able to own, control and enjoy our cultural and historical resources housed within our own community facilities."[35]

Views expressed by Fourmile that conflicted with Australian archive laws could only be indirectly included in the recommendations of the *Bringing Them Home Report*.[36] Instead, the Report recommended the formation of Records Taskforces to identify categories of records, advise where they should be held, and consider ways of returning materials to communities. In

---

Islander Children from their Families (Sydney: Human Rights and Equal Opportunity Commission, 1997): 279.

[33] Human Rights and Equal Opportunity Commission, *Bringing Them Home*, 295.

[34] Henrietta Fourmile (1989), quoted in Human Rights and Equal Opportunity Commission, *Bringing Them Home*, 307.

[35] Fourmile (1989), quoted in Human Rights and Equal Opportunity Commission, *Bringing Them Home*, 308.

[36] Human Rights and Equal Opportunity Commission, *Bringing Them Home*, 301.

the long term, repositories could be created and developed into Aboriginal-controlled 'healing centres' of history, culture, and language, with document and oral history archives and genealogies, and experience reports and histories of removal and its effects on families. Also present would be the knowledge, experience, and skills of those who had returned and of community elders and traditional healers.

The West Australian Government's response to these recommendations was lukewarm. A Records Taskforce was set up with a membership of public servants from relevant departments, a small minority of them Aboriginal, to identify, locate, and preserve government and church and mission records associated with Aboriginal families. The culmination of this work was the publication of *Looking West: A Guide to Aboriginal Records in Western Australia* (2004), which details the location of government and non-government records, the type of service, years of operation, information in the records, and contact details. Such record guides promised to further open up access to the Aboriginal records.

Meanwhile, there were significant structural changes affecting the DIA archive following the proclamation of the State Records Act in 2001. A new streamlined State Records Office (SRO) was created that operated as a separate agency from the State Library, with the State Records Commission as its controlling body. Of significance for the DIA archive was the fact that all restricted files, many of them DIA and police records, were to be reviewed within five years of the proclamation of the Act in 2006. SRO staff coordinating the work of the departments to ensure consistency across agencies found various blanket and restriction systems operating, often with no apparent good reason. An estimated forty percent of the total SRO collection was opened and, anecdotally, "thousands of files" from the DIA archive.[37]

Today, departmental permission letters are no longer required to access DIA open files and all those created before 1908 are automatically available. Some later records remain restricted to protect confidentiality of persons, but researchers can apply to the department for permission under particular circumstances. The SRO provides the initial point of contact for members of the public seeking DIA files. The Family Information Records Bureau operated by the Department for Community Development (formerly Department of Community Welfare) functions as a 'first stop shop' for Aboriginal people

---

[37] Gerard Foley, Archivist, State Records Office of Western Australia, January 2012, private communication.

seeking family information held in its archival records and controls access to personal records, which is limited to the individuals concerned or their families.

There were further advances. Access to files was facilitated by digitizing indexes and guides to the DIA records and file titles, but few of the records have been made available in digital format. SRO staff are active in their profession and follow guidelines of the Aboriginal protocols of the Australian Society of Archivists' 1997 Policy Statement on Archival Services and Aboriginal and Torres Strait and Islander Peoples (now out-dated) and the widely endorsed Aboriginal and Torres Strait Islander Library and Information Resources Network (ATSILIRN) 2005 Protocol for Libraries, Archives, and Information Services. Still, the principal formal reference to Aboriginal requirements in the 2001 Act remains the protection of matters of 'cultural sensitivity' requiring consultation with communities, and is of relevance mainly to museum collections. This is still a long way from the goals of human-rights activists advocating for change in the handling of Aboriginal archives.

Recent significant statements on human rights and the archive have come from the Trust and Technology project in Melbourne (2004–2008) and the 2010 pre-conference workshop of the Australian Society of Archivists in Melbourne, 'Archives and Indigenous Human Rights: Towards an Understanding of the Archival and Recordkeeping Implications of Australian and International Human Rights for Indigenous Australians'.[38] Both brought leading Aboriginal and non-Aboriginal archivists, lawyers, academics, and Aboriginal community members together in Melbourne and produced important outcomes for Indigenous archives and human rights.

The Trust and Technology project explored Koorie opinions and experiences with archives and how they could work with archivists to create archival systems based on "Indigenous knowledge, memory and frameworks of evidence" that will work for their communities. The findings proposed "legal, policy and professional approaches" that endorse Indigenous ways and reposition the people as "co-creators of archival records with a range of rights in the records" and as "partners in development and implementation of archival systems and services." Participants developed the 2009 'Statement of Principles Relating to Indigenous Knowledge and the Archives and the 2009 Draft Position Statement on Human Rights, Indigenous Communities in Aus-

---

[38] Gerard Foley, Archivist, State Records Office of Western Australia, January 2012, private communication (2012).

tralia and the Archives'.[39] The project identified as obstacles to change Australia's legal and archival frameworks that do not incorporate principles of Indigenous human rights or cultural rights and reported Koori sentiments that resonated with the Aboriginal lawyer Terri Janke's observation to the 2010 AIHR workshop that it was "unjust that records of great sensitivity and importance to [Indigenous people] should be owned by non-Indigenous organizations and people."[40]

AIHR workshop participants endorsed the 2005 ATSILIRN Protocol and documented examples of other national and international best practice. Like Commissioner Gooda, referred to earlier, they set out a detailed road map and action agenda based on principles of the 2007 Declaration on the Rights of Indigenous Peoples listed above. In an article published after the workshop, Sue McKemmish and her co-writers challenged archivists to consider a new participant model of "record creators," being any person who has "contributed to a records creative process and has been affected by its action" and who supports "the enforcement of a broader spectrum of rights and obligations."[41] This connects with Lynette Russell's vision for situations of trust where Aboriginal people working in innovative collaborations with archivists can make new systems where their "incommensurate ontologies" can be creatively shared and Indigenous people and Indigenous knowledge creatively added to the mix.[42] These are heady prospects for the next stage of life of the DIA archive and its evolving biography.

---

[39] Sue McKemmish et al., "Australian Indigenous Knowledge and the Archives: Embracing Multiple Ways of Knowing and Keeping," *Journal of Archives and Manuscripts* 38.1 (2009): 29.

[40] Sue McKemmish et al., "Resetting Relationships: Archives and Indigenous Human Rights in Australia," *Journal of Archives and Manuscripts* 39.1 (2010): 113–14.

[41] McKemmish et al., "Resetting Relationships," 125.

[42] Russell, *Indigenous Knowledge and Archives*, 170.

Works Cited

Babidge, Sally Marie. "Family Affairs: An Historical Anthropology of State Practice and Aboriginal Agency in a Rural Town" (doctoral dissertation, James Cook University, 2004).

Derrida, Jacques. *Archive Fever: A Freudian Impression*, tr. Eric Prenowitz (*Mal d'Archive: Une Impression Freudienne*, 1995; Chicago: U of Chicago P, 1995). Originally tr. in *Diacritics* 25.2 (Summer 1995): 9–63.

Dodson, Mick. The Rights of Indigenous Peoples in the International Year of the Family," *Family Matters* 37 (1994): 34–47; repr. in *Australian Institute of Family Studies*, http://www.aifs.gov.au/institute/pubs/fm1/fm37md.html (accessed 20 March 2012).

Flavier, Juan M., Antonio de Jesús, Conrado S. Navarro & D. Michael Warren. "The regional program for the promotion of Indigenous knowledge in Asia," in *The Cultural Dimension of Development: Indigenous Knowledge Systems*, ed. D. Michael Warren, L Jan Slikkerveer & David Brokensha (London: Intermediate Technology, 1995): 479–87.

Gifford, Brenda. "Conference report on Archiving the Iconic – Australian Society of Archivists Symposium 20th October 2011" (MS).

Gill, Andrew. "Aborigines, Settlers and Police in the Kimberleys, 1887–1905," *Journal of Studies in Western Australian History* 1 (June 1977): 1–28.

Gooda, Mick. "Towards an Understanding of the Archival and Recordkeeping Implications of Australian and International Human Rights for Indigenous Australians," in *Interdisciplinary Workshop: Archives and Indigenous Human Rights* (Melbourne: Australian Human Rights Commission, 2010): 2–8.

Hassan, Damien. "Records Relating to Aboriginal People and the Administration of Aboriginal Affairs held by the State Records Office of Western Australia," *Journal of Studies in Western Australian History* 22 (2001): 169–76.

Ketelaar, Eric. "Archival Temples, Archival Prisons: Modes of Power and Protection," *Archival Science* 2 (2002): 221–38.

Kidd, Ros. "Indigenous Archival Records at Risk," in *Australian Indigenous Knowledge and Libraries*, ed. Martin Nakata & Marcia Langton (Canberra, *Australian Academic and Research Libraries* 36.2, June 2005): 156–67.

Kinnane, Steve. *Shadow Lines* (Fremantle, WA: Fremantle Arts Centre Press, 2003).

McCoy, Thomas S. "Surveillance, Privacy and Power: Information Trumps Knowledge," *Communications* 16 (1991): 33–47.

McKemmish, Sue, Shannon Faulkhead, Livia Iacovino & Kirsten Thorpe. "Australian Indigenous Knowledge and the Archives: Embracing Multiple Ways of Knowing and Keeping," *Journal of Archives and Manuscripts* 38.1 (May 2009): 27–50.

McKemmish, Sue, Livia Iacovino, Eric Ketelaar, Melissa Castan & Lynette Russell. "Resetting Relationships: Archives and Indigenous Human Rights in Australia," *Journal of Archives and Manuscripts* 39.1 (2010): 107–44.

Marsh, Lauren, & Steve Kinnane. "Ghost Files: The Missing Files of the Department of Indigenous Affairs Archives," *Journal of Studies in Western Australian History* 23 (2003): 111–27.

Miller, Arthur R. *The Assault on Privacy: Computers, Databanks, and Dossiers* (Ann Arbor: U of Michigan P, 1971).

Nakata, Martin, & Marcia Langton. "Introduction" to *Australian Indigenous Knowledge and Libraries*, ed. Martin Nakata & Marcia Langton (Canberra, *Australian Academic and Research Libraries* 36.2, June 2005): 1–4.

Johnston, Elliott, Royal Commissioner. *National Report of the Royal Commission into Aboriginal Deaths in Custody*, 5 vols. (Canberra: AGPS, 1991–92).

Russell, Lynette. "Indigenous Knowledge and Archives: Accessing Hidden History and Understandings," in *Australian Indigenous Knowledge and Libraries*, ed. Martin Nakata & Marcia Langton (Canberra, *Australian Academic and Research Libraries* 36.2, June 2005): 169–80.

Stoler, Ann Laura. *Along the Archival Grain: Epistemic Anxieties and Colonial Common Sense* (Princeton NJ: Princeton UP, 2009).

Wilson, Sir Ronald, & Michael Dodson. *Bringing Them Home: Report of the National Inquiry into the Separation of Aboriginal and Torres Strait Islander Children from their Families* (Sydney: Human Rights and Equal Opportunity Commission, 1997).

Decolonizing Methodology in an Arnhem Land Garden[*]

MICHAEL CHRISTIE

Introduction

NOT SO LONG AGO, I was invited to take part in a government consultancy into the feasibility of a remote Aboriginal community garden. The Crops Forestry and Horticulture Division of the Northern Territory Government was seeking "feedback, input and comment" on a proposal by an international group called Community Supported Agriculture. It was proposed that a *Balanda* (non-Indigenous) gardener would establish the garden at Galiwin'ku, a Yolŋu Aboriginal island community off the north coast of Arnhem Land. On remote Aboriginal communities, unemployment rates are among the highest in Australia, and food prices, because of the transportation costs, are also among the highest. A community garden makes good sense for a range of reasons including community health, employment, and food security.

Having worked coordinating the studies of Yolŋu languages and culture at our small regional university for nearly twenty years, and having been a linguist in remote Yolŋu communities for almost twenty years before that, I knew the community and its people and languages well, and my colleague John Greatorex and I had worked with senior Yolŋu knowledge-authorities as

---

[*] Thanks to John Greatorex and Helen Verran to their contributions to this work, practical and theoretical. Thanks to the Yolŋu consultants Guthadjaka, Maratja, Garŋgulkpuy, Yurranydjil, Bepuka and Djekurr who patiently explained things in two directions. Thanks to Demala for his insight, authority and good faith. The full report to government and more details of the Yolŋu Aboriginal Consultancy Initiative can be found at www.cdu.edu.au/yaci.

co-researchers on many other research and consultancy projects including health interpreting, financial literacy, educational philosophy, and negotiations over government housing. We were constantly refining what we came to call a transdisciplinary research methodology – one that "takes seriously both academic and Aboriginal knowledge practices."[1] Yolŋu knowledge-authorities have taught us much about their situated collective epistemologies,[2] and we work together to understand how our research can be generative[3] and how it may help us work effectively within the changing worlds of north Australian research and governmentality.[4]

In each of our previous collaborations we felt we had struggled to find ways to talk to government which did not compromise the methods or epistemologies of Yolŋu knowledge making. This time, now that *land* was involved in a significant way, I was challenged to rethink my own coming-to-be a responsible researcher in the Anglo-European tradition.

The Box of Vegies

The consultants we engaged were all local Yolŋu whom we had known for many years. All were fluent in their own and other Yolŋu languages and in English, and were all connected through webs of kinship to each other, to the whole population of Galiwin'ku and to their various ancestral estates on the island and on the mainland. The task was simple: using a specially prepared poster, map, and pictures, consult with the community to seek feedback, input and comment on the proposal for the community garden.

---

[1] Michael Christie, "Transdisciplinary Research and Aboriginal Knowledge," *Australian Journal of Indigenous Education* 35 (2006): 80.

[2] See, for example, Raymattja Marika-Mununggiritj, & Michael Christie, "Yolngu metaphors for learning," *International Journal of the Sociology of Language* 113 (1995): 59–62; and Michael Christie, "Yolngu Language Habitat: Ecology, Identity and Law in an Aboriginal Society," in *Australia's Aboriginal Languages Habitat*, ed. Gerhard Leitner & Ian Malcolm (Berlin & New York: Mouton De Gruyter, 2007): 57–78.

[3] See Michael Christie, "Generative and 'ground-up' research in Aboriginal Australia," *Learning Communities: International Journal of Learning in Social Contexts* 13 (2013).

[4] See Helen Verran & Michael Christie, "The Ethnographer in the Text: Stories of Disconcertment in the Changing Worlds of North Australian Social Research," *Learning Communities: International Journal of Learning in Social Contexts* 12 (2013): 1–3.

The consultants gathered together with John to make a plan. Everyone agreed that it was crucial first to talk to Demala, a senior ceremonial figure from a significant clan group, who is recognized by everyone as the expert Yolŋu gardener. They met with Demala, who told them to "think about the land first." Each piece of land belongs to particular people, is managed by particular other people, and everyone else has one kind of relation or another to that place. When we listen to any new idea, Demala said, we need to begin with the connections we already have.

In agreement, Gotha, an elder from a related clan, told the story of the old days when we used to have harvest festival every year, people bringing their clan-based produce to the church to celebrate their life together – as well as the produce of the mission garden. Demala reminded them of how the old mission garden had eventually been taken over by the community council, and the Yolŋu felt "run over," and drifted away. Gotha agreed – unnegotiated projects are "like cyclones which come blowing through consuming energies and plans." Over the past few years, the Northern Territory Emergency Response – commonly known as the 'intervention' – has been seen as taking away from Aboriginal elders even that small amount of negotiating power they had with governments. Starting with the land and working together with the right people, said Demala, "makes people feel strong and valued."

Thinking about their connectedness to land and to kin, the consultants divided up the community for consultation into the extended family groups to which they belong. Over the following two days, discussions were held at key clan authorities' homes, outside under a tree, the senior people on the ground, and other people of all ages sitting or standing slightly further away listening, concurring, or making comments when they had something to say. The meetings were held in the various Yolŋu languages of those involved.

For a researcher in the Western tradition, these consultancy meetings often seem to lack focus. Apart from the ongoing problem of how much to pay the senior knowledge-authorities for their various contributions to the research (whose authority guarantees that others will speak forthrightly and in good faith), so much of what people say from such a perspective seems irrelevant to the problem at hand. Again it was time for tales of the ancestral and missionary past, often nothing to do with gardening, like the long diversion into the fate of the mission fishery. It made us worry about getting consensus, and pulling a well-negotiated plan together for government.

But as they worked their way towards the garden, the Yolŋu groups began by making agreement on the conditions of concern in which the garden may emerge: poor quality and expensive food, healthy and unhealthy connections to ancestral lands and to each other, poor relations with government, disaffected children and unemployed adults, the community history and before it the mission history, including the ongoing productive (and largely unrecognized) garden already at work under Demala's authority and labour.

By the time each group got down to discussing what the government really wanted to know – technical decisions about where the garden should go, and what it should grow, and general agreement for families each to pay $30 a week for a box of fruit and vegetables to be delivered to their house – the decisions were very conditional. "Of course a community garden is a good idea," was the consensus, "but if government wants to come in and set one up, it must be properly negotiated and build on what we already have. We all know what happened to the Red Cross project and the G— garden at M—." I did not really know the history of those gardens, but it was clear from the stories that they were introduced by well-meaning outsiders, and had failed because they had not been properly negotiated. And, worse, the pressure from the outsiders to make people participate and get to work before we had all come to a workable agreement generally caused disagreement leading to an impasse. Yolŋu refusal to act until there is broad authoritative agreement on action is often read as indolence.

Wherever the garden is placed, the old people made clear, the land belongs to someone. The way that people relate to the vegetables would be understood in terms of their kinship links to that land and its owners. The old 'mission farm' site now recommended by the government is not land to which Demala has a custodial connection, so it would be difficult for him to farm there. Not only does Demala need to be properly related to the land, but people who work with him need to be involved through their kin links to the land and to Demala. But everyone needs to be involved – people started talking about the school and the women's centre and the clinic, all of which would need to be brought into the action to build the community together.

Such enthusiasm, such firm principles for the unfolding of a properly negotiated community garden, but no firm plan of how to go on together with government. Back in Darwin, we struggled with the report from the consultancy. There had been seven different family meetings, on seven different sites. Each extended family made up of a good number of intermarried clans had been keen on the idea, so long as the garden could grow, so to speak, from Demala's established initiatives, and all the various families could be involved through their ancestral connections to Demala and his land. While the plan was quite straightforward in the Yolŋu imagination, it must have daunted the government, because each step would require further negotiation. There was not going to be a formal plan on paper, with pre-agreed costing and firm timelines. And even if there were, it could change at any moment. Despite the enthusiasm about community gardens, the Yolŋu were anxious about government's efforts to implant them without regard to the processes of Yolŋu life and land. The Yolŋu consultants were also developing ways of working with us university researchers. Even though they had known us for many years and we speak their languages, we still tend to want to move things forward through our own efforts and initiative.

We heard nothing back from government after they received the report, the garden never happened, and Galiwin'ku residents continue to pay exorbitant amounts for poor-quality food.

Decolonizing the Yolŋu Garden

The staggeringly complex interrelatedness of Yolŋu life, land, and history, as well as the immense good will and good faith on the part of all, infused the consultancy process, right up to the finalization and presentation of the report. The consultants were skilled at building agreed ways forward on complex community problems. They were here trying to implement an ancestral knowledge practice in collaboration with *Balanda* researchers who had quite a different research theory and practice. This agreement-making process reveals a methodology and a metaphysics underlying Yolŋu knowledge-work which challenges the received epistemology at work in the Western governmentalities at work today in remote Australia – its schools, its universities, its governments, and non-government organizations such as Community Supported Agriculture. Furthermore, the 'rules' of knowledge and agreement-making in Yolŋu society, which require ongoing polite discussion towards agreement, in a sense prevent Yolŋu knowledge-authorities from censuring us on our metaphysical commitments. It would be both bad manners and counterproductive. Knowledge, and agreement, like the garden, need to emerge from careful negotiations in good faith. I try here to unpack the epistemology of this emergence.

To begin with, the original consultancy proposal prepared for the government by Community Supported Agriculture harboured a rational assumption about the Yolŋu of Galiwin'ku. The government could see a problem of the shortage of healthy and reasonably priced fruit and vegetables in the remote

Aboriginal community, and Community Supported Agriculture could see the community garden as a possible solution. Both of those 'outside' visions entailed that the 2,200 souls at Galiwin'ku be taken in key respects as ontologically equal: all community members, all consumers, all therefore somehow significantly the same when it comes to community consultations and decision-making about a garden. From this point of view, all that is needed is enough people willing to pay $30 a week to make the employment of a gardener and the investment in the garden infrastructure (fences, sprinklers, tanks, machinery) a viable proposition. Thinking this through, I was reminded of the work of the feminist Kathryn Pyne Addelson. Addelson was an anarcho-syndicalist in the women's movement in the USA of the 1960s and 1970s, who later, as a feminist moral philosopher, reflected on her activist experiences. She was particularly interested in developing a collectivist moral theory as an alternative to that of the individualism at work in most moral philosophy. In her work on the battle over women's fertility going back a hundred years in the USA, she identified the notion of epistemic equality – the idea that anyone can potentially know anything, and everyone knows in the same way, that anyone (in principle) can know the facts of the past, and the "preconditions of action."[5] Addelson's collectivist moral philosophy seemed to me a starting point for analysing the dislocation between Yolŋu and government knowledge-practices, and the complex and (my own) interesting third position of an Australian academic working towards a decolonizing collaborative research and consultancy practice. Treating the Yolŋu townspeople as all somehow epistemically equal – because all are equally consumers – enables both the government and the agriculturalists to understand the problem of a community garden as essentially a technical one (how many people interested in paying how much money for how big a box of vegies from a garden situated where?). Epistemic equality allows the government (and academic) knowledge-makers to ignore the individuals' histories, allegiances, connections, and commitments.

When the Yolŋu consultants divided up the work among themselves and went off to talk to their own extended families, it seemed to me to be a good way to get reliable coverage of community opinion. A practical value. But to them it was the *only* appropriate way to develop agreement – the right people talking to the right people in the right place at the right time in the right order.

---

[5] Kathryn Pyne Addelson, *Moral Passages: Toward a Collectivist Moral Theory* (New York: Routledge, 1994): 139.

A moral value. The consultants engaged their Yolŋu kin *as Yolŋu* and *as kin* in everyday life. This rejection of epistemic equality entails the rejection of the common figure in academic research – whom the philosopher Kathryn Pyne Addelson refers to as the "judging observer," the

> detached knower [...] separate from time, place, social position, body and intimate relations. Judging observers require a certain kind of world, a world of objective independent facts principles and laws.[6]

The Yolŋu consultants, of course, engaged no such requirements. By rejecting first of all the role of judging observer, and working with the community members as kin, they also rejected the assumption that everyone does or can know the same things in the same way. Everyone is related to Demala and to his land, but in many different ways. Any garden that works is going to have to take account of this network of accountabilities to people, places, and stories.

By moving into the appropriate spaces to talk to their own people in the free-ranging but always refocusing ways (resisting being judging observers), and by acknowledging that there is more than just food at stake and many very different stakeholders (resisting epistemic equality), the Yolŋu consultants made the technical problem of the garden in Addelson's terms a social problem which emerges (or in our case is inserted) in arenas of public action.[7] Their fundamental concern was not the garden but the ongoing moral work of Yolŋu life. Their consultancy work consisted in "making the moral problem public"[8] – their way ultimately of encouraging the government (and us academic researchers) to listen and work collaboratively.

They refused to think of themselves and their people in government terms as all equally individual consumers of food (with associated notions of rights and accountabilities), understanding themselves as networks of kin and land (with associated notions of care, concern, and responsibilities)[9] working

---

[6] Addelson, *Moral Passages*, xi.

[7] See Kathryn Pyne Addelson, "Some Moral Issues in Public Problems of Reproduction," *Social Problems* 37.1 (1990): 1.

[8] Kathryn Pyne Addelson, "Knowers/doers and their Moral Problems," in *Feminist Epistemologies,* ed. Linda Alcoff & Elizabeth Potter (New York: Routledge, 1993): 287.

[9] See Kathryn Pyne Addelson, *Impure Thoughts: Essays on Philosophy, Feminism, and Ethics* (Philadelphia PA: Temple UP, 1991); and Addelson, *Moral Passages.*

together on how to make community life (and the garden) respond to our need to go on together faithfully, including government and the university, remembering who and where we are. The garden would build the community rather than the other way around.

This helps to explain why, in the talking about plans for a community garden, the two days of discussion with seven extended family groups centred so much on the past, and so little on the future. In Addelson's terms, the world of the judging observer relying on notions of "prediction and retrodiction [...] requires a particular understanding of time, nature, and human action and moral development."[10] Not so for the Yolŋu, for whom prediction and retrodiction must always remain open for argument.

As the Yolŋu told their stories, the past, as the raw materials for understanding how we should go on together, was reinscribed. The mission gardens, the church, the harvest festivals, the failed community gardens, ancestral connections to land were all brought up and retold in a way that made the (re)emergence of the garden viable. It brought the participants to life in new ways as we agreed upon who has the authority to decide and make decisions about what are the important issues to consider (ancestral connections to land, involvement of government departments, dealing with the Shire, growing-up young people) and who can give the go-ahead to proceed at each step.

Doing it this way, the 'community', that mythical entity with which the government imagined we were consulting, had no significant prior existence. Governments, of course, like sociologists, tend to take groups as the unit of analysis, without worrying too much about how those groups are constituted politically. But in the hands of Yolŋu researchers, the population of Galiwin'ku in all their connectedness (and the homelands and the children of the future) emerged as 'community' in a new and unique way in the complex localized discussions about the garden. And received anthropological categories of clan group, owner, authority, connectedness etc. – the stuff of academic research – also became reconstituted in new ways as the discussions progressed. "Even when the same categories seem to be used, it is a creative collective act to enact them as the same."[11]

There is an irony here – that Australian Aboriginal cultures are commonly seen to be conservative, and governments to be progressive. But the government plan assumed stable, given categories, and the Yolŋu method worked

---

[10] Addelson, *Moral Passages*, xi.
[11] *Moral Passages*, 143.

with a wide-open future which needed to be decided using very fluid, carefully negotiated and emergent categories. It depended upon abandoning the certainties and predictabilities of the techno-bureaucratic approach.

The Yolŋu consultants may have been engaged as professionals but they avoided providing what Addelson calls a "professional account"[12] – using the judging-observer position and assuming epistemic equality. Abandoning the firmness of categories (community, families, food, arable land) also entails undermining government hopes for firm and workable plans and time-lines.

In this Yolŋu metaphysics, the knowable world comes out of action, not the other way around. The *act* is primary, whether it be gardening or talking about a garden (or writing a report). Yolŋu, it could be said, understand themselves as producing what Donna Haraway has called "naturecultures"[13] in good or bad ways: good when we work together respectfully and in good faith, bad when people come in with plans and try to implement them "like a cyclone," without negotiation.

There is no difference between the correct ways to do negotiation and the correct ways to garden. Both focus on the *action* as the primary unit of meaning. For both the Yolŋu and Addelson, people and societies have their existence and meaning in the actions and experiences of making, meeting, and managing situations. *"The unit of meaning is the collective act, which generates self and the social order."*[14] Acting respectfully and collaboratively to specify the conditions for the emergence of a responsible Yolŋu garden (commitment to places, kin, ancestral histories, everyday stories of care and concern) is no different from the act of gardening itself, producing Yolŋu with commitment to places, kin, history, totems and so on.

At the end of the process, the Yolŋu community members seemed relatively happy. They had been paid for their contributions to the consultancy, and had been given a chance to make representations to the government on their own terms, in their own terms. Everything that the Community Supported Agriculture proposed – the non-Yolŋu gardener, the weekly contributions, the delivery of boxes of fruit and vegetables – was agreed to by Yolŋu as a good idea, and they made clear that there is a way of producing the garden which will guarantee its success. I, however, was in the difficult position

---

[12] Addelson, *Moral Passages*, 153.

[13] Donna J. Haraway, *When Species Meet* (Minneapolis: U of Minnesota P, 2008): 15.

[14] Addelson, *Moral Passages*, xi.

of making a report which would guarantee the government's commitment to the garden's success. I was beginning to discern a dislocation between the moral and the technical emerging as I focused on preparing the report.

While it was never made clear to us, it seems that the government decided that the complexities of implementing a negotiated emergent Yolŋu garden were more than they could ask (or trust) the Community Supported Agriculture organization to take on. It is much easier to pay a gardener to set up a garden than it is to work constantly with key representatives of seven major networks of clan groups and community organizations to negotiate, step by step, something provisional, which must be tailored to the emerging and changing collective life of the community while remaining faithful to ancestral principles of action and connection. Doing things the Yolŋu way, government could never predict how many people would need to be involved, how long it would take, or how much it would cost. The recasting of the garden from a technical to a collective moral problem set it well beyond the (perceived) capacity of government to deliver. The practices of engagement and negotiation which to Yolŋu are so natural, so necessary, and not so difficult are, to the rational practices of government, uncontrollable, expensive, and not amenable to rigorous implementation. What is an academic researcher's responsibility here?

Decolonizing the Government Consultant

In her book *Reports from a Wild Country*, the anthropologist Deborah Rose develops an "ethics for decolonisation." For Rose, time is of crucial importance. Taking up the work of Johannes Fabian (2002) in *Time and the Other*, she reminds us of the connection between the notions of salvation at work in the monotheistic religions and the notion of progress which infects governments and the academy. In this practice, the past is something to be ignored, forgotten or transcended, the present is difficult and momentary, and it is the future to which we look forward. "In our culture it is the future which is in front, that which is forward directionally, is the future (a time concept). That which is behind us [...] is the past."[15] For the Aboriginal people of the Victoria River areas, however,

---

[15] Deborah Bird Rose, *Reports from a Wild Country: Ethics for Decolonisation* (Sydney: U of New South Wales P, 2004): 151.

Decolonizing Methodology

> Orientation is towards origins. We here now, meaning we here in this shared present are distinct from the people of the early days by the fact that they preceded us and made our lives possible. We are the 'behind mob' – those who come after. [...] we face Dreaming and live our lives moving closer to Dreaming: those behind us walk in our footsteps, as we walk in the steps of those who precede us. Vic[toria] River [Aboriginal] people's time-space matrix of country and their canonical orientation towards origins (rather than towards a future state) ensure that from time to time a western person experiences a dizzying sense of historical inversion – of the past jumping ahead, or of time running backward.[16]

While the Yolŋu family groups spent so much time rehearsing all the possible conditions from which the garden would emerge, and all the histories of people and places and their ancestral connections, the focus of the government, and of our own academic research practice, was firmly focused on the future.

The government and the Community Supported Agriculture group (and we academic researchers, and the Yolŋu) saw the garden as a workable solution to a serious problem. But we all saw the problem in different ways. Learning from my Yolŋu co-researchers, I began to discern that the garden could only be negotiated ethically by looking backwards, as it were, rather than forwards. Looking forwards allows governments to ignore the past. It also allows a brutal disregard for the suffering of the present, and leaves Aboriginal people and their culture always behind somehow, never really able to catch up. It allows a "schizogenic use of time,"[17] a denial of the coeval that makes it unnecessary for government (and academics like me) to sit down, face to face with the 'Other', in real time, and negotiate a process through to its completion. I began to see the very technical and future orientation of the report as that which prevented my role of bringing Yolŋu and government together to produce a good-faith Yolŋu garden (as well as my responsibility to develop my own academic practice towards decolonization).

Some time after the consultation, I was sitting with an old Yolŋu friend who was visiting Darwin. She was disappointed that, after all the very positive discussion and agreement in good faith, the garden clearly was not going

---

[16] Rose, *Reports from a Wild Country*, 55.

[17] Johannes Fabian, *Time and the Other: How Anthropology Makes its Object* (New York: Columbia UP, 2002): x.

to happen. I was ready to blame the government, of course. We academic researchers and the Yolŋu consultants had done the right thing by everybody. The government had failed again. But I felt some sense of rebuke in the way she talked about the consultancy as if there were something I had (yet again) failed to do. Something about how, after all these years of living and working with Yolŋu, I still had not learnt the style of engagement which would cultivate the government, as it were, in bringing the garden to life. If I had not myself learned how to move a negotiated action slowly "forward" through an "orientation to origins," how could I expect to bring the government into the collective action?

I had done some shape-shifting and turned myself into a judging observer out of sight of the Yolŋu. I had written epistemic equality into the report, and in doing so I had let a few faceless bureaucrats get away with saying No to the proposal. Only if I were to engage the government workers who were clearly keen on the success of the garden as "kin in place" – that is, as committed to working face to face with Yolŋu addressing the collective problems of far-northern Australia – would I have acted honourably and productively within my "double participation"[18] as both an activist committed to justice for Aboriginal people and an academic committed to understanding and enhancing the practices of government and the academy.

My friend was sad that I had failed to practise what she and her family had taught me over forty years in order to bring the government into the Yolŋu moral universe. Turning what was clearly a moral problem in the bush into a technical problem in the report represented a sort of repudiation of my commitment to going on together in good faith. I have work to do, rethinking how I do knowledge-work with government.

A postcolonial governmentality of Australian 'Aboriginal affairs' is an impossible, contradictory goal. But working collaboratively with particular people of good faith in government to articulate with Aboriginal individuals and groups a methodology and ethics of decolonization in the context of a public problem is not impossible. It is imperative. And I am trying to learn how to do it.

---

[18] Addelson, *Moral Passages: Toward a Collectivist Moral Theory*, 158.

WORKS CITED

Addelson, Kathryn Pyne. *Impure Thoughts: Essays on Philosophy, Feminism, and Ethics* (Philadelphia PA: Temple UP, 1991).

——. "Knowers/doers and their Moral Problems," in *Feminist Epistemologies*, ed. Linda Alcoff & Elizabeth Potter (New York: Routledge, 1993): 265–94.

——. *Moral Passages: Toward a Collectivist Moral Theory* (New York: Routledge, 1994).

——. "Some Moral Issues in Public Problems of Reproduction," *Social Problems* 37.1 (1990): 1–17.

Christie, Michael. "Generative and 'ground-up' research in Aboriginal Australia," *Learning Communities: International Journal of Learning in Social Contexts* 13 (2013). Forthcoming.

——. "Transdisciplinary Research and Aboriginal Knowledge," *Australian Journal of Indigenous Education* 35 (2006): 78–89.

——. "Yolngu Language Habitat: Ecology, Identity and Law in an Aboriginal Society," in *Australia's Aboriginal Languages Habitat,* ed. Gerhard Leitner & Ian Malcolm (Berlin & New York: Mouton De Gruyter, 2007): 57–78.

Fabian, Johannes. *Time and the Other: How Anthropology Makes its Object* (New York: Columbia UP, 2002).

Haraway, Donna J. *When Species Meet* (Minneapolis: U of Minnesota P, 2008).

Marika–Mununggiritj, Raymattja, & Michael Christie. "Yolngu metaphors for learning," *International Journal of the Sociology of Language* 113 (1995): 59–62.

Rose, Deborah Bird. *Reports from a Wild Country: Ethics for Decolonisation* (Sydney: U of New South Wales P, 2004).

Verran, Helen, & Michael Christie. "The Ethnographer in the Text: Stories of Disconcertment in the Changing Worlds of North Australian Social Research," *Learning Communities: International Journal of Learning in Social Contexts* 12 (2013): 1–3.

The 'Cultural Design' of Western Desert Art

ELEONORE WILDBURGER

Introduction

WHEN EUROPEANS INVADED AUSTRALIA at the end of the eighteenth century, the continent was populated by more than two hundred Indigenous Australian nations who had inhabited the continent for tens of thousands of years. Their lives were regulated by cultural practices that provided them not only with elaborate survival skills in a very demanding environment; their (oral) cultural knowledge was also manifested in a variety of artistic forms that served as mnemonic devices. In pre-European times, however, 'art' was merely produced in response to cultural needs.

What is now commonly known as classical Indigenous Australian art goes back to the 1970s, when the young art teacher Geoffrey Bardon accepted a posting at the government-run school in the Indigenous Northern Territory township of Papunya. Bardon encouraged community elders to join in painting traditional images on a mural on the school walls. As such designs had previously only been used for cultural needs,[1] the issue of making a public painting caused much debate in the community, but the endeavour developed into the Western Desert Art whose artists produced the most prestigious artworks.[2]

---

[1] From the 1930s onwards, in an attempt to defend their culture, some Yolgnu elders had disclosed some sacred designs on bark paintings. For further details, see Judith Ryan, "Aesthetic Splendour, Cultural Power and Wisdom: Early Papunya Painting," in *Tjukurrtjanu: Origins of Western Desert Art*, ed. Philip Batty & Judith Ryan (Melbourne: National Gallery of Victoria, 2011): 11–27.

[2] For further insight into the development of the art movement, see Wally Caruana, *Aboriginal Art* (1993; New York & London: Thames & Hudson, 1996), and Howard Morphy, *Aboriginal Art* (London: Phaidon, 1998).

From the 1990s onwards, artworks of this movement have been commonly characterized as 'dot paintings', owing to their unique painting technique.

Ever since non-'Western' art has been produced for 'Western'[3] art markets, scholars have attempted to accommodate Indigenous art within established 'Western' categories of art production. Classifications would include anthropological and ethnological parameters rather than artistic key markers. Currently, Indigenous art is classified as being produced by an Indigenous person in any artistic medium, in any style and technique. In (exhibition) practice, though, 'Western' art categories seem to contradict this classification. I will first point to key concepts of Indigenous Australian cultures that form the context of classical Indigenous art, then indicate forms of cross-cultural art perception, and finally discuss curatorial concepts of art exhibitions based on cross-culturally appropriate art classification.

The Law of Indigenous Australian Cultures

The oldest continuing cultures in human communities are the Indigenous Australian.[4] In pre-European days, cultural knowledge was practised and memorized in oral forms. Mnemonic techniques included dances, songs, and artistic designs, all of which were regulated by Indigenous Law, which was inadequately termed the 'Dreaming' (or the 'Dreamtime') by the English invaders. Classical Indigenous artworks draw substantially on the concept of the Law. For non-Indigenous scholars, the concept of the Law is difficult to grasp in its complexity. In accordance with cross-culturally appropriate research protocols,[5] I give preference to the clarification offered by Indigenous voices.

Indigenous Law, established by Ancestor Beings in Creation Time, determines social and religious behaviour and defines land ownership as well as the relationship between the people and the land. The Indigenous Australian art curator Franchesca Cubillo explains:

> The Dreaming [= the Law] is the eternal moment of creation, when the spiritual Ancestors moved across the land, creating the landforms, the plants, animals, people and the languages. Rules and regulations were

---

[3] I use this term in the absence of a more appropriate one.

[4] For details, see *The Oxford Companion to Aboriginal Art and Culture*, ed. Sylvia Kleinert & Margo Neale (Oxford: Oxford UP, 2000).

[5] See, for example, Linda Tuhiwai Smith, *Decolonizing Methodologies: Research and Indigenous Peoples* (London & New York: Zed, 1999).

also established by the Ancestors in the timeless moment and are maintained by Aboriginal people in the present. The land is looked after, animals respected, ceremonies performed and social obligations adhered to according to the precepts of these traditions. Aspects of the Dreaming are taught and reinforced from an early age.[6]

The Law explains the creation of the land and all beings, and determines Indigenous identity through land ownership. A widely cited definition of what land means to Indigenous people is given by Galarrwuy Yunupingu, a renowned and long-serving Chairman of the Northern Land Council, a powerful Indigenous organization:

> The land is my backbone. I can only stand straight, happy, proud and not ashamed about my black color because I still have land. The land is art. I can paint, dance, create and sing as my ancestors did before me. My people recorded these things about our land this way, so that I and all others like me may do the same. I think of the land as the history of my nation. It tells us how we came into being and what system we must live [...]. My land is mine only because I came in spirit from that land, and so did my ancestors of the same land. [...] My land is my foundation. I stand, live, and perform as long as I have something firm and hard to stand on [...]. Without land I am nothing.[7]

Decisive features of many classical artworks relate not only to the artist's (ownership of) land, as determined by the Law, but also to the artist's kinship affiliation.[8] The kinship system is a classification that relates each person to everyone else in the community, as well as to the land and everything on the land. Each person is identified through a 'skin name'. The skin groups are gendered and are divided into two moieties. In her book on Kathleen Petyarre, Christine Nicholls explains the relevance of a person's skin name as follows:

---

[6] Franchesca Cubillo, "The Remarkable Kundu Masks of the Nyangumarta," in *Kaltja Now: Indigenous Australian Australia*, ed. Ian Chance (Kent Town, SA: Wakefield, 2001): 44.

[7] Galarrwuy Yunupingu, "Letter from Black to White," *Land Rights News* 2.6 (1976): 9.

[8] For further information, see Howard Morphy, *Becoming Art: Exploring Cross-Cultural Categories* (Sydney: U of New South Wales P, 2008); Fred R. Myers, *The Making of an Aboriginal High Art* (Durham NC & London: Duke UP, 2002); Eleonore Wildburger, *Politics, Power and Poetry: An Intercultural Perspective on Aboriginal Identity in Black Australian Poetry* (Stuttgart: Stauffenburg, 2003).

> The term [skin name] could be glossed [...] as the sociolinguistic means by which traditionally orientated Indigenous Australian people express their personal, social and spiritual orientation towards other Indigenous (and in occasion, non-Indigenous) people with whom they interact and communicate. [...] Skin names indicate not only biological relationships between people, but also classificatory relationships, which in turn act as the template for an extensive network of social obligations.[9]

Classical Indigenous Australian paintings not only confirm the artist's knowledge of her/his Law; the rules of the Law also determine the copyright of the artist in a particular way. The artist has a life-long copyright over the designs and their affiliated narratives, which means that "the use of designs belonging to others without the appropriate permission constitutes a major breach of Aboriginal law."[10] Thus, artworks express and represent individual and group identity, as Cubillo confirms:

> Different Aboriginal groups across Australia have distinct Dreamings, ceremonies, languages, social practices, kinship structures and material culture. Tradition-based artwork emerging from these groups is invariably rooted in these differentiating Dreamings.[11]

An artwork in evidence is the 'dot painting' *Bush Honey Dreaming* (1998) by the Anmatyerre artist Helen Kunoth Ngwarai from Utopia (NT), as I will demonstrate below.

'Dot-Paintings' from Utopia

Western Desert Art is closely linked to the desert towns of Papunya, Yuendumu, Lajumanu, Ernabella, and Utopia, where community artists have produced some of the most successful and renowned artworks of the movement.[12]

Utopia was established as a pastoral lease on Anmatyerre and Alywarr land in 1927, and occupies about 1,800 square kilometers northeast of Alice Springs. The name 'Utopia' was given ironically by the European invaders. The two Indigenous nations whose land was taken went through frontier viol-

---

[9] Christine Nicholls, "Genius of Place: The Life and Art of Kathleen Petyarre," in *Kathleen Petyarre: Genius of Place* (Kent Town, SA: Wakefield, 2001): 90.

[10] Wally Caruana, *Aboriginal Art*, 15.

[11] Franchesca Cubillo, "The Remarkable Kundu Masks of the Nyangumarta," 44.

[12] Howard Morphy, *Aboriginal Art*, 282–315.

ence and massacres, as did other Indigenous nations throughout colonial history. European invaders (who did not recognize Indigenous land ownership) set up pastoral industry on Anmatyerre and Alywarr territory and drove the traditional owners off their land. The people lost access to their (sacred) ceremonial grounds, which dramatically disrupted their lives in many respects. In the 1970s, it was particularly the women of Utopia who were involved in land claims, in accordance with the Aboriginal Land Rights Act (NT) of 1976. In the Land Claim Hearing (1979) they gave evidence of their land ownership by performing ceremonial dances that confirmed their knowledge of the Law (a prerequisite for Indigenous land claims).[13] The claim was successful and the land was given back to the traditional owners in 1979. The Anmatyerre/Alywarr community re-established themselves on their land and resumed practising their traditional life.[14]

The women who were active in the land-rights movement were also involved in the art movement of the region. In the beginning they did not use acrylic paint on canvas, but started to produce highly esteemed batik works in 1977,[15] and did not take up painting on canvas until the late 1980s.[16] Despite this 'late start', one might argue, Utopia is home to the most outstanding artists, such as the late Emily Kngwarreye[17] and Kathleen Petyarre.[18] The latter, in particular, and her sister Violet Petyarre are not only successful artists who also train young artists in their community; they are also very active in performing the initiation ceremonies of young women and handing on their knowledge of the Law to them.[19] In Utopia to date, artists have been producing artworks under the guidance of (and side by side with) these knowledgeable women. Kathleen Petyarre confirms the importance of the Law for her artworks (and those of her fellow artists):

---

[13] See, for example, the *Ngurrara Canvas* case, discussed in Wildburger, "Indigenous Australian art in practice and theory," *Coolabah* (Barcelona) 10 (2013): 202–12 (esp. 202–205).

[14] Eleonore Wildburger, *The 'Cultural Design' of Indigenous Australia Art*, 185.

[15] Anne Marie Brody, *Utopia: A Picture Story* (Perth, WA: Heytesbury Holdings, 1990): 9.

[16] Jennifer Isaacs et al., "Anmatyerre Artist," in *Emily Kngwarreye Paintings* (Sydney: Craftsman House, 1998): 19.

[17] See also *Emily Kngwarreye Paintings* (Sydney: Craftsman House, 1998).

[18] See also Christine Nicholls, "Genius of Place."

[19] Personal communication with Kathleen and Violet Petyarre.

The old women used to paint the ceremonial designs on their breasts, first with their fingers, and on their chests, and then with a brush called a *tyepale*, made from a stick. They painted their thighs with white paint. They painted with red and white ochres. Then they danced showing their legs. [...] The spirits of the country gave women's ceremonies to the old woman. The woman sings [recites parts of her Law], then she gives the ceremony [ceremonial knowledge] to the others, to make it strong [to keep the knowledge and hand it on].[20]

Ceremonial designs and ceremonial performances are crucial in keeping the Indigenous Law alive. As Kathleen Petyarre explains,

The old woman is the boss[21] because the spirits of the country have given her the ceremony [the knowledge of the Law]. So all women get together and sing [commemorate Law texts]. [...] The old women are also holding their country as they dance. The old women dance with that [the country] in mind. They teach the younger women and give them the knowledge, to their granddaughters, so then all the grandmothers and granddaughters continue the tradition.[22]

What Kathleen Petyarre aptly says about ceremonial performances is relevant for the interrelation of classical paintings and the Indigenous Law, as the following case study demonstrates.

The 'Cultural Design' of Indigenous Art[23]

Helen Kunoth Ngwarai, the artist of the following painting, is related to the aforementioned Emily Kngwarreye, which the skin name of both women confirms.[24] She has been introduced to the Law and incorporates her knowledge into her artworks. In line with classical Indigenous art, the painting represents the artist's country, seen from a bird's-eye view. The title of the painting suggests – as was confirmed by the artist in personal communication – that Helen Kunoth Ngwarai's Law is the Law of the Bush Honey, whose knowledge re-

---

[20] Christine Nicholls, "Genius of Place."

[21] Indigenous society is not hierarchical. Elders are respected for their knowledge.

[22] See also Nicholls, "Genius of Place."

[23] In slightly modified form, the analysis of this painting was published in Eleonore Wildburger, *The 'Cultural Design' of Indigenous Australia Art*, 202–10.

[24] The spelling of Indigenous names varies, in the absence of standardized (English) orthography.

lates her to her land and to her community in particular ways. The artist also holds the unalienable copyright to her artwork, insofar as it is rooted in her Law.

FIGURE 2: Helen Kunoth Ngwarai, *Bush Honey Dreaming* (1998; synthetic polymer paint on canvas 80x62 cm); private collection. © The artist.

Classical Indigenous paintings offer two interpretative approaches, a combination of which will be exemplified below. The hitherto more common approach is the analysis of the cultural narratives that artists may or may not share when selling their products.[25] In the case of the painting in question, Helen Kunoth Ngwarai chose to share narratives that link her artwork to her Law. In accordance with Indigenous research protocols,[26] I have been given permission by the artist to hand on this knowledge in scholarly work and publications.

The painting shows a variety of icons that are common in classical artworks:

u-shapes, representing persons, sitting on the ground;

---

[25] Wildburger, *The 'Cultural Design' of Indigenous Australia Art*.
[26] For example, Linda Tuhiwai Smith, *Decolonizing Methodologies*.

(ceremonial) body-painting patterns, representing persons (longish stripes; stripes in half-circles);
circles, representing fire places, meeting places, water holes;
(digging) sticks (mostly next to 'woman' icons); and
longish (bark) dishes [*coolamon*], often next to 'woman' icons.

The icons are grouped in settings that represent ceremonial performances of the artist's Law. In the present painting, all u-shapes and body-painting patterns represent women. Women (as well as men) apply body paint to their bodies when preparing themselves for a ceremony (when they 'paint up'). Indigenous society is gendered, including many of its ceremonies. As defined by strict rules of the Law, women artists may get permission to include another woman's Law or a man's Law (with corresponding icons) in their paintings. The same rule applies to male artists. There are also important ceremonies that are performed by men and women together. In the present painting, all icons figure as women; the ceremonial context and its implied narratives can be discerned by 'insiders' on the basis of the colour, shape, and position of icons and patterns, corresponding in detail to ceremonial performances, as the artist confirmed.

As already mentioned, the painting's title reveals that Helen Kunoth Ngwarai's Law is the Bush Honey Law. In the outback, there are diverse sources of bush honey. In Helen's Law, bush honey is collected from honey ants that store up honey in a swollen part of their body which is commonly referred to as an abdomen (see icons spread all over the painting).

FIGURE 3: Blueprint (modified) courtesy of Christine Nicholls.

I am grateful to Marcia Langton for clarifying that the honey is stored in a sort of body bag protruding from the abdomen. Honey ants hide in underground nests and women delve deep into the ground with their digging sticks to uncover them. This procedure is hinted at by the icons that represent the honey bags, the digging sticks, and the underground nests. The attentive onlooker will discern that the u-shaped icons are grouped in sets of four 'women' each, sitting around a fireplace, after having collected honey. Three groups (A, B, D) are equipped with *coolamons* that carry honey; one group of women (C) has digging sticks (for finding honey in the honey ants' nests). Each group of women represents a distinctive set of ceremonial narratives that are known in detail to the artist and particular community members according to distinct rules, given by the Law.

Helen Kunoth Ngwarai did not share with me narratives in full detail, but she did elaborate on the relevance and importance of some passages of her Law, in regard to her land and to her social obligations. She explained that the sets of narratives represented in the painting reflect texts of her Law that memorize the creation of her land, created by the Bush Honey Dreaming Ancestor; the painting also reflects particular duties and obligations on the part of herself and the women who are represented in the artwork. Besides, the narratives (in the painting) also memorize rules connected with the honey ant and its environment. Each group-narrative is related to each other set of narratives and is interconnected with all other narratives of her Law – also with those that are not painted on the canvas in question. A hint at many further narratives (untold in this painting) is the body-painting patterns in the four corners of the painting: in ceremonial contexts, persons do not sit by themselves (as the single icon in each corner suggests); on the contrary, they sit in groups of two, or more commonly in groups of four. The corner-icons suggest that further groups (of two or four women), performing further sets of ceremonial narratives, sit 'beyond' the present painting. *Bush Honey Dreaming* not only confirms the artist's ownership of her land from the time it was created by the Bush Honey Dreaming Ancestor; the inherent ceremonial narratives also reflect rules that are connected with the honey ant and its environment.

Helen Kunoth Ngwarai shared her narratives to some extent, as I said before, and this allows me to interpret a feature in her artwork, although she did not explain it in the way I will be doing here. However, I deduce from the comments she made while painting that the distinct division of the painting into four sections (emphasized by the two ant-nest axes) suggests that the four groups represent the four (female) skin groups of the eight-group kinship system of Anmatyerre people, the artist's nation. As I mentioned above, the skin names (of the kinship system) are essential factors of the Law. It is the skin names (together with the relevant Law) that testify to and confirm a person's identity. Obviously, the artist not only emphasizes in this painting the social rules that the owner of the knowledge has to obey (and to hand on to the next generation); Helen Kunoth Ngwarai's artwork is a strong confirmation of land ownership. The artist did not identify the context of the ant nests in the painting either, but I suggest (on the basis of other comparable artworks) that they also relate to land rights and to tracks in (the artist's) land as laid down by the Bush Honey Dreaming Ancestor in Creation Time.

In my view, it is also worth having a closer look at the position of the various individual honey-bags, as well as the four straight body-painting patterns in the painting. I propose that they emphasize the narrative of the respective group of woman-icons; however, they may also have a decorative function, as I will explain below. It is interesting, though, to have a closer look at the placement of the honey-bags that do not seem to belong directly to one of the groups of four women. If we read them as part of the cultural text, we may argue that they connect and interrelate the painting's sets of narratives and that they indicate that parts of one set may also be relevant in another set.

Of course, classical Indigenous paintings may also be assessed in terms of art. The painting *Bush Honey Dreaming* confirms the artist's advanced proficiency in designing and producing an artwork. The category 'dot-painting' is confirmed by the background dots, which are worth a closer look. The background appears to be brown, yet this colour is the result of a black full-surface paint that is covered with brown, ochre, and white dots. This means that the artist – in accordance with the usual dotting technique – first covered the canvas with black paint, then added the dots, and finally applied the icons and designs. In classical Indigenous paintings, the colour brown is commonly used to represent the land. Helen's choice of colours results in a vivid, brownish background that correlates excellently with the diverse shades of brown, ochre, and yellow applied to the various icons and patterns in the painting. In my view, the mixture of brown, ochre, and white dots relieves the sombre, heavy effect of an otherwise dark (back)ground. The painting confirms my point that each classical artwork demonstrates its own artistic style and technique.

The composition of the painting is well balanced; it shows subtle variations in the symmetrical design that may not catch the viewer's eye at first sight. The two 'axes' (the ant's nests) across the painting divide the composition of the artwork into four sections that are not identical, as the viewer might have expected. Minor modifications in an otherwise symmetrical composition slightly break the otherwise strict division (by the two axes) into four quarters that reflect each other. The variations are well worth noting: the four groups of four women are placed in slightly shifted positions, if we take the axes as lines of orientation; each group of four women has different 'side-objects' (group C does not include honey-bags; group A and group C, positioned opposite, include the same body-painting patterns in equal positions; but group A includes digging sticks and *coolamons*; group C shows only digging sticks; group B includes digging sticks and *coolamons*; whereas, in group D, positioned opposite, there are only *coolamons*). I proposed above that the four groups of women represent the four female skin groups of the artist's nation. This point is also confirmed by the artist's decision to represent each group with different ceremonial objects, as I pointed out. Skin groups have much in common with regard to the Law, yet in addition they own slightly different parts of the Law. Furthermore, the variations in the objects in these groups imply that the narratives relating to the four skin groups, represented by the woman-icons, are correlated and interrelated. Therefore, I argue that the modification of the four-quarter composition is an aesthetic-artistic feature that supports the cultural text of the artwork.

Another artistic strategy in Helen Kunoth Ngwarai's painting *Bush Honey Dreaming* is worth a closer look. The honey-bags in one half of the painting come in a darker shade of yellowish-brown, whereas the honey-bags in the other half of the painting come in a brighter shade of the same colour-combination. One may argue that this artistic design simply takes away the effect of a strict symmetrical composition. However, the cultural context adds another facet: the artist's emphasis on her community's subsection system, as represented in the skin groups, implies that the division of the painting into two halves (indicated by the two colour sections) points to the two moieties that make up Indigenous kinship systems. The two-section concept in the painting supports the four-section (female) skin-group concept, as is also the case with these systems in real life. Helen Kunoth Ngwarai's choice of colours and designs aptly reflects the fact that the moieties relate and divide skin groups within the kinship system. The importance of this system again resides in its relevance to the people's land ownership. Keeping this fact in mind, I would say that Helen Kunoth's artistic skills are also shown in the way she supports the importance of the details of the cultural text in her painting by the choice of colours, something that an uninformed viewer might judge to be a minor artistic feature that loosens up an otherwise symmetrical artistic composition.

It is also interesting to look at the position of the honey-bags and the four straight body-painting patterns. Of course, all of them also carry part of the main narratives relating to the four-woman skin groups; in this function, they interrelate the four sets of narratives of these skin groups, as two honey-bags (one of each moiety) extend beyond their 'main' quarters into each of the two quarters that are artistically enhanced by two straight body-painting patterns. These straight patterns, on the other hand, not only support the respective skin-group narrative, they also seem to be an excellent artistic feature in the composition of the painting. *Bush Honey Dreaming* demonstrates, in particular, how aesthetic features may support (and also 'decorate') the implied narratives, if the viewer or theorist is able to discern the 'cultural design' in the artwork. The analysis of a classical Indigenous painting as a cultural text that is supported by its 'cultural design' results in an enlightening and pleasant reception process for both scholars and art lovers. Such an interrelated analysis goes beyond the reception of a non-Western artwork as cultural artifact, as is still commonly approved of by scholars. By assessing a non-Western cultural text with 'Western' aesthetic-artistic criteria, new modes of cross-cultural understanding and communication may be established.

Indigenous 'Dot-Paintings' for Non-Indigenous Art-Lovers

Obviously, Western Desert art – like any 'other' art – does not comply with standardized 'Western' criteria of classification. I support calls for a new art category[27] that takes into account the diversity and specificity of non-Western art production. I have joined this debate with the suggestion of including what I termed the 'cultural design' of artworks in a mainly ethnographic assessment of a non-Western artwork. Such a combination of evaluative criteria clearly also influences curatorial concepts of non-'Western' art exhibitions.

The role (and epistemological importance) of museums (and art museum, for that matter) has been widely discussed.[28] Globalized interpretations of

---

[27] See Elisabeth Gigler, *Indigenous Australian Art Photography: An Intercultural Perspective* (Aachen: Shaker, 2008); Howard Morphy, *Becoming Art*.

[28] Stephan E. Weil, *Rethinking the Museum* (Washington DC: Smithsonian Institution Press: 1990); *Exhibiting Cultures: The Poetics and Politics of Museum Display*, ed. Ian Karp & Steven D. Levine (Washington DC & London: Smithsonian Institution

non-'Western' art commonly focus on culture-specific peculiarities, contextualization, and cross-cultural translation; however, exhibition curators of Indigenous Australian art even in renowned European museums struggle with this task. For example, a museum with an exhibition concept that is problematic in its peculiarity has attracted international critique: the Musée du Quai Branly in Paris.[29] A completely different (and, as I argue, innovative) approach was taken by curators in the Museum Albertina in Vienna. In 2007 the museum staged the outstanding Donald Kahn Collection of classical Indigenous paintings, produced by path-breaking artists of the Western Desert region. The exhibits were presented as artworks in their own right. This attempt did not fulfil its intention to present the paintings as artworks in their own right – nor did the exhibition value the cultural context of the artworks (as was not the museum's intention, anyway), and the display of the paintings and the debatable catalogue failed to take into account the high aesthetic-artistic quality of the thirty-seven masterpieces.[30]

In the course of my research of many years I have been to numerous exhibitions of Indigenous art in Europe and I share the concerns of Indigenous artists who have, in personal communications, occasionally voiced the view that (mainstream) Europe seems to be a difficult place for non-'Western' art. One museum that seems exceptional in that respect is certainly the Aboriginal Art Museum in Utrecht (The Netherlands), which has over the years managed to meet cross-cultural criteria *and* art-market expectations with the curatorial concept of their art exhibitions. To my current knowledge, curators at the Dutch museum cooperate closely with Indigenous artists and curators, as well

---

Press, 1991); Annie Coombes, *Reinventing Africa: Museums, Material Culture, and Popular Imagination* (New Haven CT: Yale UP, 1994); Tony Bennett, *The Birth of the Museum: History, Theory, Politics* (London & New York: Routledge, 1995); Tony Bennett, *Pasts Beyond Memory: Evolution, Museums, Colonialism* (London & New York: Routledge, 2004); Arapata T. Hakiwai, "The Search for Legitimacy: Museums in Aotearoa, New Zealand – A Maori Viewpoint," in *Heritage, Museums and Galleries: An Introductory Reader*, ed. Gerald Corsane (London & New York: Routledge, 2005); *Museums and Difference*, ed. Daniel J. Sherman (Bloomington & Indianapolis: Indiana UP, 2008).

[29] For further details, see: Sally Price, *Paris Primitive: Jaques Chirac's Museum on the Quai Branly* (Chicago: U of Chicago P, 2007); *Museums and Difference*, ed. Sherman; and Wildburger, *The 'Cultural Design' of Indigenous Australia Art* and "Indigenous Australian art in practice and theory," 208–209.

[30] See also Wildburger, "Indigenous Australian art in practice and theory," 208–10.

as with (mainstream) Australian art experts who have been active and successful in the cross-cultural art domain for years. This approach is certainly a viable strategy for exhibitions of non-'Western' art in Europe.

I propose that European art curators also take guidance from concepts of excellent cross-cultural art exhibitions in Australia, such as the *Land Marks* exhibition of Indigenous art (2006) or the exhibition *Tjukurrtjanu: Origins of Western Desert Art* (2011–2013), both in the National Gallery of Victoria. Excellent catalogues of both exhibitions support my argument.[31]

Conclusion

Western Desert art is deeply rooted in its cultural context, as this research text demonstrates. Ever since this movement has attracted art lovers, art collectors, scholars, and art market representatives, it has become obvious that Western art classification does not match the diversity, cultural context, and aesthetic features of these artworks. In response to colonial history, Indigenous artists and their supporters used to highlight the cultural context in cross-cultural debates and endeavours, rather than the aesthetic particularity of classical artworks. On the whole, this cross-cultural concern has not been dealt with appropriately in Europe, as I have indicated. A rather recent phenomenon on the European and international art scene is the attempt of art museums to focus on aesthetic criteria of non-'Western' art. There is, however, a caveat to this new approach, as intimated in my argument in the present essay, where I join the scholarly debate of the past two decades in which classificatory criteria and exhibition concepts applied to non-'Western' art have been at stake. The above sample analysis of Helen Kunoth Ngwarai's painting *Bush Honey Dreaming* indicates that it is worth discerning the 'cultural design' of art; the cultural text of an artwork may support its aesthetic features, and aesthetic features may draw the informed onlooker's attention to the cultural context. This approach is clearly also relevant for art museums and art galleries, which

---

[31] *Land Marks: Indigenous Art in the National Gallery of Victoria*, ed. Judith Ryan, with contributions by Stephen Gilchrist, Julie Gough & Paul S.C. Tacon, foreword by Gerard Vaughan (exh. cat., Ian Potter Centre, 10 February–11 June 2006; Melbourne: Council of Trustees, National Gallery of Victoria, 2006); *Tjukurrtjanu: Origins of Western Desert Art*, ed. Judith Ryan & Philip Batty, with contributions from John Kean, Dick Kimber, Fred Myers, Luke Scholes, and Paul Sweeney (exh. cat., Ian Potter Centre, 30 September 2011–12 February 2012; Musée du quai Branly, Paris, 9 October 2012–20 January 2013; Melbourne: National Gallery of Victoria, 2011).

have the potential to foster cross-culturally appropriate communication and mutual understanding. Consequently, the 'cultural design' of art may aptly serve as a classificatory criterion of non-'Western' art. There is no doubt that any artwork is embedded in its cultural context; however, the 'cultural design' of 'other' art, as discussed in this essay, transforms narratives into art, by using aesthetic features that represent particular (cultural) texts.

WORKS CITED

Anon. "Ngurrara: The Great Sandy Desert Canvas," *The Aboriginal Art Directory*, http://www.aboriginalartdirectory.com/news/feature/ngurrara-the-great-sandy-desert-canvas.php (accessed 20 March 2012).

Bennett, Tony. *The Birth of the Museum: History, Theory, Politics* (London: Routledge, 1995).

——. *Pasts Beyond Memory: Evolution, Museums, Colonialism* (London: Routledge, 2004).

Brody, Anne Marie. *Utopia: A Picture Story* (Perth, WA: Heytesbury Holdings, 1990).

Caruana, Wally. *Aboriginal Art* (1993; London & New York: Thames & Hudson, 1996).

Coombes, Annie. *Reinventing Africa: Museums, Material Culture, and Popular Imagination* (New Haven CT: Yale UP, 1994).

Cubillo, Franchesca. "The Remarkable Kundu Masks of the Nyangumarta," in *Kaltja Now: Indigenous Australian Australia*, ed. Ian Chance (Kent Town, SA: Wakefield, 2001): 42–47.

Gigler, Elisabeth. *Indigenous Australian Art Photography: An Intercultural Perspective* (Aachen: Shaker, 2008).

Hakiwai, Arapata T. "The Search for Legitimacy: Museums in Aotearoa, New Zealand – A Maori Viewpoint," in *Heritage, Museums and Galleries: An Introductory Reader*, ed. Gerald Corsane (London & New York: Routledge, 2005): 154–62.

Isaacs, Jennifer et al. "Anmatyerre Artist," in *Emily Kngwarreye Paintings* (Sydney: Craftsman House, 1998): 17–23.

Karp, Ian, & Steven D. Levine, ed. *Exhibiting Cultures: The Poetics and Politics of Museum Display* (Washington DC & London: Smithsonian Institution Press, 1991).

Kleinert Sylvia, & Margo Neale, ed. *The Oxford Companion to Aboriginal Art and Culture* (Oxford: Oxford UP, 2000).

Morphy, Howard. *Aboriginal Art* (London: Phaidon, 1998).

——. *Becoming Art: Exploring Cross-Cultural Categories* (Sydney: U of New South Wales P, 2008).

——. "Kinship, Family and Art," in *The Oxford Companion to Aboriginal Art and Culture*, ed. Sylvia Kleinert & Margo Neale (Oxford: Oxford UP, 2000): 60–67.

Myers, Fred R. *The Making of an Aboriginal High Art* (Durham NC & London: Duke UP, 2002).

Nicholls, Christine. "Genius of Place: The Life and Art of Kathleen Petyarre," in Nicholls & North, *Kathleen Petyarre: Genius of Place* (Kent Town, SA: Wakefield, 2001). 6–32.

——, & Ian North. *Kathleen Petyarre: Genius of Place* (Kent Town, SA: Wakefield, 2001)

Petyarre, Kathleen. "Women's Ceremony – Awalye," in Anne Marie Brody, *Utopia: A Picture Story* (Perth, WA: Heytesbury Holdings, 1990): 12.

Price, Sally. *Paris Primitive: Jacques Chirac's Museum on the Quai Branly* (Chicago: U of Chicago P, 2007).

Ryan, Judith. "Aesthetic Splendour, Cultural Power and Wisdom: Early Papunya Painting," in *Tjukurrtjanu: Origins of Western Desert Art*, ed. Ryan & Batty, 11–27.

——, ed. *Land Marks: Indigenous Art in the National Gallery of Victoria*, with contributions by Stephen Gilchrist, Julie Gough & Paul S.C. Tacon, foreword by Gerard Vaughan (exh. cat., Ian Potter Centre, 10 February–11 June 2006; Melbourne: Council of Trustees, National Gallery of Victoria, 2006)

——, & Philip Batty, ed. *Tjukurrtjanu: Origins of Western Desert Art*, with contributions from John Kean, Dick Kimber, Fred Myers, Luke Scholes, and Paul Sweeney (exh. cat., Ian Potter Centre, 30 September 2011–12 February 2012; Musée du quai Branly, Paris, 9 October 2012–20 January 2013; Melbourne: National Gallery of Victoria, 2011).

Sherman, Daniel J., ed. *Museums and Difference* (Bloomington & Indianapolis: Indiana UP, 2008).

Smith, Linda Tuwhai. *Decolonizing Methodologies: Research and Indigenous Peoples* (London & New York: Zed, 1999).

Weil, Stephan E. *Rethinking the Museum* (Washington DC: Smithsonian Institution Press, 1990).

Wildburger, Eleonore. *The 'Cultural Design' of Indigenous Australia Art: A Cross-Cultural Perspective* (Saarbrücken: SVH, 2010).

——. "Indigenous Australian art in practice and theory," *Coolabah* (Barcelona) 10 (2013): 202–12.

——. *Politics, Power and Poetry: An Intercultural Perspective on Aboriginal Identity in Black Australian Poetry* (Stuttgart: Stauffenburg, 2003).

Yunupingu, Galarrwuy. "Letter from Black to White," *Land Rights News* 2.6 (1976), http://www.clc.org.au/land-rights-news (accessed 20 March 2012).

Ethical and Other Encounters ⌘

Modernism, Antipòdernism, and Australian Aboriginality

IAN HENDERSON

THIS ESSAY DESCRIBES THE ENTANGLEMENT in Australia of three concepts: modernism; 'settler modernity'; and Aboriginality. Its three principal arguments are: (i) that European perceptions of Australian Aboriginal cultures were deeply influential in the development of modernism; (ii) that anxieties about the proximity of Aboriginal and settler peoples in Australia – but also resistance to European theories of Aboriginal culture not validated through personal experience of interacting with Aboriginal Australians – influenced strong anti-modernist sentiment among some Australian artists and writers; and (iii) that perhaps this 'anti-modernism' might instead be characterized as an 'alternative' modernism in Australia – an entanglement of visions of progress and degeneration – to which I will give the purposefully ugly label of 'antipòdernism'. In developing these arguments I will make reference to Sigmund Freud's *Totem and Taboo* (1913) as inflected by the work in Australia of Francis Gillen and Baldwin Spencer, and discuss writings by Miles Franklin in particular, as well as Katherine Susannah Prichard, D.H. Lawrence, A.D. Hope, and Christina Stead.[1]

---

[1] The breadth of the argument ventured here represents a new departure in my research, but part of the essay draws together and develops ideas initially published in two different contexts: Ian Henderson, "Uncommon Reading: Sight, Science and the 'Savage' Reader, 1850–1915," *Journal of the Association for the Study of Australian Literature*, 2010, www.nla.gov.au/openpublish/index.php/jasal/article/view/1507/2087; and Ian Henderson, "The Body of an Australian Girl: Miles Franklin's *My Brilliant Career* (1901)," in *Feminism and the Body: Interdisciplinary Perspectives*, ed. Catherine Kevin (Newcastle upon Tyne: Cambridge Scholars, 2009): 116–33.

Altogether, then, I will be exploring the impact of a particular construction of Australian Aboriginality on the development of modernist writing in Australia, a vast and complex subject, not least for its invocation of such contested terms as 'modernism', on the one hand, and 'Aboriginality', on the other. By virtue of providing an overview, then, I will necessarily crush significant nuances within the writing of the authors whose work I will mention; I am conscious also of working with a European figuration of Aboriginality, which is well removed from the knowledge derived from the lives, traditions, and experiences of real Aboriginal Australian men and women. I beg forgiveness for this on methodological grounds, for misconceptions of Aboriginality historically have been as influential on the cultural development of European and Australian writing as those messy and entangled truths about Indigenous Knowledge that emerge directly from interventions by Aboriginal people and from collaborations between Aboriginal and non-Aboriginal thinkers and activists.

As a starting point for this exploration I find useful a 'traditional' distinction made in discussions of Western modernity summarized by Dilip Parameshwar Gaonkar in his introduction to *Alternative Modernities* (2001). The distinction is that between societal modernization ("the growth of scientific consciousness, the development of a secular outlook, the doctrine of progress, [...] individualistic understanding of the self, contractualist understandings of society, and so on") and cultural modernity, or modernism:

> By and large, the proponents of cultural modernity were repelled by the middle-class ethos – by its stifling conformities and banalities; by its discounting of enthusiasm, imagination, and moral passion in favour of pragmatic calculation and the soulless pursuit of money; and, more than anything else, by its pretensions, complacencies, and hypocrisies as represented by the figure of the philistine.[2]

Avant-garde artists, in this reading, invoke both "the cultural patina of modernity as a spectacle of speed, novelty, and effervescence"[3] – they celebrate the positive outcomes of a technological age – and also set themselves up against regimes of social and intellectual routine, of bourgeois aspirations, and political, social, and aesthetic complacency. In doing so, they break tradi-

---

[2] Dilip Parameshwar Gaonkar, "On Alternative Modernities," *Alternative Modernities*, ed. Dilip Parameshwar Gaonkar (Durham NC: Duke UP, 2001): 1–2.

[3] Gaonkar, "On Alternative Modernities," 8.

tional forms in the making of their art, architecture, design, and writing: they 'make it new'. They also make their artwork deliberately difficult to consume: because the complacency of consumer culture is one of their targets; and because they work outwards from those new and challenging models of human subjectivity and history that rise from (i) scientific studies of nature, notably Darwin's in the nineteenth century, and (ii) those new theories of the human psyche, and materialist histories of culture, produced in the early decades of the twentieth.

By way of contrast to the scheme articulated by Gaonkar, in Australia celebrations of 'the cultural patina of modernity as a spectacle of speed, novelty, and effervescence' are precisely those works which resist stylistic innovation and facilitate, rather than obstruct, their own consumption. In particular, I have in mind the Australian nationalist pioneering saga of the second quarter of the twentieth century, a genre self-consciously rooted in the bush-realist tradition born in the 1890s. The assertion is counterintuitive for the unexpected association of bushmen and women engaged for the most part in manual labour with the modernist glint of steel, but it is one regularly made by the sagas themselves.

Let me take as a prime example the work of the key writer as regards my argument in this essay, Stella Maria Sarah Miles Franklin (1879–1954). Writing pseudonymously as Miles Franklin, she had an early hit with the novel *My Brilliant Career* in 1901 and then embarked overseas, working in Chicago and in Britain before returning to Australia in 1932 (see Jill Roe's recent, monumental biography). Most of her novels subsequent to *My Brilliant Career* sank with little trace, but writing under a new pseudonym, Brent of Bin Bin, she had a number of comparative successes, including *Up the Country* (1928), *Ten Creeks Run* (1930), and *Back to Bool Bool* (1931). In 1936, Franklin returned to fame, writing under her 'original' pseudonym for her novel *All That Swagger*, a family chronicle charting the triumph of the pioneering spirit.

All That Swagger follows the fortunes of the Delacy family from their arrival in Australia. Its ultimate hero, Brian Delacy, emphasizes that his own achievements in the modern era are directly linked to the pioneering spirit, whose future work will be realized from, and manifest in, the aeroplane. Having flown with his wife from America to Australia, Brian makes a speech to the press, paraphrased thus in Franklin's narration:

> Old Danny had come immediately after the explorers Sturt and Major Mitchell and made a home for wife and babies in the wilds. His great-grandson's announced ambition was to forward the family era in aviation and thus to banish Australian loneliness and isolation, internecine or international.
>
> We must take to the plane as the early settler took to the horse and the camel. We must all fly as a matter of course.[4]

In the next chapter he declares:

> "Fly, that's the order of the day. My old great-grandad – all his kids went from the bottle on to a horse without a pram between, and my kids and yours – if we have the luck to have any – must go from their mothers – by George! they must go with their mothers straight into planes. We'll build hangars and dromes instead of roads. Instead of the old shanty-keepers with stables and nose-bags, we're going to have bowsers and skilled mechanics with spare parts dotted about from the Roper to the Paroo and Ayer's Rock, and from the Leeuwin to Cape York. It's the greatest flying land on the globe – the best sky – blow it all, we've got about the biggest sky there is all in one piece, and that's without any bolony.'[5]

The aeroplane is here identified as a technological triumph more significant for the cultural development of Australia than for any other nation: it closes distances between Australia and the rest of the world – notably between Australia and the home of modernity, America – and it makes surveyable, comprehensible, and loveable the vast interior spaces of the continent.

Fundamental to this project also is modern woman, embodied in the cockpit by Lola, Brian's American wife, but also in the writer's seat by Miles Franklin, the world-travelled Australian woman whose saga aims to dredge the land "from oblivion by the projection upon it of human personality." "A land beloved, as a being cherished," she explains, "garners spiritual identity."[6] Not least for this reason – to popularize or, more accurately, to democratize the literary means of garnering spiritual identity – the facility of survey (and human occupation) enabled by the aeroplane begets a facility of style: there is

---

[4] Miles Franklin, *All That Swagger* (http://gutenberg.net.au/ebooks08/0800961.txt, 1936): ch 50.

[5] Franklin, *All That Swagger* (http://gutenberg.net.au/ebooks08/0800961.txt, 1936): ch. 51.

[6] *All That Swagger*, ch. 47.

nothing avant-garde or obstructionist about Franklin's writing; "the dreary, dun-coloured offspring of journalistic realism," Patrick White's summation of mainstream Australian literature, captures it, albeit maliciously.[7]

The same linking of bush pioneers and modernity's "spectacle of speed, novelty, and effervescence" is evident in Charles Chauvel's 1935 film *Heritage*, though without Franklin's redeeming feminism. (Clips from the film are freely available via the National Film and Sound Archive's 'Australian Screen' website.[8]) *Heritage* – insightfully if negatively reviewed by Franklin[9] – charts white settler history up to the marriage of a member of parliament to an aviatrix. The husband's domestic lecture about his wife's necessary submission segues into a parliamentary speech on the same subject: aviation is not to be the vehicle of female emancipation but, like white women's bodies, to become the medium ensuring a racially pure and progressive future for Australia.

Retrospectively, these rampantly nationalist sagas reveal the futurist tendency of 1890s bush-realist writing, reminding us how practitioners of bush realism, purposefully seeking out a new way of writing the Australian landscape by rejecting the conventions of anglocentric romanticism, would have seen themselves as moderns. So, too, those forging a new political landscape in Australia; for while, from the post-nationalist perspective of the twenty-first century, the Federation of the formerly individually administered British colonies as the Commonwealth of Australia in 1901 seems a dusty affair, it was a future-oriented event for its architects, albeit one built in the imperialist style. Hence, our intuited hesitation to embrace bush realists as avant-garde, or Federationists as radicals, is insightful. If Tim Armstrong reminds us that "modernism is in fact inextricably linked with the emergence of the modern nation-state from late Victorian imperialism,"[10] the modern Australian nation-state did not quite want to emerge fully. Australia might have become more politically independent from Britain than it had been hitherto, but it wanted even more both to promote the idea of coherent, progressive white Anglo-Celtic cultural expansion and to inscribe itself as central to that story. In this

---

[7] Patrick White, "Prodigal Son," *Australian Letters* 1.3 (1958): 39.

[8] Charles Chauvel, dir. *Heritage* (Sydney: Expeditionary Film, Australia, 1935; 94 min.), Australian Screen, http://aso.gov.au/titles/features/heritage/ (accessed 20 March 2012).

[9] *The Diaries of Miles Franklin*, ed. Paul Brunton (Sydney: Allen & Unwin, 2004).

[10] Tim Armstrong, *Modernism: A Cultural History* (Cambridge: Polity, 2005): 44.

regard, Australia looked back to the so-called civilizing mission underpinning the colonial project, and to social Darwinism, in order to look forward to its future as an exemplary democracy, exemplary for its acknowledgement, recognition, and promotion of the interests of white working men. In this light, the Immigration Restriction Act, the first law passed by the federal Australian parliament, might be seen as just as constitutive of "the patina of modernity" for Australians in 1901 as "the spectacle of speed" – which would make accessible for white settlers the interior and northern spaces of the continent – and the 'novelty' and 'effervescence' of new nationhood.

A similar paradox, I think, appears in the two foundational novels of the Federation period, Franklin's *My Brilliant Career* (1901) and Joseph Furphy's *Such is Life* (1903). Furphy wrote without knowledge of Franklin's work, despite its popularity, but both writers deploy unreliable first-person narration, both open with assertions of the realism of the forthcoming story, but both stories contain submerged romances: Franklin's a tale of an awkward young girl who insists on her tell-it-like-it-is Australianness is in part that of an inspired ingénue who wishes herself on the stage, who swans about in the high-class milieu of Caddagat station, bewitches every man she comes across, and is liable to give wallowing praise to poetic evocations of the bush. Furphy's narrator, while setting out to demonstrate the workings of materialist determinism, is blind to the romance of hopeless love, disguised identity, and providence operating under his very nose. In this way, both novels are forged by a hankering after realism that cannot quite relinquish the conventions of romance: instead, each is generically *unsettled*, as if neither novel can formally break through into the new while undoubtedly expressing something novel and strange. This amalgam is carried forward into Franklin's later pioneering sagas, their realist dialogue and style overlaying the neo-romanticism of her rampantly progressivist view of Australian history.

Indeed, if the latter could embrace the "patina of modernity," the formal innovations of European modernism were met with revulsion by Franklin, as expressed in her response, in her diaries and notebooks, to the work of the Australian modernist Christina Stead. A confluence of negative qualities drive Franklin's invective against this writer: Stead's expatriatism (she had left Australia for England 1928, then lived in Paris in the early 1930s before making a home in the USA); her frankness about sexual matters, cohering, in Franklin's view, around her acceptance of Freudian theories of the subject; and her subsequent 'international' (that is, not nationalist) style. In her 1935

⌘ Modernism, Antipòdernism, and Australian Aboriginality 95

notebook, reviewing Stead's 1934 novel *Seven Poor Men of Sydney*, Franklin writes:

> there seems to be a tendency to dress up the thin banality of our cities with post-Freudianism – all the license of confessions of the [word indecipherable] of the subconscious under the charter of psychoanalysis & in post-war chaos, take the vomit of Bloomsbury & Washington Square & belch it into Sydney. This will be commended by overseas intelligentsia from Washington Square to Bloomsbury & Moscow who know nothing of its relation or the contrary to Australia, but who are pleased because they can understand their own idiom.[11]

She goes on:

> The book is modern in its chaos. There has been no attempt made to organize the material. It has the post war form or formlessness of the novel resulting from the destruction of the Victorian & Edwardian patterns, a no man's land of rebellion, cynicism, licence and rush which has not yet found new patterns – undigested conglomerate. It is only saved by the vigorous talent of the author from being mere case observations of the unfit: & the investigation of perverts is only valuable insofar as it helps normality to supernormality in the upward trend of man. When perversion becomes of consequence on its own account & is respected or tolerated as sophistication it is the symptom of racial decadence. When it becomes better to be born abnormal in the sub way than born gifted in the super way disaster is overtaking the race.[12]

Significant here are Franklin's sense of the void created by the "destruction of the Victorian & Edwardian patterns" – her own novel, as suggested above, unsettled those patterns only – and the coalescence, in her attack on Stead's novel, of issues of nationality, style, sex, and race. Modernism, understood as a startling new style that takes up new theories of the subject, is rendered locally irrelevant (that is, international), sexually perverse (Freudian), morally void, and racially degenerate.

Freud is also blamed by Franklin for the dissipation of first-wave feminism's emphasis on moral purity. A 1948 review in Franklin's notebooks of Stead's *Letty Fox: Her Luck* (1945) sets her reminiscing about her first encounter in America with promiscuity among a debauched urban elite

---

[11] Miles Franklin, *The Diaries of Miles Franklin*, ed. Brunton, 26–27.
[12] *The Diaries of Miles Franklin*, ed. Brunton, 27.

prompted (in her view) by their subscription to psychoanalytic theory.[13] By way of contrast, Franklin looks back instead to a time when

> women were striving to do away with the moral monstrosity of the double standard in sexual behaviour by making men abstain equally with women, which, worked out, is mere arithmetical logic. [...] This was before 1914. When I returned to New York in 1923, Freud had swept the field. The Puritan dams were broken. [Mr.] Floyd [Dell]'s [sexually promiscuous] brand of feminism was operating. Abortions were the order of the day.[14]

Now, Franklin may have had good reason to regret women's embrace of sexual libertinism: in her view, women's acquiescing to men's desires by making themselves sexually available, even in the name of women's liberation, weakened the feminist cause. What interests me here, though, is the manner in which Franklin's early- to mid-twentieth-century attitudes to race and sex may have affected her retrospective assessment of her 1901 novel *My Brilliant Career*. We know from Elizabeth Webby's research that Franklin regularly looked back at her first work, for she wrote and re-wrote drafts of the sequel *My Career Goes Bung* which did not appear until 1946. Although the possible offence to friends and relatives is usually cited as the cause of Franklin's withdrawal of the book from publication until ten years after her death, it is tempting to suggest that as she matured and her attitudes to sex were consolidated, she found the underlying sado-masochism of the story distasteful: too Freudian. I should explain here that although the protagonist of *My Brilliant Career*, Sybylla, protests against the disempowerment of women through marriage and volubly articulates the threat her fiancé Harry Beecham represents to her career, it is none too hard to see that the character wants her lover to overcome her physically, putting a sexually charged end to virginity and career. At one point Harry seizes Sybylla, and later, when she contemplates her bruises, she ends the chapter with the notorious line "it had been a very happy day for me."[15] As Jill Roe writes, this scene was even cited by Havelock Ellis in his 1904 *Studies in the Psychology of Sex*, but "if *My Brilliant*

---

[13] Franklin, *The Diaries of Miles Franklin*, ed. Brunton, 226.

[14] *The Diaries of Miles Franklin*, 229–30.

[15] Miles Franklin, *My Brilliant Career* (1901; Sydney: Angus & Robertson, 1994): 166 (ch. 23).

Career carried the Australian novel into new territory, now recognisable as the psychology of desire, she had not intended it."[16]

And yet, sado-masochism does not stand alone as a cause of Franklin's possible distaste for her first novel: I believe its offensiveness is exacerbated by being bound up with issues of race. Tanya Dalziell has shown the number of references to Aboriginal people and culture in *My Brilliant Career*, lodged in a broader imperialist intertextual network: both Sybylla and Harry clearly understand Aboriginal men and women to be beneath contempt. But it is the novel's first reference to Aboriginality, via Sybylla's family's servant-girl Jane Haizelip, that stands out for its reference to Aboriginal gender relations. Jane declares:

> "I don't think much of the men around here. They let the women work too hard. I never see such a tired wore-out set of women. It puts me in mind ev the time wen the black fellers made the gins do all the work."[17]

The point here is that the treatment of Aboriginal women by Aboriginal men is the furthest possible conception from (gentle)manly. It is a standard trope of colonial writing, in which exploitative Aboriginal gender relations are paradigmatic of anarchically violent Aboriginal sexuality and Aboriginal tribal organization. At once, then, we have why Sybylla's sexual arousal cannot be acted upon – it is to blacken one's emphatically superior white nativity – at the moment sexual expression is most desired, forcing that expression into the sadomasochistic domain.

One senses, then, that white-settler proximity to Aboriginal people is colouring Franklin's anxieties about sex: unmediated desire becomes a sign of social anarchy and racial degeneration. Thinking not, then, abstractly, of white and 'primitive' races but of White Settler Australians and Aboriginal people specifically, nuances Franklin's 1935 statement about Stead's writing I quoted earlier:

> When perversion becomes of consequence on its own account & is respected or tolerated as sophistication it is the symptom of racial decadence. When it becomes better to be born abnormal in the sub way than born gifted in the super way disaster is overtaking the race.[18]

---

[16] Jill Roe, *Stella Miles Franklin: A Biography* (Sydney: HarperCollins, 2008): 71.
[17] Franklin, *My Brilliant Career*, 13.
[18] Franklin, *The Diaries of Miles Franklin*, 27.

Modernist tendencies threaten the maintenance of white authority on a global scale, a situation all the more precarious from Franklin's perspective, living in a nation whose 'real' natives were black and whose wide-open spaces seemed a poor defence against vast Asian populations to the north.

Positing such an attitude elucidates Franklin's view of what Australia specifically has to offer world literature in her Commonwealth Literary Fund lectures of the early 1950s, collected and published posthumously in 1956 as *Laughter, Not for a Cage*. There she characterizes Furphy explicitly, and herself implicitly, as "in every sense antipodean," "free from inherited nostalgia," "rooted so soundly in his native soil that he felt no intransigence in its rawness as material for a masterpiece. With sturdy self-reliance, he trued-up to his own pole of integrity as a writer."[19] This Furphy–Franklin alliance opposes Euro-American modernism. "Being so few in a wide clean land," Franklin writes, "we have not had time to develop those fetid jungles and ancient sinks of poverty and vice which writers in other lands have grown notable by exposing" (213). This places a peculiar moral obligation on Australian writers in the global arena.

> The Australian has an inspiring opportunity and steadying responsibility in the only continent still comparatively free from the habitations and social evils that mar the haughtiest civilizations. Let him not be ashamed of decency, of wholesome normality, of 'crime sheets' clean of 'morbid or unseemly offences' and sophisticated perversions. (126–27)

With this much at stake, it is unsurprising that expatriate New World writers like Stead are identified as significant carriers of pollution between Worlds Old and New in Franklin's lectures. (The irony that Franklin was herself an expatriate for many years passes without comment.) The rot originally set in with Henry James, who, where Furphy is "a man who writes," is a mere "writing man" enfeebled by his cultural immersion in decadent literary elites (226–27). In the Australian context, the ascent of Franklin's despised Freud is further evinced in the overseas success of the Australian expatriate Henry Handel Richardson ("The misfortunes of Richard Mahony caught this wave," 146–47, referring to Richardson's masterpiece) in the decades where Franklin experienced little literary success.

---

[19] Miles Franklin, *Laughter, Not for a Cage: notes on Australian writing, with biographical emphasis on the struggles, function, and achievements of the novel in three half-centuries* (Sydney: Angus & Robertson): 126–27. Further page references are in the main text.

The kind of modernism Franklin advocates, then, is one that looks back to a time before Freud in order to start again, as it were, with a progressive vision of morally pure white nations. This corresponds to the manner in which Franklin looks back to a time of feminist progress before Freud "swept the field":

> I am glad I am not young now, I don't desire life to stagnate inside outworn customs, and the monogamous marriage, so far, is monogamous for women only: a new experiment or extension of the pre-1914–18 one is due.[20]

It is precisely this jump-back-to-move-forward movement that characterizes, for me, what I would label antipòdernism, a settler modernism that celebrates the technological advances which apparently enable white expansion, proliferation, and success in such countries as Australia – this includes travel and medical technologies such as Robert Dixon has explored in his book *Prosthetic Gods* (2001) – that celebrates these technologies but repudiates those contemporary evolutionary (materialist) theories of the subject and of human culture that cohere around notions of the 'primitive'.

In this light, I would characterize A.D. Hope's much-anthologized 1939 poem "Australia" (readily available online) as antipòdernist. We see here cultural modernism's condemnation of bourgeois mentalities ("the river of her immense stupidity / Floods her monotonous tribes from Cairns to Perth"), but at the same time the poem repudiates European modernism as the "lush jungle of modern thought" fuelled by "the chatter of cultured apes." Implicitly mocking modernist obsession with Darwinian history and with the unconscious as phylogenetic reservoir, Hope attaches Australian vision instead to the fierce and sparse wisdom of the Hebrew fathers ("the Arabian desert of the human mind"): he jumps over nineteenth- and twentieth-century thought, looking back to see forward, rendering Australian prophecy a New Old Testament. Indigenous Knowledge of Australia's wildernesses is, it seems, absent: this is the enabling "Arabian," not Aboriginal, "desert of the human mind." And yet, if we uphold modernism's own construction of Aboriginal peoples as culturally the closest in the world to the habits of the primal horde, to apes – a point to which I will return – then Aboriginality *is* present in Hope's poem, strangely allied in it with European modernism itself.

Significant here, then, is the central place of Australian Aboriginality in the work of Émile Durkheim, James Frazer, and Sigmund Freud, to name just

---

[20] Franklin, *The Diaries of Miles Franklin*, 230.

three key thinkers in the development of "the lush jungle of modern thought." The theories of all three made extensive use of Francis Gillen's and Baldwin Spencer's work on the Arrernte people, notably *The Native Tribes of Central Australia* (1899), while Spencer in turn worked from social-Darwinist principles. Briefly, Frazer used Spencer's and Gillen's work on the Arrernte as a starting point for his concept of 'natural theology', a way of historicizing religion other than in terms of divine revelation. The Arrernte were characterized as almost wholly belonging to the 'Age of Magic', the first stage of natural theology, which included belief in physical immortality, and the belief in human-magic causes for all otherwise unexplained deaths, thus necessitating violent revenge against perpetrators. In the 'Age of Religion' this transformed into belief that spirits were responsible for unexplained deaths, meaning rites such as sacrifice developed to appease non-human deities. The Arrernte showed early signs of developing into this second Age, through their assignation of extraordinary powers to mythical ancestors, and through their showing signs of belief in just one mythical creature, a snake. Durkheim, meanwhile, repudiated Frazer's derivation of belief in a spirit world to such perishable motives as fear: the existence of spirits, rather, derived from misunderstanding those extraordinary moments of collective feeling occasioned at social gatherings. He subsequently constructed the sacred as collective wisdom garnered over generations and internalized by the individual, an internalization we might now call 'conscience'. By contrast, Freud explored conscience as born of prohibitions on childhood sexuality, prohibitions which also structured group psychology. So, if Arrernte totemism is, for Durkheim, a 'savage' precursor to hegemony, for Freud it is a 'savage' expression of psychological processes of repression. Whatever the peculiarities of each theory, Arrernte culture found itself a central place in key European works which offered a radically new way of understanding human culture and behaviour: Australian Aboriginality, albeit erroneously figured, is there at the birth of the modern.

What Freud in particular added to the modernist evolution of culture might be illustrated, if somewhat crudely, as follows. Imagine you have collected, from all over the world, artefacts from a range of 'primitive' cultures and from archaeological digs. Stratigraphic techniques have established, not least through the work of Danish archaeologists such as Christian Jürgensen Thomsen (1788–1865) and Jens Jacob Asmussen Worsaae (1821–85), a model of technological progress through three ages, where humans deploy stone, bronze, then iron implements which correspond to increasingly complex models of society and economic exchange, then extrapolated to infer more sophisticated 'levels' of culture. The same (erroneous but powerful) principle might be applied within each age. So, gathering all your stone implements into a single pile, you might arrange them according to your own ideas of degrees of technological progress, perhaps from a simple stone which has been clearly used as a tool, to stones which have been increasingly modified to form sharper and sharper blades, perhaps also with increasingly elaborate holds or even 'handles'. Adding these to implements from 'subsequent' ages, you might then display your stone artefacts as a spectrum of cultural evolution not unlike the exhibits at the famous Pitt Rivers Museum installed in Oxford in the mid-1880s (in which process Spencer assisted Professors Edward Burnett Tylor and Henry Moseley). Next, you might also group implements according to their source communities. Assessing the techniques of a particular group's manufacture, you might then look back at your first display to determine where the source community falls along the spectrum of cultural progress. What is more, measuring the age of neighbouring archaeological implements on the spectrum – the ones most like the implements you have collected from the contemporary 'primitive' source community – you would be able to determine the ancient stage in the overall history of human evolution to which the living 'primitives' belonged.

The composite effect is to develop a depth model of human cultural difference:[21] diverse living peoples were plotted according to the depth of time (the ancientness) they represent in the evolutionary process from the 'present' (and future), marked European. It is ironic, though also tragic, then, that the Aboriginal peoples of Australia, the most remote geographically from Europeans, were also considered the most remote in time, the 'deepest', projections of a 'stone age' culture (Spencer called the Arrernte a "stone-age people" in the subtitle of his 1927 tome). In the words of the anthropologist Herbert Basedow, "the Australian Aboriginal [sic] stands somewhere near the bottom rung of the great evolutional ladder we have ascended."[22]

---

[21] See Nicholas Thomas, *Entangled Objects: Exchange, Material Culture, and Colonialism in the Pacific* (Cambridge MA: Harvard UP, 1991), and Tom Griffiths, *Hunters and Collectors: the antiquarian imagination in Australia* (Cambridge: Cambridge UP, 1996).

[22] Herbert Basedow, quoted in Katherine Susanne Prichard, *Coonardoo* (Sydney: Angus & Robertson, 1985): xxii.

It is as much as to say that people way 'over there' (Aboriginal Australians) are like people 'here' (Europeans) as they used to be in the ancient past. What Freud adds to the formula is the notion that people way 'over there' still are in the unconscious; or, slightly less crudely, the formula becomes: people way 'over there' (Aboriginal Australians) are like people 'here' (Europeans) as they used to be in the ancient past, though the ancient psychic formation determining their primitive mental lives is still present 'here' in the id, a phylogenetic reservoir of former mental states.

This has implications for understanding the imagination in particular. That is because, according to Freud, the fundamental principle of primitive mentality was the projection of inner states onto phenomena in the outside world; making gods and demons of everything:

> The projection of inner perceptions to the outside is a primitive mechanism which, for instance, also influences our sense-perceptions, so that it normally has the greatest share in shaping our outer world. [...] even inner perceptions of ideational and emotional processes are projected outwardly, like sense perceptions, and are used to shape the outer world, whereas they ought to remain in the inner world. [...] Only with the development of a language of abstract thought through the association of sensory remnants of word representations with inner processes, did the latter gradually become capable of perception. Before this took place primitive man had developed a picture of the outer world through the outward projection of inner perceptions, which we, with our reinforced conscious perception, must now translate back into psychology.[23]

This statement requires more unpacking than I have space for here, but the issue is the distinction between *projection* (marked as primitive) and *perception* (marked as advanced/civilized); or, more accurately, between 'outward projection of inner perceptions' and 'reinforced conscious perception' of the 'outer world'. Thus, totemism, constituted by the projection of psychological formations, for Freud is a 'stage' in the development of cultural life that has been surpassed in more 'advanced' cultures through reality-testing. In modernity most things in nature lose their original 'richness' of meaning to become comparatively weak ('empirical') objects of science. So, too, for Freud,

---

[23] Sigmund Freud, "Totem and Taboo: Resemblances Between the Mental Lives of Savages and Neurotics" (1913), tr. A.A. Brill in *The Basic Writings of Sigmund Freud* (New York: Modern Library, 1995): 825.

science abolishes the last major remnant in 'civilized' societies of collectively projecting non-reality-tested inner processes: religion. Thus the extraordinary reality-testing enabled by scientific apparatus – modernity's prosthetic sensory organs – leaves humankind in a 'sober world where there are only material values'. Hence Freud's warning when considering 'the world of primitive man':

> We must beware of introducing the contempt for what is merely thought or wished which characterizes our sober world where there are only material values, into the world of primitive man and the neurotic, which is full of inner riches only.[24]

This recalls Frazer's comment in his 1913 Gifford Lectures:

> Outside of ourselves there stretches away on every side an infinitude of space without sound, without light, without colour, a solitude traversed only in every direction by an inconceivably complex web of silent and impersonal forces. That, if I understand it aright, is the general conception of the world which modern science has substituted for polytheism.[25]

The perceived 'inner riches' of the neurotic and the savage are precisely those tapped by stylistically experimental modernists. So, quite apart from the new ways of writing stories of the human that Freud's re-mapping of psychological development offered artists, his and others' re-articulation of the imagination not as a divine but a primeval mechanism, one richly resourced with the id's personal, racial, and species memories, presented modernist writers with further motivation to jolt readers out of conventional bourgeois patterns of thought. But, to put it crudely, that there might be a savage within was peculiarly distasteful for a settler nation busying itself dismantling the lives and cultures of its Indigenous peoples: a nation wanting to make 'them' new only by making 'them' like 'us'. That's quite a different thing from saying that modernity recognizes 'they' are *in* 'us'. It begins to explain Australia's abject relation to 'cultural modernity'.

Indeed, if some writers in Australia did take up a quasi-Freudian vision of Aboriginality, this was only belatedly coupled with stylistic innovation. In

---

[24] Freud, "Totem and Taboo," 897.

[25] James Frazer, *The Belief in Immortality and the Worship of the Dead*, vol. 1: *The Belief among Aborigines of Australia, the Torres Strait Islands, New Guinea and Melanesia* (Gifford Lectures, 1913): 21, http://www.gutenberg.org/files/20116/20116-h/20116-h.htm (accessed 20 March 2012).

1923 D.H. Lawrence literally worked out his vitalism on paper in an extraordinary novel-in-progress, *Kangaroo*, written in Australia, full of descriptions of the 'Aboriginal' landscape but entirely lacking in Aboriginal figures. His vision of the 'savage' is instead deposited in the protagonist's championing of a god of the 'lower parts'. Katherine Susannah Prichard's *Coonardoo* from 1928 intimates the eponymous character's corporeo-psychological inhabitation of space – the Aboriginal woman Coonardoo's mental and physical health is linked to the success or otherwise of the station where she works – but Prichard's novel itself is social-realist. Meanwhile, the perceived savage sexuality of Aboriginal society is transposed onto the virile and white polygamist Sam Geary in the novel. Likewise, the Jindyworobak poets attempted to vitalize their poetry with Aboriginal themes and words, but their failures were aptly characterized by Hope as the "Boy Scout School of Poetry."[26] It is, perhaps, only in the 'belated' modernism of Patrick White that we find both stylistic experimentation and a modernist vision of Aboriginality, epitomized by the fact that Alf Dubbo, White's stolen-generations Aboriginal character in *Riders in the Chariot* (1961), is an expressionist painter. Certainly White's depiction of cannibalism in *A Fringe of Leaves* (1976) recalls Freud's derivation of communion rites from the primal horde's murder and eating of the patriarchal alpha male.[27] It may be salutary also to consider White's brilliant depictions of madness and mental states occasioned by bodily trauma – and perhaps more broadly his vision of visionaries per se – in the light of Freudian notions of primitive and neurotic projection. But this flowering of modernist Aboriginalism was, as I have said, belated. The particular construction of Aboriginality that was a premise for the work of Freud and his armchair contemporaries – that Aboriginal culture was the most primitive and the least complex – was soon discredited by field-work anthropology. As a consequence, also, Australian Aboriginality lost its brief prominence in European thought.

In discussing anti-modernist sentiment in Australia, I might have focused on the Ern Malley hoax of 1944 or on A.D. Hope's notorious reference to White's 1955 novel *The Tree of Man* as "illiterate verbal sludge."[28] I have, rather, focused on race, not least because it has enabled me to identify what I

---

[26] Brian Elliott, *Jindyworobaks* (St. Lucia: U of Queensland P, 1979): 248.

[27] Freud, "Totem and Taboo," ch. 4.

[28] A.D. Hope, *Australian Literature 1950–1962* (Melbourne: Melbourne UP, 1963): 15.

have called antipòdernism as an alternative Australian modernism that occurs in the modernist first third of the twentieth century. Antipòdernism embraced what Gaonkar calls "the patina of modernity," particularly where technologies were seen to facilitate white expansion in Australia, but it balked at the stylistic innovations underpinned by materialist theories of the human subject in which, for a brief period, figurations of Australian Aboriginality were prominent. Its cohesion around issues of race reminds us that any history of modernism in Australia is contextualized by the history of white-settler oppression of real Aboriginal Australian men, women, and children. Within that history, the mid- to late 1930s was a time of domestic tragedy – the arch-assimilationist A.O. Neville became Commissioner of Native Affairs in 1936 – but, given that it also saw the birth, in 1938, of pan-Aboriginal activism, it was not a decade without hope. Indeed, it might also be seen as a significant decade for the development of *Aboriginal* modernity, a truly alternative modernity in Gaonkar's sense ... but that is another story.

WORKS CITED

Armstrong, Tim. *Modernism: A Cultural History* (Cambridge: Polity, 2005).

Brunton, Paul, ed. *The Diaries of Miles Franklin* (Sydney: Allen & Unwin, 2004).

Chauvel, Charles, dir. *Heritage* (Sydney: Expeditionary Film, Australia, 1935; 94 min.), Australian Screen, http://aso.gov.au/titles/features/heritage/ (accessed 20 March 2012).

Dalziell, Tanya. *Settler Romances and the Australian Girl* (Perth: U of Western Australia P, 2004).

Dixon, Robert. *Prosthetic Gods: Travel, Representation, and Colonial Governance* (St Lucia: U of Queensland P, 2001).

Durkheim, Émile. *The Elementary Forms of Religious Life*, tr. Carol Cosman (*Les formes élémentaires de la vie religieuse*, 1912; Oxford: Oxford UP, 2001).

Elliott, Brian, ed., *Jindyworobaks* (St Lucia: U of Queensland P, 1979).

Franklin, Miles. *All That Swagger* (1936), http://gutenberg.net.au/ebooks08/0800961.txt (accessed 20 March 2012).

——. *Laughter, Not for a Cage: notes on Australian writing, with biographical emphasis on the struggles, function, and achievements of the novel in three half-centuries* (Sydney: Angus & Robertson, 1956).

——. *My Brilliant Career* [1901] and *My Career Goes Bung* [1946], ed. Elizabeth Webby (Sydney: Angus & Robertson, 1994).

Frazer, James. *The Belief in Immortality and the Worship of the Dead*, vol. 1: *The belief among Aborigines of Australia, the Torres Strait Islands, New Guinea and*

Melanesia (Gifford Lectures, 1913), http://www.gutenberg.org/files/20116/20116-h/20116-h.htm (accessed 20 March 2012).

Freud, Sigmund. "Totem and Taboo: Resemblances Between the Mental Lives of Savages and Neurotics" (1913), tr. A.A. Brill, in *The Basic Writings of Sigmund Freud* (New York: Modern Library, 1995): 775–898.

Furphy, Joseph. *Such is Life: being extracts from the diary of Tom Collins* (1903; Sydney: Hogarth, 1986).

Gaonkar, Parameshwar, ed. *Alternative Modernities* (Durham NC: Duke UP, 2001).

Gillen, Francis, & Baldwin Spencer. *The Native Tribes of Central Australia* (1899), http://www.sacred-texts.com/aus/ntca/index.htm (accessed 20 March 2012).

Griffiths, Tom. *Hunters and Collectors: the antiquarian imagination in Australia* (Cambridge: Cambridge UP, 1996).

Henderson, Ian. "The Body of an Australian Girl: Miles Franklin's *My Brilliant Career* (1901)," in *Feminism and the Body: Interdisciplinary Perspectives*, ed. Catherine Kevin (Newcastle upon Tyne: Cambridge Scholars, 2009): 116–33.

——. "Uncommon Reading: Sight, Science and the 'Savage' Reader, 1850–1915," *Journal of the Association for the Study of Australian Literature* (2010), www.nla.gov.au/openpublish/index.php/jasal/article/view/1507/2087 (accessed 20 March 2012).

Hope, A.D. *Australian Literature 1950–1962* (Melbourne: Melbourne UP, 1963)

Lawrence, D.H. *Kangaroo* (1922; Harmondsworth: Penguin Twentieth-Century Classics, 1980).

Prichard, Katherine Susannah. *Coonardoo* (1929; Sydney: Angus & Robertson, 1985).

Roe, Jill. *Stella Miles Franklin: A Biography* (Sydney: HarperCollins, 2008).

Thomas, Nicholas. *Entangled Objects: Exchange, Material Culture, and Colonialism in the Pacific* (Cambridge MA: Harvard UP, 1991).

White, Patrick. *The Aunt's Story* (1948; Harmondsworth: Penguin, 1993).

——. *A Fringe of Leaves* (1976; London: Vintage, 1997).

——. "Prodigal Son," *Australian Letters* 1.3 (1958): 37–40.

——. *Riders in the Chariot* (1968; London: Vintage, 1996).

⌘

Material Resonance
Knowing Before Meaning

BILL ASHCROFT

WHAT IS IT TO KNOW WHAT WE KNOW? I want to talk about what we can know about the other in the interstices of cultures, in that contact zone in which subjects are mutually transformed. In particular I want to talk about the space that lies just beyond interpretation, beyond the boundary of that product we call 'meaning' to see how we might know the unknowable, might 'know' the Indigenous experience of the world, a form of knowledge outside, perhaps, the boundaries of our epistemology. I say 'beyond' but it may be better understood as a communication that occurs *before* the interpretation of meaning, in a non-hermeneutic engagement with the materiality of the text.

A beautiful demonstration of this form of 'knowing' occurs in David Malouf's *Remembering Babylon* when a group of dour Scottish farmers are confronted by Gemmy, a white boy brought up by Aborigines, whose presence destroys the comfortable boundaries of their fenced and farmed world. Trying to discover Gemmy's story, the farmers are reminded of the presence of something just beyond understanding, a form of knowing they can't put into words:

> Occasionally, in the dead light of a paddock, all bandaged stumps and bone white antlers, there would come a flash of colour, red or blue or yellow, and it would strike a man, but in a disconcerting way, as his heart lifted, that a country that was mostly devilish could also at times be playful, that there might be doors hidden here, hidden as yet, into some lighter world.[1]

---

[1] David Malouf, *Remembering Babylon* (1993; London: Vintage, 1994): 10–11. Further page references are in the main text.

Malouf's novel is about the failure of settler society to enter this lighter world, about a society that might have been if the colonizers had given themselves to the place rather than refashion it into a simulacrum of a rural Britain. The doors to this world are not so hidden, for they exist in the boundaries erected by the settlers themselves, but they remain stolidly closed. For his part, Gemmy also finds it impossible to bridge the gap, to cross the cultural boundary the settlers have erected, and he ponders the difficulty of explaining the nature of the place to the farmers who press him for explanations about the 'Absolute Dark' they see lying out beyond their fences.

> And in fact a good deal of what they were after he could not have told, even if he had wanted to, for the simple reason that there were no words for it in their tongue; yet when, as sometimes happened, he fell back on the native word, the only one that could express it, their eyes went hard, as if the mere existence of a language they did not know was a provocation, a way of making them helpless. He did not intend it that way, but he too saw that it might be true. (65)

Such knowledge seems to lie beyond language. In particular, it may lie quite outside written language, for language that inscribes itself in writing fails, because of its very power of representation, to take in the knowledge of place that exists beyond representation.

Nevertheless, it lies in the power of literary language to suggest the presence of this lighter world, a presence sometimes glimpsed without understanding by these early settlers. Jock McIvor, the father of the family that takes Gemmy in, reaches a point at which he might have broken through to a form of knowing the country, a knowledge beyond words:

> Wading through the waist high grass, he was surprised to see all the tips beaded with green, as if some new growth had come into the world that till now he had never seen or heard of.
>
> When he looked closer it was hundreds of wee bright insects, each the size of his little fingernail, metallic, iridescent, and the discovery of them, the new light they brought into the scene, was a lightness in him – that was what surprised him – like a form of knowledge he had broken through to. It was unnameable, which disturbed him but was also exhilarating; for a moment he was entirely happy. (107)

Remembering Babylon is a brilliant allegory of settler society: of its refusal to countenance the unknown, its refusal to harvest the bounty the earth already provides, its unthinking importation of the familiar. The society that huddles behind fences protecting it from the Absolute Dark of the bush is a society in which possibility is diminished. The novel is a story of what might have been if the relentless imperial control of time and space, and the adamant belief in the mission of white culture, had not so enveloped the colonizing society. Gemmy's very existence shows the possibility of a different way of being. But he is also a threat, because he subverts, by implication, the ordered world of white society. Ultimately, the extensive implications of this allegory focus in language. For the settlers, no matter how open to the experience, the unnameable recedes into meaninglessness. Even the most open, such as Jock McIvor, come up hard against the edges of words:

> The things he had begun to be aware of, however fresh and innocent, lay outside what was common, or so he thought; certainly, since he could have found no form in which to communicate them, outside words. (108)

This is perhaps the price a language, a written language in particular, exacts from experience. While it provides us with an intersubjective world, it places limits on that world. As Wittgenstein says in the last line of the *Tractatus*, "Whereof one can not speak, thereof one must be silent."[2] This is sage advice for philosophers, but what does it mean for poets? T.S. Eliot says, on the other hand:

> It is not necessary to understand the meaning first to enjoy the poetry, but [...] our enjoyment of the poetry makes us want to understand the meaning.[3]

Enjoyed indeed! But the question I am asking is: what kind of *knowing* may exist before understanding? It is precisely that whereof one cannot speak that concerns me, because it is the resonance of the unsaid and unsayable that both enriches and mystifies the aesthetic object.

But there is another piece to this puzzle. Aileen Moreton–Robinson makes the familiar claim that the Aboriginal relationship to the land is an ontological one that white people can never share.[4] No one would dispute this. But how useful are such binaries? What happens when we delve into the space be-

---

[2] Ludwig Wittgenstein, *Tractatus Logico Philosophicus* (London: Routledge & Kegan Paul, 1922): 189.

[3] T.S. Eliot, *Dante* (London: Faber & Faber, 1929): 56.

[4] Aileen Moreton–Robinson, *Whitening Race: Essays in Social and Cultural Criticism* (Canberra: Aboriginal Studies Press, 2004): 248.

tween the ontological polarities of white and Aboriginal relationship to place? Can we *understand* that which we cannot share? Can we 'know' before we understand? And, if so, what is it to know in this way? Clearly, to even ask these questions is to begin to reconfigure our idea of epistemology. Of the first question post-colonial writing shows categorically that understanding is not to be confused with shared experience. But the second question is much more challenging. To what extent does the created object or, more broadly, the creative act itself intimate a form of knowing? To what extent is this form of knowing something that exists beyond the cognitive, in the affective response of the body? Does a poem, or any other work of art, communicate before it is understood? Does such communication take us beyond epistemology into the body? If so, how does transcultural communication proceed before understanding?

I begin with Malouf's example of Gemmy because he stands in a space between languages – one occupied by Indigenous writers who write in the language of the colonizer, a space familiar to many colonized writers. By appropriating the language of the colonizer, these writers have chosen a world audience and taken hold of the power of self-representation. The story of postcolonial literature is a story of resistance through the transformation, as English is appropriated to the exigencies of a vernacular tongue. The space of this writing is a transcultural space, and I want to investigate the extent to which transcultural space is transformative in both a hermeneutic and epistemological sense.

The term 'transcultural' was coined in the 1940s by the sociologist Fernando Ortiz in relation to Afro-Cuban culture,[5] and incorporated into literary studies by the Uruguayan critic Ángel Rama in the 1970s.[6] Ortiz proposed the term to replace the paired concepts of acculturation and deculturation that described the transference of culture in reductive fashion, one imagined from within the interests of the metropolis.[7] The contact zone has often been

---

[5] Fernando Ortiz, *Cuban Counterpoint: Tobacco and Sugar*, tr. Harriet de Onís, intro. Bronisław Malinowski, prologue by Herminio Portell Vilá, new intro. Fernando Coronil (*Contrapunto cubano del tabaco y el azúcar*, 1940; tr. 1947; Durham NC: Duke UP, 1995).

[6] Ángel Rama, *Transculturación narrativa en América Latina* (Montevideo: Siglo XXI, 1982).

[7] Mary Louise Pratt, *Imperial Eyes: Travel Writing and Transculturation* (London & New York: Routledge, 1992): 228.

framed as a contestatory space, but we can see it producing a more constructive dialogue, a process of intersubjective contact and mutual change. One contact zone clearly open to analysis is the transcultural text. In Indigenous writing this zone becomes increasingly subtle, as writers' familiarity with Indigenous culture may well occur after or simultaneously with their schooling in English.

The transcultural text is a space of negotiation, a heterotopic space in which the boundary between self and other blurs, a space in which meaning is negotiated, where, in a sense, both writer and reader are changed in constitutive collusion. Bakhtin is interesting here because he contends that *all* novels involve a cross-cultural engagement between readers and writers. He is interested in the novel because for him the novel form provides a particularly rich medium for the many-voiced appearance of different languages. For the novelist, the object is always "entangled in someone else's discourse about it, it is already present with qualifications" and is inseparable from the "heteroglot social apperception of it."[8]

Significantly, Bakhtin is talking about a putatively monoglossic text, unhampered by issues of cultural communication. For him, such a text is already heteroglossic, already engaged in dialogue *within* the text, a dialogue which, to all intents and purposes, is a *cross-cultural* dialogue between 'belief systems'. All forms involving a narrator

> open up the possibility of never having to define oneself in language, the possibility of translating one's own intentions from one linguistic system to another, of fusing "the language of truth" with "the language of everyday," of saying "I am me" in someone else's language, and in my own language "I am other."[9]

The dual dynamic of saying "I am me" in another's language and "I am other" in my own language captures precisely the dual achievement of the second-language writer. For such a writer demonstrates, in heightened form, the writer's negotiation of the forces brought to bear on language

> Every concrete utterance of a speaking subject serves as a point where centrifugal as well as centripetal forces are brought to bear [...] the

---

[8] Mikhail Bakhtin, *The Dialogic Imagination: Four Essays by M.M. Bakhtin*, ed. Michael Holquist, tr. Caryl Emerson & Michael Holquist (Austin: U of Texas P, 1981): 330.

[9] Bakhtin, *The Dialogic Imagination*, 314–15.

> utterance not only answers the requirements of its own language [...] but it answers the requirements of heteroglossia as well; it is in fact an active participant in such speech diversity.[10]

One of the preeminent advantages of cross-cultural writing in English is the capacity to translate ways of seeing into the 'bilingual' text without making any concessions to the 'way of seeing' of the reader. This is because the text is already a heteroglot profusion of ways of seeing. But it is also because the post-colonial text manages to extend Bakhtin's view of dialogue with the discovery that *true dialogue can only occur when the difference of the other is recognized.*

Constitutive Reading

Although I don't have room to fully outline it here,[11] since we are not focusing on meaning and interpretation, I want to suggest a model of reading that demonstrates the way in which transculturality operates in the text. To do this, I want to propose that the dialogism of the text shapes it as a *social situation*. It is important to see the text as a material object, a *thing*, because its materiality affects the communication. But we must not forget that the writing is an intense and socially mediated *act*. If we accept the reality of writing as a practice, we can then understand the text as a *social situation* in which the 'objective' meanings of writing come about through a process of 'social' accomplishment between the writing and reading participants. If we understand the 'meaning event' as a negotiation of social actors who present themselves to each other as functions in the text, we can then posit the negotiation of *cultural* meaning in the cross-cultural text as a 'transcultural' event. People living in different cultures may live in totally different, and even incommensurable, worlds: different worlds of experience, expectation, habit, understanding and tradition. Nevertheless, meaning is *accomplished* between writing and reading participants in ways that may confound theories of cultural incommensurability. Meaning and understanding occur because the language

---

[10] Bakhtin, *The Dialogic Imagination*, 272.

[11] I first proposed this model in "Constitutive Graphonomy," *Kunapipi* 11.1 (1989): 53–78, to address arguments about cultural 'authenticity,' but it is eminently adaptable to the question of transcultural negotiation. See also the updated version, "How Books Talk," in Ashcroft, *Caliban's Voice: The Transformation of English in Post-Colonial Literatures* (London & New York: Routledge, 2008): 143–58.

encodes the reciprocity of the experiences of each conversant. It is the situation, the *'event'* of this reciprocal happening, that 'tells', 'refers', 'informs'.

The transcultural contact zone, then, is not so much a space of shared experience as a space of acknowledged difference, a space of negotiated meaning. The particular facility of that writing which uses English as a second language, and invites the reader into the mental and emotional horizon of the 'other' culture, is to bridge the gap between cultures, to reveal that understanding is a function of the linguistic situation. The dialectic of writer and reader functions within this situation is particularly significant. Such writing re-emphasizes the constitutive nature of the meaning event and the varied nature of the usage in which meaning is accomplished.

The Production of Presence

The question is: does this constitutive function also extend beyond what we understand as the interpretation of meaning? For Bakhtin, transculturality is a condition of the novel. Each fictional text embeds an engagement of various voices in a way that changes each voice. We can extend this to see the text as a social situation in which meaning is negotiated by writer and reader functions. However, I want to go further than this to suggest that the text produces knowledge beyond the multiple voices of heteroglossia and even beyond interpretation itself in an experience of unmediated Presence. In using this term I am prompted by its importance in Hans Ulrich Gumbrecht's *Production of Presence*, which challenges "a broadly institutionalised tradition according to which interpretation, that is, the identification and/or attribution of meaning, is the core practice, the exclusive core practice indeed, of the humanities."[12] Interpretation is so institutionalized in the humanities that we take its core function for granted. But Gumbrecht's dissatisfaction arose from a sense that 'materialities of communication' were completely ignored in the humanities. The term 'materialities of communication' refers to the idea that different media affect the meaning they carried. The 'production of presence' implies that the tangible effects of the particular communication media (sound, print, and computer screen, for instance) will affect the meaning, and this production

---

[12] Hans Ulrich Gumbrecht, *Production of Presence: What Meaning Cannot Convey* (Stanford CA: Stanford UP, 2004): 3. This discussion was first developed in my "Transcultural Presence," *Storia della Storiografia* 55 (2009): 76–93. See this chapter for its relevance to transculturality in general.

of presence will occur in any form of communication, in which its material elements will "touch" the bodies of the persons communicating.[13] Gumbrecht has not been alone in this. The materiality of the artwork was a feature of the 'Group Zero' school of painting and particularly Lucio Fontana, whose Tagli paintings, in which the canvas was slashed to emphasize the material surface of the artwork, seemed to urge the viewer to engage with the pre-hermeneutic materiality of art. Indeed, more than urging, the violence of Fontana's 'abuse' of the canvas shocks us into a recognition of the materiality of art.

In literary writing, poetry is one of the most obvious examples of the importance of materiality, producing a simultaneity of presence effects and meaning effects, "for even the most overpowering institutional dominance of the hermeneutic dimension could never fully repress the presence effects of rhyme and alliteration, of verse and stanza."[14] This is clearly apparent when we read the printed lyrics of a song, for example, compared to hearing it performed. But it is also detectable in poets' performances of their own poetry, for instance. Such a resonance between the 'presence effects' and the 'meaning effects' of the communication, particularly if it is a work of art or a ritual enactment, appears fairly obvious, even trivial, once we begin to think about it. But it seems to have been completely forgotten in the West "ever since the Cartesian cogito made the ontology of human existence depend exclusively on the movements of the human mind."[15]

Material Resonance

Perhaps T.S. Eliot was delving deeper into epistemology than he knew when he alluded to the 'thinghood' of the text, a concept that thing theory has recently taken up with a vengeance. The textual materiality that seems most evocative is the domain of music, whether situated in performance or in text, whether in music itself or in the musicality of language. Indeed, I am tempted to call this particular quality the 'music' of the text, but to cover the range of textual formations in which this may occur we can call this the 'material resonance' of the text. When we hear the Indigenous poet Romaine Moreton reciting her poetry, we encounter not so much a different meaning as a different presence offered by the material resonance of the spoken text. Material

---

[13] Gumbrecht, *Production of Presence*, 17.

[14] *Production of Presence*, 18.

[15] *Production of Presence*, 17.

resonance is obviously most pronounced in music itself, for instance, when we hear Gurrumul singing in Yolgnu.

What we encounter through the Aboriginal language in Gurrumul's singing is a form of knowing before interpretation and perhaps above all a knowing of the otherness of the other. Aldous Huxley claimed that "After silence, that which comes nearest to expressing the inexpressible is music."[16] The example of music suggests that Presence is, in a sense, carried by affect. It is *carried* by affect but not identical with it, and is carried equally in the written as well as the musical object. But, more importantly, Presence may be the point at which true dialogue begins, because, in Bakhtin's terms, it is the point at which the difference of the other is recognized.

Where the production of presence becomes useful for understanding a transcultural literary space in Australia is in its suggestion that there are ways of experiencing, responding to, of 'understanding' the world apart from structures of meaning: i.e. apart from the kind of interpretation that can be fixed in language. The fact that these moments can be suggested in art, music, and especially literature is an important discovery, for the concept of presence privileges the aesthetic moment. This is not limited to transcultural writing, but in many writers it takes the form of moments of luminous comprehension – what we could call 'revelation' – emerging out of and sinking back into lives of general incomprehension. But their works always resolve into particular moments of epiphany drawn out of the material world. It is in such moments, which appear comprehensively aesthetic moments, that the presentation of the unpresentable occurs. In the words of Les Murray,

> Everything except language
> knows the meaning of existence.
> Trees, planets, rivers, time
> know nothing else. They express it
> moment by moment as the universe.[17]

"Everything except language / Knows the meaning of existence." This is perhaps because it simply *is*. This poem itself, like all fine poems, gestures to a horizon of meaning beyond language, and it is within that 'beyond' of lan-

---

[16] Aldous Huxley, "The Rest is Silence" (1931), in *Music at Night and Other Essays, including Vulgarity in Literature* (London: Chatto & Windus, 1949): 10.

[17] Les Murray, "The Meaning of Existence," in Murray, *Poems the Size of Photographs* (Sydney: Duffy & Snellgrove & Manchester: Carcanet, 2002): 104, http://www.lesmurray.org/pm_tme.htm (accessed 22 January 2012).

guage, the space beyond interpretation and perhaps even beyond articulation, that Presence is situated.

The 'Beyond' Before Interpretation

The importance of the materiality of the transcultural text compels us to face the possibility that Presence is not something added onto the interpretation, but something on which interpretation is grounded. If we think of Presence as initiated by the material resonance of the text – in the case of poetry, for instance, by the texture, music, and linguistic transformation of the lines – then we must see the 'beyond' of metaphysics as in fact the ground or starting point of an interpretation. Although we might engage with Presence, *after* we have engaged with the meaning, we must begin with the *substance* of Presence, so to speak. In one respect this is obvious – we must start with the physical (or aural or visual) text before we can even read, much less engage in, an interpretation. But I want to suggest by means of a diagram of the hermeneutic spiral that what we term the *beyond* – the non-semantic – may be seen as the *before*, the pre-linguistic.

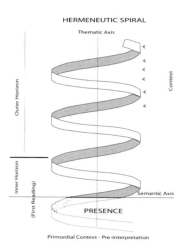

FIGURE 4: The hermeneutic spiral. (Bill Ashcroft.)

This idea of the hermeneutic spiral proposes that the Presence of the text, and I am thinking particularly of the transcultural text, might become the ground of interpretation rather than the excess or the additional engagement with the text's 'meaning'. We see in the diagram that the horizontal axis (the 'semantic' axis) is the axis of articulation, and the vertical axis (the 'thematic' axis) is the temporal or historical axis of interpretation, an axis that leads to progressive cycles of the hermeneutic circle changing through time and in different historical, cultural, and even theoretical contexts. In this simple diagram of the hermeneutic process we may see that the axis of engagement begins *below* the axis of articulation. This is the realm of Presence, the point at which the materiality of communication, the 'music' of the text, sets up a resonance between presence effects and meaning effects.

One may test for Presence by attending an art exhibition in which you are given a handset with guided commentary. After a while you find that your response is guided wholly by the commentary on the history, the art movement, the technical aspects of the painting. Your response is trapped in a hermeneutic enclosure. Put the commentary aside, perhaps for later comparison, and you will encounter that luminous moment that may be described as experiencing your experience of the work before it 'means' anything.

The depiction of the relationship between the dimension of Presence and that of interpretation suggests that our approach to the work begins below the axis of articulation and continually returns to it. Presence may not therefore be the added-on factor to the hermeneutic process but the ground on which that process occurs. In Eliot's terms, it is a domain of enjoyment preceding understanding, but with the right attention it is also a domain of knowing that doesn't necessarily become closed off by interpretation. This is particularly so in music and art, as well as song and recited poetry, but in literature it is a key function of the transcultural text. Why Presence has been so obscured by interpretation is probably explained by the historical dominance of the hermeneutic attitude in the humanities. The suggestion I want to make here is that the transcultural text, by insisting on Presence, gives easier access to this prelinguistic section of the hermeneutic spiral. We don't do away with representation, nor with the requirements of meanability, but we find them considerably augmented by the resonance in such a text.

Material resonance has a marked effect on written language, and it is shared in various transcultural situations, as we can see in Lionel Fogarty's poetry. Fogarty uses a range of strategies within a single poem to create a metonymic gap in the English text. In the following poem, untranslated words, creolized syntactical forms, ethno-rhythmic prose all serve to draw readers into the poem through the rhythms of a lullaby yet hold them at an invisible edge of Aboriginal culture.

Joowindoo Goonduhmu

Ngujoo nye muyunube
Little black buree
You must respect golo
You must praise to junun
You must seek love with googee
little black buree hear your
song 'nuyeeree munu juwoon'
The gendergender
will bring the message
The googuhgu
will laugh when you cry sad
to make your world happy
Gugun gugun buree 'gukoore doongge'
Wake up little buree your
old gulung boome
all gnumgnin to
love mooroon gunggen ge
Oh little buree goonduhmu sing
goonduhmu the feelings of
gurring ina narmee, gurring ina narmee
nha gun goon na nhorn goo
yea little buree our binung love
your sounds in the boorun
now miremumbeh and
monu goondir helps
little black gukoore your gumee
loves you. Even mumu love you.[18]

Language operating in this way achieves something a simple translation could never achieve: it foregrounds Aboriginality in a transformed English and constructs difference in two ways. On the one hand, the linguistic features simultaneously install and bridge a cultural gap between Aboriginal subject and English-speaking reader by replicating the rhythms of oral language in the

---

[18] Lionel Fogarty, "Joowindoo Goonduhmu," in *Aratjara: Aboriginal Culture and Literature in Australia*, ed. Dieter Riemenschneider & Geoffrey V. Davis (Cross/Cultures 28; Amsterdam & Atlanta GA: Rodopi, 1997): 53.

⌘ Material Resonance

structure of a poem. On the other, the reader makes an unspoken commitment to accept radically transformed language as Aboriginal English. This dialectic is the essential feature of the literature of linguistic intersection and its particular facility in this context is its capacity to intimate a cultural reality though the music, the 'bodily presence' of the words.

By stretching the 'Englishness' of the poem to the very limit, a limit so extensive that the poem is filled to excess with the words, rhythm, and sound of the Aboriginal language, the poet arrives at, or at least gestures towards, that zone of untranslatability that all aesthetic objects occupy. But in this case the transformation of English, the production of the poetic object, demonstrates the political accessibility of a space beyond translation, a space of Presence that exists prior even to the structures of meaning on which a translation, either inner or outer, must rely. The poem is in the form of a lullaby, as if to show that poetic language itself is a zone of pure potentiality.

The Volume of the Text

There is much more *meaning* in the poem than an interpretative gloss would encompass, and by balancing the requirements of meanability and difference the poem *insists* on presence. The 'much more' that constitutes cultural Presence is in fact beyond meaning, for it exists in the *sound*, the music, of the lines, a dimension very aptly described by Gadamer's term 'volume':

> But, can we really assume that the reading of such texts is a reading exclusively concentrated on meaning? Do we not sing these texts [*Ist es nicht ein Singen*]? Should the process in which a poem speaks only be carried by a meaning intention? Is there not, at the same time, a truth that lies in its performance [*eine Vollzugswahrheit*]? This, I think, is the task with which the poem confronts us.[19]

The 'volume' of Fogarty's poem is encompassed in the 'performance' of the sound and shape of the lines, a materiality that opens up the non-hermeneutic dimension of reading. This is not an aesthetic volume alone: it is an extension, a 'beyond' of cultural difference as well. Gumbrecht makes the point that this tension between the semantic and non-semantic dimensions of a poem reflects the distinction between 'earth' and 'world' that Heidegger makes in his essay

---

[19] Hans–Georg Gadamer, *Wahrheit und Methode: Grundzüge einer philosophischen Hermeneutik* (1960; *Gesammelte Werke* I; Tübingen: Mohr Siebeck, 2010): 36, quoted in Gumbrecht, *Production of Presence*, 66.

"The Origin of the Work of Art." "It is the component of 'earth' that enables the work of art, or the poem, to 'stand in itself'; it is 'earth' that gives the work of art existence in space."[20] We must imagine the cultural earth of the poem, then, to be that which is adumbrated by the physical texture of the lines. In the cross-cultural text, the earth is that which is approached through the world, but because the 'world' of the text is hybrid, the earth is engaged in a transcultural negotiation, a constitutive negotiation of writer and reader functions.

Knowing Time: The Dialectical Image

The second medium of transcultural Presence is one I will refer to as the dialectical image, the specific function of which is "knowing time." I take this term from Benjamin's use of it in *The Arcades Project* (*Das Passagen-Werk*), which was to be a theory of modernity, a philosophy of history, and a reflection on the meaning of consumer culture generated from a close analysis of the dilapidated shopping arcades of nineteenth-century Paris. The dialectical image is Benjamin's most radical contribution to the revision of History. The fleeting image arrests the false logic of historical development while illuminating the unresolved tensions that lie dormant within modernity. History becomes arrested in the dialectical image, such that its key moments are no longer presented in narrative succession but, rather, history becomes a frozen image at the crossroads of modernity's unresolved tensions.

There are two fundamental ways of revising history in post-colonial writing. The first is an interpolation of history in which the literary text enters, rewrites, contests, and in other ways disrupts the seamless historical narrative. This is a more demotic form of knowing time, a form Kim Scott achieves to great effect in *That Deadman Dance*. The novel is structured historically, with the "Parts" dated from 1833 onwards. The novel doesn't so much give a different account of history, although it avowedly relies on the historical record, as turn history inside out by providing a wholly different perspective on the history of white Aboriginal contact. This perspective from the Nyungar builds on "their readiness to appropriate new cultural forms – language and songs, guns and boats – as soon as they became available," says Scott, consciously

---

[20] Martin Heidegger, "Conversation on a Country Path about Thinking" ("Gelassenheit," 1959), in Heidegger, *Discourse on Thinking*, tr. John M. Anderson & E. Hans Freund (New York: Harper & Row, 1966): 66.

alluding to his own appropriation of the cultural form of the novel. "Believing themselves manifestations of a spirit of place impossible to conquer," says Scott, "they appreciated reciprocity and the nuances of cross-cultural exchange."[21] Such a creative interpolation of history has a profoundly transformative effect going far beyond the presentation of an alternative memory. The re-conception of a past in which the Aboriginal is an active participant in the 'dance' of modernity forms the basis of cultural recovery, in what Scott calls the 'literature of recovery'.

Another form of historical revision is to re-constitute or re-imagine the very idea of the imperial discourse of History, and one way this is achieved is to 'know time' through what may be called a dialectical image. In Benjamin's formulation, the dialectical image is the centre of a robust critique of history and of modernity. The reason I borrow this term is less to use Benjamin to explicate the function of the image in Aboriginal literature than to show that Benjamin's positing of a dialectical relationship between the past and the present within the image is *already* a feature of Indigenous knowledge. Aboriginal place is a way of knowing time. Certainly, while it is often accepted that this dialectical feature of the now-time in the image is a tool to be used by those marginalized and excluded by the passage of History, we encounter an even more radical sense that this dialectical image already exists in the function of Indigenous place to immobilize time.

In Aboriginal use, the dialectical image comes not from the atavistic desire to retrace the path of history – that is, it is not so much dominated by a concern with time as with an overwhelming concern with place or, more specifically, of time *as* place. The image emerges from a cultural consciousness in which time and place are conflated, an identification we can understand in the concept of the Dreaming. Stephen Muecke, for instance, remarks:

> In outback Aboriginal communities strangers arrive who ask the Aborigines, 'Why do you do as You do?' [...] the answer was, and is, 'Come back tomorrow and I'll take you to a *place* that is important to us.'[22]

In this respect, place absorbs and signifies time in the way a word embodies its referent, and the two are interchangeable in the Dreaming. This involves a continual cycling of an ancient past within the present. Time is not so much

---

[21] Kim Scott, "Appendix" to Scott, *That Deadman Dance* (Sydney: Picador, 2010): 398.
[22] Stephen Muecke, *No Road* (Fremantle WA: Fremantle Arts Centre Press, 1997): 84.

immobilized as embodied in place, and this embodiment captures the function of the dialectical image. We are well aware, I think, of the ways in which traditional painting fixes a sense of time in the spatial image such as Clifford Possum Tjapaltjarri's "Man's Love Story." But this persists in contemporary Aboriginal representations of time and place. An interesting example of this is Lin Onus' *Road to Redfern*, which demonstrates what Édouard Glissant calls a "prophetic vision of the past": "The past," he says, "to which we were subjected, which has not yet emerged as history for us, is, however, obsessively present."[23] It is the function of the dialectical image to know time in this way by situating it.

FIGURE 5. Lin Onus, *Road to Redfern* (1988; synthetic polymer paint on canvas, 60x120cm). © Lin Onus Estate, licensed by Viscopy 2013.

Road to Redfern is a dialectical image not because it immobilizes time but because it captures the unity of past and future in a mobile present. The past is

---

[23] Édouard Glissant, *Caribbean Discourse: Selected Essays*, ed., tr. & intro. J. Michael Dash (*Le discours antillais*, 1981; CARAF Books; Charlottesville: UP of Virginia, 1989): 64.

apprehended in terms of the future and vice versa. It offers an image that is both a prophetic vision of the past and a utopian assurance of the future of Aboriginal identity. The painting is crucially framed by the title: the 'road to Redfern' is the road towards a Sydney suburb that has been the centre of urban Aboriginal resistance, a modern urban sacred site. The rainbow serpent in the rear-view mirror is the sustaining metaphor for the continuation of the past in the present. The fact that the head of the serpent is a truck is a cunning metaphor for the persistence of Aboriginal identity in modernity and the importance of mobility and transformation. The image is dialectical because it resists closure.

The importance of the rainbow serpent in knowing time comes from its capacity to blur the boundary between myth and reality, past and future, tradition and modernity. Alexis Wright's use of the image in *Carpentaria* is a project of reclamation: of reclaiming the North to the Aboriginal voice, and also to an Aboriginal cosmology. Take this description in the opening pages:

> Picture the creative serpent, scoring deep into – scouring down through – the slippery underground of the mudflats, leaving in its wake the thunder of tunnels collapsing to form deep sunken valleys. The sea water following in the serpent's wake, swarming in a frenzy of tidal waves, soon changed colour from ocean blue to the yellow of mud. The water filled the swirling tracks to form the mighty bending rivers spread across the vast plains of the Gulf country.[24]

The question here is: what is the status of the voice narrating? Is it ironic? Is it simply animistic and mythological? Or is it re-narrating the nature of place in a way that situates the metaphoric and metonymic reality of the Aboriginal Dreaming in the demotic English text? Though poetic and oracular, the lines also seem to be pushing the boundaries of realism. The last sentence states: "It *is* all around in the atmosphere and is attached to the lives of the river people like skin." In that sentence, in the *Presence* of the Aboriginal reality, the boundary between reality and myth is crossed and the re-narration, re-creation, of place begins to occur.

Second, the description includes no concessions to the contemporary reader. By simply inserting the perception of place into the text, a metonymic gap is established, and the assertion of Aboriginal reality is made in the contemporary English text. The author has chosen her audience and the audience

---

[24] Alexis Wright, *Carpentaria* (Sydney: Giramondo, 2006): 1–2. Further page references are in the main text.

must enter into dialogue with the continuing reality of the Aboriginal Dreaming.

> Imagine the serpent's breathing rhythms as the tide flows inland, edging towards the spring waters nestled deeply in the gorges of an ancient limestone plateau covered with rattling grasses dried yellow from the prevailing winds. Then with the outward breath, the tide turns and the serpent flows back to its own circulating mass of shallow waters in the giant water basin in a crook of the mainland whose sides separate it from the open sea. (2)

In this long passage, the narrator addresses the reader – "picture" and "imagine" – words that belong to the ocular dimensions of the English text and to the modern reader. As with all literature, the reader 'imagines', constructs the reality of, the novel and it becomes real. Oracular though the language is, it invites the reader to enter a dialogue with difference, to *know* the other. It invites the reader to know Aboriginal time, not as fractured but as continuous, a dialectic of past and present located in place. This is something Max Otto comes to understand in Alex Miller's *Landscape of Farewell* when he sees that the country, to Dougald,

> was still the country of his Old People, as he called his ancestors, the term familiar and intimate, as if they were not remote beings whose individual features had been forgotten long ago, but were known to him, and were a people still in occupation of their lands. (233)

In his analysis of time in the African novel, Emmanuel Eze suggests that the African writer not only writes of the brokenness of African cultures but also imports a sense of broken time into the writing. Yet, when we examine the strategy of the dialectical image we see time as *layered* rather than broken. No community could more justly be said to exist in a state of 'broken' time than Aboriginal people, yet the event of Mabo revealed that the 'erased' reality of Aboriginal place could re-assert itself even within the apparently unavoidable reality of Australian modernity. Although the narrative of Aboriginal place, through the discourse of land rights, stolen generations, exile, and exclusion might appear to be one of unremitting loss and absence, the fusion of the past and the future in place is a profound realization of Ernst Bloch's notion of utopia.[25] The relationship to place through the Dreaming is a demonstration of *Vorschein* – the 'anticipatory consciousness' of *Heimat* – Bloch's term for the home that we have all sensed but have never experienced or known. While the persistent identification of the Indigenous subject with and in place appears to participate in a discourse of mourning and loss, it is, by its very determination to rehearse that identification with time, a confirmation of the utopian force of place.

In *Carpentaria*, the serpent maintains a sense of the past in the present, transforming history by a process of layering time. The unapologetic irruption of the rainbow serpent into the temporal form of the novel is an act that reconfigures the 'broken time' of colonized experience with a layering of time that counters the apparent closure of historical discourse. This is why the material resonance of the text is so important in the kind of knowledge of time we may call Presence. The dialectical nature of the image of the rainbow serpent refuses closure. It is not historical, but its temporality is fixed in the dialectical relationship with the topography of Carpentaria.

Reading for Presence

The engagement with the cross-cultural text occurs in a 'transcultural space', a contact zone in which both reader and writer functions are changed. We can see how the writer of the second-language text sets up the conditions for this engagement through a use of language that pushes the attentive reader past the demands of interpretation. This is an elaboration of the power of all literature to present the luminous effects of its materiality. But what of the reading? If texts are constitutive, how can readers approach them in a different way to engage with Presence? Like viewers at an art exhibition, readers are surrounded by a great deal of noise, both positive and negative, concerning Aboriginal creative production. Should readers be open to the beyond of meaning – ready to enjoy before understanding, to be open to the material resonance of the text before interpretation? Indeed, there is a way of being open to the text without 'representing', a way of (not)thinking that Heidegger calls *Gelassenheit*. It becomes very obvious, when we examine this concept, that Heidegger's admonition to engage in a form of meditation without willing, an attitude of

---

[25] Ernst Bloch, *The Principle of Hope*, tr. Neville Plaice, Stephen Plaice & Paul Knight, 3 vols. (*Das Prinzip Hoffnung*, 1954–59; Minneapolis: U of Minnesota P, 1995).

'being open' – what he refers to as 'releasement', and what we could also interpret as 'being composed' and simply waiting – is ideally designed to apprehend Presence in the text, to 'know' that which lies beyond meaning. "Releasement towards things" and "openness to the mystery" are two aspects of the same disposition, a disposition that allows us to inhabit the world "in a totally different way."[26] By letting go of willing, we actually give ourselves the possibility of being open to *Gelassenheit* and, in *Gelassenheit*, remain open for be-ing itself.[27] What this may mean in a practical sense is being open to Otherness in the transcultural text by being open to the materiality of its language – is to enter into a subtle ethical engagement in which true dialogue is enabled, as Bakhtin suggests, but where the reader goes further by refusing to capture that Otherness in an act of interpretation. Far from diminishing the experience, being open to the beyond of meaning, that we may apprehend *before* interpretation in the material resonance of the text, is the way in which the true wonder of Indigenous knowledge may begin to be apprehended.

WORKS CITED

Ashcroft, Bill. "Constitutive Graphonomy," *Kunapipi* 11.1 (1989): 53–78.

——. "How Books Talk," in Ashcroft, *Caliban's Voice: The Transformation of English in Post-Colonial Literatures* (London & New York: Routledge, 2008): 143–58.

——. "Transcultural Presence," *Storia della Storiografia* 55 (2009): 76–93.

Bakhtin, Mikhail. *The Dialogic Imagination: Four Essays by M.M. Bakhtin*, ed. Michael Holquist, tr. Caryl Emerson & Michael Holquist (Austin: U of Texas P, 1981).

Benjamin, Walter. *The Arcades Project*, ed. Rolf Tiedemann, tr. Howard Eiland & Kevin McLaughlin (*Das Passagen-Werk*, ed. 1982; Cambridge MA: Harvard UP/Belknap Press, 1999).

Bloch, Ernst. *The Principle of Hope*, tr. Neville Plaice, Stephen Plaice & Paul Knight, 3 vols. (*Das Prinzip Hoffnung*, 1954–59; Minneapolis: U of Minnesota P, 1995).

Eliot, T.S. *Dante* (London: Faber & Faber, 1929).

Eze, Emmanuel Chukuwudi. "Language and Time in Postcolonial Experience," *Research in African Literatures* 39.1 (Spring 2008): 24–47.

---

[26] Heidegger, "Conversation on a Country Path about Thinking" ("Gelassenheit," 1959), 56.

[27] "Conversation on a Country Path about Thinking," 61.

Fogarty, Lionel. "Joowindoo Goonduhmu," in *Aratjara: Aboriginal Culture and Literature in Australia*, ed. Dieter Riemenschneider & Geoffrey V. Davis (Cross/Cultures 28; Amsterdam & Atlanta GA: Rodopi, 1997): 53.

Glissant, Édouard. *Caribbean Discourse: Selected Essays*, ed., tr. & intro. J. Michael Dash (*Le discours antillais*, 1981; CARAF Books; Charlottesville: UP of Virginia, 1989).

Gumbrecht, Hans Ulrich. *Production of Presence: What Meaning Cannot Convey* (Stanford CA: Stanford UP, 2004).

Heidegger, Martin. "Conversation on a Country Path about Thinking" ("Gelassenheit," 1959), in Martin Heidegger, *Discourse on Thinking*, tr. John M. Anderson & E. Hans Freund (New York: Harper & Row, 1966): 58–90.

Huxley, Aldous. *Music at Night and other Essays, including Vulgarity in Literature* (London: Chatto & Windus, 1949).

Malouf, David. *Remembering Babylon* (1993; London: Vintage, 1994).

Miller, Alex. *Landscape of Farewell* (Sydney: Allen & Unwin, 2007).

Moreton–Robinson, Aileen. *Whitening Race: Essays in Social and Cultural Criticism* (Canberra: Aboriginal Studies Press, 2004).

Muecke, Stephen. *No Road* (Fremantle, WA: Fremantle Arts Centre Press, 1997).

Murray, Les. "The Meaning of Existence," in Murray, *Poems the Size of Photographs* (Sydney: Duffy & Snellgrove & Manchester: Carcanet, 2002): 104, http://www.lesmurray.org/pm_tme.htm (accessed 22 January 2012).

Ortiz, Fernando. *Cuban Counterpoint: Tobacco and Sugar*, tr. Harriet de Onís, intro. Bronisław Malinowski, prologue by Herminio Portell Vilá, new intro. Fernando Coronil (*Contrapunto cubano del tabaco y el azúcar*, 1940; tr. 1947; Durham NC: Duke UP, 1995).

Pratt, Mary Louise. *Imperial Eyes: Travel Writing and Transculturation* (London & New York: Routledge, 1992).

Scott, Kim. *That Deadman Dance* (Sydney: Picador, 2010).

Wittgenstein, Ludwig. *Tractatus Logico Philosophicus* (London: Routledge & Kegan Paul, 1922).

Wright, Alexis. *Carpentaria* (Sydney: Giramondo, 2006).

Waiting at the Border
White Filmmaking on the Ground of Aboriginal Sovereignty

LISA SLATER

Introduction

T HERE IS A PHOTO OF TRUGANINI, the so-called 'last Tasmanian Aborigine', with cropped hair and wearing a shell necklace, her intense gaze meeting the viewer's eyes, defying the colonial fantasy of her own or her people's passing. Her gaze demands a response.[1] Jeni Thornley's poetic filmic essay, *Island Home Country* (2008), could be thought of as one such, albeit belated, response. Thornley is driven by the question of how she can connect the war against Aboriginal people with her peaceful family memories of growing up in Tasmania, Australia. As a documentary maker, she undertakes a filmic journey to learn about what she seemingly didn't know: the disturbing history of colonial Tasmania, erased during her own 1950s childhood. Thornley is confounded by how to negotiate ethically and affectively all that she has come to learn about her childhood home and Aboriginal protocols. Nearing the end of the film, the Palawa elder[2] Jim Everett asks and answers, "Well, how do you become responsible?":

> Well it's simple. It's like the old traditions where one Aboriginal group visited another, they waited at the borderline, the boundary of that cultural country, until they were invited in.[3]

---

[1] See Andrys Onsman, "Truganini's Funeral," *Island* 96 (2004): 10.

[2] Palawa are the Aboriginal people of the island state of Tasmania, Australia.

[3] Jeni Thornley, "'Island Home Country': working with Aboriginal protocols in a documentary film about colonisation and growing up white in Tasmania," in *Passionate Histories,* ed. Frances Peters–Little, Anne Curthoys & John Docker (Canberra:

I want to begin at the end: with waiting as a practice of responsibility and ethics. Waiting at *the* border is dependent upon some form of recognition of another country and sovereignty. The moment of 'impossibility' of recognizing the sovereignty of Aboriginal laws, Irene Watson writes, provides Australians with an opportunity to take responsibility and create an opening to a future that has not existed before.[4] What clues might Thornley's stepping onto the ground of impossibility offer up for settlers' *becoming* responsible? Engaging with the 'impossibility' of Indigenous sovereignty, Thornley says, "I lose my thread, the film is dissolving."[5] Is dissolving different from, and more ethically productive than, white worrying and anxiety? I want to examine whether "dissolving' might be a way to unlearn and re-invent new models for knowing 'our' place, and in so doing forging anti-colonial modes of coexistence.

After Truganini, there were no Tasmanian Aboriginal people. Or so Australians were taught at school. (A strange acknowledgement of mainland Aboriginal people.) Tasmania was to bear the horror of colonialism for the rest of the country. Truganini, of the Nuenone people, died in 1876 in Hobart, and she was heralded as the last Tasmanian Aboriginal. Her passing ushered in the myth of the imminent extinction of all Aboriginal people. But, as Andrys Onsman writes, "her death began long before her final breath."[6] The Black War (c.1828–32), was a time of mass killings by the colonists, and came close to annihilating the Tasmanian Aboriginal people.[7] The Black Line, Lieutenant-Governor George Arthur's initiative of forming a human chain of able-bodied male colonists to herd Aboriginal people onto the Tasman Peninsula, might have failed, but it succeeded in galvanizing the settlers and sending a message to the Aboriginal people that the colonial force was intent on dispossession and destruction. Except for a few, the Black War is undisputed

---

Australian National University E-Press, 2010): 247. Further page references are in the main text.

[4] See Irene Watson, "Aboriginal Sovereignties: Past, Present and Future (Im)Possibilities," in *Our Patch: Enacting Australian Sovereignty Post-2001*, ed. Suvendrini Perera (Network Books Symposia Series; Perth, WA: Australia Research Unit, Curtin University of Technology, 2007): 26.

[5] Jeni Thornley, dir. *Island Home Country* (Anandi Films, Australia, 2009; 52 min.).

[6] Onsman, "Truganini's Funeral," 2.

[7] See Onsman, "Truganini's Funeral," and Lyndall Ryan, *The Aboriginal Tasmanians* (St Leonards, NSW: Allen & Unwin, 1996).

by scholars, but the nineteenth-century scientific conviction that Tasmanian Aboriginals were a doomed race persists. As Greg Lehman writes,

> For Aborigines in Tasmania, the period [over the last two centuries] has been about defending a place called home, and then, following profound displacement, reclaiming that place.[8]

Early in Thornley's film *Island Home Country*, the Palawa elder Jim Everett recalls:

> We always knew we were blackfellas because we were treated like blackfellas at school and in public & stuff. But we didn't know what kind because my parents and grandparents wouldn't talk about where our roots as black people come from. And I always suspected, although we're at school, we're being taught there are no Tasmanian Aboriginals. So what the devil are we. When I got back here and met our mob on Flinders Island, I knew straight away. It was like a lightning strike. I knew we were Tasmania Aboriginal although they say we're not.

Despite Aboriginal peoples' self-identity, there is still little recognition by settlers of Palawa sovereignty and cultural heritage, and Palawa voices get lost in the din of an old persistent myth and resentments and fear. Thornley's impulse to take responsibility is shared by many. Yet how do settlers practise, or make, ethical engagement?

For Everett, taking responsibility should be a simple matter. Respectfully, it is not simple for non-Indigenous Australians. Settlers need to conceive of the possibility of shared sovereignty.

> In the struggle for Aboriginal sovereignty the prevailing 'reality' is that the sovereignty of Aboriginal laws is an impossibility [...]. Yet for many Aboriginal people, Aboriginal laws, or sovereignty, simply exist [...] Aboriginal laws live.[9]

For most non-Indigenous Australians, Aboriginal law and sovereignty are no longer relevant to a modern nation. Indeed, they can barely be imagined. Many advocate for social justice, equality, and recognition of cultural difference and heritage: including a share of the country's wealth of resources. But for most Australians the existence of multiple sovereignties proves to be unthinkable. I would suggest that it is not always because the notion is outwardly rejected

---

[8] Greg Lehman, "Editorial," *Island* 96 (2004): 1.
[9] Watson, "Aboriginal Sovereignties," 24.

but, rather, because it is something that cannot be thought: the thinking is impossible.[10] Western ontology grasps Indigenous sovereignty through appropriation – generalizing it as the same or similar – or dismissing it as non-sensible or not modern. It is outside of how I make sense of the world. I do not have the capacity, or what I need, to comprehend the reality of Indigenous sovereignty. Following Derrida, Watson urges that our thinking begin on the ground of impossibility. Settler Australians need to test the (im)possibility of recognizing Aboriginal sovereignty and law in order to take responsibility for creating an anti-colonial future. As Watson asks, "what makes the sovereignty of Aboriginal law impossible?"[11]

Island Home

"I am white, born on a stolen island. This is a story of my journey." So begins Thornley's film *Island Home Country*. Throughout the making of the film, she wrestled with how to name herself, and arrived at what became the film's opening. Her voice is haunting, a little ethereal, brimming with earnest responsibility, and it sets the tone: it is a serious pursuit to uncover silence, which causes her anguish and deep questioning of her family history. The two central elders, Jim Everett and Aunty Phyliss Pitchford, then individually address the camera. Both speak with gentle determination. Everett emphasizes what he believes is the most important principle of being Aboriginal: "The country is us, as much as we are it." If this is lost, he laments, the colonial construct will take an even greater hold. Pitchford recites her poem of loss, "Sad Memories." Their concerns and passions order and determine the film's themes: Indigenous sovereignty and ethical living in and on country and the pain of colonial violence and continued non-recognition.

"Growing up here, I knew nothing about colonization," Thornley tells her viewers. She wonders if making a film will allow her to reckon with colonial amnesia. In an attempt to un-forget and "shed her colonial skin," she returns to Tasmania to film with her family – sister, aunt, and cousin – who reflect upon their memories, silences, and (lack of) understanding of Aboriginal Tasmania. She says, "white Australian history haunted me,' which she represents

---

[10] See Jacques Derrida, "Time and Memory, Messianicity, the Name of God," in Derrida, *Deconstruction Engaged: The Sydney Seminars*, ed. Paul Patton & Terry Smith (Sydney: Power, 2001): 57–69.

[11] Watson, "Aboriginal Sovereignties," 26.

with a ghostly figure of a girl running through the bush. Taking up the Murri poet Sam Watson's counsel to "use Aboriginal sources as primary sources,"[12] the film pursues, and becomes deeply informed by, the creative work, voices, and questioning of Palawa writers and artists: Everett, Aunty Phyliss Pitchford, Julie Gough, and PennyX Saxon. She writes:

> Alongside this creative force, were works of cultural recovery and continuity, [...] which expressed the resilience of the Tasmanian Aboriginal community culturally and their fundamental relationship to country.[13]

Sovereign Palawa confront the filmmaker with her own "possessive whiteness," her blindness and complicity in neo-colonialism. Near the close of the film, Jim Everett and Aunty Phyliss Pitchford remind Thornley that the film was to be about her, not them. The turning of the gaze upon herself and negotiating Aboriginal protocols is deeply unsettling – causing her to "experience *un-possession*."[14] She is no longer able to hold the film in her mind. The film's dissolving is represented stylistically as montage – juxtaposition of images, where multiple voices, interruptions, and reflections, and past and present, coexist. Her idea of home, history, and self is ruptured.

The impetus for the film was the work of Tasmanian historians, such as Cassandra Pybus and Lyndall Ryan. It is from their work that she initially learned of the attempted genocide of the Palawa – the removal of Aboriginal people to make way for the "peaceful pastoral idyll" of her childhood. Pybus's call for settlers to "do a reckoning" – to learn of and take responsibility for colonial violence – led Thornley to undertake her own reckoning. She writes:

> I wanted to penetrate the 'silence' around my childhood imaginary of this island, and then connect it, somehow, to the reality of colonization – the attempted genocide of the Tasmanian Aboriginal people – and the community's resilient and dynamic struggle to re-establish sovereignty of their country.[15]

Although, early in the film, she says "growing up here I knew nothing of colonization," her central concern is not 'not knowing' but amnesia: forget-

---

[12] Sam Watson, quoted in Thornley, "'Island Home Country'," 259.
[13] Thornley, "'Island Home Country'," 259.
[14] "'Island Home Country'," 258.
[15] "'Island Home Country'," 248.

fulness. To reckon with settler amnesia, she returns to Tasmania, to question her "*idea* of a peaceful island."[16]

The making of the film was framed by the 'history wars' – does Australia have a blood-stained past or a slightly blemished but largely noble history? – and then by Prime Minister Kevin Rudd's national apology to Indigenous people, on 13 February 2008. This period – of approximately a decade – proved to be a rich time for settler Australians to remember colonial violence and to seek forms of reconciliation and redemption. However, settler remembering is routinely interrupted by a habit of forgetting Indigenous presence and colonial violence. The habit persistently troubles Australian scholars, cultural producers and public alike. The renowned historian Henry Reynolds famously named his memoir of growing up in 'peaceful' Tasmania, *Why Weren't We Told* (2000). Despite all the evidence to the contrary, most especially Aboriginal people's protests and proclamations against injustice, be it in song, story, or politics, settler Australia continues to claim ignorance about the extent and impact of colonial violence.

Remembering the white body

Why and how do settler Australians remember and forget? A central concern of Chris Healy's book *Forgetting Aborigines* (2008) is the cycle of forgetting and remembering of 'Aborigines' in Australian public culture. Taking his cue from Marcia Langton, he argues that mainstream perceptions of 'Aborigines' and Aboriginality have little or nothing to do with experiences of historical or contemporary Indigenous peoples; rather, he is referring to a particular cultural assemblage and intercultural space that is the product of stories inherited from colonists and colonialism.[17] The dominance of the assemblage 'Aborigine' enables the forgetting of contemporary Indigenous people: everyday encounters, with people or self-representations, and Australia's troubling history. He explores the paradox of remembering and forgetting 'Aborigines':

> Non-indigenous Australians imagine again and again that they have only just learned about indigenous disadvantage – mortality rates, poverty, poor health, housing and educational opportunities, high imprisonment rates, substance abuse or sexual assault, take your pick – as

---

[16] Thornley, "'Island Home Country'," 259. (My emphasis.)

[17] Chris Healy, *Forgetting Aborigines* (Sydney: U of New South Wales P, 2008): 4–5.

if for the first time. These endless (re)discoveries of, and about, Aborigines are only possible because non-indigenous Australians forget their own forgetting.[18]

What we experience in Australia is periodic "dramatic remembering." Healy is not arguing that there is a need to replace forgetting with remembering or more knowledge about Aboriginal people, history, and culture but, rather, that we need to remember our own forgetting. Non-Indigenous Australians habitually forget contemporary Indigenous poverty and social distress, and indeed their flourishing life, shared present, and sovereignty, because the cultural memory of primitivism, extinction, and strangers in modernity is so prevalent.

Like Healy, my concern is not individual memories, but remembering as a shared cultural process or performance.[19] When non-Indigenous people, like those in Thornley's film, say that, in their growing-up, they did not learn about colonial history and the violent removal of Palawa, or don't have knowledge of assimilation policies and practices or little awareness of ongoing Aboriginal presence, they aren't necessarily lying or being absent-minded. It is much more a telling of a shared culture: inheritances that produce social rules, practices, and boundaries. As Roslyn Diprose argues,

> Under the guidance of law and its regulatory moral and disciplinary mechanisms, bodies are trained to repeat what are considered good acts and to discard the undesirable.[20]

The repetition of acts forms habits. The self does not have an identity except through habitual action, which Diprose refers to as body-identity: "the deed, act or performance is the self actualized."[21] Styles of interactions with people, places, and things define one socio-culturally and cultivate subjectivity. We know who we are and where we belong through consistent and like-minded (bodied) performances. As Healy posits, memory is not an individual invention but a collective enterprise: to belong to a particular culture, I am beholden to certain styles, habits, of remembering and forgetting. It holds me in place, *makes* me at home, and constructs my subjectivity. I am arguing that there is a particular colonial body-identity that *has* the settler body and produces a parti-

---

[18] Healy, *Forgetting Aborigines*, 204.

[19] *Forgetting Aborigines*, 9.

[20] Roslyn Diprose, *Corporeal Generosity: On Giving with Nietzsche, Merleau–Ponty, and Levinas* (Albany: State U of New York P, 2002): 63.

[21] Diprose, *Corporeal Generosity*, 61.

cular memory-making culture. Healy advises that we learn to forget the race-thinking of the term 'Aborigine', and instead remember our entangled histories.[22] I agree, but I want to suggest that settler Australians cannot remember their entangled histories, because boundaries and uniformity are essential to the consistency and integrity of settler body-identity, which in turn produces a habit of forgetting, or a careless body.

We need to remember the cultivation of the white body. In the age of Imperialism and prior to the acceptance of Darwinism, one dominant race theory was based on the notion that racial groups were distinct, and that they evolved from their environment – that the environment determined racial characteristics. Race as a discursive construction was used to denote discrete biological types that determined the various capacities for civilization. Warwick Anderson suggests: "Each colour decreed a way of life and a capacity for civilisation, with whites at the top and African blacks at the bottom of the hierarchy."[23] There were various hierarchies, including some that placed Australian Aboriginal people at the very bottom. The marker of territorial possession was bodily harmony with the environment. The marker of European civilization, and therefore racial superiority, was the ability to thrive and prosper in the 'new world' – to inhabit a place with propriety.[24] European bodies, the repositories of civilization, which were understood to have, over centuries, evolved from and acclimatized to a particular environment, were displaced into foreign territories. It could be argued that the very act of acclimatization to a foreign environment potentially dispossesses the colonizers of the shared characteristics integral to Europe's constitution of humanity and racial superiority. The Imperial era's discursive construction of race as distinct and evolving from a particular environment was, therefore, not consistent with colonial expansion; in the "struggle for material possession [the colonizers] could be dispossessed."[25]

The Australian continent was being brought into modernity and it was expected that, with changes to the land, Indigenous people would die out. According to race theories reconfigured under colonialism, the distinct Indigenous racial groups could not survive outside of their pristine, original environ-

---

[22] Healy, *Forgetting Aborigines*, 215.

[23] Warwick Anderson, *The Cultivation of Whiteness* (Melbourne: Melbourne UP, 2002): 171.

[24] Anderson, *The Cultivation of Whiteness*, 5.

[25] *The Cultivation of Whiteness*, 40.

ment, or in contact with 'superior' races and cultures. The settlers (the 'civilized' white subjects), in an attempt to separate their selves from, and limit the effects of, what was understood to be the chaos of nature, cultivated the land and built settlements. In the colonial imaginary, Australia was a vast, unsettled land, and the boundary between cultivation and 'savage' nature was very thin. The frontiers, which arguably made up much, if not all, of Australia, exposed the vulnerability of the European body in this foreign environment, hence the vulnerability of its 'natural' sovereignty. What the colonizers were recognizing, even in their fear and prejudice, was that the land is a site which shapes bodies and perceptions, shapes knowledge, and informs a sense of the aesthetic.[26] The frontier was a problematic environment, as it was a site in which the British might be dispossessed of their 'civility'; the body politic would become reconfigured.

Australia was made white, and, with it, the white body was made sovereign. Thornley, in *Island Home Country*, recalls her family's attachment to England: her grandmother's tears at the death of Queen Victoria and a home movie of her first visit to England in 2008. "The signs of the British colony are everywhere," she says – place-names, monuments to Captain Cook and the monarchy, cobbled streets and colonial sandstone buildings. Racial logic connected Australia to the 'mother country', and separated us from our near northern neighbours: we were not a part of Asia, despite the geographical closeness and hundreds of years of networks and flows between the peoples of these diverse islands. One thinks of the Macassans, trepangers from Sulawesi, who for hundreds of years traded with Indigenous peoples from across northern Australia, until, in the late-nineteenth and early-twentieth century, the imposition of customs duties and policies to protect Australia's 'territorial integrity' brought an end to the regional exchange.[27] Racial boundaries marked and demarcated territorial boundaries, severed regional connections, and affirmed the white diaspora as British. Suvendrini Perera writes:

> The island will operate as a 'plot' that organizes bodies and histories within its boundaries into a narrative that serves the ends of nations. The plotting of Australia as an insular formation both expels the 'foreign' bodies around its edges and encloses Indigenous peoples

---

[26] See Radhika Mohanram, *Black Body: Women, Colonialism and Space* (St Leonards, NSW: Allen & Unwin, 1999).

[27] See Peta Stephenson, *The Outsiders Within: Telling Australia's Indigenous-Asian Story* (Sydney: U of New South Wales P, 2007).

> more closely within clearly demarcated national borders. [...] transborder and cross-regional relations are abruptly terminated and Indigenous bodies secured within the new national unit in ways that increase their subjection to it and suppress their links to other places. The inauguration of this new geography confers a new territorial as well as racial corporeality on the geo-body of the island-continent.[28]

Racial corporeality of the insular island is never more apparent than in what was known as the White Australia policy: the founding statutes that restricted non-white immigration to Australia and the removal of 'prohibited' immigrants, which led to, in particular, Pacific Islander, Chinese, and Japanese workers being deported. Colonial racial logic categorized and condemned Indigenous people as savage, a mind-set enforced through frontier violence and policies, from elimination and segregation to assimilation. The nation was imagined as being *for* one white people, and excluded "bodies that compromised the project of the white island."[29] The marker of territorial possession is bodily integrity with one's environment. Racialized bodies threaten territorial possession, thus they are a threat to self-possession, which in turn shapes what might be called a social geography. The geo-body of the insular island continent is a plot that organizes social bodies and cultural memory. To be a good white Australian, one cannot associate with non-white bodies on equal terms or as fellow citizens. The country is not shared, and national memory is the providence of white bodies. Exclusion and forgetting become second nature.

The body is a site of chaos for colonizing Europe, as it is resistant to colonialism's desire to manage and order. This resistance was politically threatening because Europe's insistence on its ability to manage and order the world was the basis of its claimed right to expansion. As Zygmunt Bauman argues,

> Agencies are sovereign in as far as they claim and successfully defend the right to manage and administer existence: the right to define order and, by implication, lay aside chaos, as the left-over that escapes definition.[30]

The body, particularly the black body, became (and continues to be) burdened as a site upon which the colonizers, determined to maintain sovereignty,

---

[28] Suvendrini Perera, *Australia and the Insular Imagination* (New York: Palgrave Macmillan, 2009): 27.

[29] Perera, *Australia and the Insular Imagination*, 29.

[30] Zygmunt Bauman, *Modernity and Ambivalence* (Cambridge: Polity, 1991): 286–87.

played out their desire to define order. Eugenics and the subsequent practices of child removal were but two interlinked historical manifestations of the management of existence. So is the frontier violence of the Black Line, and the dispossession and removal of Palawa people to Flinders Island. The colonizers focused their fears and anxieties on the black body, which bore the burden of the colonizers' fears of being engulfed by the strangeness that Imperial conquest engenders.[31] Indigenous people, and the strangeness of the country, posed a direct threat to the colonizer's self-recognition as the rightful heirs of modernity and civilization. Coming too close to strangers, being pulled into the body of *other* lives, one can too easily trip into a liminal space, where, as Paul Carter writes, the "property of selfhood falls into doubt."[32] Arguably, written into the settler body-identity is the colonial fear of being engulfed by strangeness and enmeshed in the body of other lives. One response to this is to institute order, boundaries, by clearing places of interference and difference: to live, as Thornley says in *Island Home Country*, as if behind a hedge, keeping history and ambiguity out.

Encounters

Thornley set out to undertake her own reckoning: to penetrate the silence around her own childhood memories and understand the reality of historical and contemporary Aboriginal Tasmania. But she could not do so on her own. It required filming with her family and the Tasmanian Aboriginal community, which involved negotiating ethics and protocols – the "ethical encounter," she writes, with Aboriginal protocols deeply affecting the filmmaking process and the film itself.[33] Following European filmmakers who examined Nazism, as well as the Australian scholars Ross Gibson and Bain Attwood, Thornley considered the potential of her film to be a "work of mourning."[34] Here might lie the means to explore settler Australia's amnesia around colonial violence and how it informs national identity, imaginaries, and the public culture of remembering and forgetting. This was just the beginning of the project, and what the film was doing and why were radically re-thought through the pro-

---

[31] Anne McClintock, *Imperial Leather: Race, Gender and Sexuality in the Colonial Context* (New York & London: Routledge, 1995): 24.

[32] Paul Carter, *Living in a New Country* (London: Faber & Faber, 1992): 3.

[33] Thornley, "'Island Home Country'," 249.

[34] "'Island Home Country'," 249–50.

cess of negotiating Aboriginal protocols, which involve developing relationships, trust, a dialogic and self-reflexive relationship, and a valuing of the agency of Aboriginal participants and their ownership of cultural heritage. Thornley's notion that her film could be a work of mourning received short shrift. Presenting her ideas at a Hobart-based conference, she was confronted with: "What makes you think you're welcome at our mourning sites?"[35] Throughout the filmmaking process, she was repeatedly challenged, which led her to examine her own assumptions and her "possessive whiteness": settler Australians' ownership of the country and its stories, and 'our' innate understanding of what is good for the nation and its people.[36]

Thornley wants to shed her colonial skin – through learning about colonial history and connecting with Palawa people, she wants to see with different eyes. This is a very familiar pursuit of good white Australians, and often produces a strange mix of anxiety and not a small amount of self-righteousness. Working with Aboriginal protocols required her to "let go of control of the project into a process of negotiation and dialogue"; the "protocols [...] really pushed me to question my motives, further de-centering my control. I had to learn to wait for negotiations to unfold in their own time."[37] She questioned whether the film would get made. When Julie Gough was undertaking a critique of the film's first edit, a breakthrough came: Gough suggested that Thornley return to Tasmania to work more closely with the Aboriginal community. In the following year, when watching revised edits, Jim Everett said: "I think the storyline should be more yours – looks too much like our story." She writes that his observation triggered her telling a story of white unsettlement. She turns the gaze back on herself: "onto the interior space of my own colonized–colonising mind."[38] Who is she when she isn't in control of the narrative? She writes:

> In this contested site, as if in the midst of the 'politics of sovereignty', I was no longer able to hold the film in my mind. It was slipping away into quicksand. It was not that it was becoming an Aboriginal film; it

---

[35] Thornley, "'Island Home Country'," 258.

[36] See Aileen Moreton–Robinson, "Towards a New Reserarch Agenda? Foucault, Whiteness and Indigenous Sovereignty," *Journal of Sociology* 42 (2006): 383–95.

[37] Thornley, "'Island Home Country'," 253.

[38] "'Island Home Country'," 255.

was the challenge of *whose story is being told here, and who is the storyteller?*[39]

Initially, she takes shelter in the well-rehearsed white-settler subject-position of hardship and suffering.[40] Her story is that of the anxious white filmmaker made to suffer while undertaking the good deeds of civilizing and cultivating Australia's bad history and race relations. But this is an evasion and resistance to an ethical encounter, and allows a return to a protective subject-position that assures the ego of one's own goodness and selflessness. It blocks being put into question and, as Diprose argues, "being-in-question amounts to responsibility for the other." In Diprose's terms, benevolence and pity for the other's suffering (and self-pity) are not practices of responsibility; rather, "one's truth must be contested and one's affirmation of ourselves and our confidence in our culture must be questioned."[41] The more she engages with Aboriginal protocols, the more her "Tasmanian idyll is breaking down."[42] The film dissolves and, arguably, the filmmaker with it. However, Thornley's becoming responsible begins with dissolving; but dissolution is not enough.

Irene Watson proposes that what is needed is for settlers to be in a place that enables uncomfortable conversations but questions whether this is even possible. I would suggest that there is a need to stay with the bad feelings, rather than to take refuge in anxiety. To do so, Watson asks,

> [can] we move from places where whitefellas feel truly uncomfortable into what I call 'a meditation on discomfort' – to places there the settler society is made to answer these questions: what brings them to a place of lawfulness?[43]

What might allow settlers to stay in places of discomfort and still be responsive and answerable? As the filmmaking progresses, Thornley experiences "race relations *within my own skin*"[44] Neo-colonialism is not out there, upheld and exercised by those bad white Australians, nor something that can, with the right intentions, be easily shed: it is embodied. One's response to another,

---

[39] Thornley, "'Island Home Country'," 254.

[40] "'Island Home Country'," 268.

[41] Diprose, *Corporeal Generosity*, 164.

[42] Thornley, "'Island Home Country'," 259.

[43] Irene Watson, "Settled and Unsettled Spaces: Are we free to roam?," in *Sovereign Subjects: Indigenous Sovereignty Matters*, ed. Aileen Moreton–Robinson (Crows Nest, NSW: Allen & Unwin, 2007): 30.

[44] Fiona Nicoll, quoted in Thornley, "'Island Home Country'," 260.

Diprose writes, is saturated with the cultural-historical: it has our bodies and directs my response, is written into my body and makes me consistent.[45] One such response is to live with a body that cares for some but not others – that literally cannot feel some bodies.

In the film, there is a particularly compelling scene in which Thornley's sister, Jan, puzzles over her inability to feel the reality of the death, destruction, and continuance of Aboriginal sovereignty. Grappling for the right words, she says:

> I can hardly, it is like it was a dream, even reading in the books. I haven't been to those places where I can feel it is actually real. Seeing Truganini's memorial up there on the hill, it didn't seem real. It is hard to imagine. There are sights, we are on Aboriginal land.

It is unusual to witness such honesty about an inability to empathize: to feel. But it is an important scene for thinking through Diprose's idea that the cultural-historical *has our body*. I would argue that feeling race relations in and on one's own skin commonly produces anxiety and confusion, and there is a refusal to stay with this discomfort, as Jan does. Remembering colonial violence questions my cultural inheritance, making my people strange to me, and empathy draws me into the life of another. Both threaten my body-identity. The cultural-historical artifact that is my body directs my response. To maintain my settler body-identity, I *cannot* remember and I *cannot* become enmeshed in another body. I can stand in the place of violence, and am numb: memories that offer me consistency have my body.

I set out a rather gloomy predicament: how is decolonization to occur if settler Australians are bound to colonial modes of encounter? How can different possibilities for existence be opened?[46] Again, the scene with Thornley's sister is instructive. When Jan revisits Truganini's memorial, she weeps, is *touched*: her body shifts and opens to the sentient landscape. Thornley says, "she cries my sister," and suggests it is not out of guilt but sadness. What allows this opening? Her idea of peaceful Tasmania is ruptured. Might it be that Jan's troubling over her inability to feel for Truganini's life and death, and the devastation that the memorial bears witness to, opens her to her own contradiction and ambiguity? She is not lost in anxiety and worrying about her own lack of 'goodness' (moral worth), nor does she repress these 'bad feelings' but is gently disordered by feeling her own carelessness. The imaginary *has*

---

[45] Diprose, *Corporeal Generosity*, 192.
[46] *Corporeal Generosity*, 23.

the body, Diprose writes, but my body is not finished and is thus open to others.[47] Jan is disturbed, touched, and animated by other bodies – human and non-human – sentient landscape, Truganini, and bodies of history. She gives of herself, or is given, and in this ambiguous space of inter-corporeality is affected and affects.

Jan's response holds the possibility of a new relation with 'home', and I would contend that it is suggestive of Diprose's notion of corporeal generosity. Generosity, Diprose argues, is essential for social justice, and, I would, add for anti-colonial or decolonializing modes of sociality. But her generosity is not based on an economy of exchange, social contract, or duty between sovereign individuals. It does not enhance one's virtue or make one a more magnanimous or morally worthy person: such claims undermine generosity, by serving self-interest. Corporeal generosity, Diprose writes,

> is an openness to others that not only precedes and establishes communal relations but constitutes the self as open to otherness. Primordially, generosity is not the expenditure of one's possessions but the dispossession of oneself, the being-given to others that undercuts self-possession. Moreover, generosity, so understood, happens at a prereflective level, at the level of corporeality and sensibility, and so eschews the calculation characteristic of an economy of exchange. Generosity is being given to others without deliberation in a field of inter-corporeality, a being given that constitutes the self as affective and being affected, that constitutes social relations and that which is given in relation.[48]

Generosity is a disposition of the self. But Diprose's analysis troubles the position of the 'good white woman' who enjoys a greater sense of her own progressiveness and virtue by practising benevolence or kindness or dutifully following the perceived moral necessity in an era of reconciliation.[49] In the uneven exchange of charity, the white body is recognized and valued as the source of goodness. Obligation or magnanimity forgets the 'gifts' of Aboriginal people, such as their dispossession from their sovereign lands and ongoing social injustice. Rather, Diprose conceptualizes generosity as a dispossession of the self: being given to "intercorporeal relations that are open to difference,

---

[47] Diprose, *Corporeal Generosity*, 193.

[48] *Corporeal Generosity*, 4–5.

[49] See also Gay Hawkins, *The Ethics of Waste: How We Relate to Rubbish* (Sydney: U of New South Wales P, 2006): 113–15.

that are affective, and that overcome self-sovereignty and the egotism that underpins it."[50] Other bodies disturb and disrupt – get under one's skin – and direct one to perform the self differently.

What most disturbs and disrupts Thornley, I would argue, is not just the learning about colonial violence – 'the remembering' that reveals the lie of the idea of the peaceful island home; rather, what is eroded in ethical intercultural engagements is her body-identity. What does it make of her? If, as I suggest, the settler body-identity is given to a habit of securing an identity, an image, as the rightful heir of modernity and civilization, and to do so one practises careless and forgetting, then her entanglement in the lives of others creates new relations and bodily practices. Waiting at the border, she is exposed: "learning to listen, stay open and *pass through* 'anxious whiteness'."[51] Here might lurk a model for anti-colonial sociality: the emergence of caring bodies.

Waiting

At the close of the film, Thornley heeds Jim's advice: "For now I am waiting at the border." She is learning how to enter Aboriginal country and she will wait to be invited in. But how does she wait? What orientation does she bring to her waiting?[52] I can only guess at an answer (the film ends here), and say that her willingness to wait demonstrates that she understands herself as answerable to Palawa people and country. It is a mode, or orientation, of responsibility and negotiation, hence relationality. She must not only remember Aboriginal sovereignty but also observe it. But if Aboriginal sovereignty is an impossibility – settler Australia cannot recognize it on its own terms – then she needs to wait for it to be revealed to her: to turn her attention to signs she cannot yet see. Crucially, waiting on others, Monica Minnegal writes,

> confers on them agency and subjectivity equivalent to one's own, recognizing the need to wait for them to reveal themselves rather than presuming to know what they are.[53]

---

[50] Hawkins, *The Ethics of Waste*, 114.

[51] Thornley, "'Island Home Country'," 270.

[52] See Christopher Cordner, "Waiting, Patience and Love," in *Waiting*, ed. Ghassan Hage (Melbourne: Melbourne UP, 2009): 176.

[53] Monica Minnegal, "The Time is Right: Waiting, Reciprocity and Sociality," in *Waiting*, ed. Ghassan Hage (Melbourne: Melbourne UP, 2009): 92.

She must forget what she thinks she knows and must engage intensely with the present: be responsive to the human and non-human world whose announcement of presence she awaits.

One never waits alone: it is always already a co-performance. (Waiting for the bus requires a bus, driver, roads, infrastructure, other commuters etc.) Initially, it is the writing of settler historians that leads her to *want* a reckoning with colonial history: to respond to colonial violence, Aboriginal sovereignty, and settler amnesia. Then, as mentioned, she responds to Sam Watson's call for Aboriginal sources to be one's primary sources. The work of Tasmanian Aboriginal writers, poets, and artists 'rushes in' and affects her, and she puts aside settler academic research.[54] Palawa experiences expose her to the pain of racist policies and practices, and to importantly ongoing Indigenous sovereignty and its attendant responsibilities. She is moved by their work, and her way of seeing the country shifts. The force of these works animates and disturbs her, prising open a space for her to begin to connect with Jim Everett's appeal to move "beyond the colonial construct."[55] Importantly, working with Palawa people and cultural material, she encounters Aboriginal sovereignty and protocols, and has to wait for things to unfold in their own time. Waiting re-orientates Thornley: she ceases to want a reckoning with or to learn about colonial history. The film is no longer an individual creative endeavour to fulfil her moral obligation or release her from colonial complicity. She is not made a better person through the process but, rather, is left waiting, wondering and deeply uncomfortable.

What is Thornley's story? She identifies herself as "white, born on a stolen island."[56] She is put into question, and puts herself under question. Palawa elders and artists respond to Thornley's desire for a reckoning by claiming and forging a creative space for dialogue and experimentation. The anxious white filmmaker takes a back seat to negotiating Aboriginal sovereignty, and she (and her peaceful island home) is made strange. Aboriginal protocols involve "communication, negotiation and relatedness."[57] For all the difficulty (if not impossibility) of the process, protocols bring her into an anti-colonial intercultural encounter. I am not suggesting that protocols ensure success; rather, what they demand is the very things that colonialism refuses, most

---

[54] Thornley, "'Island Home Country'," 259.
[55] "'Island Home Country'," 259.
[56] "'Island Home Country'," 255.
[57] "'Island Home Country'," 253.

especially relatedness. Palawa are not 'native informants' but have agency and equivalence to her. Taking Aboriginal protocols seriously compels a new bodily disposition and performance: she is open to Palawa history, law, and sovereignty, and is touched, moved, and enmeshed in the body of other lives. Those who have been excluded – even more: their very existence denied – become central to her documentary. Palawa history, knowledge, and law shift from non-recognition – forgetfulness – to fundamental determinants of her understanding of Tasmania – her childhood home, hence herself. She is indebted to Aboriginal sovereignty. Even if, as a settler Australian, she cannot know Indigenous sovereignty, she registers the trace of it in herself.[58] I would argue that registering the affective force of encountering Indigenous sovereignty and the pain of colonial violence is the beginning of responsibility and generosity. It is not responsibility in and of itself but inhabiting that space and exposing oneself to questioning without taking shelter in sympathy, anxiety or resentment that constitutes, in the words of Irene Watson, a "meditation on discomfort." Thornley is in a place neither of white comfort nor of guilt but, rather, in a space of upheaval and reflection where one might begin to have conversations about the lawfulness of settler sovereignty.[59] She waits on the ground of impossibility.

WORKS CITED

Anderson, Warwick. *The Cultivation of Whiteness: Science, Health, and Racial Destiny in Australia* (Melbourne: Melbourne UP, 2002).

Bauman, Zygmunt. *Modernity and Ambivalence* (Cambridge: Polity, 1991).

Carter, Paul. *Living in a New Country* (London: Faber & Faber, 1992).

Cordner, Christopher. "Waiting, Patience and Love," in *Waiting*, ed. Ghassan Hage (Melbourne: Melbourne UP, 2009): 169–83.

Derrida, Jacques. "Time and Memory, Messianicity, the Name of God," in *Derrida, Deconstruction Engaged: The Sydney Seminars*, ed. Paul Patton & Terry Smith (Sydney: Power, 2001): 57–69.

Diprose, Rosalyn. *Corporeal Generosity: On Giving with Nietzsche, Merleau–Ponty, and Levinas* (Albany: State U of New York P, 2002).

Hawkins, Gay. *The Ethics of Waste: How We Relate to Rubbish* (Sydney: U of New South Wales P, 2006).

Healy, Chris. *Forgetting Aborigines* (Sydney: U of New South Wales P, 2008).

---

[58] Diprose, *Corporeal Generosity*, 23.

[59] See Watson, "Settled and Unsettled Spaces: Are we free to roam?," 30.

Lehman, Greg. "Editorial," *Island* 96 (2004): 1–4.
McClintock, Anne. *Imperial Leather: Race, Gender and Sexuality in the Colonial Context* (New York & London: Routledge, 1995).
Minnegal, Monica. "The Time is Right: Waiting, Reciprocity and Sociality," in *Waiting*, ed. Ghassan Hage (Melbourne: Melbourne UP, 2009): 89–96.
Mohanram, Radhika. *Black Body: Women, Colonialism and Space* (St Leonards, NSW: Allen & Unwin, 1999).
Moreton–Robinson, Aileen. "Towards a New Research Agenda?: Foucault, Whiteness and Indigenous Sovereignty," *Journal of Sociology* 42.4 (2006): 383–95.
Onsman, Andrys. "Truganini's Funeral," *Island* 96 (2004): 1–12.
Perera, Suvendrini. *Australia and the Insular Imagination: Beaches, Borders, Boats, and Bodies* (New York: Palgrave Macmillan, 2009).
Reynolds, Henry. *Why Weren't We Told?: a personal search for the truth about our history* (Ringwood, Victoria: Viking, 2000).
Ryan, Lyndall. *The Aboriginal Tasmanians* (St Leonards, NSW: Allen & Unwin, 1996).
Stephenson, Peta. *The Outsiders Within: Telling Australia's Indigenous–Asian Story* (Sydney: U of New South Wales P, 2007).
Thornley, Jeni, dir. *Island Home Country* (Anandi Films, Australia, 2009; 52 min.).
——. "'Island Home Country': working with Aboriginal protocols in a documentary film about colonisation and growing up white in Tasmania," in *Passionate Histories*, ed. Frances Peters–Little, Anne Curthoys & John Docker (Canberra: Australian National University E-Press, 2010): 247–78.
Watson, Irene. "Aboriginal Sovereignties: Past, Present and Future (Im)Possibilities," in *Our Patch: Enacting Australian Sovereignty Post-2001*, ed. Suvendrini Perera (Network Books Symposia Series; Perth, WA: Australia Research Unit, Curtin University of Technology, 2007): 23–43.
——. "Settled and Unsettled Spaces: Are we Free to Roam?" in *Sovereign Subjects: Indigenous Sovereignty Matters*, ed. Aileen Moreton–Robinson (Crows Nest, NSW: Allen & Unwin, 2007): 15–32.

Wounded Spaces/Geographies of Connectivity
Stephen Muecke's *No Road (bitumen all the way)*,
Margaret Somerville's *Body/Landscape Journals*,
and Katrina Schlunke's *Bluff Rock: Autobiography of a Massacre*

KAY SCHAFFER

L ANDSCAPE HAS ALWAYS BEEN a defining feature of Australian identity; the imagined aspect of the English white settler colony and later nation that seemed to best characterize its uniqueness to the world. In 1876, twenty-five years before Federation, Marcus Clarke penned his memorable and enduring comments on the landscape of Australia as opposed to other climes. In his preface to an early collection of Australian poetry, he opined that, far from the knightly songs of England, the weighty recollections of Asian's past magnificence, or the glittering, insatiable rush of American nature writing, "in Australia alone is to be found the Grotesque, the Weird, the strange scribblings of Nature learning how to write":

> the dweller in the wilderness acknowledges the subtle charm of this fantastic land of monstrosities [...] where all is fear-inspiring and gloomy [... as] he learns the language of the barren and the uncouth.[1]

Clarke's only mention of Indigenous peoples comes at the end of a paragraph describing the ghostly sights and sounds of animal life, thus metonymically aligning 'the natives' with nature at a time when they were facing near-extinction and were thought to be a dying race. There he adds that in the corner of

---

[1] Marcus Clarke, "Preface to a New Edition of Adam Lindsay Gordon, Sea Spray and Smoke Drift," in *Portable Australian Authors: Marcus Clarke*, ed. Michael Wilding (St Lucia: U of Queensland P, 1976): 646, 647.

the silent forests "natives painted like skeletons" dance around their fires, to the rising sounds of a "dismal chant."[2]

These dismal colonial and colonizing imaginings form the backdrop for contemporary writing about "uncanny Australia," the title of a landmark book (1998) by Jane Jacobs and Ken Gelder, in which the authors reflect upon Indigenous peoples' sacred and indivisible relation to the land as opposed to the colonial frameworks of land ownership and possession that resulted in Indigenous dispossession. Colonial conflict, often resulting in violence and massacre, bloodied the landscape and contributed to the near-annihilation of native populations in the nineteenth century, not so very long before Clarke penned his gloomy assessments. The enduring imaginings that Clarke's preface inspired, coupled with the haunting memory of white settler violence and the nation's resistance to addressing its wounded spaces and the psychic legacies of frontier violence, suggest that perhaps Clarke revealed something more than he could have known concerning the fears, anxieties, and insecurities that underwrote the colonial enterprise and continue to haunt the present.

In recent years, a number of texts written by non-Indigenous authors have emerged that attempt to come to terms with Australia's colonial and colonizing history. These decolonizing texts of reconciliation, sometimes written in collaboration with Indigenous people, sometimes intent on addressing and rewriting the neo-colonial mind-set of white settler selfhood, start from a different set of premises. They address white settler guilt and acknowledge the legacies of colonization. At the same time, they acknowledge that Indigenous people have very different understandings of white colonial history and different epistemological, ontological, and cosmological understandings that inform their relationships together and their ways of being in the land.

In this essay, I explore three texts written by white Australians that either attempt to explore Indigenous relationships to land or address the legacies of white settler violence. All of them might be considered as texts of reconciliation growing out of concerns generated by the *Bringing Them Home Report* (1996) on the separation of mixed-race children from their families and the 1990s Decade of Reconciliation.[3] All three texts seek new ways of belonging

---

[2] Clarke, "Preface to a New Edition of Adam Lindsay Gordon," 646.

[3] The *Bringing Them Home Report* documented the removal of Aboriginal and Torres Strait Islander children from their families in every state and territory in Australia in the period from 1910 to 1970. It concluded, among other things, that "Indigenous families and communities have endured gross violations of their human rights.

to country and new connections with peoples and landscapes. The narratives include Steven Muecke's *No Road (Bitumen All the Way)* (1997), Margaret Somerville's *Body/Landscape Journals* (1999), and Katrina Schlunke's *Bluff Rock* (2004).[4] These hybrid, provisional texts exceed disciplinary and generic classifications. They self-consciously reflect upon the complex attachments and messy entanglements involved in white settler belonging, challenging what Aileen Moreton–Robinson calls the "possessive logic of white patriarchal sovereignty."[5] Weaving together autobiographical material with postcolonial and postmodern theory, ethnography, spatial history, cultural geography, ecological ethics, and decolonizing critique, their narrators speak across cultures, attempting to negotiate a contested ground of knowledges, cosmologies, and modes of being; to forge an ethics of being together.

Several questions motivate my interest: how do the writers structure their narratives and figure 'the self' between Western and Indigenous knowledges and ways of being? What risks are involved and what potentials for 'becoming Other' are offered when white scholars, dealing with a history of colonial violence, attempt to renounce white privilege, acknowledge Indigenous cultural practices and relations to country, and seek out reciprocal relations across

---

These violations continue to affect Indigenous people's daily lives. They were an act of genocide, aimed at wiping out Indigenous families, communities and cultures, vital to the precious and inalienable heritage of Australia" (conclusion). In 1991 the then Prime Minister Paul Keating established a Council on Aboriginal Reconciliation to lead the nation through a decade of dialogue designed to redress the abuses of the past and build bridges between Indigenous and non-Indigenous Australians.

[4] One might also add the mixed-genre historical narratives like that of Mark McKenna, *Looking for Blackfellas' Point: An Australian History of Place* (Sydney: U of New South Wales P, 2002), and Martin Thomas, *The Artificial Horizon : Imagining the Blue Mountains* (Carlton, Victoria: Melbourne UP, 2003). In addition, several cross-cultural life narratives have recently been published, such as that by Ros Moriarity, *Listening to Country* (Sydney: Allen & Unwin, 2010), a story which details her family's journey to her husband's Indigenous community at Borroloola, and John Bradley's memoir written in collaboration with Yanyuwa elders, *Singing Saltwater Country: Journey to the Songlines of Carpentaria* (Sydney: Allen & Unwin, 2010), a text that details his three decades of living with the Yanyuwa people of the Gulf region and coming to understand their ways of being.

[5] Aileen Moreton–Robinson, "The Possessive Logic of Patriarchal White Sovereignty: The High Court and the Yorta Yorta Decision," *borderlands e-journal* 3.2 (2004).

difference in local and specific acts of connection? On what basis do we decide whether these texts succeed or fail?

Muecke's *No Road* and Somerville's *Body/Landscape Journals* grew out of years of personal interaction and professional collaboration with Aboriginal people in remote areas of Australia. In each of the texts, the narrators enact a crisis within the self that results from their situated knowledge and experience of Western and Indigenous cultures and ways of knowing. Both look to Aboriginal cultures in order to find a way to be other than what one is. In this regard, Katrina Schlunke's *Bluff Rock* is the exception. Her narrator returns 'home', to the place of her childhood, to mine the landscape for traces of its violent, and all but silenced, colonial past. All three texts were published by small academic presses, in small print-runs, and addressed a limited range of white readers. Their reverberations might be registered as minor in effect but seismic in potential, as the questions they raise continue to rumble through the fissures of a deceptively settled landscape. These edgy texts deal with issues of cultural translation, taking white knowledge frameworks to the limit and bringing "unsettling, postcolonial anxieties to bear upon the act (or styles) of writing itself."[6]

The personal histories of the three writers under consideration have relevance, as each author is specifically and uniquely positioned to both literally and figuratively 'see' the land differently. Prior to *No Road*, Stephen Muecke had co-authored or edited several cross-cultural texts engaging with Paddy Roe, a senior Indigenous storyteller from the remote Kimberley region of northern West Australia, and Krim Bennterak, a Moroccan-born Australian artist from Broome, Western Australia. These include *Gulurabulu: Stories from the West Kimberley* (1983) and *Reading the Country: Introduction to Nomadology* (Benterrak, Muecke and Roe, 1984).[7] In *Reading the Country*,

---

[6] Fiona Probyn, "A Poetics of Failure Is No Bad Thing: Stephen Muecke and Margaret Somerville's White Writing," *Journal of Australian Studies* 75 (2002): 19, 25.

[7] In *Reading the Country*, Stephen and his co-authors visit Roebuck Plains, an area in the north of Western Australia which until less than a century ago had been inhabited by Aboriginal people. Today the plains form part of a pastoral lease, and no Aboriginal people live there. As the publisher's blurb explains, "The book provides an account of the authors' exploration of the meaning of place, and their attempt to chart the relationships between people and those specific places in which they must find a place to live. Readings include traditional and contemporary Aboriginal narratives and songs, European history of 'discovery' and 'settlement' and geological and geographic

Muecke, a French-influenced cultural theorist, transcribes traditional stories by Paddy Roe and provides a parallel text in which he adopts a Deleuzean perspective to come to terms with Aboriginal ways of being in the world: imagining Aboriginal elders "as nomads set against the State, and as storytellers who live out 'rhizomatic' connections to country and community."[8] A Deleuzean sense of nomadic movement, which, he asserts, is a characteristic of Aboriginal culture, informs Muecke's writing practice. As he explains, "movement is more important to Aboriginal modes of being than territoriality, and lines (or pathways of movement) more than boundaries."[9] In *Gulurabulu*, he invents a new mode of transcription to render the Indigenous elder Paddy Roe's traditional stories more 'authentic' in keeping with their original oral form. *No Road* continues his nomadic journeying, but from a more embodied and self-reflexive stance than he had adopted in the previous works. Here, he presents "an inventive mix of storytelling and ideas, and a personal account of travels in outback Australia, Europe, Africa [...] and suburban Newtown" (publisher's blurb) in an attempt to inscribe himself and 'Australia' differently.

Prior to the *Body/Landscape Journals,* Margaret Somerville had published two collaborative texts with Aboriginal women, *Ingelba and the Five Black Matriarchs* (1990) and *The Sun Dancin': People and Place in Coonabarabran* (1994). Both projects, which involved the skills of an ethnographer and oral historian, had been initiated by Aboriginal women from country New South Wales who enlisted Margaret, as a feminist historian from the area, to help them tell the story of their lives in community. Charged with the responsibility to represent a culture other than her own, she becomes keenly aware of the distance between oral and written cultures and the radical instability of Western interpretative frameworks in dealing with them. The collaborative work takes her out of her comfort zone. Through her work, she not only seeks to challenge Western knowledge paradigms, she also begins to identify with the Aboriginal women in their attachment to kin and country, which she desires for herself. In *Body/Landscape Journals* she attempts to turn the gaze

---

knowledge, paintings and photographs, and a series of exploratory, linking essays." *Gulurabulu* contains Paddy Roe's traditional stories of country.

[8] Ken Gelder & Jane M. Jacobs, *Uncanny Australia: Sacredness and Identity in a Postcolonial Nation* (Carlton, Victoria: Melbourne UP, 1998): 1.

[9] Stephen Muecke, *Ancient and Modern: Time Culture and Indigenous Philosophy* (Sydney: U of New South Wales P, 2004): 16.

back onto herself and to her own unsettled sense of embodied belonging in country. Positioned in a liminal space between different ways of knowing, she suffers a breakdown. *Body/Landscape Journals* grow out of this time of crisis in/of the body.

In *No Road*, Steven Muecke positions himself as an 'accidental tourist' in remote north-western Australia, a 'tangential intellectual' moving into a territory where there are no roads, no signposts, no words. The narrator asks: "what language can I use to *carry* this story?"[10] How can he make it move? Here, writing is movement, interdisciplinarity the chosen mode of transport. Like an 'accidental tourist', the narrator mixes the anecdotal with the banal, backed up (and some readers would say distanced and contained), by the 'solidity' of theory (32).[11] But theory, like Toyota four-wheel drives, can get bogged in unfamiliar territory; drivers can get lost. Accidents require improvisation, risk, negotiation with strangers; getting lost requires setting off in unfamiliar directions. Muecke offers these metaphors of the journey as a way of breaking away from Western knowledge frameworks and adapting to the movement of the nomad. He directs his tale at an audience of postmodern and postcolonial readers, intending to move us out of a zone of settled belonging; admitting that accidents which spell danger are likely. Muecke constructs an allegory for the intellectual journey into nomadology by staging an accident early in the narrative. His accidental tourist en route to Broome, Western Australia, bogs his four-wheel-drive vehicle on Eighty-Mile Beach, where it sinks back into the ocean, leaving him and his travelling companion stranded, a twelve-hour walk away from the nearest highway (73–74). From this point of no return, Aboriginal strangers become his guides.

No Road is divided into nine sections, each of them having numerous digressions as the text weaves together a matrix of journeys. It combines autobiographical material and snippets of anecdote, story, letters, postcards, film, and music with philosophical ruminations in dialogue with Continental and North American cultural theorists that include Gilles Deleuze, Roland Barthes, Michel de Certeau, Homi Bhabha, Trinh Minh-ha, Brian Massumi,

---

[10] Stephen Muecke, *No Road (Bitumen All the Way)* (South Fremantle, WA: Fremantle Arts Centre Press, 1997): 15. Further page references are in the main text.

[11] See Gelder & Jacobs, *Uncanny Australia*, and Michèle Grossman, "Xen(Ography) and the Art of Representing Otherwise: Australian Indigenous Life-Writing and the Vernacular Text," *Postcolonial Studies* 8.3 (2005): 277–301, for different critiques of his methodology.

Mikhail Bakhtin, Jean Baudrillard, and Maurice Blanchot, as well as numerous Australian cultural critics such as Paul Carter, Myra Morris, Jennifer Craik, Ross Chambers, and Deborah Bird Rose. The clash between Aboriginal and Western cultures motivates the journey, but the voice of the Western intellectual presides.

He writes:

> We can know this, to know is not to perish quickly in the deserts of endless deferral of meaning, but getting to know may mean leaving home and getting lost for a while, to admit that there may not be a road going anywhere that we all agree on, but that somewhere along that road is a local guide who knows a story we may never have heard before, a story that leads to a place in the desert [...] where there is plenty of food and water. (130)

By staging a series of nomadic journeys and imaginings in the text, Muecke attempts to say something different about Australia; to envisage "a new architecture for the environment" and "a house in which one can more comfortably reside."[12] He does not entirely succeed. Although moving across a landscape of untranslatable differences, the text-as-vehicle comes with heavy theoretical baggage. A number of critics have expressed concerns about Muecke's self-conscious use of autobiographical materials and personal interactions with Aboriginal modes of being to explicate French cultural theory. As David Brooks comments, "what makes [... the book] exemplary," Muecke's movement towards an Aboriginal alterity, "also holds it back, or rather twists it, rather seductively, from within, conveying to the reader that it isn't always agreeing with itself."[13] Intellectually, the author critiques and resists the pull of Oedipal relations of sex/textuality, what Barthes posits as the origins of all narrative, but he is never quite able to achieve the ontological abandonment he seeks; in his stylistic play he retains the control of the text as a sovereign, knowing, authoritative, Oedipal subject. Brooks suggests that herein lies the paradox: that "in order to have what one desires, one cannot be what one is."[14]

Muecke and Somerville both engage with the desire to become other. Both seek ways of living in a decolonized landscape, of finding non-exploitative

---

[12] Stephen Muecke, quoted in David Brooks, "On the Road Again: Review of Muecke, Stephen. *No Road (Bitumen All the Way)* (1997)," *Meanjin* (Melbourne) 56.3–4 (1997): 487.

[13] Brooks, "On the Road Again," 487.

[14] "On the Road Again," 494.

ways of belonging to country. Both of their narratives stage breakdowns as they crash through the barriers of their own frames of knowing, of being. Muecke plays with tropes of accidents and danger as an allegorical counterpoint to his intellectual dilemma. Although often intimately engaged with his Aboriginal hosts, in his enunciative mode he retains a critical distance from them. Somerville's sexual/textual immersion is more immediate. As she vacillates between Western knowledge frameworks and fluid, unsettled longings, her 'breakdown' becomes quite literal.

Margaret Somerville relates that she began the *Body/Landscape Journals* after experiencing a "crisis in the body."[15] The crisis occurs in the space and time between two collaborative oral history projects with the Aboriginal women. Having sensed the intimacy of body/place connections in the stories of the women while working with Patsy Cohen on *Ingelba and the Five Black Matriarchs*, she craves it for herself. She writes: "I felt that I had been born in this landscape, the Aboriginal stories were inside me."[16] Desiring of, yet excluded from, the intimacy and union she feels the women share together and in their connection to country, she experiences a dissociation of self, divided between her desire to be located inside the landscape of these stories and her state of being shackled by the inadequacy of her critical tools. Her crisis in and of the body occurs while writing an article about her relationship to place, in the early phases of her work with the Aboriginal women of Coonabarabran who are the subject of *The Sun Dancin'*:

> I sensed the body and body/place connection always already there in the stories but didn't know how to do it for me. I thought and thought about the problem intellectually, and the more I thought the more distressed I became. I felt weak and exhausted, my heart pounded, even to walk up the stairs was an effort. I had strange and frightening dreams about a fragmented body. [...] I had fallen into the abyss of Western dualistic thinking predicated on separation rather than connection.[17]

Somerville experiences a crisis both of representation and of selfhood. The narrator fears she cannot represent the women, who have enlisted her to write their stories, without performing epistemic violence. Abandoning her original

---

[15] Margaret Somerville, *Body/Landscape Journals* (North Melbourne: Spinifex, 1999): 1.

[16] Somerville, *Body/Landscape Journals*, 9.

[17] *Body/Landscape Journals*, 12.

aim to critique patriarchal relations of colonization, she seeks absorption with the women, into country. The Indigenous women take her to their country and include her in their ceremonies but cannot share their meanings. She gets lost between the two cultures; her guilt and shame driving her out of one, her (impossible) desire to achieve oneness with the women propelling her into the Other.

Intellectually and psychologically unable to proceed, she fears that she will fail the women and fail herself. Riddled with guilt, she falters in her writing practice. Somerville desires the desire of the Other to the extent that the *Body/Landscape Journals* become "a liminal space in which [she] cannot represent otherness, but only perform the effects of that otherness on [her] self."[18] The problem is one of reactive desire. Margaret does not want to have what the Other has; she desires the desire of the Other.

Lisa Slater perceptively reads the *Body/Landscape Journals* as a study of the postcolonial subject-in-crisis. Each chapter stages a performance, beginning with the author's involvement with Aboriginal and white women during the Pine Gap Women's Peace Camp in 1983, moving through her oral history collaborations with Aboriginal women, and finally arriving 'home' in the mid-1990s to find herself without a home, a place of belonging, or a language to express her fragmented selfhood.

Each chapter becomes a memory site that mixes personal reflection with photographs, journal entries, poems, and critical commentary, feminist and postcolonial theory. As the narrator progresses through the journals, she intersperses perceptions of her experiences with the women with quotations from French feminist and Australian poststructural critics such as Hélène Cixous, Luce Irigaray, and Elizabeth Grosz, seeking to find an in-between space of sexuality/textuality or pleasure/production.[19] As she moves "to the limit edge of self," the journals dissolve into an incoherent babble of words and images.[20] The narrative falls apart as intertextuality and quotation replace narrative and take over the anxious gasps of desiring selfhood. This broken, disordered text becomes haunted by both the murmur of voices of the marginalized Aboriginal women and the boom of mainstream Western academics. It "cannot

---

[18] Lisa Slater, "Intimate Australia: *Body/Landscape Journals* and the Paradox of Belonging," *Cultural Studies Review* 13.1 (2006): 152.

[19] Somerville, citing Grosz, in *Body/Landscape Journals*, 172.

[20] *Body/Landscape Journals*, 221.

hold the excess of her creative, intellectual play."[21] In the impossible desire to become the Other, Somerville assumes the place of the repressed. A sickness takes over and propels her journals, one that "could be understood to result from the fear of being consumed by indeterminacy and thus set adrift like an insane discourse."[22] Perhaps, as Slater suggests, it is not possible for her white-settler self to 'go beyond' colonialism without moving back through it, exploring its dark spaces, its messy entanglements.

There is much of value in these texts as they unsettle notions of white settler belonging to country. In their writing practice, Muecke and Somerville invent hybrid styles to engage with different epistemes in order to acknowledge Indigenous life-ways, understandings, cosmologies, and ontologies of being. They attempt to destabilize old and re-establish new ethical grounds for reciprocal relations between Indigenous and non-Indigenous Australians. They also become caught in epistemological and affective faultlines, where the propulsive energies of these exploratory texts are immobilized. Whereas Muecke's *No Road* risks appropriating Indigenous stories into his theoretical project, the (im)possible desires that drive Somerville's *Body/Landscape Journals* put her at risk of madness. While potentially transformative, these provisional texts privilege an examination of anxieties concerning white colonial subjectivity, authority, and epistemology. This approach has limited purchase when forging new directions for a decolonized, postcolonial Australia.[23] It seems we have arrived at another impasse.

Katrina Schlunke's *Bluff Rock: Autobiography of a Massacre* (2004) attempts another turn. Unlike *No Road* and the *Body/Landscape Journals*, the text does not attempt to establish new grounds for reciprocal relations with Indigenous Australians in remote or rural communities. Rather, it is situated in a white-settler place of unsettled belonging, where it attempts to look critically at *whiteness*. Schlunke uses a homeopathic metaphor to explain her writing practices and methods – to use the ideas and practices that have caused damage in order to heal damage.[24] Here, the body in question is the corporeal

---

[21] Slater, "Intimate Australia," 152.

[22] "Intimate Australia," 166.

[23] For a more in-depth discussion of this dilemma, see Fiona Probyn, "A Poetics of Failure Is No Bad Thing: Stephen Muecke and Margaret Somerville's White Writing," and David Brooks, "On the Road Again."

[24] For a discussion of her methodology, see her "Historicising Whiteness: Captain Cook Possesses Australia," in *Historicising Whiteness: Transnational Perspectives on*

body of colonized Australia viewed historically, imaginatively, and affectively, with reference to both temporal and spatial relations between non-Indigenous and Indigenous peoples and cultures.

Bluff Rock opens with the question "how do we know the past?"[25] The narrative concerns a massacre that occurred in the early days of white settlement, possibly in 1844, at Bluff Rock, in the New South Wales tablelands, near the farm where the author was raised and where her sister continues to live. As a child growing up in the 1950s, the author, now a cultural theorist and an historian, knew and did not know about the local massacre. As with many white Australians who grew up in areas marked by frontier conflict, her lips could call out familiar place-names like Slaughterhouse Creek, Blackfellows Ridge, and Niggers Leap without a shudder or a stutter (184). The cultural amnesia of forgetting what had happened in these places and gave rise to their naming shrouded her formative years, characterized by a shutting-down of history, an attempt at closure so that the uncanny remnants of a violent colonial past might be silenced and buried; left only in the traces of place-names in a wounded landscape.

The author returns to the scene not to discover what really happened at Bluff Rock, but, in her words, to "unknit *how* we know something [...] to unravel how stories can both fix ideas (and our ways of knowing) and intimately and intricately undo those certainties" (14). She uses a variety of modes and techniques in an attempt to embody the presence of the past in the people and places "that are simultaneously past, present and emerging" (16). The sub-title of the narrative, "autobiography of a massacre," signals something of her critical method: to imagine a massacre site as a character in the theatre of colonialism. Her text enunciates the performance of "a tragedy of epic proportions" where most of the action happens off-stage, is silenced, and leaves a miasma of pollution in that place (her place, her home) that continues to haunt. On silences she writes:

> Silences can be the trembling of desire for the deeply unsaid, but when does silence become a sustained forgetting? A forgetting so constant that even when you want to speak you find, with a shock, that your

---

the Construction of an Identity, ed. Leigh Boucher, Jane Carey & Katherine Ellinghaus (Melbourne University Conference and Seminar Series 16; Melbourne: RMIT Publishing/School of Historical Studies, University of Melbourne, 2007): 41–50.

[25] Katrina Schlunke, *Bluff Rock: Autobiography of a Massacre* (Perth, WA: Curtin UP, 2004): 11. Further page references are in the main text.

> dumb fumbling lips cannot say what should be said, never having heard the right words. Are we kept or do we keep 'as quiet as possible'? (116)

Schlunke mines the site of Bluff Rock for traces that bring the remnants of the past into the present. She registers the affects and displacements of history in the remembered and recorded stories of place. Although local, her massacre story is not unique. Her site, like those to be found across the landscape of white-settler Australia, encompasses a two-hundred-year history of colonial relations. With specific variations and contingent permutations, it was performed elsewhere. Schlunke collects and sifts through its textual artefacts in the place she calls 'home' to detect the flaws, ambiguities, discontinuities, and contradictions in the production of knowledge about Bluff Rock, which the massacre site shares with other white mythologies of place, born of liminal longings for place and belonging.

Like Muecke and Somerville, Schlunke produces a multi-modal, excessive text, littered with the detritus of history – in her case, the material artefacts include tourist leaflets, family diaries and letters, official historical records, gossip, and journals, to which she adds field-notes of journeys to sites, her own personal reminiscences and diary entries of her partner Susan, and their feelings and reactions to events as they unfold in the lived process of historical research, to cobble together a narrative of disorder; a writing practice of decolonization. For example, in investigating reports of the massacre, the historian determines that there was not one massacre but several, which had occurred over a number of years and in widespread areas of the New South Wales pastoral tablelands. The one attached to Bluff Rock that is now mentioned in tourist brochures could not have been one that she could trace through historical artefacts. Diaries and local histories themselves dissemble when massacres are touched upon. There are many equivocations in the historical records.

Like Muecke and Somerville, Schlunke employs metaphors of knitting, unravelling, weaving, and entanglement to open up the complex fabric of history for inspection, to register its fabrications, its fragility, and to test its ability to become something else. Like them, she studies the ambiguities of language and how *words* contain meaning. Words *contain* meaning. Take the word 'massacre', derived from Old French for 'to butcher', meaning a general slaughter or indiscriminate killing of human beings. In the historical sources, white settler Australians find different words to describe their murderous activities. The pioneering whites

> went 'blackbird shooting',
> formed a 'black line',
> encouraged and organised 'expeditions',
> formed a 'bush party' and
> took 'decisive measures'. (184)

Euphemisms found in recorded memoirs disguise the murder of unarmed opponents in a war of guns against shields.

Schlunke's narrative also shares with the other texts a concern with the (white) writing self, the written self that registers dis-ease in its complicity with the past and its dissatisfactions with the present. And, like them, the narrator sometimes finds herself in danger, wedged uncomfortably in between spaces of abjection and disorder that threaten to overwhelm the subject as witness. Like Somerville, she begins to disappear into an abyss of non-being, prompted by a deep disaffection with her own whiteness. As the narrator becomes more knowing, the text takes on a breathless cadence; the voice falters as she nears "a crisis of excruciating self-consciousness, of grisly overidentification" (228). Writing in solitude, she finds the contours of the land of her childhood, the land she loves, becoming ugly. Guilt-ridden as she shoulders the weight of the past, she reflects that, no matter how much she pays, no matter how much the country pays, it will never be enough for the damage done.

Sinking and wallowing with every new empathic connection, every new awareness of deception and dissimulation in the materials she studies, she envisages a metaphoric space that parallels her condition:

> But now I'm thinking of myself as a boat listing over on the water nearly drowning. And now the imagining of the tragic boat, alone on a vast sea (make it dark as well), looks so stupid, ludicrous, so sorry for oneself – *Get ON with it!* But I can't without imagining, and everything I think is wrong. (228)

The Bluff Rock massacre is no longer untouchable; the perpetrators not distant but close in imagination, and they are "white like me" – "I have an investment in knowing them so that I might know myself" (17). Reading this, I am transported into another theatre in the history of colonial violence and another scene of grisly over-identification leading to self-loathing. Schlunke's locatedness in an assemblage of colonial relations, her over-identification with the actors in another scene of history, her dumbfounded stumbling for meaning, calls to mind Antjie Krog's *Country of My Skull*. As Krog's narrator becomes more conscious of her own white-settler complicity with her country's history of violent encounter, she grows sick, her hair and teeth begin to fall out, she loses her ability to speak.[26] With abhorrent recognition, she hears the harsh Afrikaans voices of perpetrators. "They are familiar as [her] own brothers, cousins, school friends. Between us all distance is erased" (121):

> I shrink and prickle. Against. Against my blood and the heritage thereof. Will I forever be them – recognizing them as I do daily in my nostrils? Yes. And what we have done will never be undone. (171)

And:

> Whence will words now come? For us. We who hang quivering and ill from this soundless space of Afrikaner past? What does one say? What the hell does one do with this load of decrowned skeletons, origins, shame, and ash? (168)

Krog worked as a journalist for the South African Broadcasting Commission for the duration of the Truth and Reconciliation hearings. Her witnessing to apartheid violence was direct and immediate. Schlunke imaginatively re-creates scenes of earlier violence which she bears like a wound on the edge of her skin. Like Krog in South Africa, Schlunke in Australia enacts a performance in the (post)colonial theatre of violence. Like Krog, she owns and embodies, even as she recoils from, the intimacies of history, of what Allen Feldman calls the "materiality of the violent particular."[27] As an historian and cultural theorist, with deep attachment to country, she attempts to stay rooted in the local, acknowledging the place of her youth, the site of multiple massacres, the area where her family still resides. She stutters, dumbfounded, lost in shame and grief for what is not recoverable. Like Krog, and Somerville at the limits of settler selfhood, she begins to dissolve in shame at the fact of her whiteness, until a voice calls her back from the endpoint: "GET REAL!" (227).

At different times in the text, the narrator seeks to 'know herself' differently, to examine "the intimacies of both History (as officially documented) and history (as a fiction in the present)" (202). In one of the most controversial sections of the text, she returns to the times of colonial massacre to stage a perverse, erotic imagining of herself as a wife in liaison with the white

---

[26] Antjie Krog, *Country of My Skull: Guilt, Sorrow, and the Limits of Forgiveness in the New South Africa* (New York: Three Rivers, 1998): 65. Further page references are in the main text.

[27] Allen Feldman, "Memory Theatres, Virtual Witnessing, and the Trauma-Aesthetic," *biography* 27.1 (Winter 2004): 169.

station owner and murderous historical actor Irby, whose diaries inform a large part of the Bluff Rock massacre history. Her imagined, historicized self moves from the steamy bed of Irby to that of a woman, the beer-stealing wife of his friend Bates. These imagined liaisons defy defensive assertions of contemporary white Australians that they would not have participated in massacres, that they are somehow different from their pioneering settler ancestors due to their more enlightened location in the present. In part, these dramatic scenes locate women (however unstable the category) in an imagined rewriting of History, mainly composed of men's reports. In part, they queer history, not to recuperate lesbians in the historical canon (as one might want to recuperate women), but to write beyond the limits of history yet not beyond the imaginable, "to provide a limit at which we produce our own locatedness" (205).

The sexed intensities of these bedroom scenes are also informed by actual rather than invented memories of the narrator's early lesbian experiences. These experiences connect to other fragments, other desires, other productions, "where the imaginary line between past and present [...] and so future" (205) coalesces in a Deleuzean assemblage of colonial relations. Schlunke asks:

> Were the impossibilities of being lesbian connected to the impossibilities of acknowledging Aboriginal presence? [... Did those impossibilities also] follow well-worn colonial paths of opening us up to the new, investing ourselves in spaces and places – always into country owned by no-one else? (206, 207)

Schlunke follows these imagined bedroom scenarios in the narrative with a visit that she, as a research historian, and her partner, Susan, make to the home of the descendants of Irby, who own the original Irby journals. They welcome the curious strangers into their home and issue a dinner invitation. The women are pleased: "we fit, you see" (210), she writes. At dinner she is appalled by her polite participation in forms of everyday, garden-variety racism, when she chooses not to speak out against the casual racist remarks of her hosts, for fear of offending them. Irby was, she is, complicit in the category: 'white like us'.

This section of the text disarms many Australian critics. Reviews have been minimal. Those which have appeared range from a kind of careful appreciation of the presentation of a decolonized history to utter disdain for the excessively sexual, affective dimensions of the text and the imaginative rewriting of the past, what Schlunke calls the queering of the text. The critics complain that she crosses too many boundaries, goes too far in her imaginative fictions. In other words, she touches raw nerves.

Schlunke admits that her text fails her own purpose at important moments – how could it not, when the murderous destruction of a people and their culture is brought home in such intimate proximity? She seeks a way out of the crisis of the white-settler self by entering into new intersubjective relations with others in the present. Underlying this movement is an understanding of the self as undecided, volatile, always embodied, and always in a state of becoming and connecting in unpredictable ways with others. Her final performance in the text, her way of 'making ends meet', is to place herself in the shared Indigenous and non-Indigenous spaces of the present. Spaces of hope. With her partner, Susan, two nieces and nephew, she takes a Wooloo Wooloo Aboriginal Cultural Tour with a local Aboriginal guide. Generous and good-humoured, the guide acknowledges the violence of the past and its effects on his community, but is more alive to the present spaces of possibilities. His culture survived. He is relearning the traditional language of his people, creating opportunities for a shared future. His generosity provides a fragile delight, a tentative path into new histories and cultures that allow us to live together. For this she gives thanks. It is perhaps a small moment on which to end the narrative, a fragile beginning, an ethical relation of connection.

Much is missing from the historical record of colonial Australia. Our knowledge of the past is partial, broken, and obscured by denial. In response to this dilemma, the historian Greg Dening has written that "the most important historical work happens when historians apply imagination to evidence."[28] He does not advocate that historians should write fiction or fantasy but, rather, that they should use their imagination, with a fealty to all the evidence that can be supplied by the historical records. In her autobiography of a massacre at Bluff Rock, Schlunke constructs an historiography of the imagination and the senses as well as the mind, a palpable history, a history directed towards reconciliation. The text engages the reader in an unmaking and a remaking of subjectivity, time and space, an immersive recovery of the presence of the past, in all its messy densities. An ethical aesthetic informs her writing. She assembles an open-ended narrative of non-linear emergences, entanglements, and transformations. Schlunke imagines Bluff Rock as a place of death, an abiding presence, and a landscape of new beginnings (244). Those

---

[28] Greg Dening, quoted in Ross Gibson, "Palpable History," *Cultural Studies Review* 14.1 (2008): 185.

beginnings, like the Aboriginal cultural tour, in its moment of delight and its promise of a generous exchange, allow white Australians to be something else, something other than what they are. The text rests on this glimmer of hope, this imagining of the unknowable.

The three texts, taken together, connect the challenging work of decolonizing the landscape to the work of reconciliation in Australia. In their complex weaving and unravelling of body and body/place connections, they attempt to knit a new fabric for the nation. Each text in its own way takes a risk, what we might understand as a "propulsive risk," to deploy a term from Félix Guattari's *Chaosmosis*,[29] one that moves the subject out of familiar groundings into transformed environments, allowing for recognitions of difference to emerge in which singular moments occur and outcomes are unknown. These moments of singularity can fail, of course, or become banal, and there are moments in all three texts when the narrative falters. But they can also open up new possibilities, new beginnings. Guattari writes: "it's sometimes necessary to jump at the opportunity to approve, to run the risk of being wrong," and, in so doing, to "respond to the event as the potential bearer of new constellations of Universes of reference."[30] The future of reconciliation in Australia may require many moments of white-settler immersion in territories of confusion and contradiction, the outcomes of which are as yet unknown and unmappable. These texts of Muecke, Somerville, and Schlunke, for all their epistemological and ontological accidents, gaps, collisions, and chasms, also build bridges of possibility and hope, however fragile, that clear a space for new geographies of connectivity.

WORKS CITED

Australia, Commonwealth of. *Bringing Them Home Community Guide* (Canberra: Human Rights and Equal Opportunity Commission, 1997).

——. *Bringing Them Home: National Inquiry into the Separation of Aboriginal and Torres Strait Islander Children from Their Families*, ed. Sir Ronald Wilson & Michael Dodson (Canberra: Human Rights and Equal Opportunity Commission, 1997).

---

[29] Félix Guattari, *Chaosmosis: An Ethico-Aesthetic Paradigm*, ed. Julian Pefanis, tr. Eva Hung (Bloomington: Indiana UP, 1995): 18.

[30] Guattari, *Chaosmosis*, 18.

Benterrak, Krim, Stephen Muecke & Paddy Roe. *Reading the Country: Introduction to Nomadology* (Fremantle, WA: Fremantle Arts Centre Press, 1984).

Brooks, David. "On the Road Again: Review of Muecke, Stephen. *No Road (Bitumen All the Way)* (1997)," *Meanjin* 56.3–4 (1997): 486–94.

Clarke, Marcus. "Preface to a New Edition of Adam Lindsay Gordon, *Sea Spray and Smoke Drift* (Melbourne: Clarson, Massina & Co., 1876) Signed 'Marcus Clarke'," in *Portable Australian Authors: Marcus Clarke*, ed. Michael Wilding (St Lucia: U of Queensland P, 1976): 643–47.

Cohen, Patsy, & Margaret Somerville. *Ingelba and the Five Black Matriarchs* (North Sydney: Allen & Unwin, 1990).

Feldman, Allen. "Memory Theatres, Virtual Witnessing, and the Trauma-Aesthetic," *biography* 27.1 (Winter 2004): 163–202.

Gelder, Ken, & Jane M. Jacobs. *Uncanny Australia: Sacredness and Identity in a Postcolonial Nation* (Carlton, Victoria: Melbourne UP, 1998).

Gibson, Ross. "Palpable History," *Cultural Studies Review* 14.1 (2008): 179–86.

Grossman, Michèle. "Xen(Ography) and the Art of Representing Otherwise: Australian Indigenous Life-Writing and the Vernacular Text," *Postcolonial Studies* 8.3 (2005): 277–301.

Guattari, Félix. *Chaosmosis: An Ethico-Aesthetic Paradigm*, ed. Julian Pefanis, tr. Eva Hung (Bloomington: Indiana UP, 1995).

Krog, Antjie. *Country of My Skull: Guilt, Sorrow, and the Limits of Forgiveness in the New South Africa* (New York: Three Rivers, 1998).

Moreton–Robinson, Aileen. "The Possessive Logic of Patriarchal White Sovereignty: The High Court and the Yorta Yorta Decision," *borderlands e-journal* 3.2 (2004).

Muecke, Stephen. *Ancient and Modern: Time Culture and Indigenous Philosophy* (Sydney: U of New South Wales P, 2004).

——. *No Road (Bitumen All the Way)* (South Fremantle, WA: Fremantle Arts Centre Press, 1997).

——, & Paddy Roe. *Gularabulu: Stories from the West Kimberley*, ed. Stephen Muecke (Fremantle, WA: Fremantle Arts Centre Press, 1983).

Probyn, Fiona. "A Poetics of Failure Is No Bad Thing: Stephen Muecke and Margaret Somerville's White Writing," *Journal of Australian Studies* 75 (2002): 17–26.

Schlunke, Katrina. *Bluff Rock: Autobiography of a Massacre* (Perth, WA: Curtin UP, 2004).

——. "Historicising Whiteness: Captain Cook Possesses Australia," in *Historicising Whiteness: Transnational Perspectives on the Construction of an Identity*, ed. Leigh Boucher, Jane Carey & Katherine Ellinghaus (Melbourne University Conference and Seminar Series 16; Melbourne: RMIT Publishing/School of Historical Studies, University of Melbourne, 2007): 41–50.

Slater, Lisa. "Intimate Australia: *Body/Landscape Journals* and the Paradox of Belonging," *Cultural Studies Review* 13.1 (2006): 150–69.

Somerville, Margaret. *Body/Landscape Journals* (North Melbourne, Victoria: Spinifex, 1999).

——. et al. *The Sun Dancin': People and Place in Coonabaraban* (Canberra: Aboriginal Studies Press, 1994).

Recovering the Past
Entangled Histories in Kim Scott's *That Deadman Dance**

SUE KOSSEW

LT. WILLIAM BRADLEY'S WATERCOLOUR PAINTING "View in Broken Bay" (1788) provides an early and vivid example of a visual allegory of first contact. Amid a vast landscape of sky and sea, cliffs and gum trees, the painting shows two distinct cultures: "native" canoes and European sailing ships on the water; naked Indigenous peoples and uniformed European men on the shore presumably encountering each other for the first time. What is striking about this painting is that these two groups of people appear to be dancing together or to be engaged in animated cross-cultural communication: not fighting but dancing. It is no coincidence that this image was chosen by Inga Clendinnen for discussion in her aptly-titled historical reimagining, *Dancing with Strangers*, as an index of the potential of the colonial encounter for sympathetic understanding, "with friendship between unlike peoples a blossoming hope."[1] Clendinnen suggests that "the Australians [her preferred term for Indigenous Australians] and the British began their relationship by dancing together"[2] in what she surmises is the British style, "hand in hand, like children at a picnic."[3] Similarly, she suggests that the British "invoked the power of song" for its "pacifying power"[4] in their interactions with the Eora people of Botany Bay. Clendinnen's hope, expressed in the Introduction,

---

* This is a version of a paper first presented at "Disciplining the Margins or Relocating Postcolonial Studies," Stuttgart/Freudenstadt, 21–24 July 2011.

[1] Inga Clendinnen, *Dancing with Strangers* (Melbourne: Text, 2003): 26.

[2] Clendinnen, *Dancing with Strangers*, 5.

[3] *Dancing with Strangers*, 9.

[4] *Dancing with Strangers*, 10.

that, in retracing the potential problems as well as promises of such intercultural communication, her text is contributing to a discourse of wider social justice[5] clearly links it to those discourses of reconciliation that, as Gillian Whitlock suggests, "place emphasis on deeply personal and individual acts of recognition and contrition" in a "cross-cultural dialogue that is of national importance."[6] This desire expressed by Clendinnen is also a measure of the distance still to be travelled in achieving such understanding.

On receiving his second prestigious Miles Franklin Prize in 2011, for his novel *That Deadman Dance*, the Noongar[7] author Kim Scott[8] baulked at one of the judge's description of it as a "post-reconciliation" novel. Rather, he suggested, Australian Indigenous literature has worked through two stages and has arrived at a third: from Stolen Generations and Continuity narratives to what he identifies as describing his own text – a Recovery narrative, one that has to do with "reconciling ourselves to our shared history," something, he added, that is yet to happen.[9] The notion of a "recovery narrative" is one that has potentially different connotations for Indigenous and non-Indigenous writers and historians in Australia. The word 're-cover' has a number of nuances: it is to return to the past in order to rethink it; to reconnect with Indigenous history and language in a spirit of revival and regeneration; but also to participate in a process of national recovery that can be read (however optimistically) as a pathway to potential healing. For Kim Scott, recovery is closely tied to re-connecting with an endangered language like Noongar that forms an integral part of his novels and his own personal heritage and identity. And language is, of course, closely tied to stories, so that retelling and sharing stories that did not make it into the historical archives enables a participatory narrating and listening that amounts to a 'shared' national history. As

---

[5] See Clendinnen, *Dancing with Strangers*, 5.

[6] Gillian Whitlock, "Becoming Migloo," in *The Ideas Market: An Alternative Take on Australia's Intellectual Life*, ed. David Carter (Carlton, Victoria: Melbourne UP, 2004): 248.

[7] This is the spelling that Kim Scott uses in *That Deadman Dance* and in the articles cited in this essay. Other spellings may also be used.

[8] He won it in 2000 for his first novel, *Benang*, sharing it with Thea Astley for her novel *Drylands*. *That Deadman Dance* was also the 2011 Commonwealth Writers' Prize regional winner.

[9] Anon, "Kim Scott Wins Prestigious Miles Franklin," *Australian Broadcasting Corporation News* (22 June 2011), http://www.abc.net.au/news/2011-06-22/kim-scott-wins-prestigious-miles-franklin/2768022 (accessed 23 June 2011).

Rosanne Kennedy has suggested in her analysis of Kim Scott's first novel, *Benang*, it "contributes to a transnational project of commemorating Indigenous losses and celebrating survival while providing insight into the destruction of culture that complicates any act of return."[10] Its engagement with both memory and mourning, while linking it to other "reparative works"[11] in a spirit of recovering from the past, also draws attention to the ways in which the past has been covered up in the "great Australian silence."[12]

While Ross Poole has suggested that "the responsibility to come to terms with the Australian past is a morally inescapable component of what it is to be Australian,"[13] there is a current of theoretical and critical commentary in Australia that regards this tendency as offering only a temporary "postcolonial trauma-therapy" for white Australians that allows for the perpetuation of colonialist views and that commodifies victim narratives and traumatic historical events.[14] I have written elsewhere of what I termed the "sorry novel," a contemporary genre of Australian novels by non-Indigenous writers that seeks to participate in a process of national apology for the traumas visited upon Indigenous Australians as a result of the colonial history of settlement and dispossession.[15] Kate Grenville's novel *The Lieutenant* and Gail Jones's novel *Sorry* provide examples of a rewriting of the past in order to directly or obliquely comment on debates in the present about political responsibility, guilt and the need to say sorry. In admitting to and embracing the "sins of the nation,"[16] a dialogue of restitution is generated that encourages a sharing of what have previously been diametrically opposed historical perspectives.

---

[10] Rosanne Kennedy, "Indigenous Australian Arts of Return: Mediating Perverse Archives," in *Rites of Return: Diaspora, Poetics, and the Politics of Memory*, ed. Marianne Hirsch & Nancy K. Miller (New York: Columbia UP, 2011): 101.

[11] Kennedy, "Indigenous Australian Arts of Return," 102.

[12] This now-famous phrase was used by the Australian anthropologist W.E.H. Stanner in his 1968 Boyer Lectures, published as *After the Dreaming: Boyer Lectures* (Australian Broadcasting Commission, 1969): 18; 27.

[13] Ross Poole, *Nations and Identity* (London & New York: Routledge, 1999): 141.

[14] See Ghassan Hage, *Against Paranoid Nationalism: Searching for Hope in a Shrinking Society* (Sydney: Pluto, 2003): 96.

[15] See Sue Kossew, "Saying Sorry: The Politics of Apology and Reconciliation in Recent Australian Fiction," in *Locating Postcolonial Narrative Genres*, ed. Walter Goebel & Saskia Schabio (Abingdon & New York: Routledge, 2013): 171–83.

[16] Danielle Celermajer, *The Sins of the Nation and the Rituals of Apology* (New York: Cambridge UP, 2009).

However, as Peter Read has suggested in his memoir *Belonging*, such acknowledgement of "white guilt" often results in a moral dead end: "I belong but I do not belong [...] I understand our history but it brings me no relief."[17]

There are other ways of engaging with this history of complicity. Kay Schaffer, for example, in her analysis of Katrina Schlunke's *Bluff Rock* in this volume, describes its "ethical aesthetic" that enables an "immersive recovery of the presence of the past"[18] while it simultaneously probes the "wounded landscape" of a nation that "has taken no steps to resolve a past but merely denies it."[19] The text achieves this, Schaffer shows, through its deliberate use of "the ideas and practices that have caused damage in order to heal damage."[20] The idea of an obsessive return to the traumatic wound in order to facilitate healing has become a familiar trope in reconciliation discourse, originally employed by Archbishop Desmond Tutu in the context of the South African Truth and Reconciliation Commission. Recovery, then, is a national project, one for both Indigenous and non-Indigenous Australians.

It is striking that the metaphor of unravelling the past is one that, as Schaffer points out in the same essay, is used in a number of non-Indigenous texts of reconciliation. The metaphor draws attention to the fabricated materiality of the past, to its various threads and connections and also to the ease with which these can be torn apart. Kate Grenville, too, employs the metaphor of "picking up the stitches" when she suggests that, in returning to the difficult questions of the past, "the only thing you can do is go back to the point where it went wrong [...] and you unpick it, like knitting," to work out "why you dropped it, what your choices were, and then you go on."[21] While this belated return to the "dropped stitch" of the past may seem somewhat optimistic, the metaphor of knitting and materiality is a useful one for imaging the entangled histories of Indigenous and non-Indigenous Australians. An historical study entitled *Botany Bay: Where Histories Meet* by Maria Nugent exemplifies this approach, as the writer suggests that oral Indigenous stories are as important

---

[17] Peter Read, *Belonging: Australians, Place and Aboriginal Ownership* (Cambridge: Cambridge UP, 2000): 21.

[18] See Kay Schaffer, "Wounded Spaces/Geographies of Connectivity," in this volume, 164.

[19] Katrina Schlunke, "Home," *South Atlantic Quarterly* 108.1 (2009): 22.

[20] Schaffer, "Wounded Spaces/Geographies of Connectivity," 158.

[21] Grenville, quoted in Diane Stubbings, "Picking up the Dropped Stitches of our History," *Canberra Times* (24 September 2005): 12.

as European historical monuments, so that the history of place is not just about one or the other of these contested histories but about the "entanglement of, and interactions between, these various pasts and presences."[22] However, as Nugent is aware, this meeting place is always unstable, and, in the rush to reconciliation, often once again hides the domination of the colonizing culture even as it proclaims itself as equal rather than dominant. For Katrina Schlunke, too, an awareness of the troublingly contested investments of colonial and Indigenous history – made material when she encounters an Eora shield from the time of Cook's landing in the ironically named Enlightenment Gallery of the British Museum – produces a "fascination and fury."[23] She recognizes both her own inescapable complicity as a settler Australian and her own "melancholia" or mourning without end, the "inability to resolve [...] grief and ambivalence."[24] Recovering from the past is a tricky process for non-Indigenous Australians.

It is perhaps only in a space of sharing, where telling stories and listening to them coexist in a changed power relationship, that a process of recovery can begin to take place. In an interview with Anne Brewster, Kim Scott responds to a question about his thoughts on reconciliation by suggesting the need for continuing "'cross-cultural' exchange [...] for negotiation, and the reconciling to history – our different parts in it."[25] It is in this space of entangled strands of history and cross-cultural encounters that Kim Scott's novel *That Deadman Dance* inserts itself. It is inspired by the history of contact in the early 1800s (1826–44) between the Indigenous Noongar people of Western Australia and Europeans in the area of Scott's hometown, Albany, known as King George Town in the novel, which historians have termed "the friendly frontier." The whaling and sealing industry, which was indeed a global one involving French, British, Chinese, Spanish, German and many other nationalities, and one with vast global reach, forms the background for this encounter and is represented as providing the possibility of a brief period of mutuality and reciprocity between Indigenous and European cultures. From the be-

---

[22] Maria Nugent, *Botany Bay: Where Histories Meet* (Crows Nest, NSW: Allen & Unwin, 2005): 4–5.

[23] Schlunke, "Home," 21.

[24] "Home," 22.

[25] Anne Brewster, "Can you Anchor a Shimmering Nation State via Regional Indigenous Roots? Kim Scott talks to Anne Brewster about *That Deadman Dance*," *Cultural Studies Review* 18.1 (2012): 245.

ginning of the sealing industry in 1798 to the late 1860s which marked the trailing off of the whaling industry, Aboriginal men and women were deeply involved in this maritime trade, often travelling vast distances from their homelands. As Lynette Russell suggests in her book on this period of history entitled *Roving Mariners*,

> There can be no denying that for most Australian Aboriginal people the impact of colonialism was blunt – dispossession, dislocation, disease, murder and missionisation. Yet there is another, largely untold story of Australian colonial history. It's a story of enterprise and entrepreneurship; of Aboriginal Australian people seizing the opportunity to profit from participation in the colonial economy and pursuing life at sea as sealers and whalers.[26]

While, for some, this was not a free choice, particularly for Aboriginal women, involving kidnapping and forced labour, Russell, citing her own family history as inspiration for her study of this period, points out that "in many cases the people involved maintained and exercised a degree of personal autonomy and agency within their new circumstances."[27]

It is in this transnational threshold space that Scott's novel is set. Described in the cover-notes as a "story for our times," one that "shows that first contact did not have to lead to war," this novel revisits history in order to assert the agency of local Indigenous people in this early phase of the colonial process. It is a "story for our times" because it is a story that is relevant to contemporary discourses of nation and globalization: one that moves beyond the notion of colonizer/colonized to take into account the more complex relations of that particular time in history. It is important here to insert a caveat and to insist on the difference between Kim Scott's representation of this cultural exchange and the so-called alternative version of frontier history propagated by the white conservative historian Keith Windschuttle:

> a great many Aborigines willingly accommodated themselves to the transformation that occurred after 1788. Many Aborigines were drawn to, fascinated with and became part of the new society.[28]

---

[26] Lynette Russell, *Roving Mariners: Australian Aboriginal Whalers and Sealers in the Southern Oceans, 1790–1870* (Albany: State U of New York P, 2012): 19.

[27] Russell, *Roving Mariners*, 20.

[28] Keith Windschuttle, "The Construction of Aboriginal History: Fact or Fiction?," *University of New South Wales* (29 May 2003), http://www.sydneyline.com/UNSW%20debate.htm (accessed 1 June 2011).

As the Indigenous cultural critic Aileen Moreton–Robinson counters, this "white blindfold view"[29] of history assumes that Aboriginal people "did not mind the disease, dispossession and displacement that occurred because the benefits of civilization far outweighed any negative consequences"[30] and that they were compliant and passive in their own colonization. In Kim Scott's novel, on the contrary, the space of cultural contact and exchange is represented as a space of potential *agency* for Indigenous people and of *mutual* transformation rather than in the simpler binaristic terms of an exploitative encounter between colonizer and colonized with the weaker colonized culture being easily negated because of the perceived desirability of the colonizing and civilizing culture. Here, rather, Scott's return to this period of history is an assertion of the power, adaptability, and transformative survival of local Indigenous culture in the face of the colonizing process rather than only a mourning of its passing. It is, of course, both memory and mourning.

Scott's novel highlights a number of instances that he uses to represent what he calls "a certain power relationship between them [the British] and the Nyoongar people" and the Indigenous belief that "the spirit of place could never be conquered."[31] What Scott images in his novel is a number of examples of "Nyoongar heritage containing and encapsulating aspects of the colonial experience" that he terms "cultural sampling."[32] Where his version of the colonial encounter crucially differs from that suggested by Keith Windschuttle alluded to earlier is his more positive spin on the exchange: he talks about "the compassion, the curiosity, the inclusiveness, the risk-taking and the trust in one's own heritage"[33] that characterizes and accompanies the process of accommodating the colonizer that Windschuttle sees only as cultural weakness. On the contrary, for Scott, rather than demonstrating the susceptibility and vulnerability of Indigenous culture, this inclusiveness is indicative of the

---

[29] Aileen Moreton–Robinson, "Indigenous History Wars and the Virtue of the White Nation," in *The Ideas Market: An Alternative Take on Australia's Intellectual Life*, ed. David Carter (Melbourne: Melbourne UP, 2004): 233.

[30] Moreton–Robinson, "Indigenous History Wars and the Virtue of the White Nation," 223.

[31] Ramona Koval, "Kim Scott's Latest Novel," *The Book Show*, ABC Radio National (4 November 2010), http://www.abc.net.au/rn/bookshow/stories/2010 /3056907.htm (accessed 1 June 2011).

[32] Koval, "Kim Scott's Latest Novel."

[33] Koval, "Kim Scott's Latest Novel."

cultural strength and cultural confidence of the Noongar people of the time. For Scott, this is the mark of the postcolonial, or, in his words, "an admirable postcolonial position: a grafting of the newcomers' culture and being onto Indigenous roots."[34] Using the Noongar historical figure of Mokare as his example, Scott suggests that Mokare's appropriation of a British song, "Oh where have you been all the day, Billy boy, Billy boy" in a "witty, even 'postcolonial' way"[35] was an act of cultural exchange rather than one of colonization. Scott comments, on Mokare's use of this line to greet his brother, that he is "showing his knowledge of the immigrants' cultural forms" and melding this new insight with traditional Noongar knowledge where "people knew one another by their sound."[36] In the novel *That Deadman Dance*, Scott restages this incident using the character of Wunyeran, who sings out this line to Wooral as he comes in through the doorway of a hut. Unlike Clendinnen's colonial version of the shared dancing and singing referred to earlier, with the British teaching the Indigenous people their ways, Scott suggests a postcolonial exchange of cultural forms that was not just a one-way process but one that was mutually transformative in a process of "exchange and dialogue."[37] Indeed, the distinction between "newcomers' culture" and "Indigenous roots" with an emphasis on the latter draws attention to the grounded strength and deep confidence of Indigenous cultural practices.

It is striking that there are a number of recent texts that, like Scott's novel, return to this brief period of Australian colonial history based around the whaling and sealing industries in order to tell "another, largely untold story," and that similarly emphasize the mutuality of this cultural encounter. For Lynette Russell, herself an historian of Aboriginal heritage, revisiting this period of history enables her to explore the idea that

> [...] both native and newcomer are transformed by their encounter with the other [...] It was not only the Aboriginal men and women that were changed by coming into contact with European and other newcomers, but they exerted change on the newcomer men that lived and worked amongst them [...]. Within this new social form, people

---

[34] Kim Scott, "Covered Up with Sand," *Meanjin* 66.2 (2007): 122.

[35] Scott, "Covered Up with Sand," 122.

[36] Kim Scott, "Apologies, Agency and Resilience," in *Frontier Skirmishes: Literary and Cultural Debates in Australia after 1992*, ed. Russell West–Pavlov & Jennifer Wawrzinek (Heidelberg: Winter, 2012): 61.

[37] Scott, "Covered Up with Sand," 124.

were able to perform and maintain their traditions and at the same time adapt to changing circumstances. Far from assimilating into the dominant European culture, Aboriginal people and their cultural forms simply, to use Sleeper-Smith's term, hid "in plain view."[38]

Both Russell in her historical text and Kate Grenville in her novel *Sarah Thornhill* (2011), which is also set at this time, make reference to the historical figure of Tommy Chaseland (the character is named Jack Langland in Grenville's novel). Chaseland was a part-Aboriginal whaler and sealer who left the Hawkesbury region of New South Wales (the setting for Grenville's first novel of her historical trilogy, *The Secret River*) to live and sail in New Zealand, where he became a respected local figure, marrying a high-ranking Māori woman. For Russell, Chaseland represents a glimpse of how "Aboriginal people were able to participate in the new social structures which had emerged from the establishment of European colonies."[39] and how his entrepreneurial skills enabled him to set his own destiny. She interprets the way in which Tommy was revered for his achievements as an indication of his escaping from other ways of classifying him, such as colour or race,[40] so that his life "in many ways defied the very categories that were ascribed to him."[41] By exhibiting agency and autonomy, he was able to "move beyond the victimisation of colonialism."[42] For Grenville, by contrast, Jack, while mimicking the racist language of a white man and even being able to 'pass' for white ("you wouldn't pick him straight away" [as Indigenous]), is never able to escape the symbolic category of 'black man' assigned to him by the settlers, even though he is disconnected from his own people and views them as 'other': he "talked about *the* blacks the same way everyone did. They were strange to him the same way they were strange to us."[43] Thus, Jack's love affair with Sarah is doomed to failure, as each is trapped in an inescapable colonial identity.

The reconstructing and return to this period of history, then, by Indigenous and non-Indigenous writers in both fictional and historical genres seems to have been generated by a present-moment discourse of agency rather than

---

[38] Russell, *Roving Mariners*, 30.

[39] Lynette Russell, "'A New Holland Half-Caste': Sealer and Whaler Tommy Chaseland," *History Australia* 5.1 (2008): 8.1.

[40] See Russell, *Roving Mariners*, 88.

[41] *Roving Mariners*, 100.

[42] *Roving Mariners*, 101.

[43] Kate Grenville, *Sarah Thornhill* (Melbourne: Text, 2011): 34.

subjection; by a desire to escape from the unremittingly victim-oriented history of that encounter and to engage in an "ethics of recognition." This is not to diminish what Russell terms the "horror of much of that history" but, rather, to suggest that, within the colonial structure, there are, in Russell's words, "moments when we can observe the exertion of personal freedom and agency"[44] in the complex cultural relationships that emerged during this period in the history of the maritime industry.

The friendship that emerges in *That Deadman Dance* between Dr Cross, the original Governor, and Wunyeran, for example, is represented by Kim Scott as "a tribute to the good relationships at King George Town [the name the settlers gave to Albany]" (25).[45] These two men communicate by singing to one another. But, unlike Clendinnen's version of this encounter, where the British employ song as a way of pacifying the "natives," in Scott's account it is "Wunyeran [who] initiated it, Cross accepting. It was a way to communicate, to say more of oneself than was possible with their limited shared vocabulary" (129). Each of them is using song to express a cultural subjectivity. For Cross, this is nothing less than the beginning of a new language: "We are two men of such different backgrounds, thought Cross, and, attempting to fuse them, we are preparing for the birth of a new world" (129). This utopian sense of potential exchange and learning is at the heart of this early encounter, an exchange between equals rather than a mechanism of subjection.

As in Grenville's *The Lieutenant*, it is in language itself that this entanglement is recorded. Drawing on historical accounts (such as Daisy Bates's diaries), Scott has his main character, Bobby Wabalanginy, as a young boy showing great aptitude for learning to speak and write in English – indeed, being able to mimic the voice of Dr Cross, his first teacher, so that "it might almost have been Cross talking" (45). But it is Bobby's songs and dances that become the repository for the cross-cultural relationship symbolized also by his Noongar name (translated as 'all of us playing together'). Listening to his whale-hunt song, the whalers "smiled and laughed, recognising the mime and also, among the incomprehensible words and infectious melody, the names of their tools and hunting cries" (311). But by the end of the novel, Bobby's song and dance, with its offer to share the land with the settlers, does not win them over, ending instead with gunshots (395) and the loss of any further trust,

---

[44] See Russell, *Roving Mariners*, 26.

[45] All quotations from and comments on *That Deadman Dance* refer to Kim Scott, *That Deadman Dance* (Sydney: Picador, 2010).

symbolized by the title of the final chapter, "With friends like these we break apart." As the old man Bobby, now performing for tourists, tells them,

> We thought making friends was the best thing, and never knew that when we took your flour and sugar and tea and blankets that we'd lose everything of ours. We learned your words and songs and stories, and never knew you didn't want to hear ours. (106)

The potential for mutuality is lost, the cross-cultural encounter replaced by a one-sided colonial assertion of 'civilization' and 'progress'.

Similarly, the performing of the Dead Man Dance begins with sharing and ends in tragedy. The dance is based on the local Noongars' interpretation of the British soldiers' military drill: the Noongars' own cultural practices lead them to believe that these strangers, with their stiff marching steps, are sharing with them one of their own European culture's dances. Bobby dances this Dead Man Dance as "a lively dance for people to do together [...] a dance from way past the ocean's horizon, and those people give it to our old people" (67). By the end of the novel, though, the Noongar people have come to understand the "fierce, strategic intention" of the Dance by recognizing it for what it is: not a gift to signify cultural exchange but a menacing and predictive military drill. The Noongars have added to it new dances with movements that now represent the consequences of first contact: "crowds of coughing bodies, hands brushing clouds of flies from around mouths, barking rifles and falling bodies and stiff limbs" (376). Thus, the history of colonial contact is recorded through the dance, including the history of apparent friendship and ultimate betrayal.

This pattern of friendship and betrayal is repeated throughout the novel. The mutual respect and, indeed, love shown between Dr Cross, the original Governor, and Wunyeran, Bobby's uncle, is epitomized not only in the "gladbag bastard language the two of them used together" (120) but also in Cross's order that he be buried in the same grave as his great friend Wunyeran. At the end of the novel, this symbolic act of brotherhood is undone when Cross's body is moved to a grave in the new settlement's graveyard (in a move that, the settlers and the Governor agree, is "more appropriate to Cross's important role in the history of King George Town," 354), while Wunyeran's bones, dug up in the process, are left lying around for the local animals to gnaw on. This disrespect is represented as a measure of the miscarriage of the "birth of the new world" (129) that Cross had imagined would arise from this first contact among what he considered equals. Equally significantly, this "terrible change" (356) is registered at the level of language, too: "No one said Noongar no more; it was all blackfellas and whitefellas" (353). As he suggests in his author's note, Kim Scott sees the initial trust and respect afforded to the British as a measure of the strength of Noongar culture: "Believing themselves manifestations of a spirit of place impossible to conquer, they appreciated reciprocity and the nuances of cross-cultural exchange" (398). This belief, of course, tragically only made it easier to betray them, as the novel inevitably shows.

It is significant that, despite this, Kim Scott has suggested that "the story of our history is not over yet: I like to go back to early models and build on them rather than solely talk about damage done in our shared history."[46] In the same interview, he describes his writing as "a means to have a more inclusive and compassionate way of living in current society."[47] These are two important insights: first, he posits the notion of a history that is not simply about traumatic encounters of "damage done" but that could be described as a process of "sharing histories": that is, as an "exchange of knowledge between differently situated or positioned people – a place where they both tell their histories and listen to others."[48] Secondly, Scott emphasizes the conjunction of past and present, an aspect of Indigenous storytelling about the past that highlights the ongoing presence of the past. It is into this space of sharing that Australians are perhaps moving, as cultural forms work through the process of guilt and apology to, in more hopeful mode, recovery. But, as Scott continues to stress, there is still much cross-cultural work to be done – in his words quoted earlier, "particularly reconciling ourselves to our shared history – that is yet to happen."[49] Despite this tentativeness, I am particularly struck by the word "our." It expresses the potential hope for a shared postcolonial future. And, as Scott acknowledges, too, this sharing has the potential to lead to empowerment.[50] The doubleness of this mourning and memory is encapsulated in the phrase used on the novel's first page – "Roze a wail…" (1). The intersection of orality and writing in the homophonic "wail" that describes both the totemic whale and the sound of mourning in one word is emblematic of

---

[46] Koval, "Kim Scott's Latest Novel."

[47] "Kim Scott's Latest Novel."

[48] Bain Attwood, *Telling the Truth about Aboriginal History* (Crows Nest, NSW: Allen & Unwin, 2005): 190.

[49] Anon, "Kim Scott Wins Prestigious Miles Franklin."

[50] See "Kim Scott's Latest Novel."

Scott's project of creating through his novel a meeting-place for his readers, "an intimate butting up of difference,"[51] thereby "making space [...] for other ways of thinking."[52] But Bobby's writing of the words on "a thin piece of slate [...] on stone" with "damp chalk, brittle as weak bone" (1) exemplifies the fragility of his "moving between languages" even as it celebrates his achievement.

WORKS CITED

Anon. "Kim Scott Wins Prestigious Miles Franklin," *Australian Broadcasting Corporation News* (22 June 2011), http://www.abc.net.au/news/2011-06-22/kim-scott-wins-prestigious-miles-franklin/2768022 (accessed 23 June 2011).

Attwood, Bain. *Telling the Truth about Aboriginal History* (Crows Nest, NSW: Allen & Unwin, 2005).

Brewster, Anne. "Can you Anchor a Shimmering Nation State via Regional Indigenous Roots? Kim Scott talks to Anne Brewster about *That Deadman Dance*," *Cultural Studies Review* 18.1 (2012): 228–46.

Celermajer, Danielle. *The Sins of the Nation and the Rituals of Apology* (New York: Cambridge UP, 2009).

Clendinnen, Inga. *Dancing with Strangers* (Melbourne: Text, 2003).

Grenville, Kate. *Sarah Thornhill* (Melbourne: Text, 2011).

Hage, Ghassan. *Against Paranoid Nationalism: Searching for Hope in a Shrinking Society* (Sydney: Pluto, 2003).

Hutchison, Geoff. "Who are you? Kim Scott," *ABC Perth Radio podcast* (1 June 2011), www.abc.net.au/local/audio/2011/06/01/3232852.htm (accessed 22 June 2011).

Kennedy, Rosanne. "Indigenous Australian Arts of Return: Mediating Perverse Archives," in *Rites of Return: Diaspora, Poetics, and the Politics of Memory*, ed. Marianne Hirsch & Nancy K. Miller (New York: Columbia UP, 2011): 88–106.

Kossew, Sue. "Saying Sorry: The Politics of Apology and Reconciliation in Recent Australian Fiction," in *Locating Postcolonial Narrative Genres*, ed. Walter Goebel & Saskia Schabio (Abingdon & New York: Routledge, 2013): 171–83.

Koval, Ramona. "Kim Scott's Latest Novel," *The Book Show, ABC Radio National* (4 November 2010), http://www.abc.net.au/rn/bookshow/stories/2010/3056907.htm (accessed 1 June 2011).

---

[51] Brewster, "Can you Anchor a Shimmering Nation State via Regional Indigenous Roots?," 237.

[52] Scott, "Covered Up with Sand," 123.

Moreton–Robinson, Aileen. "I Still Call Australia Home: Place and Belonging in a White Postcolonising Society," in *Uprootings/Regroundings: Questions of Home and Migration,* ed. Sarah Ahmed, Claudia Castaneda, Anne–Marie Fortier & Mimi Sheller (London: Berg, 2003): 23–40.

——. "Indigenous History Wars and the Virtue of the White Nation," in *The Ideas Market: An Alternative Take on Australia's Intellectual Life*, ed. David Carter (Melbourne: Melbourne UP, 2004): 219–35.

Nugent, Maria. *Botany Bay: Where Histories Meet* (Crows Nest, NSW: Allen & Unwin, 2005).

Poole, Ross. *Nations and Identity* (London & New York: Routledge, 1999).

Read, Peter. *Belonging: Australians, Place and Aboriginal Ownership* (Cambridge: Cambridge UP, 2000).

Russell, Lynette. "'A New Holland Half-Caste': Sealer and Whaler Tommy Chaseland," *History Australia* 5.1 (2008): 8.1–8.15.

——. *Roving Mariners: Australian Aboriginal Whalers and Sealers in the Southern Oceans, 1790–1870* (Albany: State U of New York P, 2012).

Schlunke, Katrina. "Home," *South Atlantic Quarterly* 108.1 (2009): 1–26.

Scott, Kim. "Apologies, Agency and Resilience," in *Frontier Skirmishes: Literary and Cultural Debates in Australia after 1992,* ed. Russell West-Pavlov & Jennifer Wawrzinek (Heidelberg: Winter, 2012): 57–68.

——. "Covered Up with Sand," *Meanjin* 66.2 (2007): 120–24.

——. *That Deadman Dance* (Sydney: Picador, 2010).

Stanner, William Edward Hanley. *After the Dreaming: Boyer Lectures* (Australian Broadcasting Commission, 1969).

Stubbings, Diane. "Picking up the Dropped Stitches of our History," *Canberra Times* (24 September 2005): 12–13.

Whitlock, Gillian. "Becoming Migloo," in *The Ideas Market: An Alternative Take on Australia's Intellectual Life,* ed. David Carter (Carlton, Victoria: Melbourne UP, 2004): 236–57.

Windschuttle, Keith. "The Construction of Aboriginal History: Fact or Fiction?," *University of New South Wales* (29 May 2003), http://www.sydneyline.com/UNSW%20debate.htm (accessed 23 June 2011).

Reading Transformations ⌘

The Geopolitical Underground

Alexis Wright's *Carpentaria*, Mining, and the Sacred

PHILIP MEAD

I N A 2006 ARTICLE in the *Australian* which appeared under one of Tracey Moffatt's images from her 1998 photographic exhibition, "Up in the Sky," Marcia Langton began by recalling two events of that year that had rekindled her interest in "the complicated relationship, ranging from the brutally and pragmatically financial to the highly emotional that Australians have had with the mining industry":

> And they framed the question of how we will understand the new boom and the way mining is still changing Australia.
>
> In April, the media broadcast every detail of the Beaconsfield mine tragedy in Tasmania, from the impact of the death of Larry Knight on the community to the emotion and heroism of the tense and laboriously slow 14-day rescue of Todd Russell and Brant Webb. As if I had read about them in a novel, I now have an odd imaginary relationship with a small Tasmanian mining town and the two fortunate men rescued from its mine.
>
> The previous month [March] I was struck by the death of artist and sculptor Pro Hart. A miner in his youth, Hart lived most of his life in the mining city of Broken Hill in far western NSW, where he painted the people and streetscapes, the landscapes and the mines. Long ignored by urban art industry elites as merely a naïve artist, Hart struck a chord with ordinary Australians, especially the mining folk who were his subjects. After his death, the print and broadcast media provided tributes to his life that repeatedly reminded us of the irony that

the National Gallery of Australia does not own a single work by Australia's most popular artist.[1]

Langton recalls Moffatt's images of the "obliquely referenced" Broken Hill landscapes – "no romance under the big western skies [...] only discontented souls, treeless gullies, the highway, storm drains and corrugated-iron shacks" – in connection with her experience of the mediatized Beaconsfield drama and the news of Pro Hart's death. Her article speculates on the aesthetic and social contradictions she perceives in these two events and that have their resonances in her own history of growing up as an Aboriginal person in southern Queensland, and in her knowledge of the history of mining in Australia. The tensions run deep. Moffatt's photographs, "acute [studies] of the edges of an imagined mining landscape and society," were in fact commissioned by New York's Dia Art Foundation and therefore circulate within a globalized contemporary art world, which includes the internationally oriented Roslyn Oxley9 gallery in Sydney, where the series was first exhibited. The "Up in the Sky" series is highly allusive and technically innovative photographic work, including the image that heads the *Australian* article of a "beefed-up Amazonian chick swinging a mallet on top of a burnt-out car." While overall the impact of Moffatt's series for Langton is "apocalyptic and banal," she also recognizes the "mise en scène" as "undeniably Australian, [...] the desiccated inland, hinting at history and the new global citizens" of a resource-industries-driven economy. All the same, as Langton feels, Moffatt's work is as distant as possible on the spectrum of Australian cultural expression from the work of the "non-urban and naïve" Pro Hart, however much they both might reference the landscape of Broken Hill. Back in 1989, Langton had played a leading role in Moffatt's "rural tragedy" *Night Cries*, her short film that, like "Up in the Sky," is in dialogue with international media history and avant-garde image-making.[2] So Langton clearly feels implicated in the "urban art industry elites" that have spurned Pro Hart just as she feels that the experience of the Beaconsfield miners, as miners, is "alien."

---

[1] Marcia Langton, "Intimate Places and Terrifying Spaces," *The Australian* (17 September, 2006): 1, http://www.theaustralian.com.au/arts/intimate-places-and-terrifying-spaces/story-e6frg8px-1111112227516 (accessed 20 March 2012).

[2] See Meaghan Morris, "Beyond Assimilation: Aboriginality, Media History and Public Memory," in *Identity Anecdotes: Translation and Media Culture* (Thousand Oaks CA & London: Sage, 2006): 109–10.

Motivated by such contemporary contradictions, "dualities" she calls them, Langton ranges widely across Australian literature, historiography, film, and art – from Fred Williams's Conzinc Riotinto commissions (the Pilbara and western Cape York landscapes), to Geoffrey Blainey's history of the gold rushes (and S.T. Gill's visual chronicle of that colonial history), little-known literary works like Walter Mills Bradshaw's poem about the 1901 South Mine Tragedy in Broken Hill, to Randolph Stow's novel of the mining ghost-town Tourmaline, Colin Thiele's *The Fire in the Stone* (about opal mining), the Kimberley artists Lena Nyadbi and Paddy Bedford's prints (of the Argyle mine country) at the Musée de Quai Branly in Paris (opened in 2006), Vance Palmer and Katherine Susannah Prichard's anthropocene sagas, the Golconda and goldfields trilogies.[3] It is the contradictory and heterogeneous status of these cultural expressions that intrigues Langton:

> even though the wealth generated by mining, and the death too often involved in earning it, has always happened a long way from most Australians, a rich vein of our artistic and literary heritage consists of a search for beauty and meaning amid the ruins of the industry. And a great deal of it eschews academicism in favour of the Australian need for authenticity.[4]

Mining may provide the economic subsidization of landscape art (Indigenous and non-Indigenous), the subject of popular, frontier fiction, but never the serious attention of a cosmopolitan culture.

Langton is also well aware of mining's role in the despoliation of Aboriginal land and society, having spent much of her childhood, as she says, "in a town like Tourmaline, where I learned the Australian history I later unlearned at university." She recalls, at one point in her article, the first sentence of Stow's novel *Tourmaline* with its reference to a "bitter heritage." The specific resonance Stow's novel obviously has for her is reflected in her perspective on settlement history:

> Mostly small outback towns are Aboriginal communities, left behind as generation after generation from the old white families moved to the

---

[3] The problematic role of Nyadbi and Bedford's paintings in the postcolonizing of the Paris museological landscape is told in the "Glass, Gardens and Aborigines" chapter of Sally Price's *Paris Primitive: Jacques Chirac's Museum on the Quai Branly* (Chicago: U of Chicago P, 2006): 129–39.

[4] Marcia Langton, "Intimate Places and Terrifying Spaces."

cities. The demographic of the remote inland is becoming a majority Aboriginal world broken up by islands of mine workers and few service towns.[5]

As well as this archaeological evidence of the lust for mineral wealth, Langton recognizes the profound social and economic changes that contemporary mining is having on Australian life and landscape,

> as the hyper-technological world of modern mining sweeps aside the world portrayed by [Pro] Hart, [Russell] Drysdale, [Janette Turner] Hospital, Nyadbi, Bedford and so many other brighter or dimmer luminaries in our cultural heritage.
>
> Whereas the front bar of the pub in these towns was once full of droll, tough, almost feral white men in battered rabbit-felt hats, there are now mostly Aboriginal people. The white men have retreated to their clubs and bars, many located on mine sites, which use membership regulations to exclude locals. There are no tick-ridden, comatose dogs lying at the door of these establishments. These men are richer than their fathers. They work generous two-weeks-on, two-weeks-off shifts. They might have mining engineering degrees or own subcontracting companies that bid for multimillion-dollar earthmoving contracts.
>
> Slowly, some few thousand Aboriginal people have entered these ranks and are qualified, well paid and in high demand. There are more than 100 modern impact-benefit agreements negotiated by mining companies and Aboriginal groups. The old certainties of the anti-mining protest movements no longer exist.
>
> There is a significant literature from the social and political sciences on these matters, and yet the cultural workers in literature, art and film have barely kept up with them. The environmental movement has a great deal to do with them turning their backs on these traditions. And so too does the power of Aboriginal art. It dominates all else that purports to speak for the heart of our land. The modernist period into which Hart, Drysdale and Williams were born is a fading memory and rapidly becoming an interesting historical period only.[6]

But Langton is also deeply knowledgeable about the resource economy in relation to the Aboriginal population, and its communities and estates. Her study with Odette Mazel explores the lack of "socio-economic improvement"

---

[5] Marcia Langton, "Intimate Places and Terrifying Spaces."
[6] Langton, "Intimate Places and Terrifying Spaces."

that the mining boom, including Indigenous Land Use Agreements, has meant for Aboriginal communities.[7] In the heart of the country, then, there coexist the ruins of a settler-development history and its heterogeneous aesthetic mode, and a contemporary, economic, and cultural reality of incommensurate ideologies and knowledges. The participant anthropology of Marcia Langton's writing on Aboriginal knowledge and belief systems and the social and spiritual relations of Aboriginal people to country and landscape exists alongside (for example) the anthropologist David Trigger's studies of narratives of development and progress as they constitute the life-worlds of mining engineers:

> those who drive the resource development industries are understood as pursuing the tasks of mineral exploration and development with a surety about its cultural and moral significance, as well as its economic importance. Their convictions in this respect constitute a dimension of ideology situated at the centre of Australian culture.[8]

As it happens, later in 2006 Alexis Wright's *Carpentaria* was published, and had she been able to read it for her article, Langton would instantly have recognized the important role that mining plays in the novel, just as it does in the history and contemporary life of the Gulf country where the novel is set. Indeed, Wright's novel provides a further complex literary representation of the historical and social contradictions Langton observes, and which Trigger studies, and one with just as deep a personal connection to mining and its role in Aboriginal Australia's past and present.[9]

---

[7] Marcia Langton & Odette Mazel, "Poverty in the Midst of Plenty: Aboriginal People, the 'Resource Curse' and Australia's Mining Boom," *Journal of Energy and Natural Resources Law* 26.1 (2008): 31–70.

[8] David Trigger, "Mining, Landscape and the Culture of Development Ideology in Australia," *Cultural Geographies* 4 (1997): 163. Trigger interviews people involved in mining exploration and the discovery of ore-bodies to analyse the specific human embodiment of "cultural assumptions underlying the pro-development ideology" (162).

[9] There is another historical conjunction here, not strictly relevant to this article, but which is certainly relevant to any understanding of Wright's work more generally. The day of the announcement that *Carpentaria* had won the Miles Franklin Award (21 June 2007), Australia's most prestigious literary prize, was also the day that the Howard government announced its 'Northern Territory Emergency Response', commonly known as the NT Intervention; see Alexis Wright, "Open Letter: Talking about an Indigenous tomorrow," *Unleashed* (30 March 2011), http://www.abc.net.au/unleashed/45734.html (accessed 20 March 2012).

Carpentaria begins with a contrapuntal evocation of two incommensurable myth systems: the Christian eschatology and the Aboriginal dreaming of the Gulf country. The conjunction of these cultural master-narratives in volatile historical events and the human life-worlds of settlement generate the trajectory of the novel in a kind of narrative fission. This opening chapter is titled "From Time Immemorial," reminiscent of the biblical 'in the beginning' but subversive as well, in its suggestion of a cosmography beyond mythographic narrative enclosure. And the specific narrative modes and lexicons already signal what will be the novel's thematic outworkings. The present continuous of the short opening section seems deliberately to recall the mission setting of Wright's earlier novel *Plains of Promise* (1997) and its disembodied voice of 'national' denial: *"But we know your story already."*[10] There is a similar tone in the ghostly voice of Pilot, the murdered Chinese in *Plains of Promise*: *"Draw no simple conclusion my friend. All are implicated."*[11] In this first sentence of *Carpentaria*, though, a "nation chants" – like menacing children in the schoolyard? Like politicians coached to stay on message? At any rate, in a collective, bullying act of illocutionary dismissiveness. We know your story from the time of sovereignty (as the lawyers say); we know your story, even if you don't. When it comes to narrating the nation, we've moved on, further along the trajectory of postmodernity, from where animistic narratives of creation have only a quaint, anthropological interest, and narratives of dispossession and injustice are discounted as "black arm-band" history. Australians don't like "clinging to the past."[12] What is also happening in this brief prologue – a kind of prose poem – is that the colonizing language of Christian evangelism is being turned back on itself, folding in the history of missionizing violence, and adding a note of post-nuclear apocalypse:

> Church bells calling the faithful to the tabernacle where the gates of Heaven will open, but not for the wicked. Calling innocent little black girls from a distant community where the white dove bearing an olive branch never lands. Little girls who come back home after church on

---

[10] Alexis Wright, *Carpentaria* (Artarmon: Giramonda, 2006): 1. Further page references are in the main text.

[11] Alexis Wright, *Plains of Promise* (St Lucia: U of Queensland P, 1997): 140 (italics in the original).

[12] Meaghan Morris, "Afterthoughts on 'Australianism'," in *Identity Anecdotes: Translation and Media Culture* (Thousand Oaks CA & London: Sage, 2006): 34.

Sunday, who look around themselves at the human fallout and announce matter-of-factly *Armageddon begins here*. (1)

This is simultaneously the historical time of colonial violence and national biopolitics – the girls have been removed from their distant families and communities by assimilationist policy. It is also the time immemorial of Christian mythogenesis, as well as the imaginary time of debased and abused spiritual progress, from "witchdoctors to modernity,' to use the bookend terms of Vic Akehurst, the missionary-descendant historian of Doomadgee Mission.[13]

The 'last things' of the Christian mythos, in one of its developed iterations, include both an alpha and an omega, genesis and the end of the world, an Eden and an Armageddon, the plain below Mount Carmel where the human population is herded while the war in heaven takes place. There will be a final day, when human history is wound up and cosmic power finalized. At the time of Parousia, according to the Book of Revelations, the New Jerusalem will descend from heaven, at its centre the tabernacle of the new heaven and new earth. There is always the ethnographic question of how much weight, how much belief, a text like the Revelation of John on Patmos might have carried with a missionized community, how effectively it was deployed in the process of colonization. Revelations is a non-canonical narrative in Calvin's gospel, as it happens, so there is an uncertainty there at the heart of fundamentalist Christian discourse. And its deployment would have had to be adapted to all kinds of pre-existing narrative heritages. In whatever kriolized form, the story has been transmitted, the concept of apocalypse has been introduced in the desire for conversion, to be used for ethnocentric, coercive purposes, for quietening down the Aboriginal people, after the wild time.[14]

The opening chapter then switches dimensions from this selective fragment of mission bible story and settlement fallout to a satellite view of the Indigenous creation and its sacred geography. This "creative drama," as Marcia Langton refers to it, establishes "the appearance and patterns of life experienced today" and features "typically the bird's-eye view and the abbreviated

---

[13] Vic Akehurst, *A Light in the Darkness: An Anecdotal History of Doomadgee Mission; Fifty-Three Years of Faithful, Fearless Endeavour by Assembly Missionaries* (Petaling Jaya, Malaysia: Market Intelligence, 1993).

[14] See David Trigger, *White Fella Comin': Aboriginal responses to colonialism in northern Australia* (Cambridge: Cambridge U P, 1992): 18. For an account of the 'pastoral' colonization of the Gulf country, see Tony Roberts, *Frontier Justice: A History of the Gulf Country to 1900* (St Lucia: U of Queensland P, 2005).

cartographic representation of landscapes whose places and species are familiar and familial."[15] The paratactical effects of these two beginnings is a rhetorical strategy to draw attention to the status of origins, both cultural and narrative. The attenuated story of the end of the world is followed by the alternative Aboriginal cosmography. The linearity of all narrative that is at work here is inflected in ways that are no doubt political. In the novel's first beginning, the bitter, missionizing application of the Christian Armageddon precedes the dreaming, giving it inevitably a kind of primacy, it has an historical reality after all. But it will be overwhelmed by the previously unheard narratives of Aboriginal-Carpentarian history, and the traditionally sacred and secular, that the novel dramatizes. The devastation of Aboriginal landscapes and life-worlds is packed into the volatile narrative singularity of Christian colonization, a story with a beginning and, more significantly for the Aboriginal people of Carpentaria, an ending. But the limitations of the Christian story, of all such narratives with no relation to familial and ancestral places, will be repeatedly limited and overlaid by the narrative density and complexity of *Carpentaria*'s Aboriginal storytelling.

The rest of this first chapter extends the temporal narrative down to the present, and at the same time thickens and re-layers the radical polarity that is inaugurated on the first page, including generational memory-loss. One of the first narrative moves Wright makes in this section is to subsume geological time under Aboriginal creation:

> Looking down at the serpent's wet body, glistening from the ancient sunlight, long before man was a creature who could contemplate the next moment in time. It came down those billions of years ago, to crawl on its heavy belly, all around the wet clay soils in the Gulf of Carpentaria. (1)

The 'ancestral serpent' creates this landscape of many rivers and vast plains of the Gulf country, the plains of promise as John Lort Stokes named them in 1841 in an act of christianizing appropriation of the Gulf homelands, part of the toponymy of *terra nullius*.[16] But geological time and space are still bound up with this version of the creation:

---

[15] Marcia Langton, "Sacred Geography," in *Aboriginal Religions in Australia: An Anthology of Recent Writings*, ed. Max Charlesworth, Françoise Dussart & Howard Morphy (Aldershot: Ashgate, 2005): 131.

[16] Nicholas Jose, *Black Sheep: Journey to Borroloola* (South Yarra: Hardie Grant, 2002): 208. Marcia Langton, "Earth, Wind, Fire and Water: the Social and Spiritual

⌘   *The Geopolitical Underground*   193

>   This is where the giant serpent continues to live deep down under the
>   ground in a vast network of limestone aquifers. They say its being is
>   porous; it permeates everything. It is all around in the atmosphere and
>   is attached to the lives of the river people like skin. (2)

There follow two paragraphs about how learning about country is learning about the omnipresence of the ancestral, creating serpent: its breathing rhythms in tides and floods, its breath in winds, its presence in human events and locales, including tragic ones (the accidental hanging of "Cry-baby Sally" by "up-to-no-good" "mission-bred kids" (2), its stretch from Boodjamulla (Lawn Hill) Gorge, a significant place for Alexis Wright's Waanyi heritage, across the tidal planes to Mornington Island. Whereas Christian mythography was coeval with human creation (within the space of five days at least) and aerial in its epic settings, the Aboriginal myth system is oppositely and differently structured: the serpent descended from the skies in time immemorial, aeons before humans, but his life is eternal and underground (and undersea). The Aboriginal belief and knowledge systems are subterranean in all their referentiality:

>   The inside knowledge about this river and coastal region is the Aboriginal Law handed down through the ages since time began. Otherwise, how would one know where to look for the hidden underwater courses in the vast flooding mud plains, full of serpents and fish in the monsoon season? (3)

Aboriginal knowledge is also particular to the serpent dreaming:

>   It is about there being no difference between you and the movement of water as it seasonally shifts its tracks according to its own mood. A river that spurns human endeavour in one dramatic gesture, jilting a lover who has never really been known, as it did to the frontier town built on its banks in the heyday of colonial vigour. A town [Desperance] intended to serve as a port for the shipping trade for the hinterland of Northern Australia. (3)

Thus, the narrative modulates from the cosmographic opening into the time of settlement and the geography of the recent past. Aboriginal worlds are defined by an animism that frequently moves groundward – the reader imagines trans-

---

Construction of Water in Aboriginal Societies," in *The Social Archaeology of Australian Indigenous Societies*, ed. Bruno David, Bryce Baker & Ian J. McNiven (Canberra: Aboriginal Studies Press, 2006): 139.

ition wipes moving from the sky down into underground levels and caverns. Although the novel will also have its moments of near-apocalyptic conjunctions of earth and sky, deep weather follows deep country.[17]

This may sound like too much interpretative pressure to put on the opening of the novel, but these opposing cosmo-spatialities and their generic hybridity emblematize the novel's unfolding drama of the clash of ideologies of resource extraction (mining) and the sacredness of burial, both subterranean and at sea. As this first chapter gradates into postcolonial and modern times, the narrative increasingly shifts between two domains: "one temporal, epic and European, the other magical, poetic and linked to Aboriginal lore."[18] This will be the predominant narrative mode of the rest of the novel, both more historically concrete and less realist. This opening section foreshadows the geopolitics of the underground that the novel narrativizes, including the contest of discourses about country. In relation to this thematic, the aspect of the novel I would like to focus on is where the disjunction of industrial colonization and Aboriginal spirituality is most starkly and violently enacted, in the adjoining chapters, 11 and 12, "The mine" and "About sending letters."

But at this point I think it is important to add a perspective on Wright as author, and on *Carpentaria*, that is contextual rather than textual-analytical alone. It's important because understanding the authorial experience out of which the novel emerges is crucial to understanding its project as a work of fiction. The matrix of Aboriginal experience and culture out of which *Carpentaria* evolves is not just a 'context', it is crucial to understanding both the novel's structure and meaning and the way these are simultaneously high-postmodernist, Indigenized, and socially, locally grounded.

Alexis Wright has been involved in the political-activist and social-policy work of Aboriginal self-determination and land rights since the mid-1970s, working "extensively in government departments and Aboriginal agencies across four states and territories as a professional manager, educator, researcher and writer."[19] In 1978 she worked for the Queensland Aboriginal Legal Service as a representative of the Lardil people on Mornington Island, in the political fallout from the winding-up of the Uniting Church mission.

---

[17] The cyclone is at least as important an aspect of the story of *Carpentaria* as the mine; for another perspective on Alexis Wright's understanding of weather and Aboriginal knowledge, see "Deep Weather," *Meanjin* 70.2 (Winter 2011): 70–82.

[18] Jose, *Black Sheep*, 203.

[19] Alexis Wright, *Grog War* (Broome, WA: Magabala, 1997): half-title page.

This was about self-determination in the face of attempts by the then Bjelke–Petersen Queensland government to control the island. In 1984–85 she was involved in the McLelland Royal Commission on Maralinga Nuclear Tests, in the 1985 Nicholson River Land Claim (aka the Waanji/Garawa claim), and as a coordinator in 1993 of the Northern Territory Aboriginal Constitutional Convention. In 1996 she was commissioned by the Warramungu people of Tennant Creek to produce a study of the effect of alcohol on their community, published as *Grog War* in 1997. At the time she was writing *Grog War* she was community writer-in-residence for the Central Land Council, in Alice Springs. In 1997 Wright also coordinated the Kalkaringi Convention, a response to a convention for Northern Territory statehood held in Darwin earlier that year and that refused to significantly acknowledge Aboriginal rights of self-determination and self-government. Kalkaringi is next to the Aboriginal community at Daguragu, where "Vincent Lingiari led his people, the Gurindji, when they walked off Wave Hill cattle station in 1966 because of the way they were being treated by the owners of the property, the British pastoral company, Vesteys."[20] In 1998 Wright also edited *Take Power: Like this Old Man Here: An Anthology of Writings Celebrating Twenty Years of Land Rights in Central Australia, 1977–1997*, an historical account of the first twenty years of the Land Rights movement in Central Australia, drawing on archival research and interviews with Aboriginal people involved in the movement, as well as lawyers and anthropologists.

But in the 1990s Wright's activism took a turn from political organizational involvement in Aboriginal causes to fiction writing. In a 2001 talk, "The Politics of Writing," Wright explains:

> By the time I had come to making the decision to write a novel in the 1990s, I guess it was at a time of deep inner personal crisis I was experiencing about everything I had ever believed in about our rights as people. I was questioning the failures of our hopes for just about everything we fought for. Every idea and goal was overtaken by others. Governments found new ways of making our lives harder. We did not seem to gel as a political movement at either the national, state or regional level. As individuals, as communities, as peoples with Indigenous rights, everything we did to accomplish anything seem to

---

[20] Alexis Wright, "Breaking Taboos: Alexis Wright at the Tasmanian Readers' and Writers' Festival, September 1998," *Australian Humanities Review* (1998), http://www.australianhumanitiesreview.org/archive/Issue-September-1998/wright.html (accessed 20 March 2012).

> be a meaningless exercise because the force of ingrained racism stood against us.
>
> I wrote *Plains of Promise* to deal with my inner crisis and loneliness of the soul. [...] I felt literature, the work of fiction, was the best way of presenting a truth – not the real truth, but more of a truth than non-fiction, which is not really the truth either.[21]

While creative storytelling offered Wright a way through this personal crisis in Indigenous and political selfhood, it's not as though narrative fiction presented an unproblematic alternative to political work, with all its formal challenges and its questions of existential origins and social utility. Wright has written, for example, about her worries concerning *Carpentaria*'s non-standard narrative style:

> I also knew that I would pay a price for my decision to write a novel as though some old Aboriginal person was telling the story. I think what I feared most was that this kind of voice and style of telling would be flatly rejected in Australia. Every day I was writing the novel, I would begin the day by arguing with myself about how a manuscript written in this voice was taking a big risk.
>
> I knew that by using a story-telling narrative voice in a language that was as much my own as it is of Aboriginal people in the Gulf, I was setting myself up for failure.[22]

Part of the formal crisis here has to do with the extremity of the social history Wright wants to encompass, the ground zero of human experience the novel narrates, the devastation of culture and life-worlds represented by the violence and dispossession of colonization and the poverty and despair that came in its wake, right down to the present. There is an influential connection here to global postmodern fiction (Eduardo Galleano, Elie Wiesel, Keri Hulme, Carlos Fuentes, Gabriel García Márquez, Toni Morrison, Amos Oz), all enabling writers for Wright. In her essay "Breaking Taboos," Wright categorized

---

[21] Alexis Wright, "Politics of Writing," *Southerly* 62.2 (Summer 2002): 10–20. Wright's role in Aboriginal political movements was in fact more 'writerly' perhaps than this talk suggests: *Grog War*, for example, "contains two chapters of fiction because I was asked not to identify members of the community who have suffered from the consequences of alcohol and the state of cross-cultural relationships in that town" ("Breaking Taboos") and while she was working for the Central Aboriginal Land Council she published short stories and creative essays.

[22] Alexis Wright, "Gulf Music," *Australian* (9 June 2007): http://www.theaustralian.news.com.au/story/0,20867,21853571-5001986,00.html (accessed 20 March 2012).

Carpentaria, for example, via Salman Rushdie's discussion of the literature of post-World War Two Germany and Günter Grass, as Rubble Literature. The essay of Rushdie's that Wright is thinking of here is his 1981 review of *The Meeting at Telgte* where he writes:

> [Grass's] subject is how German writers after a war that did its work of destruction 'at six times the speed' of the Thirty Years war, responded to ruination [...] how they tore their language down and rebuilt it anew; how they used words to assault, excoriate, accept, encompass and regenerate; how the phoenix poked its beak out of the fire.[23]

At the centre of the project of Wright's novel, then, is a sense that the rebuilding of Aboriginal culture in Australia might happen via language, in the form of storytelling. Or, at least, that the rebuilding of narrative capacity from the ruinations of a catastrophe holds out the hope of rebuilding, eventually, a culture, a society, even a nation. The first scene of *Carpentaria* takes place in a rubbish dump, the direct metaphorical equivalent of Grass's postwar European rubble.

Given these authorial frames, merely sketched here, together with the counter-cosmography the novel represents – a non-Western temporal universe, the refusal of national modernity, the co-valuing of dream and waking realities – perhaps it is not surprising that critical responses so far have tended to circle around the novel, even when they are unreservedly admiring (like Adam Shoemaker): "the most inventive and most mesmerizing Indigenous epic ever produced in Australia."[24] Shoemaker attempts to find a way into its world using the discourses of reading and cultural analysis as they are available in contemporary Australia. But *Carpentaria* is both more hybridly In-

---

[23] Salman Rushdie, "Günter Grass" (1981), in Rushdie, *Imaginary Homelands: Essays and Criticism 1981–1991* (London: Granta, 1991): 273. There is another link from language to Nazi Germany and British imperialism (within) in Rushdie's essay "The New Empire Within Britain" (1982), also in *Imaginary Homelands* (131–32). Compare the strange reversals of political history: white Australia as an 'immigrant' nation – in the Thatcherite sense – and the Indigenous people as the colonized people within. See also p. 137ff about language: integration, assimilation etc.

[24] Adam Shoemaker, "Hard Dreams and Indigenous Worlds in Australia's North," *Hecate* 34.1 (2008): 55. Anne Brewster's important article "Indigenous Sovereignty and the Crisis of Whiteness in Alexis Wright's *Carpentaria*," *Australian Literary Studies* 25.4 (November 2010): 85–100, reads the novel in terms of concepts of Aboriginal sovereignty and storytelling/storykeeping.

digenous-postmodern and more specifically responsive to the realities of contemporary land management and land tenure, including the politics of the extractive industries and the ideology of development, than such critical discourse can easily articulate. This essay is a preliminary attempt to understand the geopolitical fiction of Alexis Wright, representing as it does the cultural and political truth (albeit fictional) of an altered geography, of what business research and forecasting firms like BIS Shrapnel refer to as the Carpentaria Minerals Province.[25] *Carpentaria* is also postnational in Marcia Langton's sense that it both critiques, implicitly, the idealized cultural history of mineral exploitation (the gold rushes) and re-narrativizes the mythology of every dimension of the Australian settlement.

Subterranean

Leading up to the final cyclonic cataclysm of *Carpentaria*, where the troubled town of Desperance is swept into the sea and reconstituted as a floating island of garbage, there are two important episodes: the blowing-up of the Gurfurrit International mine; and the burial of the three young boys, Mozzie Fishman's sons with Angel Day, Tristrum and Luke, and Aaron Ho Kum, who have died in custody in the Desperance lock-up. Both are subterranean episodes; both take place in dangerous and sacred proximity to the ancestral spirit of the land, the great serpent who shaped and continues to live in the earth, who constitutes the "holocene homeland."

In Chapter 11, the blowing-up of the mine is an act of industrial sabotage, masterminded by the charismatic Aboriginal religious lawman Mozzie Fishman and operationalized by the hero of the novel, Will Phantom. Mozzie's seditious rhetoric of direct anti-globalization action had rallied the young Aboriginal men to the cause:

> 'You know who we all hear about all the time now?' he asked us. 'International mining company. Look how we got to suit international mining people. Rich people. How we going to do that? Now, even we, any old uneducated buggers, are talking globally. We got to help United Kingdom money. Netherlands lead air problems. Asia shipping. United States of America industry, and we don't even know

---

[25] See BIS Shrapnel, *Future Development of Queensland's Carpentaria Minerals Province*, http://www.mitez.com.au/docs/project_devresourcescorridor.pdf (accessed 20 March 2012).

German people. 'I says,' he says like he is singing, 'we mobs got to start acting locally. Show whose got the Dreaming. The Laaaw.' He liked to empathise [emphasize] 'The Laaaw' whenever he was heating up around the ears on the subject of globalization. (408–409)

The chapter is a tour de force of descriptive as well as parodic action-thriller generics and one of the most narratively complex chapters in the novel. The pace of the narrative varies from fast to slow-mo, the POV shifts from the ground-bass third person of the novel as a whole to the excitable first-person plural of the group of Aboriginal saboteurs ("The finale was majestical. Dearo, dearie, the explosion was holy in its glory," 411), the action shifts from die-hard mode (good and bad guys, chases, fights, shooting, etc.) to media reportage, cutting between sequences of present action and the immediate past.

At the beginning of the chapter, Will is on the run from a squadron of police sent to Desperance by the State Premier, for his sabotage two years earlier of the thirty-million-dollar pipeline that runs from the mine to the export terminal in the Gulf. But he is captured by security thugs working for the mining company and brought back to the mine site in a helicopter. The cynical and divisive strategies of the multi-national mining company have further riven the Aboriginal community of Desperance:

> Some people were talking about the jobs they would be getting. *You very, very wrong.* They were arguing against the pro-land-rights brigade. [...] Others were saying they wanted the mining company to give the country back. Others were opposed to having any mines on their sacred country. *Full stop.* Some people said how they would kill anybody going against country. (392)

This industrial-thriller scenario of the operation against Will Phantom and Mozzie's Aboriginal saboteurs by the mining company mercenaries Cookie and Chuck ends with their deaths (ECU shot) and the mine explosion:

> Guns were being fired. The two lads heard the strange sound for the first time in their lives as the bullets whistled by, inches past their ear, and both yelled. 'Duck man, they are shooting at us.' Both ran faster, bolting for their lives like jack rabbits, and Will, where was he? They had seen him disappear into the ground like he was made out of thin air. And they did duck, unbelievingly, as they ran [...] not even looking back to see that glorious fire tonguing down to the underground storage tanks, nor knowing there were only moments to go, and they

would be all feeling what it was like to be blown sky-high, if they did not make it out over the fence and into the hills. (405)

After the giant fireball, Will and his accomplices are "thrown down for shelter behind the boulders, in the fold of the ancestral spirit who governed the land" (407).

Following this action thriller version of events the narrative switches to the register of eye-witness media reporting. The effect is to shift the sabotage/explosion action to behind the scenes:

> The multi-million dollar mine, from infancy to its working prime, was probed, described and paraded to network viewers. Interviews and footage of scenery went jig-jogging along in soap opera intensity, before finally shifting to pan, and viewers were encouraged to dissect what become of this showcase of the nation.
>
> [...]
>
> The face of a scientist, speaking behind his glass-fronted mask with a muffled voice which had to be transcribed into English on the bottom of the television set, like the SBS channel, became the anchorman for the task that lay ahead. On the first day he reported that a fire had spread from the main transport hangars to the fuelling bowsers. It was lucky no one was killed. On day two, the wash-up at the end of the day was like at the beginning, this was a major explosion in the remote Gulf of Carpentaria at Gurfurritt, the biggest mine of its type in the world.
>
> [...]
>
> After a week of the hooded scientist, another bald, Mars-faced scientist appeared on the television screen. [...]
>
> 'The fuel line to the mine operations connected to the main fuel tanks caused further major damage to occur. The intense heat rising into the atmosphere from the initial explosions generated a chain reaction of explosions throughout the mine. (Footage to air of mass destruction.) An incidental fuel leakage running throughout the 300-kilometre pipeline to the coast caused it to be extensively damaged. (Pause.) [...] The force from this simultaneous explosion uncovered the entire pipeline and pieces were found many kilometres from their original site.' (Pan shot: bits of pipeline sticking out of the ground and throughout the surrounding bushland like an exhibition of post-modern sculpture outside the Australian National Gallery or the Tate Modern in London on the Thames.) (414–16)

After the explosion, the mine site looks like an avant-garde work of landscape photography, like Tracey Moffatt's. Further, the parallels with Marcia Langton's "odd imaginary relationship" with Todd Russell and Brant Webb, via television broadcast, but as if she had "read about them in a novel," are apparent, and uncanny, given that Wright's novel must have been in production at the time of the Beaconsfield event. Like the Tasmanian mine disaster, where the real-life action was happening underground and not available to the media, the Gurfurritt sabotage is also a national media event, televised to a highly emotionally engaged audience that can only follow what is going on on the surface. The novel's thematic thread about the rapacious, colonizing exploitation of the mine and its dangerous disregard for the Law that governs culture, society, and country, and the responsibility of humans for ancestral guardianship of the land, is satirically and parodically dramatized in this episode, but its violence nevertheless comes as a shock.

The mine conflagration is immediately followed by the chapter in which Mozzie Fishman leads his convoy of young male followers, including Will Phantom, on a burial ritual of the three young boys, who have died in custody, into a subterranean sea. The group eludes the helicopter operation that has been dispatched to capture them. In confirmation of Mozzie's anti-globalization rhetoric, this operation is masterminded by the mining company executive, by mobile phone, from a boardroom in Manhattan. The file of men, carrying the three bodies, walks for nearly two days along a secret track, to where Mozzie leads them to an entrance to a cave, behind a dingo's lair, that opens out into an ancient site of burial. Mozzie reveals his TO's knowledge of the site, his "authority of prior presence," the right way to approach it, the song cycles associated with it, and appropriate rituals of burial.[26] Where the previous chapter was all fast cuts, confusion, and fireballs, this one, in its hushed silence and solemn prose, conveys the awe of the young Aboriginal men as they follow Mozzie's ritual in the waterworld:

> And the walls, they screamed at you with the cryptic, painted spirits of the Dreamtime. And inside the walls, was the movement of spirits, moving further and further forward, so the surface appeared to be falling into the frightened eyes of the Fishman's men. They all stood there inside, crowded like that. Old Fishman was in another world, crying and talking the dead language, walking around, gently pushing past anyone standing in his way. His staff pounded on the living wall,

---

[26] Langton, "Earth, Wind, Fire and Water," 149.

and the men looked away, down at the dusty floor, before seeing the Fishman moving forward through a narrow opening inside the resting spirit's body. The entrance must have been there already, but it was impossible to have noticed it, because the cave seemed so crowded and occupied with relics from other times. The song cycles' arias of devotion that had droned on in this place for days like locusts before rain, which came from forever in the old, musty air inside, were heard now. The men felt the sound lingering inside their bodies. (436–37)

Led by Mozzie, the men are moving within the subterranean, porous being of the serpent who, we remember from the first page of the novel, "continues to live deep down under the ground in a vast network of limestone aquifers" (2). The underground lake has been a site of burial for eons and the bodies of the three boys are laid in paperbark canoes that are there on the edge of the underground sea, tied to a mooring with ancient rope. Thus the "canoes moved away, navigating the routes to the spirit world, across the sea," returning the spirits of the boys to the waterplaces their beings emanated from originally (440). After this ritual is completed and the men ascend from the underworld, evading the mine mercenaries, the "tracks they followed were the very same as an underground river several kilometers wide, travelling from one side of the continent to the other" (446). Travel across the country, then, is also travel within it. The action sequences of the mine sabotage all take place on the surface and the media-reporting mode of the narrative is a further anti-realist distancing of the subterranean reality. The explosion of the underground fuel tanks destroys the rapacious exploitation of the Carpentarian homelands by the rogue multi-national Gurfrritt and the "Fishman's men [...] agreed that only the greatness of the mighty ancestor had saved them" (416). The code-switching of the narrative allows Wright to distance the cinematic parody of the mine action drama from the deep, sacred episode that follows.

There is more to these two episodes than there is space to convey here. There is the thematic phrasing, for example, between the underground lake burial and the sea burial of Elias Smith in the groper hole, by Norm Phantom after an epic two weeks of rowing out into the Gulf. "Relations with water are always social relations," and this is embodied in these two scenes of the novel, as well as in the death of Elias Smith in the lagoon.[27] In the earlier underworld scene, Norm steers along a "corridor above a steep underwater canyon":

---

[27] Langton, "Earth, Wind, Fire and Water," 133.

> He noticed a different breaking pattern in the current line and when he touched the water, felt its temperature had risen. He thought he saw glimpses of the giant spirits as they clung, swimming closely to the sides of the underwater chasm. (251)

Later, after he lowers Elias Smith to his final resting-place, Norm sleeps and dreams of the "many levels of a Mesozoic bluff"; the "deep hole could have been the result of a Dreamtime volcano, or a meteorite the size of a mountain, or a city that had sunk deep down into the earth" (257). As well as the thematics of the terrestrial and marine underworld, there is the complexly shifting narrative modes in which these thematics are enacted, including the translation of non-Aboriginal realities into the hybridized storytelling of the novel.

I might summarize the multiply layered narrative of *Carpentaria* as a fictional representation of the deep ideological contests at work within the Australian nation, since the time of sovereignty and into the present. As the recent global financial crisis has reminded us – in the way that only a serious threat to economic growth and prosperity can – the link between Australia's natural resources (that is, the land), regional trade, economic policy and governmentality is part of an ecocidal ideology of growth and prosperity at any cost. On the surface, it may seem like a time of world-historical reconciliation, symbolized by Kevin Rudd's 2008 apology, on behalf of Parliament, to Australia's Indigenous people, but underneath the rhetoric, governmental neo-colonialism continues, as the NT Intervention. Marcia Langton recognized these stresses in contemporary Australia, as they express themselves in photography, fiction, and art. Alexis Wright's novel also reminds us, powerfully, of the subterranean forces at work within our region of the world, locally and globally, that include, side by side, violence and unsustainable exploitation, the moral priority of development ideology, and the coexistence of ritual, magic, spirituality, and Indigenous knowledge. I don't wish to suggest that Wright's novel represents a reconfiguration of the cultural domain in relation to economic and social reality, although I am arguing that its narrative modes and dissonances and the obvious complexities of reception it has occasioned are signs of its radical critique of the culture of literature in Australia. The novel raises, I think, profound and urgent questions about the realm of literary knowledge, about the functions and institutions of critical discourse, about the relations of power between a metropolitan, global critical theory and a peripheral, postnational literary work.

Works Cited

Akehurst, Vic. *A Light in the Darkness: An Anecdotal History of Doomadgee Mission; Fifty-Three Years of Faithful, Fearless Endeavour by Assembly Missionaries* (Petaling Jaya, Malaysia: Market Intelligence, 1993).

BIS Shrapnel. *Future Development of Queensland's Carpentaria Minerals Province* (March 2010), http://www.mitez.com.au/docs/project_devresourcescorridor.pdf (accessed 20 March 2012).

Brewster, Anne. "Indigenous Sovereignty and the Crisis of Whiteness in Alexis Wright's *Carpentaria*," *Australian Literary Studies* 25.4 (November 2010): 85–100.

Jose, Nicholas. *Black Sheep: Journey to Borroloola* (South Yarra, Victoria: Hardie Grant, 2002).

Langton, Marcia. "Earth, wind, fire and water: the social and spiritual construction of water in Aboriginal societies," in *The Social Archaeology of Australian Indigenous Societies*, ed. Bruno David, Bryce Baker & Ian J. McNiven (Canberra: Aboriginal Studies Press, 2006): 139–60.

——. "Intimate Places and Terrifying Spaces," *Australian* (17 September 2006): 16–17, http://www.theaustralian.com.au/arts/intimate-places-and-terrifying-spaces/story-e6frg8px-1111112227516 (accessed 20 March 2012).

——. *Anthology of Recent Writings*, ed. Max Charlesworth, Françoise Dussart & Howard Morphy (Aldershot: Ashgate, 2005): 131–39.

——, & Odette Mazel. "Poverty in the Midst of Plenty: Aboriginal People, the 'Resource Curse' and Australia's Mining Boom," *Journal of Energy and Natural Resources Law* 26.1 (March 2008): 31–70.

Morris, Meaghan. "Afterthoughts on 'Australianism'," in Morris, *Identity Anecdotes: Translation and Media Culture* (Thousand Oaks CA & London: Sage, 2006): 34–51. Originally in *Cultural Studies* 6.3 (1992): 468–75.

——. "Beyond Assimilation: Aboriginality, Media History and Public Memory," in Morris, *Identity Anecdotes: Translation and Media Culture* (Thousand Oaks CA & London: Sage, 2006): 104–23. Originally (abr.) in *Aedon* 4.1 (1996): 12–26.

Price, Sally. *Paris Primitive: Jacques Chirac's Museum on the Quai Branly* (Chicago: U of Chicago P, 2006).

Roberts, Tony. *Frontier Justice: A History of the Gulf Country to 1900* (St Lucia: U of Queensland P, 2005).

Rushdie, Salman. "Günter Grass" (1981), in Rushdie, *Imaginary Homelands: Essays and Criticism 1981–1991* (London: Granta, 1991): 273–75.

——. "The New Empire Within Britain" (1982), in Rushdie, *Imaginary Homelands: Essays and Criticism 1981–1991* (London: Granta, 1991): 129–38.

Shoemaker, Adam. "Hard Dreams and Indigenous Worlds in Australia's North," *Hecate* 34.1 (2008): 55–61.

Trigger, David. "Mining, Landscape and the Culture of Development Ideology in Australia," *Cultural Geographies* 4 (April 1997): 161–80.

——. *White Fella Comin': Aboriginal responses to colonialism in northern Australia* (Cambridge: Cambridge UP, 1992).

Wright, Alexis. "Breaking Taboos: Alexis Wright at the Tasmanian Readers' and Writers' Festival, September 1998," *Australian Humanities Review* (1998), http://www.australianhumanitiesreview.org/archive/Issue-September-1998/wright.html (accessed 20 March 2012).

——. *Carpentaria* (Artarmon, NSW: Giramonda, 2006).

——. "Deep Weather," *Meanjin* 70.2 (Winter 2011): 70–82.

——. *Grog War* (Broome, WA: Magabala, 1997).

——. "Gulf Music," *Australian* (9 June 2007), http://www.theaustralian.news.com.au/story/0,20867,21853571-5001986,00.html (accessed 20 March 2012).

——. "Open Letter: Talking about an Indigenous tomorrow," *Unleashed* (ABC, 30 March 2011), http://www.abc.net.au/unleashed/45734.html (accessed 20 March 2012).

——. *Plains of Promise* (St Lucia: U of Queensland P, 1997): 140.

——. "Politics of Writing," *Southerly* 62.2 (Summer 2002): 10–20.

Identity and the Re-Assertion of Aboriginal Knowledge in Sam Watson's *The Kadaitcha Sung*

HEINZ ANTOR

THE COLONIZATION OF AUSTRALIA by white Europeans triggered a long and woeful history of genocide, oppression, and exploitation in the course of which Aboriginal Australians were marginalized and submitted to the regimes of white capitalist culture. This had serious consequences for their own Indigenous cultures, which, as we all know, were constructed in white European representations as primitive, savage, and inferior Others in need of being superseded by the supposed blessings of the progress of white civilization. The orality of Aboriginal cultures further contributed to the silencing and suppression of a literature and an epistemic system which were not granted any status in the cultural taxonomies of the colonizers with their emphasis on written texts. Not only did this lead to a serious denigration and in some instances even the disappearance of Aboriginal knowledge, but it also damaged Indigenous Australians' sense of identity.

The twentieth century, however, in a long, slow, and arduous process and in the face of continuing discrimination, saw a gradual and at least partial recovery of Aboriginal culture and identity. Indigenous Australians raised their voice again, and this time they also used writing to make themselves heard, from David Unaipon's early interventions in the 1920s via the first budding of a black Australian literature in English in the 1960s to the present, in which it can be said that there is a sizeable body of anglophone Aboriginal writing. The Empire has indeed begun to write back, in Salman Rushdie's famous phrase, and it does so with a vengeance indeed, as the following remarks will show. I have chosen Sam Watson's novel *The Kadaitcha Sung*, published in 1990, as my central text and example here because it illustrates how the issues I have just mentioned are negotiated in contemporary Aboriginal literature in a way that both salvages and re-asserts Indigenous knowledge and in doing so also re-asserts Aboriginal identity.[1]

The Kadaitcha Sung is a hybrid text insofar as it is many things at the same time. It is an action-packed adventure novel,[2] a revenge story, a piece of magical realism[3] combining social documentary with mythological and fantastic as well as gothic elements,[4] a confrontational story accusing the perpetrators of colonialist crimes in a shrill and often violent narrative that also contains lyrical and subtly meditative passages, but it is also a morality story about the struggle between good and evil and a postcolonial comment on race relations in contemporary Australia. It tells the story of the half-caste Tommy Gubba, son of Fleur, a white Australian woman, and of Koobara, one of the gods from the Dreamtime. Tommy is one of the last two members of the powerful Kadaitcha, "an ancient clan of sorcerers from the heavens," sent

---

[1] Katrin Althans affirms that "a regained Aboriginal identity [...] is at the centre of *The Kadaitcha Sung*"; Althans, *Darkness Subverted: Aboriginal Gothic in Black Australian Literature and Film* (Göttingen: V&R unipress & Bonn UP, 2010): 90. Sam Watson himself points out: "The great theme of 1988 [the Bicentennial] was that we, as a people, have survived. The theme of the nineties is that we will come back – we have absorbed the terror, we had our holocaust but now we are re-numbering, we are re-populating our communities, we are making a strong and energetic come-back." Elizabeth Dean, "An Interview with Sam Watson," *Famous Reporter* 11 (June 1995), http://walleahpress.com.au/int-watson.html (accessed 23 November 2011).

[2] Estelle Castro refers to the book as a "fast pace narrative" and "an action-packed novel" as well as "an entertaining novel, unrestricted by literary conventions and transgressing genres or sub-genres"; "Imaginary (Re)Vision: Politics and Poetics in Sam Watson's *The Kadaitcha Sung* and Eric Willmot's *Below the Line*," *Anglophonia: French Journal of English Studies* 21 (2007): 160, 168.

[3] See Eva Rask Knudsen, *The Circle & the Spiral: A Study of Australian Aboriginal and New Zealand Māori Literature* (Cross/Cultures 68; Amsterdam & Atlanta GA: Rodopi, 2004): 270 ("Aboriginal science fiction"). See also Roslyn Weaver, "'Smudged, Distorted and Hidden': Apocalypse as Protest in Indigenous Speculative Fiction," in *Science Fiction, Imperialism and the Third World: Essays on Postcolonial Literature and Film*, ed. Ericka Hoagland & Reema Sarwal (Jefferson NC: McFarland, 2010): 99–114 ("speculative fiction").

[4] See Suzanne Baker, "Magic Realism as a Postcolonial Strategy: *The Kadaitcha Sung*," *SPAN: Journal of the South Pacific Association for Commonwealth Literature and Language Studies* 32 (1991): 59 ('functions on one level as a kind of 'fantastic' adventure").

down to the earth there to represent the great god Biamee.[5] The other remaining Kadaitcha is Tommy's uncle Booka Roth, who, in a struggle for power, killed his own brother: i.e. Tommy's father, and banished Biamee from the realm of the mortals by stealing the sacred heart of the rainbow serpent. Booka Roth[6] then took on a white identity by inhabiting a migloo (i.e. white) body; ever since, he has been seeking earthly power by collaborating with white Australians. Booka becomes a Captain of the Native Mounted Police and in that capacity commits many crimes, murdering Aborigines and raping women. Tommy Gubba is elected by the gods to re-establish order and justice. He is to seek the stolen sacred heart of the rainbow serpent and return it to Biamee, thereby ending the latter's banishment from earth as well as making Booka's punishment possible.

The novel begins with a prologue which is printed in italics and provides the mythological framework as well as the prehistory of the plot of the novel. This prologue is interesting because it already encapsulates in a nutshell some of the salient principles on which the book's postcolonial and anti-racist discourse, its process of writing back,[7] is founded. The very beginning of the novel implicitly juxtaposes an Aboriginal creation story with the biblical book of Genesis and thus challenges the latter's authority and its claims as a white master-narrative:[8]

---

[5] Sam Watson, *The Kadaitcha Sung* (Ringwood, Victoria: Penguin, 1990): 1. Further page references are in the main text.

[6] Booka Roth's status as an Aboriginal traitor is underlined by his name, which "is most likely a fictionalised version of Dr Walter Roth, Protector of Aborigines in Queensland 1898–1906." Kate Hall, "'All are implicated': Violence and Accountability in Sam Watson's *The Kadaitcha Sung* and Alexis Wright's *Plains of Promise*," in *Frontier Skirmishes: Literary and Cultural Debates in Australia after 1992*, ed. Russell West–Pavlov & Jennifer Wawrzinek (Anglistische Forschungen 409; Heidelberg: Winter, 2010): 207.

[7] The prologue is thus part of what Suzanne Baker refers to as "a fairly recent development, [in which] Aborigines are now challenging white-constructed versions of history, and attempting to write themselves back into Australian life" ("Magic Realism as a Postcolonial Strategy," 55).

[8] The novel thus performs what Robert Ariss considers to be an important task of Aboriginal discourse: namely, "to deconstruct European representations and to re-present Australian history from the perspective of the oppressed, the indigene rather than the colonialist." Ariss, "Writing black: the construction of an Aboriginal dis-

> When time was still young the gods created substance from the firmament. They made the land and the waters, and then they made life. The land and the waters would serve to reflect the void, and life would bow down and worship the gods, as the gods needed to be worshipped. They brought forth fowl for the air, fish for the oceans and beasts for the land. Men and women were created to have dominion over all; they would live upon the land. The men and women must worship the gods and keep the laws of the gods, and they must ensure that the natural order of all things was kept. One god, a greater being, made his camp on the rich veldts and in the lush valleys of the South Land. He was called Biamee and he loved all life. In time he came to love the tribes of man above all others, for they revered him and his laws. For many aeons the land and the people basked in Biamee's beneficence, and all was well. (1)

The parallels with the beginning of the Book of Genesis are striking here. The heaven and the earth are mentioned, just as the initial void, the waters, birds and fish, and humans, who, in both the Aboriginal and the Christian version of creation, are to dominate the earth. We are told that "all was well" at the end of the passages quoted above, and indeed, what we have here is an Indigenous Garden of Eden.[9] The only major difference we can discern so far is that next to the main god Biamee there are other gods, so that the monotheistic Christian theology here is replaced by a polytheistic one. In addition, the Aboriginal paradise described in the passage is clearly located in the 'South Land': i.e. in Terra Australis, Australia.

The Indigenous paradise described here is about to witness a crisis when Biamee decides to return to the stars, which leaves the human tribes fearful because "the world was still a savage place" (1). That the dangers of the world lurk beyond the waters: i.e. outside Australia, becomes clear when, in order to protect the land, Biamee "made a veil of mists that hung upon the South Land and hid it from all" (1). In addition, the Kadaitcha are to guard and protect the land and its people so that Biamee can ascend into the heavens from Uluru, "his most sacred altar" (1). The situation erupts into crisis when the Kaidatcha

---

course," in *Past and Present: The Construction of Aboriginality*, ed. Jeremy Beckett (Canberra: Aboriginal Studies Press, 1988): 134.

[9] Cf. Kevin Gilbert, who refers to the Dreaming and the days of creation as "the Aboriginal version of the 'Garden of Eden'." Gilbert, "Introduction" to *Inside Black Australia*, ed. Kevin Gilbert (Ringwood, Victoria: Penguin, 1988): xix.

Booka, not having been chosen as his father's heir, kills his brother in a rage. This is contextualized in a significant way in the prologue:

> Booka waged a long and terrible campaign against his brother, and great was the devastation and loss of life. The evil one caused the mists to lift from the land and other mortals saw its wealth and abundance; they came in their hordes and they slaughtered the helpless tribes with a monstrous lust. [...] The fair-skinned ones laid waste to the garden and the chosen people.
> Denied his birthright by his own tribe, Booka joined with the new settlers so he would secure position within their order. (3)

What is described here is what happened in 1788 and after.[10] However, this is told here from an Aboriginal perspective. Colonialism is associated with the deed committed by Booka, who is an alternative version of what in the Bible is described in the story of Cain and Abel as well as of the tale of Lucifer, the fallen angel who rebelled against god. Booka is here referred to as "the evil one," and the whole project of white colonialism in Australia is thus characterized as evil right from the start, through its association with Booka, who made it possible in the first place, and through the colonialist genocide and the ecological catastrophe caused by the whites.

The beginning of the novel thus not only presents an Indigenous mythology challenging the Biblical account of creation but is also an instance of alternative historiography, in which colonialism is explained differently from the standard accounts of white Australians. Not only is Aboriginal culture given back its voice here, but it is also re-invested with agency, because it was the Indigenous figure of Booka who, although a negative character and a traitor, triggered the events that led to the white colonization of Australia. This is a strategy in postcolonial Indigenous writing, which uses Aboriginal counter-narratives to unhinge and subvert the authority of white master-narratives.[11] Not only is white knowledge relativized in such texts by being

---

[10] Watson himself points out that "what I did was I took the entire history of white settlement and compressed it into living memory." Watson, "I Say This To You: Sam Watson, Manager of Brisbane Aboriginal Legal Service and Author of *The Kadaitcha Sung* (Penguin 1990), talks to 'Meanjin'," in *Meanjin* 53.4 (1994): 591.

[11] Another such example from a different world region would be the Native Canadian Thomas King's novel *Green Grass, Running Water*, which also uses Indigenous creation stories and pitches them against the Biblical account and in addition in many passages re-tells the history of the white settlement of the North American West from a

juxtaposed with Indigenous knowledge, but the latter is also foregrounded, captured in writing, documented, and preserved in the process, in an act of defiant refusal against the forces of cultural extinction produced by the dominant white culture, the very act of writing thereby turning into a subversive intervention.

In the prologue to Sam Watson's *The Kadaitcha Sung*, the linkage between Booka and colonialism establishes a moral taxonomy which gives Aboriginal culture an ethical advantage. Moreover, in the novel's account of events, it is Indigenous culture that is central, and white civilization is marginalized as the result of an act of transgression and betrayal, a breach that needs to be healed. This is why the prologue ends on an ambiguous note which prepares for the main plot of the novel:

> As time passed the violence lessened and the tribes that survived began to rebuild. They started to adapt to life under the new masters [...]. Booka [...] murdered Koobara and became the last of the Kadaitcha clan. Such had been the scale of the killings that none other remained to deny him.
>
> But Koobara's son had been born of a white woman, and Biamee promised his people that the Kadaitcha child would deliver them. (4)

On the one hand, Aboriginal Australians now are subjected to white power and the murderous renegade Booka has established himself in a powerful position among them. On the other, the prologue ends on a note of promise, heralding deliverance from the yoke of colonialism of Indigenous Australians, who are here referred to as a chosen people: namely, Biamee's. We are told that they will be freed by a hybrid saviour, and that figure is Tommy Gubba,[12] the protagonist of the novel, the plot of which is the story of the deliverance and revenge carried out by him.[13]

Native-Canadian point of view, thus shedding doubt on the narratives of white historiography.

[12] As Kimberley McMahon–Coleman points out, "Even the name of [the] protagonist, Tommy Gubba, designates his hybrid status, for his surname, Gubba, is a common colloquial insult for white people, derived from the Aboriginal-English 'gubbament'"; "Arctic and Outback: Indigenous Literature at the 'Ends of the Earth'," *Australasian Canadian Studies* 26.1 (2008): 51. On the name Gubba, see also Ken Gelder & Jane M. Jacobs, *Uncanny Australia: Sacredness and Identity in a Postcolonial Nation* (Melbourne, Victoria: Melbourne UP, 1998): 110.

[13] Cf. Don Fletcher: "There is an assertion, then, of a traditional Aboriginal warrior identity, overwhelmed to date by superior weapons [...], and of Aboriginal cultural

The prologue thus ends on a note of urgency, which creates a sense of suspense and expectation. The reader is then catapulted into the narrative present of the 1980s, and the first part of the main narrative establishes a link between the mythological and transcendent realm of the Dreamtime and the world of the here and now. In the initial scene, Tommy Gubba flies through the air on the back of "Purnung, the giant dingo spirit of the dreaming time" (5). Their destination is Uluru, "the vast red rock that sat upon the heart of the land" (1), as it is solemnly called in the prologue, because it is from there: i.e. from the very centre of Australia, that the saviour figure Tommy is to meet the emissaries of the gods and to be sent on his mission of delivery and redemption. Significantly, we are told that "Uluru awaited them" (5) so that a special relationship is established between the land and the half-caste boy as well as the people in whose cause he is to fight in the book. With regard to Purnung, we learn that a "growl of hatred rumbled from deep within his shaggy body, but a human hand [i.e. Tommy's] grasped his ear and settled him" (5), which both heralds the violence that is about to take place in this revenge story[14] and already hints at the need for such excesses to be curbed. Tommy Gubba and the giant dingo Purnung, during their flight to Uluru, can smell the three white members of the Native Mounted Police, who have been ordered to camp near the red rock by the suspicious Booka Roth, now a captain in the NMP, in order to keep an eye on the Aboriginals there. One by one, they are brutally killed by Jonjurrie, an Aboriginal trickster figure accompanying Purdung and Tommy Gubba. The Jonjurrie are described as "mischievous little imps [who] delighted in playing tricks on the living" (9), but here the prankster spirit is dead serious and takes bloody revenge for the cruelties of whites against his own people.

---

values as a counter discourse, personified in the conflict of Tommy Gubba versus Booka Roth." Fletcher, "Australian political identity: Aboriginal and otherwise – Carey/Malouf/Watson," in *Proceedings of the 2000 Conference of the Australasian Political Studies Association*, ed. Francis Castles & John Uhr (Canberra: Australian National UP, 2000): 5.

[14] Castro justifies the description of violence in *The Kadaitcha Sung* as "inherent to a poetics of unmasking and disruption [...], conveying the sense that breality causes bloodshed" and suggesting "that some truths must be told in their sheer brutality and without guises" ("Imaginary (Re)Vision," 167). Similarly, Don Fletcher points out: "Aggression may be necessary to break the monopoly of white interpretations of Australian history" ("Australian political identity," 6).

It is interesting to see how this is narrated in the novel. In the second scene of the book, following the description of Purnung's and Tommy's trip to Uluru, we are given a description of the camp of the white NMP officers. This turns into an uncanny scene of the return of the repressed. To begin with, the fact that the men are members of the Native Mounted Police in itself constitutes a resurrection from the dead of an organization which was dissolved in 1900.[15] The gruesome massacres in which its members were implicated, claims of which are often denied by right-wing racists, here come alive again when the men openly reminisce and brag about their cruel deeds:

> 'We've hunted friggin' coons all over the country, mate. Me and Ed and some of the other boys, we worked in Tassie and Victoria, right up through the friggin' Territory. I seen days when we come back to camp soaked in blood, drippin' blood and brains and shit from our arseholes to our friggin' eyebrows.' (11)

This is supplemented by tales of Aboriginal waterholes poisoned by the NMP, of killings of Indigenous women and children, "gins and piccaninnies" (15), as they are disparagingly referred to by the men, and of other atrocities. This resurrection of the racist genocide from the past fulfils various functions. It signals a refusal to forget in this novel by an Aboriginal writer and it lays the moral foundation for the plot of revenge that is to follow.[16] The NMP officers are characterized as raw and uncivilized men, totally brutalized and devoid of human feelings. The coarse language they use contrasts sharply with that in the almost lyrical prologue[17] describing the epistemic system of Indigenous Australians and thus characterizes the white NMP killers as primitive. Uluru, which, in the prologue for example, was referred to in respectful words, is irreverently called "a dirty great lump of rock" (10) in the conversation of the white men. Through this linguistic discreditation, the conventional white-racist primitivization of Aboriginal culture is reversed in a counter-discursive manoeuvre that subverts the assumptions of colonialism.

---

[15] See Katrin Althans, *Darkness Subverted*, 91.

[16] Owing to the dominance of the revenge motif, Kate Hall refers to Watson's text as "a 'payback' novel" ("'All are implicated'," 201).

[17] Susan Lever refers to "the pseudo-Shakespearean language of the mythological sequences." Lever, "The Bicentennial and the Millennium: The Dissident Voices of David Foster and Sam Watson," in *'And What Books Do You Read?': New Studies in Australian Literature*, ed. Irmtraud Petersson & Martin Duwell (Brisbane, Queensland: U of Queensland P, 1996): 104.

The resurrection of the Native Mounted Police in the present of the late-twentieth century also signals that the dangers of racism are still very much alive in contemporary Australia,[18] as expressed in the wishes the men have for the future of their country and their hopes for the complete extinction of Aboriginal people:

> 'Fuck me! This could be a real white man's country if only those big mouths would just give us a go. Have a look at how friggin' quiet Tasmania is now you and Roth and all the rest shot out the niggers. The place is shit-free. [...] Yes, mate, we did a good bit of work down there. And made a pile. They were paying us a quid for every coon's head we brought in.' (13)

The murderous commodification of Indigenous human lives at the hands of such brutes is still a danger to be reckoned with, the text implies, as long as such ideas have a certain currency. The moral framework in which this is to be seen is underlined when one of the men complains about the bad press the NMP has had: "'One of them Sydney papers even called us Nazis and mass murderers'" (13). In an authorial comment about the NMP officers' unquestioningly following Booka Roth's orders, we are also left in no doubt as to the evil we are confronted with here, and the identification of Booka with Lucifer in the prologue is underlined once again:

> It hadn't occurred to them to question Roth, who was the coldest and most violent man any of them had encountered. The blacks called him 'moogi man', or devil man, and he was that all right. The Chief of the Native Mounted Police was the Prince of Darkness. Old Satan himself! (12)

The repressed returns, though, in another, more concrete way here: namely, in the form of the revival of Aboriginal agency. This is heralded by uncanny events described from the point of view of the white NMP officers. For example, when one of the men leaves the campfire to relieve himself, he disappears in the darkness and never returns, an inexplicable event which has disquieting and disorientating effects on the others remaining. The wristwatch of one of the men stops working, thus further contributing to their growing confusion. The linear time of the whites and the taxonomies of white culture do

---

[18] Watson himself has stated: "Racism is endemic within Australian society and it will not just fade away. It must be confronted and it must be exposed and those things will not happen naturally." Elizabeth Dean, "An Interview with Sam Watson."

not work here any longer.[19] Indeed, the borderline between what white culture would refer to as the real and the supernatural become blurred, and this has eerie and uncanny effects – for example, when we are told that

> The howl of the giant dingo shattered the air and rolled on beyond the camp. It came from the Rock and was a noise that neither white man had ever heard before. It was as if the very gates of hell had been torn apart. (21)

This is the Aboriginal battle-call which gives rise to the killing in revenge of all the NMP officers. It is heard while they rape Worimi, an Aboriginal woman who was kidnapped by them and whose whole family, including her little daughter, was killed by the NMP. Her reaction to the howling of Purnung differs significantly from that of the white men:

> Even in the midst of her spasms, Worimi's heart sang to Bora. Purnung, the great dingo god, had pledged to avenge her and now she could prepare to join her husband and child. [...]
> 'Friggin' hell!' Chambers [one of the NMP officers] jumped for his rifle. 'What the fuck's happening here?'
> 'I reckon we ought to bolt, mate. Roth or no fuckin' Roth! This place gives me the fuckin' willies.' (21)

The NMP men here are catapulted out of their active role; the repressed fear of the Aboriginal Other returns and takes on concrete shape while agency is about to be transferred to Worimi, who is handed a sharpened kangaroo bone by Jonjurrie with which she stabs her tormentor, while the spirit kills Chambers. Although the latter manages to kill Worimi before dying himself, this moment marks a point of reversal because, while the NMP men are dying, Tommy Gubba undergoes his final step of initiation at Uluru and is sent on his mission of revenge. Agency now is returned to Aboriginal Australia and,

---

[19] Incidentally, this is a ploy also used by Joan Lindsay in her 1967 novel *Picnic at Hanging Rock*, where the otherness of the Australian landscape is constructed from a white point of view and where the watches of the members of the picnic party also stop as they approach Hanging Rock. Baker, referring to an interview with Watson, points out that the "collapsed time frame" of *The Kadaitcha Sung* relates to the Aboriginal Dreamtime, where time and space are nothing, a direct contrast to the European concept of progressive linear time. Baker, "Magic Realism as a Postcolonial Strategy: *The Kadaitcha Sung*," 61. On "temporal confusion" in Watson's novel, see also Knudsen, *The Circle & the Spiral*, 289ff.

as we are told, "the time of the Kadaitcha was nigh. Soon the payback would begin" (27).

The payback mentioned here is a double one. It takes the form of overcoming Booka Roth through the taking-away of his magic moogi stones and the restitution of the heart of the rainbow serpent to its appropriate place, thus re-establishing Biamee's access to and power over the earth. But it also means the breaking of white colonial power, the taking-revenge on Booka's racist allies. All this is told in the gothic mode in the novel because it means that the repressed fears of white Australians concerning their Aboriginal Other surge again and come true. Booka himself, the evil devil figure, is constructed as a gothic villain. He is partly imprisoned in Brisbane because, like a vampire, he cannot cross water (e.g., 41), and, although he is not described as a vampire, he is a body-snatcher: "A lost and lonely prospector had been relieved of his body and his mind so the renegade Kaidatcha could walk more easily in the camp of the migloo" (41). His NMP headquarters in Brisbane are a fortress with some of the characteristics of the dark castles of classic eighteenth- and nineteenth-century gothic fiction.[20] Although the part of the fortress that is situated above the earth seems to be nothing but a venue for social occasions where the NMP Captain Booka entertains his corrupt and racist friends among the politicians of Queensland, its cellar houses dark secrets. There, the same politicians rape and sometimes even kill Aboriginal women abducted by Booka and his men,[21] and there is also a secret cave hidden by a wall of blood and guarded by the Bunyatt, an Aboriginal version of a monster, which "guards the heart of the Serpent" (39) that is to be recovered by Tommy and to be put back where it belongs. Booka is to meet his end in the Native Compound at Cribb Island, which is also described in gothic terms:

> The compound on Cribb Island was built over an old colonial fort. Even though access to the fort had been barred by the incumbent Jesuits, [Tommy's Aboriginal friend] Pinni had forced her ways into the network of underground passageways and abandoned storm water

---

[20] See Althans, *Darkness Subverted*, 95 (referring to the "horrid Gothic quality [...] of Booka's very own headquarter").

[21] Apparently, the first draft of the novel was even more critical of white Australian politicians and described their misdeeds in such a drastic way that the publisher "felt that it would spend more time in the courts than on the bookstands," as a consequence of which Watson changed the manuscript so that "the white political figures only play very minor roles" (Watson, "I Say This To You," 593).

> channels, one of which was of crucial importance. It would be there that Booka would be lured into the trap that would begin the end of his mortal dominion. (82–83)

The old colonial fort on which the compound is built is an imperial equivalent to the gothic castles of British literature, and the labyrinthine chaos of underground passageways below the deceptive surface of a Jesuit mission is not only an architectural heir to the dungeons, dark cavernous cellars and confusing maze-like corridors underneath many a gothic castle but also the petrified version of the repressed fears of Booka and his colonialist friends – Booka's fear of water and the colonizers' fears of possible reprisals by the victims of the oppression that originated in the old fort.

Even the weather, in a pathetic fallacy, is described as supporting the Aboriginal subversion of the reign of the white colonizers and their murdering minion Booka in a scene which again assumes gothic dimensions:

> The port of Brisbane battened down for the freak storm that had swept in from the west with little warning. As it hit the outer suburbs and hurled itself in towards the city, bolts of bluish lightning crackled through the night air. Thunder pealed out as if to herald some momentous happening, and greenish clouds rolled forward to hunt.
> [...] frightened whites sought cover from the elements. For exactly one hour, the centre of Brisbane was assaulted by wave after wave of fury. It was as though the old gods of the land were attacking the newcomers and their camp, to smash them and to drive them back into the sea. But these new tribes did not know the old gods, and did not know when to fear them. (40)

What is inexplicable to the white Australians in Brisbane, a "freak storm," becomes explicable with the knowledge of the Indigenous cosmos we as readers of the novel are in a privileged position to have, and again the empowerment of the Aboriginal people's epistemic system here goes hand in hand with the weakening of explanatory potency and accuracy of white knowledge. Power and agency are shifted back to Aboriginal Australia,[22] signifying the end of Booka's reign: "A roar of thunder bellowed, as if mocking Roth and his assertion of sovereignty" (43).

The colonial project which was made possible by Booka's act of treachery when he lifted the mists surrounding the South Land is described by this evil

---

[22] Watson explicitly states that he "wanted to write about Aboriginal power" (Watson, "I Say This To You," 590).

protagonist himself in a sober and undeluded way that in itself amounts to a condemnation of the capitalist ideology behind colonialism and shows that Booka, although he uses white society as a framework in which to achieve the status he was denied by the gods, ultimately also despises the migloo, as the following conversation with his Aboriginal NMP underling Sambo shows:

> 'These migloo are very busy, Sambo. They are the lords of all the land and they have very strong magic.'
> 'What! Them mob know poorie way?' The simple-minded black was taken aback.
> 'No, boy,' Booka reassured him. 'Their magic is nothing to do with that. They don't have any deep feelings at all about the land, so they don't draw any power from there. They don't have any great regard for each other, so they don't draw any power from each other. [...] Their special sort of poorie comes from deep within them. They are driven by a restless sort of energy that sends them onwards. They are ruled by greed, sambo, greed and an evil sort of hunger that won't allow them any peace.' (42)

Booka's own connections with the white colonizers are depicted in the novel as having an alienating effect on him insofar as he loses his connection with the land, which is described as a protagonist in its own right, animated and endowed with a certain intentionality, agency, and purpose.[23] During Tommy's final initiation, the spirit of his father tells him that Booka "'is now weak. The further he drifts from the mysteries of the land, the faster he loses his strength'" (37), and, indeed, Booka experiences the freak storm in an NMP vehicle as something deeply disturbing: "the rain had unsettled him. Water was the key to his mortal death and it battered wildly, mindlessly against the windshield, trying to get at him" (41). Conversely, Tommy's connection to the land, his Aboriginal rootedness, is stressed as a strong source of power, something that supports him in difficult situations and provides him with the energy he needs to resist the iniquities of the white colonial system of oppression and injustice. For example, after the imposition of the death penalty on his friend Bulley Macow, we are told: "Tension had all but drained him" (69). However, it is his special link to the land that refreshes him:

---

[23] Cf. Castro: "This theme, an inscription within the texts that the land is a living entity, is a recurrent trait in Aboriginal and more broadly Indigenous literatures" ("Imaginary (Re)Vision," 164). Cf. also Knudsen, who talks about the "life force of the land" in *The Kadaitcha Sung* (*The Circle & the Spiral*, 284).

> Reaching down through the concrete and steel, Tommy made contact with the land beneath. New blood began to pump through him and in a short time he felt completely rejuvenated. (69)

It is not only the land, though, that seems to turn against Booka and favour Tommy Gubba, but the whole cosmos. The novel is set in early 1986 when Halley's comet approached the earth and became visible again. In an act of Aboriginal re-interpretation, this is used in characteristic fashion to pit an Indigenous conceptualization of the comet as Biamee's Eye against the explanations of white science:

> The Eye of Biamee. The migloo called it a comet, but even the youngest child in the tribe knew that the hurtling mass was really the great one's watchdog. (68)

The epistemic power of native conceptualizations of natural phenomena is also re-valued through a white character, Tommy's girlfriend Mary, who tells Tommy that she

> 'once studied a tribe in central Africa that worshipped this star [...] this tribe worshipped a star that wasn't even discovered until this century. [...] how did those people who had never even seen a pair of binoculars know about that star? It took a powerful radio-telescope to even locate it.' (151–52)

Native knowledge, it is implied here, is just as powerful as white science, if not more so, and this episode thus turns into a strong re-assertion of Aboriginal epistemology.

The appearance of Halley's comet in this novel is also attributed a role in the power-struggle between good and evil, Aboriginal and colonialist Australia, which is staged in the text. This is why Tommy is told by Koobara: "'The Eye of Biamee is coming and it will help to pull the sacred heart out of Booka's grasp'" (38). Thus, when Booka tries to reassure himself by affirming that "I am the last of the Kadaitcha," this is commented on in the following words: "But the night sky mocked him, the land knew" (44). Both the land of Australia and the whole cosmic order are opposed to the forces of evil embodied by Booka.

Despite these signs of Booka's impending downfall, the novel stages Tommy's victory over the evil renegade Kadaitcha as an arduous struggle, the decisive phase of which stretches over four days. This provides Watson with a fictional space in which he can unfold a tale of adventure and conflict full of suspense which, on the one hand, entertains the reader and, on the other, allows the author to expose the racist discrimination that is still rife in postcolonial Australian society. Watson thus has it both ways: He presents a critical realist text[24] and at the same time uses the advantages of other genres such as the adventure tale, the fantastic narrative, and gothic fiction. The ideological foundations of the latter, which in a colonial context often depicts Indigenous people as exotic representatives of an inferior but nevertheless dangerous alterity, are thus inverted and the construct of the negative Aboriginal Other is turned upside down, with the white racist abuses and cruelties committed by the whites showing who are the real barbarians.

The setting of part of the novel is Coontown, an Aboriginal suburb of Brisbane, which to Tommy symbolizes the perversions of colonialism and gives rise for him to the vision of a vengeful and restorative turn towards a better past before the advent of the white conquerors: When walking through Coontown, Tommy is aware of "the misery and degradation of the inmates of this perverted asylum":

> Words of many ancient dialects were thrown drunkenly at him. Blurred faces dulled by cheap wine and starvation passed by in a stream and Tommy's soul became heavy with despair. He was reaching a point from which he would finally confront the white man's total conquest. In his mind he went back to the happy camps of the sleek, fat hunters, laughing women, playing children, and the wise old eyes of the elders who saw everything. (109)

Aboriginal knowledge in this context becomes a weapon with which Tommy Gubba can fight the white oppressors as well as Booka Roth and his minions. For example, after having been kidnapped and sodomized by Roth and Sambo, Tommy scrapes his attackers' hair and juices from his raped body and uses these substances to "sing" the two evil men: i.e. to cast an evil spell and curse on them (54).

Tommy also uses his special abilities as a sorcerer to "sing" a corrupt white policeman (who had raped and murdered his Aboriginal friend Bulley Macow's sister) so that Bulley can draw him into a trap and kill him by eviscerating him, thus administering the Aboriginal "traditional punishment for rapist-murderers" (57). This episode fulfils various functions in the novel. For example, it shows the racist injustices of the practice of white law in Australia.

---

[24] The social-realist elements of the novel link up with early Aboriginal texts which used realism "to make a clear statement about the conditions under which Aborigines lived in white Australia" (Baker, "Magic Realism as a Postcolonial Strategy," 55).

Bulley feels the urge to take such direct revenge on the policeman in the first place because no legal action had been taken against the perpetrator although a "black man who had witnessed the girl's murder had come forward to give evidence" but was "found floating in the Brisbane River soon after" (56). In the face of such obvious legal misconduct and perversion of justice, Bulley's act of revenge appears in a different light from reports in the white press, where it is constructed as yet another example of Aboriginal savagery. Bulley, unlike the violator and killer of his sister, is imprisoned and tried for murder, and Tommy, who works as a translator for the court, visits Bulley in his cell. The latter is remarkably resilient in view of the unfair trial he gets and the capital punishment that is in store for him. Once again, it is Aboriginal knowledge and a special link to the land that gives strength to this Indigenous Australian and gives him a feeling of superiority over the Anglo-Saxon colonizers. As Bulley tells Tommy: "'These mob got no love in them. They like stone! I been all over my own country but I never found one migloo that knew anything. They bad seed, boy'" (56). Bulley uses his rootedness in the land as a weapon with which to spiritually resist white oppression:

> 'Every time them migloo punch me and kick me, when they tried to drown me and all that. I bin call to the land then, I bin call to my own special land and my own spirit push. No fear there, Tommy.' (58)

In contrast to the Aboriginal people's special relationship to the land, that of the white colonizers to their new environment is characterized from an Indigenous perspective as one of violent exploitation, destruction, and abuse, an ecological crime in which nature is imprisoned and violated just as Aboriginal men and women are. This is expressed in a conversation between Tommy and his Aboriginal friend Jarroo, in which the latter condemns the whites:

> 'Their words, their clothes ... everything about them. They don't belong to this land. Why did they come here? [...] But now that they're settled here and should be making a permanent camp out of it they rip up the land! They pull down the trees and change the courses of our rivers. This land will be devastated even within our own generation.'
>
> Tommy nodded in agreement. [...] His heart was burning and tears crept into his eyes. *My land! My land! What have the migloo done to you? They have bound you in chains of concrete and steel! They have raped you. How can you live with such terrible shame?*
>
> The river heard Tommy's call and whispered back to him. *Grieve not, young Kadaitcha. We will be strong again.* (132–33)

The episode of Bulley Macow's trial in the novel not only demonstrates the incompatibility of Aboriginal and white concepts of justice but it also serves to characterize the white legal system from an Indigenous point of view as an alien colonialist imposition without any real legitimation in Australia. Both court and jury are wholly indifferent to the cultural framework which is the basis for Bulley Macow's deed of revenge. White justice as practised in the case of Macow's trial is shown here to be perverted and self-contradictory insofar as it does not honour its own principles, because the defendant's point of view is wilfully and studiedly ignored. Watson here turns the tables on the representatives of white justice by reversing white sterotypes of Aboriginal savagery and making the jury members into savages rather than the Indigenous defendant. The culture of the colonizers here becomes a disease; indeed, this narrative is not only a novel of revenge but also a story of healing from an Aboriginal point of view after the trauma of colonization – the therapy taking violent forms, however.

The violence of the process of colonization is stressed in a scene which once again underlines Tommy's special relationship with the land. After the sentencing of Bulley Macow, Justice Jones asks Tommy to come to his office, where he offers him a job as foreman on his newly acquired cattle farm, thus trying to make him an accomplice in the process of exploiting the local Aboriginal people: "'we can't get any work out of our coons and we need someone like you to get through to them'" (77). Not only is the judge part of the racist system of judicial discrimination against Aborigines but he also participates in the system of white domination as a private landowner. He is turned into a symbol of racist abuse and colonial iniquity in the novel, which comes out most clearly in the description of his desk when Tommy enters the judge's office:

> Tommy reached out casually and put his hand on the varnished timber. He almost jumped at the scream of rage that leapt up at him.
> [...]
> '[...] This is a fine desk. Where did you get it from?'
> 'A lovely piece of work, isn't it? It comes from up north, some place west of Cairns. The dealer told me that it belonged to one of the local pioneers and was carved from a single tree. He said that it had been used as a burial tree or something by one of the nigger tribes.' The white man scoffed. 'But I'm not superstitious, are you?'
> Tommy relaxed. The old lines had been re-established and he was back in known territory. 'No sir, I'm not superstitious.' (75)

Here the judge unwittingly reveals himself as an heir to and exponent of a system of racist colonialist oppression and cultural denigration in a scene which plays with discrepant awareness and thus achieves bitter ironic and critical effects. Justice Jones's desk was carved from a sacred tree, the cultural function of which was disregarded by the pioneers, their only concern being the material qualities of the wood. The Indigenous spiritual knowledge connected with the tree is nothing but an instance of primitive superstition to the judge, who is unwilling to respect the epistemic system of Indigenous Australians and in an act of cultural imperialism refuses to value any cultural vision other than his own white perspective. His coarse and derogatory choice of words to refer to aborigines ('coons' and 'niggers') marks him as somebody whose attitudes do not differ from those of the colonial pioneers who cut down the tree. Since the reader, together with Tommy, witnesses the angry outcry of the timber the desk is made of, however, s/he is placed in an Aboriginal position and thus made to share the point of view of the victims of colonial dispossession and discrimination. When Tommy tells the judge that he is not superstitious, this is ironic – Jones interprets this as a sign of Tommy's assimilation to white cultural perspectives, whereas the reader knows that this is not the case. On the contrary, Tommy means what he says – he is not superstitious – and yet he believes in the sacred qualities of the burial tree because he has experienced the Aboriginal spirit-world as real, and so has the reader in the magical-realist scenes of the novel, so that we are aware of the fact that what is deemed to be mere superstition by the judge is Aboriginal knowledge for Tommy, with very real consequences, as is demonstrated in the text.[25] It is also significant that Tommy relaxes when the judge uses abusive language with reference to Indigenous Australians, because this re-establishes the orientational markers Tommy is used to. The judge plays his role according to the script of the binary confrontation between white and black in the context of a racist society, and this reinforces Tommy's determination to take revenge on white Australians. The scene ends with Justice Jones condescendingly and

---

[25] This is a good example of the ways in which "magic realism, as an alternative form of literary discourse, may provide Aboriginal writers with new ways of presenting their views." Baker, "Magic Realism as a Postcolonial Strategy: *The Kadaitcha Sung*," 57. Mudrooroo refers to this use of the supernatural in a realist framework as "maban realism" and cites Watson's novel as a pioneer in this "new realm of reality." Mudrooroo, *The Indigenous Literature of Australia: Milli Milli Wangka* (Melbourne, Victoria: Hyland House, 1997): 46.

patriarchally advising Tommy not to identify too much with the Aboriginal defendants for whom he translates in the trials, but while the white man thinks that through this avuncular attitude he is doing the supposedly inferior man a favour, the reader is granted an insight into Tommy's mind, which turns the power-constellation assumed by Jones on its head:

> His [Tommy's] inner spirit was thirsting for the blood of this man who had just ordered the execution of a tribal brother. He deserved to die as well. Jones' shiny head looked to be as fragile as an egg and Tommy knew that he could kill the man with a single hit. But that would not gain anything and the spirits locked into the wood of the desk warned for caution. (76)

The scene thus ends with the re-empowerment of the young Aboriginal protagonist and the merely strategic sparing of the representative of the white legal system, which has been deconstructed as a system of injustice. Moreover, the death penalty imposed on Bulley Macow is also rendered harmless and thus subverted when Tommy points out that ultimately it doesn't mean a thing to the Aboriginal man – "At the exact moment of physical death his spirit will be taken up to the dreaming time" (80). It is this Aboriginal knowledge that takes the sting out of the white punishment, which thus becomes ineffective on a deeper level.

Justice Jones, in a later scene, is shown to be not just an exponent of the injustices of the white legal system but also a violent perpetrator himself, even in the framework of white justice. In Booka Roth's headquarters, he sexually abuses Aboriginal women kidnapped by Roth for that purpose, even killing them for his own pleasure (221–22).

Tommy turns into the avenger of such injustices and iniquities in the novel, For example, racist slights are punished immediately by him through his use of spiritual powers which quickly administer justice from the Aboriginal point of view, as in the following scene in which Tommy finds himself in the streets of Brisbane with his Aboriginal friend Pinni:

> A white face leaned out of a taxi as it zoomed past and Pinni stepped back as a gob of spit spattered at her feet. Tommy stared hard at the rear of the vehicle and about two hundred yards further on it sailed into the back of a stalled bus. The driver leaped out unhurt but the passenger's head hung across the lip of the window, blood dripping from a head wound. (82)

Justice in such scenes functions along the lines of instant retribution, and what the reader is confronted with is not an instance of Aboriginal vengeful wish-fulfilment but the redressing of a certain imbalance in black–white relations in an Australia that is characterized as unashamedly racist and inattentive to the dignity and human rights of Aboriginal people.

This is also stressed in a scene in which the Irish lawyer Finlay visits the Jesuit missionary in the Native compound on Cribb Island, in which the supposedly benevolent attitude of the missionary is exposed as nothing but a shameless façade behind which there lurk racist contempt, white attitudes of cultural superiority, and hidden vices. The Jesuit father likes punishing Aboriginal girls by smacking their naked bottoms (87), satisfies his sadistic needs by brutally striking those he is supposed to care for (88), refers to Aborigines as savages (87), and describes them as superstitious and primitive people in need of being civilized: "'It saddens me a great deal, but what can you do? Life goes on, [...] and we must bring these poor ignorants into the modern age'" (89). At the same time, the priest is characterized as a lazy glutton and drunkard who could not care less for the aborigines he is in charge of. He is the living stereotype of the racist colonial missionary.

Although Tommy is the representative of Aboriginal Australia in the novel as well as the instrument of postcolonial revenge, he is not a fundamentalist representative of a nativist position. Significantly, he is a half-breed – half-Aboriginal and half-white – and this allows him to take up less extreme positions than some of the other Aboriginal characters in the novel, who are fundamentalists and have a nativist position. For example, when he meets Jarroo, a full-blood Aboriginal and "sub-chief of a fierce southern tribe" (95), the latter complains about the fact that some of the Indigenous Australians he has met in Brisbane "'seem to get on pretty well with the white fullahs'" (96). This, however, is countered by Tommy, who takes up a more understanding position when he says: "'They do what they have to in order to live. I wouldn't think any less of them for that'" (96). On the other hand, this does not mean that Tommy no longer cherishes Aboriginal customs. He insists on the acceptance of tribal rules, such as those concerning taboos. Thus, when two young Aboriginal men dance one of the sacred initiation dances of their tribe in front of women in a pub, Tommy allows his native friend Boonger to hit them and to reprimand them for this infringement (103). Aboriginal justice also has to be meted out in the episode of the blacktracker Bunda of the Gullilee tribe, who has worked for the Native Mounted Police and had a part in the killing of many Aboriginal people, including his own, whom he delivered to the white oppressors. Tommy decides to deliver him to the spirits of his own tribe, whom he betrayed, and Bunda's sufferings are described in drastic terms, conjuring up a vision of hell:

> Tommy closed his ears to Bunda's screaming. He would scream for a long time yet and beg for oblivion. But the people of the now-extinct Gullilee blood had learnt much from their migloo tormentors and would see to it that Bunda remained conscious until the end of eternity [...]. (127)

The suspense created in this novel is greatly heightened by the fact that such demonstrations of Aboriginal revenge are linked with obscure hints at the impending doom awaiting white Australians in the context of the scheme devised by the Indigenous gods described in the prologue. Thus, Tommy claims: "'No migloo who walks on this land is innocent. They are all guilty! And they shall all be punished for what they have done'" (131).

It is interesting to see the ways in which the novel establishes transcultural postcolonial solidarity[26] among the oppressed victims of white colonialism in Australia and beyond. For example, Bulley Macow is defended by Jack Finlay, a white Australian of Irish descent (61): i.e. a member of the very ethnic group which during the colonial period provided the greatest number of convicts, people who were more frequently transported than others and most consistently discriminated against and abused, Ireland having been England's first colony. As a member of an ethnic group that has often been racialized as an inferior Other, Finlay can understand Aboriginal grievances much better than any of the other white Australians in the novel; hence, he works as "the voluntary president of the Native Charity League" (61). Tommy himself is explicitly aware of his own race's fellowship with the Irish as another people suffering from the iniquities of British colonialism:

> Watching the whites with a wry smile, Tommy again thought about the incredible damage that the English race had done to the world. The Irish people had also developed a noble civilisation, but the likes of Cromwell had crushed them without mercy, taking their land and reducing them to enslavement. The tribes of Uluru were not the only victims. (182)

It is significant that the saviour figure of this novel is not a full-blooded Aboriginal, but a half-breed. This is one of various signifiers in the text that

---

[26] Castro talks about the novel's "international and pan-indigenous context" ("Imaginary (Re)Vision," 160) and Knudsen refers to "the obvious multicultural influence on Watson's narrative" (*The Circle & the Spiral*, 271).

point in the direction of a relativization of the harsh binary opposition between black and white, good and evil, despite the very clear condemnation of colonialism and white injustice. Even the authority of the gods is relativized in a scene in which the wise spirit Ningi tells Tommy, his pupil:

> 'In time you will join us and will come to know that you revere the gods too highly, Tommy Gubba. They are an ancient race, too preoccupied with their vanities and their stupidities to warrant such respect from a Kadaitcha as skilled as yourself.'
> Ningi's words had a terrible impact. The old bird was talking sacrilege, betraying Biamee and his pantheon of greater beings. His words opened up a shattering vista of a world that was barren and colourless, a chilling wasteland without gods. Tommy's mind reeled, unable to countenance so meaningless an existence. (226)

Aboriginal mythology here is de-absolutized by the words of Ningi, and Tommy's reaction makes it clear to the reader that the Indigenous gods are first and foremost a cultural agent for the vanquishing of human existential loneliness. This is a remarkable hint at cultural relativism in a text whose strategic essentialism throughout the greater part of the novel re-asserts Aboriginal values against those of white culture.

Tommy's status as a saviour figure is underlined in the novel by imagery reminiscent of the Biblical story of the birth of Christ. The events take place around Christmas (see 170), and Tommy impregnates his Aboriginal girlfriend Jelda so that, at the end of the novel, a baby is indeed soon to be born. Jelda's impregnation by the young Kadaitcha takes place in a graveyard for white Australians, a place Tommy is particularly fond of:

> his psyche was being appeased by the symbolism of the graveyard. After all, the whites who had been given back to the land in this place had probably spent much of their earthly time desecrating the same soil within which they were now entombed. (161)

As if to re-assert their Aboriginal identity against the white colonizers, Tommy and Jelda make love in the graveyard under "the huge Moreton Bay fig that had been born long before the coming of the migloo" (200), thus symbolically erasing the latter's existence in Australia (see 203; 206). The description of a sexual act turns into an Indigenous rejection of the whole colonialist period and looks forward to a future which returns to the pre-colonial past. Revenge will be taken and the traces of white colonialism will be obliterated so that the pre-colonial status will be re-established.

Aboriginal and white ways of conceptualizing the world, we are told here, are totally different, and an Indigenous, organic, socially responsible and caring mode of existence is challengingly pitted against white culture, which is characterized as mindlessly hedonistic, self-centred, and potentially destructive. This comparison constitutes an act of re-assertion of Aboriginal knowledge and identity.

Aboriginal and white conceptualizations of nature are contrasted by Watson in order to deconstruct the hypocrisies and inconsistencies of white culture from an Indigenous point of view. Moreover, the text shows how facts and knowledge of the past are manipulated by the perpetrators of white racist crimes.

The novel stages the various steps of Aboriginal revenge in graphic terms, and all the evil-doers get their due, from Judge Jones and Booka's other white friends, who are all killed in a ferocious way, through Sambo, to Roth himself, whom Tommy heroically vanquishes in a duel. But the vengeful fighter Tommy in the end takes up a conciliatory position despite his hatred of the migloos and his contempt for their black collaborators. When Ningi tells him that the black possum people, among them Jelda, are marked for death, Tommy contradicts him:

> 'there has been too much killing, too much death [...] Let Biamee now give life and he shall be honoured for it. [...] I shall take no action against any of the black possum blood.' (301)

Tommy here refuses to do Biamee's bidding and pits a more peaceful position against that of the highest god. And even as far as the migloo themselves are concerned, Tommy does not destroy them all but asks Biamee to impose "a terrible retribution" upon them, which, after all, turns out to be a comparatively mild punishment: "For every one hundred migloo, there had to be one that knew depthless tragedy and sorrow" (310). The ultimate destruction of the migloo is thus avoided. However, Tommy has to pay dearly for his meddling with the will and plans of Biamee: the god allows Tommy to be put on trial by the whites and to be sentenced to death by hanging. This is commented on in a way which yet again turns Tommy into an Aboriginal Jesus figure:

> So many lives had been extinguished, so many destinies reduced to nothing. Such was the lot of the Kadaitcha blood; it was they who had to atone for the sins of the land. (309).

The novel thus does not have an undiluted happy ending, which would have been unconvincing in view of the problems depicted. But Aboriginal knowledge and identity have been re-asserted in what is one of the most violent and multi-faceted anglophone texts written by an Indigenous Australian in recent years.

WORKS CITED

Althans, Katrin. *Darkness Subverted: Aboriginal Gothic in Black Australian Literature and Film* (Göttingen: V&R unipress & Bonn UP, 2010).

Ariss, Robert. "Writing black: the construction of an Aboriginal discourse," in *Past and Present: The Construction of Aboriginality*, ed. J.R. Beckett (Canberra: Aboriginal Studies Press, 1988): 131–46.

Baker, Suzanne. "Magic Realism as a Postcolonial Strategy: *The Kadaitcha Sung*," *SPAN: Journal of the South Pacific Association for Commonwealth Literature and Language Studies* 32 (1991): 55–63.

Castro, Estelle. "Imaginary (Re)Vision: Politics and Poetics in Sam Watson's *The Kadaitcha Sung* and Eric Willmot's *Below the Line*," *Anglophonia: French Journal of English Studies* 21 (2007): 159–70.

Dean, Elizabeth. "An Interview with Sam Watson," *Famous Reporter* 11 (June 1995), http://walleahpress.com.au/int-watson.html (accessed 23 November 2011).

Fletcher, M.D. "Australian political identity: Aboriginal and otherwise – Carey/ Malouf/ Watson," in *Proceedings of the 2000 Conference of the Australasian Political Studies Association*, ed. Francis Castles & John Uhr (Canberra: Australian National University, 2000): 1–8, apsa2000.anu.edu.au/confpapers/fletcher.rtf (accessed 23 November 2011).

Gelder, Ken, & Jane M. Jacobs. *Uncanny Australia: Sacredness and Identity in a Postcolonial Nation* (Melbourne: Melbourne UP, 1998).

Gilbert, Kevin. "Introduction" to Gilbert, *Inside Black Australia* (Ringwood, Victoria: Penguin, 1988): xv–xxiv.

Hall, Kate. "'All are implicated': Violence and Accountability in Sam Watson's *The Kadaitcha Sung* and Alexis Wright's *Plains of Promise*," in *Frontier Skirmishes: Literary and Cultural Debates in Australia after 1992*, ed. Russell West–Pavlov & Jennifer Wawrzinek (Anglistische Forschungen 409; Heidelberg: Winter, 2010): 199–214.

Knudsen, Eva Rask. *The Circle & the Spiral: A Study of Australian Aboriginal and New Zealand Māori Literature* (Cross/Cultures 68; Amsterdam & Atlanta GA: Rodopi, 2004).

Lever, Susan. "The Bicentennial and the Millennium: The Dissident Voices of David Foster and Sam Watson," in *'And What Books Do You Read?': New Studies in Australian Literature*, ed. Irmtraud Petersson & Martin Duwell (Brisbane: U of Queensland P, 1996): 101–11.

McMahon–Coleman, Kimberley. "Arctic and Outback: Indigenous Literature at the 'Ends of the Earth'," *Australasian Canadian Studies* 26.1 (2008): 43–58.

Mudrooroo. *The Indigenous Literature of Australia: Milli Milli Wangka* (Melbourne: Hyland House, 1997).

Watson, Sam. "I Say This To You: Sam Watson, Manager of Brisbane Aboriginal Legal Service and Author of *The Kadaitcha Sung* (Penguin 1990), talks to *Meanjin*," *Meanjin* 53.4 (Summer 1994): 589–96.

——. *The Kadaitcha Sung* (Ringwood, Victoria: Penguin, 1990).

Weaver, Roslyn. "'Smudged, Distorted and Hidden': Apocalypse as Protest in Indigenous Speculative Fiction," in *Science Fiction, Imperialism and the Third World: Essays on Postcolonial Literature and Film*, ed. Ericka Hoagland & Reema Sarwal, foreword by Andy Sawyer (Jefferson NC: McFarland, 2010): 99–114.

Gallows Humour and Stereotyping in the Nyungar Writer Alf Taylor's Short Fiction
A White Cross-Racial Reading

ANNE BREWSTER

> Within the context of black/white relations, a
> laugh [is not] just a simple laugh[1]

MIKHAIL BAKHTIN POINTS TO THE CAPACITY and universal spread of literary humour, arguing that laughter is as important as seriousness in posing significant 'problems' in literature.[2] In Australia, Aboriginal writers have deployed humour across a range of literary and extra-literary genres. Indigenous life stories have their fair share of comic narratorial modes: books that come to mind are Ruby Langford Ginibi's *Don't Take Your Love to Town* (1988), Alice Nannup's *When the Pelican Laughed* (1992) and Monty Walgar's *Jinangga* (1999). Many works of fiction also made use of humour in a wide range of styles. These include Marie Munkara's *Every Secret Thing* (2009), Alexis Wright's *Carpentaria* (2006),[3] Vivienne Cleven's *bitin' back* (2001), Gayle Kennedy's *Me, Antman & Fleabag* (2007), Jared Thomas's *Sweet Guy* (2006), and Herb Wharton's *Un-*

---

[1] Betsy Huang, "Ralph Ellison's Offense of Laughter," paper presented at the 2000 Modernist Studies Association (MSA) Conference (Philadelphia, 2000), http://www.clarku.edu/activelearning/departments/english/huang/huang.cfm (accessed 12 May 2011).

[2] Mikhail M. Bakhtin, *Rabelais and his World*, tr. Hélène Iswolsky (Bloomington: Indiana UP, 1984): 66.

[3] I have written about satire in Brewster, "Indigenous Sovereignty and the Crisis of Whiteness in Alexis Wright's *Carpentaria*," *Australian Literary Studies* 25.4 (2010): 85–100.

branded (1992). Poets who mobilize humour include Anita Heiss, especially *I'm not racist but…* (2007). There are many comic Indigenous plays such as Jimmy Chi's *Bran Nue Dae* (1990; movie adaptation by Reg Cribb and Rachel Perkins, 2010) and, more recently, Tony Briggs's *The Sapphires* (2004), Scott Rankin's *Namatjira* (2010) and (with Leah Purcell) *Box the Pony* (1997), Ningali Lawford's *Ningali* (1995), and Reg Cribb's *Krakouer!* (2009, adapted from Sean Gorman's novel *Brother Boys*, 2005). However, in spite of the abundance of humour in contemporary Aboriginal literature and its evident significance in both Indigenous cultural production and Indigenous day-to-day life, there has been almost no analysis of Aboriginal humour or how it works cross-racially. One of the few people who has written on Aboriginal humour, the Aboriginal commentator Lillian Holt, observes that humour is "one of the least researched areas"[4] in Aboriginal culture, although, she wryly adds, in other fields Aboriginal people have been "researched to death by experts."[5] This last comment sounds a warning to me as a white 'expert'; in thinking about the kind of attention I bring to bear on this literature, I hope my enquiry will not contribute to the tradition in which Aboriginal people, in Holt's words, have been "dissected," "studied," and "labelled."[6]

I find Aboriginal humour powerful and compelling, and in this essay I want to address the ways in which it compels and is taken up by white readers such as myself. This is not to assume that I occupy the position of a universal reader or that white readers such as myself are the definitive or primary audience for Aboriginal literature. Aboriginal literature convenes many different kinds of audiences – including Aboriginal and other non-white audiences – locally, nationally, and globally. Its humour is polysemous and fluid, and speaks to this range of audiences in a variety of ways. Given its slipperiness and semantic complexity, there are dimensions of Aboriginal literary humour that inevitably elude me. In this essay I speculate, as a white reader, about ways it renegotiates cross-racial relationality.

Many Aboriginal commentators have talked about the important role that humour has played and continues to play in Aboriginal cultures (for example, Holt). I am interested in the role it plays for white audiences. I would suggest

---

[4] Lillian Holt, "Aboriginal Humour: A Conversational Corroborree," in *Serious Frolic: Essays on Australian Humour*, ed. Fran de Groen & Peter Kirkpatrick (St Lucia: U of Queensland P, 2009): 93.

[5] Holt, "Aboriginal Humour: A Conversational Corroborree," 85.

[6] "Aboriginal Humour: A Conversational Corroborree," 85.

that humour has been a highly effective strategy by which Aboriginal authors and performers have intervened in white public spheres, and that this visibility and audibility have functioned to interrupt the white self-preoccupation and solipsism that have tended to disavow the fact that, since arriving in Australia, white people have been intimately, if painfully, connected, materially and psychically, to Aboriginal people. The telling of jokes and stories places Indigenous writers in the strong position of commanding the attention of white readers and audiences. Through its linguistic skill and aesthetic effects, Aboriginal humour, as I will argue with reference to Freud, has a strong impact on white people bodily and cognitively in ways that are sometimes beyond their immediate control; it gains their attention almost without their knowing it.

Many theorists of humour have commented on the contagious nature of laughter. Freud said it is one of the most "highly infectious expressions of psychical states,"[7] and Jung stated that "nothing is more contagious than [...] laughing."[8] Nevertheless, the Victorian novelist and poet George Meredith allowed that there are people who refuse to laugh. He suggested that a refusal to engage in laughter can be political; the "non-laugher," he observed, invariably "dignifies [...] dislike as an objection in morality."[9] Being wooed to laugh, to engage with Indigenous humour, can constitute a shift in the authority of whiteness. Aboriginal humour can thus function as a powerful political and cultural weapon not only to consolidate Aboriginality but also to counter the effects of coloniality and to critique whiteness. In his study of the literature of the Harlem Renaissance, Mike Chasar suggests that the "black laugh could go where the physical black body in many cases could not and thus could uniquely challenge white control of public space."[10] I would argue that the same is true of Aboriginal literary humour.

Analysts of humour from Sigmund Freud and Henri Bergson onwards have commented on the decidedly social nature of humour – the fact that it in-

---

[7] Sigmund Freud, *Jokes and their Relation to the Unconscious*, tr. James Strachey (*Der Witz und seine Beziehung zum Unbewussten*, 1905; tr. 1960; Penguin Freud Library; Harmondsworth: Penguin, 1976): 209.

[8] Jung, quoted in Mike Chasar, "The Sounds of Black Laughter and the Harlem Renaissance: Claude McKay, Sterling Brown, Langston Hughes," *American Literature* 80.1 (March 2008): 63.

[9] George Meredith, *An Essay on Comedy and the Uses of the Comic Spirit* (London: Archibald Constable, 1905): 9.

[10] Chasar, "The Sounds of Black Laughter and the Harlem Renaissance," 58.

volves us in relations with others.[11] Bergson, for example, says that "our laughter is always the laughter of a group."[12] Nevertheless, in spite of the recognition of its social dimensions, humour is often characterized as unchanging and ahistorical.[13] Bakhtin advises against the notion that "laughter is the same in every time and age, that a joke is always nothing more than a joke,"[14] insisting upon the historicity of laughter. I would argue that the same is true of contemporary literary humour. In this essay, I investigate the psychical and cultural work that humour performs in an embodied white cross-racial reading of Aboriginal literature. I attend to the intersubjective and interactive 'scene' of literary humour, which, like the scene of irony that Linda Hutcheon examines in another context, "involves relations of power based in relations of communication."[15] I take Paul Lewis's suggestion that humour has the potential to "redefine the relationship between [social] groups"[16] as a starting point to speculate on how Aboriginal humour draws me, as a white reader, into relations of proximity with Aboriginality and as a result, bodily and cognitively estranges me from whiteness. I draw on Freud's discussion of joking in order to think about the psychical operations of humour in cross-racial readings of Aboriginal literature. Although Freud's analysis of jokes focuses on the 'real-life' genre of the joke, his model, I would suggest, lends itself to the analysis of realist fiction, because fiction's narrative fashioning of worlds and characters in some degree mimics the embodied interpersonal exchanges of 'real-life' actors telling jokes and performing humorous incidents. I start from the obvious but important point that to narrate a joke, funny story or anecdote (in literature as in 'real life') is to assume a speaking posi-

---

[11] Freud, *Jokes and their Relation to the Unconscious*; Henri Bergson, *Laughter: An Essay on the Meaning of the Comic*, tr. Cloudesley Brereton & Fred Rothwell (*Le rire: Essai sur la signification du comique*, 1900; London: Macmillan, 1911).

[12] Henri Bergson, "Laughter" (from *Le rire*, 1900), in *Comedy: "An Essay on Comedy" by George Meredith and "Laughter" by Henri Bergson*, ed. & intro. Wylie Sypher (1956; Baltimore MD & London: Johns Hopkins UP, 1994): 64, quoted in Joseph Boskin, *Rebellious Laughter: People's Humor in American Culture* (Syracuse NY: Syracuse UP, 1997): 201.

[13] Mike Chasar makes the same observation ("The Sounds of Black Laughter and the Harlem Renaissance," 78 fn 14).

[14] Bakhtin, *Rabelais and his World*, 134.

[15] Linda Hutcheon, *Irony's Edge* (New York & London: Routledge, 1994): 2.

[16] Paul Lewis, *Comic Effects: Interdisciplinary Approaches to Humor in Literature* (Albany: State U of New York P, 1989): 37.

tion. It is to establish a set of contractual relations which facilitate the psychical process of humour. It is the relations contracted in a white cross-racial reading of Aboriginal literary humour that are the object of my analysis.

In the following discussion, I study the impact of humour in the Nyungar writer Alf Taylor's story collection *Long Time Now* (2001) on a white reader such as myself.[17] Taylor is part of a Nyungar literary tradition which includes writers such as Rosemary van den Berg, Glenyse Ward, Jack Davis, Richard Wilkes, Graeme Dixon, and Kim Scott. His stories emerge from the rich density of Nyungar vernacular, culture, and sociality. The world they present seems to me both bleak and warm. While they depict the dispossession of the Stolen Generations and document the domestic violence, poverty, and alcoholism that are the legacies of this history, they also depict Nyungar culture as strong, inventive, loving, and funny. I examine here the humour in one story from *Long Time Now*, "Toby." This is an apparently simple tale with a straightforward, open-ended plot. As in many of Taylor's stories, it ends with the death of one of the characters. Its thematic focus is alcohol, whose impact on contemporary Aboriginal communities and families is nothing short of devastating. I analyse how Taylor's humour in "Toby" negotiates the fraught issue of alcoholism, focusing in particular on gallows humour. The narrative impetus of the story is largely carried by micro-stories – the anecdotes, jokes, and yarns embedded in the interactions and the dialogue of the characters.

The story focuses on a group of drinking Nyungars and the jokes and yarns they tell each other; drinking gives rise to laughter and vice versa. They joke about the car in which the group travels to the bush for their drinking session. At the conclusion of the story, the driver, Sam, who has gone to buy more alcohol, is reported to have died in a crash in this car on the way back. This event carries the 'moral' of the cautionary tale – that alcohol is literally deadly. Here is a section from that story:

> "This thing sounds as if it's running on one spark plug," said Toby, wincing at the noise coming from the motor.
> "Don't worry, the other spark plugs will catch up to the one working on its own," said Sam, smiling to the blokes at the back.
> "Yeah, Toby, you can't beat a Valiant."

---

[17] This essay builds on my initial study of Alf Taylor's humour, extending the exploratory argument of that article. See Brewster, "Humour and the Defamiliarisation of Whiteness in the Short Fiction of Australian Indigenous Writer Alf Taylor," *Journal of Postcolonial Writing* 44.4 (2008): 427–38.

"Looks to me," said Toby, "that somebody already beaten it about the body with a crowbar or an axe." Sam was too busy putting the Valiant into motion to take any notice of Toby's smart remarks.

As they chugged off, there was a shout of joy from Sam. He didn't believe he was moving. There was a sickening noise coming from the motor. Yes, if the cops got hold of this car, they would blow it to pieces just to *keep Australia beautiful*. Reckon the occupants would go with it.[18]

Sam's car functions as a metonym, both of the poverty of these characters' lives and of their alcohol addiction. The car provides the means for the group to continue its drinking (by moving from the pub to the bush). It is the agent of Sam's alcohol-infused death. But the car is also a vehicle of humour. The explanation of how Sam has acquired it – through a complex process of bartering – is one of the story's funniest anecdotes. It turns out that Sam swapped a dog and the family TV for the car while his wife was away for the day. Toby muses that the person who swapped the car would end up giving the 'mangy mutt' (37) away and that 'the TV would do the full cycle of [bartering between] Nyungar families before it would eventually get back to Sam and his wife' (37). The very difficult issues of poverty and alcoholism which beset the Nyungar community represented in these stories are thus approached through the mechanism of humour.

There are many different styles of humour in Taylor's fiction; I will focus on two instances of gallows humour in "Toby." Gallows humour is often the product of particularly dire social, political, or physical circumstances, emerging from a 'precarious or dangerous situation' and, sometimes, impending death.[19] Various sociological and literary studies have located this type of

---

[18] Alf Taylor, "Toby," in Taylor, *Long Time Now: Stories of the Dreamtime, the Here and Now* (Broome, WA: Magabala, 2001): 34–35. (My emphasis.) Further page references are in the main text.

[19] Antonin J. Obrdlik, "'Gallows Humor': A Sociological Phenomenon," *American Journal of Sociology* 47.5 (March 1942): 709. Gallows humour is sometimes used in circumstances where death is immanent or unavoidable. In this essay, I use it to refer to humour used in a number of situations in Taylor's stories which depict the 'precarious and dangerous situations' that arise for Aboriginal people as targets of systemic white power and violence. I also use it to refer to humour used within the fiction in situations of self-abuse which is severe, ongoing and debilitating and may also lead to death (for example, the abuse of alcohol).

humour in war zones, military occupations or concentration camps[20] and as a legacy of slavery;[21] it has also been seen as characteristic of many minority-group cultures.[22] In a study of American popular culture, Joseph Boskin argues that, "perched on the edge of personal destruction, gallows humour confronts a seemingly hopeless situation."[23] He sees gallows humour as an index of 'group morale' and 'resistance' in extreme conditions.[24] The literary theorist Paul Lewis discusses gallows humour in Alice Walker's fiction, arguing that it functions for her characters "to create distance from [their] pain, to liberate [them], at least temporarily, from otherwise inescapable torment"; as such, it is "an assertion of independence from the brutalising conditions of life."[25] In the extensive literature on the Jewish Holocaust, gallows humour is identified as a mechanism for providing distance from and protest about an "intolerable" reality.[26] The very act of survival itself is a reason for triumph.[27] In my reading of "Toby," I suggest that gallows humour buoys up the characters by affirming intra-group bonding (and is thus indeed an index of morale and resistance). Also, I draw on Freud to argue that the humour works cross-racially to critique racialized violence. In both of these functions, I argue, the humour works for me as a white reader to invert negative stereotypes of Aboriginal people and alcohol.

In his *Jokes and their Relation to the Unconscious* (1905), Freud links joking to hostility and aggression. He focuses specifically on "tendentious"

---

[20] Obrdlik, "'Gallows Humor': A Sociological Phenomenon"; Boskin, *Rebellious Laughter*.

[21] Lewis, *Comic Effects*. See also, for example, Jerry W. Ward, Jr., who identifies Richard Wright's humour as deriving from a black heritage of "gallows humour [that] flavoured the every day racial life in the southern United States as one lived the ethics of Jim Crow"; Ward, "Two Research Notes on Richard Wright," *Southern Quarterly* 48.2 (Winter 2011): 79.

[22] Joseph Boskin, *Rebellious Laughter*; Alf Taylor, in Brewster, "That child is my hero," interview with Alf Taylor, *Aboriginal History* 31 (2007): 165–77.

[23] Boskin, *Rebellious Laughter*, 41.

[24] *Rebellious Laughter*, 41.

[25] Lewis, *Comic Effects*, 80.

[26] Sidra DeKoven Ezrahi, "After Such Knowledge, What Laughter?" *Yale Journal of Criticism* 14.1 (Spring 2001): 300.

[27] Mark Cory, "Comedic Distance in Holocaust Literature," *Journal of American Culture* 18.1 (Spring 1995): 36.

jokes: i.e. jokes that are "directed against someone,"[28] and it is this interest in the tendentious that makes Freud's work germane to my project of thinking about Aboriginal literature's engagement with and critique of whiteness and racism. Freud figures the psychical process of joking as a scene of three people: the teller of the joke, the butt of the joke, and a third person – the hearer or the audience. (I will refer to this person as the 'reader'). He argues that tendentious jokes allow the teller "to exploit something ridiculous in [their] enemy."[29] The teller does this by 'enlisting' the audience against its 'enemy' through the telling of the joke. In this analysis, Freud focuses largely on the relationship between the teller and reader, arguing that the "collaboration" between the two represents an important bond that facilitates the joking process. The teller, in effect, "bribes the hearer with [the joke's] yield of pleasure to take sides with [him or her]."[30] In applying Freud's ideas in a reading of Taylor's fiction, I will explore the transaction in his fiction between the narrator, the reader, and the butt of the joke, and argue that a white readerly encounter with the text may mirror in some respects Freud's transactional model. I argue that the 'jokes' related by the characters and the narrator in Taylor's fiction mimic the interchange between the three key actors or agents of joking modelled by Freud (the teller, the listener, and the butt). However, I argue that, in a white *cross-racial* reading of Aboriginal humour, the relationship between these three actors is modified through a destabilization of the structural hierarchy of whiteness and racial difference, thus calling for a revision of Freud's model.

I focus below on the narratorial 'joke' about the police blowing up the car and its occupants as an example of Taylor's gallows humour. We are told: "'if the cops got hold of this car, they would blow it to pieces just to *keep Australia beautiful*. Reckon the occupants would go with it'" (35; my italics). The humour in the episode up until this point has been mocking, affectionate, and self-deprecating; the witty, disparaging remarks about the car contrast with Sam's absurd but endearing pride in his vehicle. The joke about the police blowing up the car and its occupants to "keep Australia beautiful"

---

[28] Virginia Richter's gloss on the word 'tendentious' (from Strachey's translation) is illuminating and apt. See Richter, "Laughter and Aggression, Desire and Derision in a Postcolonial Context," in *Cheeky Fictions: Laughter and the Postcolonial*, ed. Susanne Reichl & Mark Stein (Amsterdam & New York: Rodopi, 2005): 63.

[29] Freud, *Jokes and their Relation to the Unconscious*, 147.

[30] *Jokes and their Relation to the Unconscious*, 147.

continues the mood of Nyungar self-deprecation but, for me, it also introduces an undercurrent of bleakness. We could say that the butt or target of this final joke is not only the Nyungars with their clapped-out car but the racialized violence that has become institutionalized in practices of law enforcement.

The phrase "keep Australia beautiful" is a reference to a high-profile national campaign which deploys discourses of ecology, philanthropy, corporatism, civic pride, and moral responsibility to promote 'Tidy Towns', 'Sustainable Cities', and 'Clean Beaches'.[31] The iconic images of this campaign, which has been running for forty years, are the cleaning-up of litter and rubbish. The joking remark in Taylor's story correlates not only the car but its Indigenous occupants with the detritus that mars 'beautiful Australia' and in doing so the joke segues from self-deprecation to something more pointed. The characterization of Indigenous people as rubbish is, for me, disturbing and embarrassing; it rehearses the habitual white positioning of Indigenous people outside modernity as the sub- or infra-human[32] remnants of a bygone era, and excludes them from the promissory future of the white nation. However, it is also a trope for all that whiteness fears to contain or confront within itself – criminality, uncleanliness, addiction, and guilt. The Murri novelist Sam Watson gives us an insight into how postcolonial guilt, for example, is channelled into racialized aggression:

> To be Black in Australia is to live in an alien place - a world of fear, hatred and loathing. Each and every time that we set foot on the white streets, we [...] hear that great unasked question – why are you still alive? What right do you have to be here now, within out midst? [...] Those of us who have survived [...] are made to feel that we have no place within this new white world that the settlers have built upon our land and we are made to carry forever, the bloody cross of our own stubborn refusal to die.[33]

---

[31] See the "Keep Australia Beautiful" website, http://www.kab.org.au (accessed 31 January 2011).

[32] See Kay Anderson, *Race and the Crisis of Humanism* (London & New York: Routledge, 2007). See also Aileen Moreton–Robinson: "The existence of those who can be defined as truly human requires the presence of others who are considered less human," Moreton–Robinson, *Whitening Race: Essays in Social and Cultural Criticism* (Canberra: Aboriginal Studies Press, 2004): 76.

[33] Sam Watson, "Hanson: A Murri Perspective," in *The Rise and Fall of One Nation*, ed. Michael Leach, Geoffrey Stokes & Ian Ward (St Lucia: U of Queensland P, 2000): 193.

In this essay, I am arguing that Taylor's gallows humour critiques the aggressive subjection and exclusion that subtend the pedagogical nationalism of 'Keep Australia Beautiful' and disavow Indigenous people's prior and continuing occupation of their territories. Taylor's gallows humour reminds me as a white reader of the precariousness of Indigenous lives.[34] As a white reader I am ambivalently positioned by Taylor's gallows humour. I am 'brought over to the side' of the teller (the narrator) as I witness the effects of this violence. In Freud's model of the joke, laughter is enabled by the teller and the reader forming a coalition in order to laugh at the butt of the joke. But what happens in white cross-racial readings of Aboriginal humour where whiteness is the butt? How do racial difference and whiteness inflect and complicate Freud's model of the psychical transaction between teller, listener/reader, and butt? In the joke about the blowing-up of the car, the narrator[35] is Aboriginal and the reader (in my case) is white. Moreover, the persons constituting the butt or the target of the joke – the police (an index of the ongoing systemic violence of coloniality) – are also white.

It is commonly observed in studies of humour that humour often works "down the hierarchy."[36] Aristotle, in *The Poetics*, for example, asserts that comedy makes us laugh at "low characters."[37] But what happens when Aboriginal people 'laugh up'?[38] What happens when the hierarchy of the psychical

---

[34] "Life expectancy for Aboriginal and Torres Strait Islander men is estimated to be 11.5 years less than for non-Indigenous men [...]. For Aboriginal and Torres Strait Islander women, the difference is 9.7 years [...]. For the period 1999–2003, for both Indigenous males and females, there were almost three times as many deaths for all causes as would be expected based on the rates of non-Indigenous Australians. Data from national surveys in 1994, 1995 and 2001 and 2004–05 show that Indigenous Australians were more likely than other Australians to smoke, consume alcohol at hazardous levels, be exposed to violence, and to be categorised as obese, all of which are significant health risk factors that could lead to mortality" (Australian Bureau of Statistics. Deaths, Australia. Latest Issue Released 10 November 2010).

[35] It is not necessary at this point to distinguish between the author and the narrator, as both constitute Taylor's Aboriginal literary subjectivity.

[36] Lewis, *Comic Effects*, 36.

[37] *Comic Effects*, 33.

[38] I gesture here to the common Aboriginal phrase of 'talking up' to white people. See, for example, the title of Aileen Moreton–Robinson's influential book *Talkin' Up to the White Woman: Aboriginal Women and Feminism* (St Lucia: U of Queensland P, 2000).

process of telling the joke is inverted from the outset – that is, when an Aboriginal subject/narrator tells a joke in which the reader is white and the butt is whiteness?

This is the position in which I find myself with Taylor's gallows humour. The joke skates along the borderline of pleasure and discomfort. What am I, as a white person, laughing *at*? Is the Aboriginal author/narrator laughing *with* or *at* me? The answers to these questions are difficult to disentangle from the unsettling ambiguity of cross-racial humour. In fact, the work that cross-racial humour undertakes, I'd argue, is precisely to foreground the entanglement of the white reader in a mesh of cross-racial proximities and relationality. The discomfort of white laughter in a cross-racial context arises from the levelling of white power and the democratization of speaking positions. In contradistinction to the white public sphere, which is largely sealed off from the intervention of its others and where the dominant white subject attempts to retain mastery of cross-racial intersubjectivity, the *multiracial* public sphere convened by cross-racial humour dispels the distantiation or separation of the white listener/reader. No longer occupying an unmarked position of power, the white listener/reader is convoked alongside non-white subjectivities and points of view.

This process, as I have suggested, is enabled precisely through the slipperiness and ambiguity of humour. Humour enables Indigenous writers such as Alf Taylor to expose or address issues surrounding racism that are difficult to raise overtly. In circumstances where a direct critique of coloniality might be rebuffed, humour can be efficacious in gaining a white public's attention. To quote Mike Chasar again, the "black laugh [can] go where the physical black body [can]not."[39] It can slip a negative critique past the conscious, analytical mind of the white reader who may not want to compromise her control of the intersubjective situation. Freud explains that jokes are conveyed to hearers/readers in a way that side-steps their conscious mind. Laughter, he says,

> is in fact the product of an automatic process which is only made possible by our conscious attention's being kept away from it... we scarcely ever know what we are laughing at in a joke.[40]

---

[39] Chasar, "The Sounds of Black Laughter and the Harlem Renaissance," 58.
[40] Freud, *Jokes and their Relation to the Unconscious*, 207.

As Freud says, "while we are beginning to wonder [about the logic of the joke] we are already laughing; our attention has been caught unawares."[41] Laughter (or at least amusement) leads me as a white reader into relation with the Aboriginal narrator whose point of view I momentarily share.

Freud's model, however, doesn't accommodate the fundamental inversion of white authority which the emergence of Aboriginal subjectivity in white discursive space enacts. I am suggesting that, when both the reader and the butt of Indigenous humour are white, the psychical transaction between the three subject-positions of the joke modelled by Freud (the teller, the butt, and the reader) becomes multidirectional as the white gaze doubles back on itself. Aboriginal literature changes the focus of the literary and critical gaze and, concomitantly, challenges the white "possessive investment"[42] in literary subjectivity that has subtended the tradition of white Australian literature. No longer is the white reader simply analysing the Indigene from a putatively unmediated point of view. Rather, she recognizes (or, in Michelle Fine's term, "witnesses"[43]) her own whiteness from the Indigene's point of view.

The work of Freud's contemporary, the black American intellectual W.E.B. Du Bois, on the psychical operations of racialized intersubjectivity picks up where Freud's model leaves off, giving us a way of thinking through the effects of Aboriginal humour on whiteness. His foundational study, *The Souls of Black Folk* (1903), was published two years before Freud's *Der Witz und seine Beziehung zum Unbewussten*. Du Bois defined the black American experience as one of "double-consciousness" in which the black subject has the sense of "always looking at one's self through the eyes of others."[44] Concomitantly, I'd suggest, Aboriginal literary subjectivity reverses the white gaze to instantiate a sense of double-consciousness in white readers; it defamiliarizes whiteness. This disidentification involves in some measure a surrendering of authority. In being the butt of Aboriginal humour and by being captivated and manoeuvred by the aesthetic skill and the linguistic dexterity

---

[41] *Jokes and their Relation to the Unconscious*, 205.

[42] George Lipsitz, *The Possessive Investment in Whiteness: How White People Profit* (Philadelphia PA: Temple UP, 1998).

[43] Michelle Fine, "Witnessing Whiteness," in *Off White: Readings on Race, Power and Society*, ed. Michelle Fine, Linda C. Powell, L. Mun Wang & Lois Weis (New York & London: Routledge, 1997): 57–65.

[44] W.E.B. Du Bois, *The Souls of Black Folk* (1903; London: Archibald Constable, 1905): 3.

of the writer, a white reader must afford the Indigenous author a symbolic victory. The Anishinaabe writer Gerald Vizenor, for example, asserts that the white reader "salutes" the trickster of Indigenous storytelling.[45]

⌘

Much of the humour in the stories of *Long Time Now* appears to revolve around drinking. The comedy arises from the 'micro-stories' – the jokes, repartee, and anecdotes – generated by the sociality of Nyungars drinking together. This kind of humour might seem at odds with the pedagogical function of the cautionary tale in "Toby." Indeed, throughout the stories of *Long Time Now* there is an awareness of the impact on contemporary Aboriginal communities of alcohol, which is linked to the high mortality rates of Aboriginal people, to domestic violence, welfare dependence, and poverty. One of his books of poetry, *Winds* (1994), documents this painful struggle. Taylor has linked alcohol with the suffering he underwent as a child at New Norcia Mission where he first started drinking as a child.[46] In a comment reminiscent of the way theorists talk about the role of Jewish humour in the Shoah, Taylor says that humour enabled his survival as a child during his intolerable 'confinement' at New Norcia Mission. Of that childhood he has said: "without humour I would have been dead."[47] Taylor is passionate about the survival of Nyungar people and their culture. He has said of *Long Time Now* that "my message is mainly for the younger generation today: look, if you keep drinking and using drugs today, you won't even [reach] the age of these old guys."[48] To observe Taylor's sense of embeddedness in and commitment to the Nyungar community and its current political, social, and cultural concerns is not simply to restrict his fiction to an instrumentalizing function or even to suggest that it is *primarily* pedagogical. As I hoped I have implied, his humour is polyvalent and ambiguous. Social critique is only one of its effects, the range of which inevitably exceeds the present investigation.

How, then, does Taylor use humour in *Long Time Now* to mediate the difficult issue of alcohol abuse? In the concluding brief section I take up the issue of how Taylor's fiction explores the triangulation of humour, storytell-

---

[45] Gerald Vizenor, *The Trickster of Liberty: Tribal Heirs to a Wild Baronage* (Minneapolis: U of Minnesota P, 1988): xi.

[46] Brewster, "That child is my hero," 167–68.

[47] "That child is my hero," 169.

[48] "That child is my hero," 173.

ing, and alcohol. To do this, I examine the stereotype of the inebriated Aboriginal person. Virginia Richter says that "at the core of the joke is the stereotype"; she argues that the recognition and reproduction of the stereotype can be seen as "the basis for the 'coalition'"[49] between the teller and the reader. They distance themselves from the butt who personifies the stereotype. Racialized stereotypes function to differentiate and distance Aboriginal people from the white 'mainstream'. Marcia Langton describes the 'drunken Aborigine' as "the most common and enduring stereotype" of Aboriginal people; this "icon," she asserts, performs the work of transforming "the dangerous native into the pathetic mendicant 'Abo'."[50] She argues that, in the political and cultural economy of colonization, the stereotype has been used to criminalize Aboriginal people and to generate panic and alarm in mainstream society about "standards of civilised living falling."[51] She asserts: "Alcohol was used from the very beginning of British settlement [as] a crucially important strategy in dealing with Aboriginal people."[52]

> From the first settlement and throughout the frontier period, alcohol was used to engage Aboriginal people in discourse, [to] attract Aboriginal people into settlements, in barter for sexual favours from Aboriginal women, as payment for Aboriginal labour and to incite Aboriginal people to fight as street entertainment.[53]

She says that alcohol has been used as "an agent of seduction."[54] In the assimilationist era, for example, exemption certificates promised Aboriginal people access to alcohol but conspired to break community links by forbidding exempted people from drinking with family and friends. She argues that eugenicist discourse, which promulgated the spurious argument that Aboriginal people were genetically unable to tolerate alcohol, has been used to serve assimilationist agendas and justify the "extraordinary arrest rates of Aboriginal people, removal of Aboriginal children, exclusion of Aboriginal

---

[49] Richter, "Laughter and Aggression, Desire and Derision in a Postcolonial Context," 64.

[50] Marcia Langton, "Rum, Seduction and Death: 'Aboriginality' and Alcohol," *Oceania* 63.3 (March 1993): 197.

[51] Langton, "Rum, Seduction and Death," 195.

[52] "Rum, Seduction and Death," 201.

[53] "Rum, Seduction and Death," 196.

[54] "Rum, Seduction and Death," 196.

people from employment, education and a range of other services."[55] The stories in *Long Time Now* are set against the backdrop of colonialist violence, aggression, and contempt that Langton documents, and their characters are metonymic of the colonial relations she critiques. The rich network of humour which animates the stories is complex and polysemous, ranging from sentimental wishful humour to gallows humour. While the affectionately drawn inebriated characters in Taylor's stories might seem to a white reader to reiterate the damaging and offensive stereotype of the 'drunken Aborigine' that Langton identifies, I'd suggest that the operations of his humour are more complex.

Joseph Boskin has noted the elastic polarity of humour regarding the stereotype: "On the one hand, it reinforces pejorative images; on the other it facilitates the inversion of such stereotypes."[56] Taylor's humour embodies the tension that Boskin identifies: while it might be seen to reinforce racist stereotypes, it actually works to undo them. His humour mocks Nyungars in a gentle, self-deprecating way but its sharp (tendentious) edge also works to unmask the aggressive drives of colonizing whiteness, giving the lie to demeaning white stereotyping. In Taylor's gallows humour, white readers witness the role that violence plays in the historical production of degrading stereotypes, a history in which they themselves are embedded. Readers such as myself, I suggest, find not only their stereotypes of Aboriginal people defamiliarized but also those relating to the putative superiority and authority of whiteness.

There is a second brief instance of gallows humour in "Toby" which arises in the context of alcohol consumption. Willie, on opening his first bottle of beer, proposes a toast: "The white man maketh, the black man drinketh" (35). This comment parodies biblical language and holy communion, yoking alcohol and religion[57] together as twin vehicles of colonization. The remark addresses the serious issue of alcoholism in Aboriginal communities directly

---

[55] Langton, "Rum, Seduction and Death," 198–99.

[56] Boskin, *Rebellious Laughter*, 38.

[57] Christianity is critiqued elsewhere in "Toby" in the gentle satire of the two women. Aunty Flo is a "strong Christian" (32) who complains that "all Nyoongar kids today, soon as they get out of their nappies, straight to the pub. Ask them to come to church they say, 'No, I can't, gotta sore ankle'" (29). The other Christian in the story is Sam's hapless wife, who is away at an all-day 'Christian meeting' and is yet to learn of the loss of their family TV and dog, which have been bartered by Sam for the useless car. As a pious Christian she is an obvious butt – like Auntie Flo – for the jokes of the drinking Nyungars.

but with grim humour. It allows both the speaker and the author to step back from and acknowledge the issue, not with shame but with acerbity, as the joke recognizes Aboriginal alcoholism as a legacy of colonialism. This aphoristic joke thus puts colonial relations in a nutshell. It also performs intense affective work; its humour accommodates and expresses pain and anger but also provides some relief from them, obviating the emotional wear and tear that they usually exact. Lillian Holt quotes the American Indian novelist and humorist Thomas King on the subject of the interplay of pain, anger, and humour; he says:

> Those things that hurt in life, those things that continue to hurt about being Native in North America, I can handle those things through humour. I can't handle those through anger because, if I get angry about something, it just gets away from me. It just consumes me.[58]

I would argue also that the character Willie, who makes the remark "The white man maketh, the black man drinketh," is not seen as foolish at this point. Taylor has said that he aims to give his characters dignity, pride, integrity, and compassion,[59] and in this short story Willie and his friends exhibit all these characteristics. Any shame deriving from the jokes feels to me as though it attaches to the liberal white reader in the light of the history that Langton outlines. I am reminded of the fact that alcoholism, which is commonly seen as an 'Aboriginal problem', is actually endemic in *white* Australia, as indicated by recent, widely disseminated governmental campaigns to curb its role in the mainstream contexts of youth binge-drinking, drunk driving, and domestic violence.[60]

But alcohol and Christianity are not the only options for the Nyungars in "Toby." Toby finds an alternative source of hope in his ancestors' spirits. They have the power to speak to and regenerate his "spirit" (39) and they guide him away from alcohol in their forewarning of Sam's death. The sustenance that Toby draws from his ancestors' spirits is an affirmation of Indigenous sovereignty, which Aileen Moreton–Robinson defines as being

---

[58] Holt, "Aboriginal Humour: A Conversational Corroborree," 86.

[59] Brewster, "That child is my hero," 173.

[60] For a minority comedic critique of white attribution of 'a drinking problem' to Aboriginal people, see Fear of a Brown Planet, "White People": "No-one in this country has a scarier drinking problem than white people"; http://www.youtube.com/watch?v=38j8pSOekiY (accessed 27 June 2011).

"grounded within complex relations derived from the intersubstantiation of ancestral beings, humans and land."[61] This vision of embodied Indigenous sovereignty debunks the white utopian ideal of 'Beautiful Australia', which Taylor's fiction characterizes as necro-political.

Thus far in my analysis of Taylor's humour, I have largely been viewing humour from Freud's perspective in *Jokes*: i.e. as generated essentially from aggressive and hostile impulses. However, in a later brief article on humour, some twenty years after *Jokes*, Freud displayed a slightly different take, seeing humour not only as a hostile and aggressive force but also as one with positive and 'liberating' effects. In "Humour" (1928), he argues that "the humorous attitude" is one in which the subject refuses to be "compelled to suffer."[62] It acts to "protect" and "comfort" the subject; in doing so, it is essentially "rebellious" in its "repudiation" of a painful or damaging environment.[63]

In his pioneering study *The Signifying Monkey* (1988), Henry Louis Gates, Jr. examines the emergence and significance of humour in African-American literature. He argues that black humour enacts a semantic appropriation in which words and signs become "decolonised."[64] This happens through an emptying of a signifier, which is then filled with new (black) content. We can see this process in Taylor's humour where Indigenous literary subjectivity occupies the space of white signification and resignifies Nyungar subjectivity through the aesthetic skills and the troping of the Aboriginal English vernacular. Taylor's humour arises from and figures the complex and multilayered links between alcohol, storytelling, and friendship; it is both a weapon of critique and a bodily imperative which affirms Aboriginal resignification and continuance.

While his humour indexes suffering, Taylor's comic world-view and its engagement with the white reader belie the "heroic" method and tragic-loss paradigm of white anti-racist scholarship[65] and its melancholy. The liminality and ambiguity of Aboriginal tendentious jokes, I'd argue, instantiate a mode

---

[61] Aileen Moreton–Robinson, "Introduction" to *Sovereign Subjects*, ed. Aileen Moreton–Robinson (Crows Nest, NSW: Allen & Unwin, 2007): 2.

[62] Sigmund Freud, "Humour," *International Journal of Psycho-Analysis* 9 (1928): 3.

[63] Freud, "Humour," 6, 3, 5.

[64] Henry Louis Gates, Jr., *The Signifying Monkey: A Theory of African-American Literary Criticis* (New York: Oxford UP, 1988): 50.

[65] Vizenor, *The Trickster of Liberty*, xvi.

of awareness, in particular a renewed awareness of relationality.[66] They index a mode of cross-racial coexistence or cohabitation which proffers different terms of relationality, which are not, of course, invariably comfortable for white people. As Alf Taylor says, for example, "Nyoongars [...] can tell you anything, if you're silly enough to believe them."[67] In re-establishing proximal cross-cultural relations, Aboriginal humour challenges the distance established by racialized stereotyping and the authority that this distance shores up. Once control of the space of intersubjectivity is ceded by white readers, they may consciously register the fact that whiteness itself has become the object of satire and laughter. In turning attention onto the white reader, Taylor's humour opens up the complex question of relationality, foregrounding white people's investment and stake in the stereotyping of Aboriginal people.

⌘

In an early study of Australian humour, Keith Willey relates an instance of Aboriginal gallows humour. His preamble to the joke rehearses the tragic discourse of the 'dying race' which provides the frame for the telling of the joke:

> The loneliness and despair felt by an old man who had seen the first Europeans arrive in his district and lived on to be the last of his tribe, is beyond comprehension. Yet when settlers asked such a man what would happen when he, too, had gone, he roared with laughter. 'Then all the white fellers get lost in the bush; die finish,' he said. 'No blackfellow left to find 'em.'[68]

Willey reads the joke as indexing the admirable strength of character that allows Aboriginal people to "extract a laugh from moments of hardship" and to "bear the unbearable."[69] While his delivery of the joke points to Aboriginal people's fortitude in the face of suffering, the joke itself is directed at whiteness. The old Aboriginal man's prescient remark highlights the discursive dependency of whiteness upon Aboriginality and the paradox of the constitutive centrality of Aboriginal culture to the ways in which white Australia

---

[66] Ghassan Hage formulated this relationality from a minority point of view as "I need you to recognize that I don't need you" (comment made at the EASA conference Prešov, Slovakia, 14 September 2011).

[67] Brewster, "That child is my hero," 174.

[68] Keith Willey, *You Might As Well Laugh, Mate: Australian Humour in Hard Times* (South Melbourne, Victoria: Macmillan, 1984): 6.

[69] Willey, *You Might As Well Laugh, Mate*, 6.

defines itself. I'm thinking, for example, of the badging of the nation and its claims to a deep history and cultural distinctiveness through the deployment of symbols and motifs drawn from traditional Aboriginal culture and the ways in which Aboriginal culture is called upon in the production of marketable images of the nation.

The old man's scenario of white people being lost in the bush without a blackfellow to find them resonates with the perceived loss of white authority and legitimacy. However, while Willey's account of the old Aboriginal man's joke draws on pious white anti-racist liberalism in its (re)formulation of the tragic paradigm of Aboriginality as loss, the joke's humour debunks the tragic-loss paradigm and opens up new spaces of cross-racial relationality which, as I have suggested, may refuse white modes of framing.

Works Cited

Anderson, Kay. *Race and the Crisis of Humanism* (London & New York: Routledge, 2007).

Bakhtin, Mikhail M. *Rabelais and his World*, tr. Hélène Iswolsky (Bloomington: Indiana UP, 1984).

Bergson, Henri. *Laughter: An Essay on the Meaning of the Comic*, tr. Cloudesley Brereton & Fred Rothwell (*Le rire: Essai sur la signification du comique*, 1900; London: Macmillan, 1911).

——. "Laughter" (from *Le rire*, 1900), in *Comedy: "An Essay on Comedy" by George Meredith and "Laughter" by Henri Bergson*, ed. & intro. Wylie Sypher (1956; Baltimore MD & London: Johns Hopkins UP, 1994): 59–190.

Boskin, Joseph. *Rebellious Laughter: People's Humor in American Culture* (Syracuse NY: Syracuse UP, 1997).

Brewster, Anne. "Humour and the Defamiliarization of Whiteness in the Short Fiction of Australian Indigenous Writer Alf Taylor," *Journal of Postcolonial Writing* 44.4 (November 2008): 427–38.

——. "Indigenous Sovereignty and the Crisis of Whiteness in Alexis Wright's *Carpentaria*," *Australian Literary Studies* 25.4 (2010): 85–100.

——. "That child is my hero," interview with Alf Taylor, *Aboriginal History* 31 (2007): 165–77.

Chasar, Mike. "The Sounds of Black Laughter and the Harlem Renaissance: Claude McKay, Sterling Brown, Langston Hughes," *American Literature* 80.1 (March 2008): 57–81.

Cory, Mark. "Comedic Distance in Holocaust Literature," *Journal of American Culture* 18.1 (Spring 1995): 35–40.

Du Bois, W.E.B. *The Souls of Black Folk* (1903; London: Archibald Constable, 1905).

Ezrahi, Sidra DeKoven. "After Such Knowledge, What Laughter?" *Yale Journal of Criticism* 14.1 (Spring 2001): 287–313.

Fine, Michelle. "Witnessing Whiteness," in *Off White: Readings on Race, Power and Society*, ed. Michelle Fine, Linda C. Powell, L. Mun Wang & Lois Weis (New York & London: Routledge, 1997): 57–65.

Freud, Sigmund. "Humour," *International Journal of Psycho-Analysis* 9 (1928): 1–6.

——. *Jokes and their Relation to the Unconscious*, tr. James Strachey (*Der Witz und seine Beziehung zum Unbewussten*, 1905; tr. 1960; Penguin Freud Library; Harmondsworth: Penguin, 1976).

Gates, Henry Louis, Jr. *The Signifying Monkey: A Theory of African-American Literary Criticism* (New York: Oxford UP, 1988).

Holt, Lillian. "Aboriginal Humour: A Conversational Corroborree," in *Serious Frolic: Essays on Australian Humour*, ed. Fran de Groen & Peter Kirkpatrick (St Lucia: U of Queensland P, 2009): 81–94.

Huang, Betsy. "Ralph Ellison's Offense of Laughter," paper presented at the 2000 Modernist Studies Association (MSA) Conference (Philadelphia, 2000), http://www.clarku.edu/activelearning/departments/english/huang/huang.cfm (accessed 12 May 2011).

Hutcheon, Linda. *Irony's Edge* (New York & London: Routledge, 1994).

Kris, Ernst. "The Psychology of Caricature," *International Journal of Psychoanalysis* 17.3 (1936): 285–303.

Langton, Marcia. "Rum, Seduction and Death: 'Aboriginality' and Alcohol," *Oceania* 63.3 (March 1993): 195–205.

Lewis, Paul. *Comic Effects: Interdisciplinary Approaches to Humor in Literature* (Albany: State U of New York P, 1989).

Lipsitz, George. *The Possessive Investment in Whiteness: How White People Profit* (Philadelphia PA: Temple UP, 1998).

Meredith, George. *An Essay on Comedy and the Uses of the Comic Spirit* (London: Archibald Constable, 1905).

Moreton–Robinson, Aileen. "Introduction" to *Sovereign Subjects*, ed. Aileen Moreton–Robinson (Crows Nest, NSW: Allen & Unwin, 2007): 1–11.

——. *Talkin' Up to the White Woman: Aboriginal Women and Feminism* (St Lucia: U of Queensland P, 2000).

——. *Whitening Race: Essays in Social and Cultural Criticism* (Canberra: Aboriginal Studies Press, 2004).

Obrdlik, Antonin J. "'Gallows Humor': A Sociological Phenomenon," *American Journal of Sociology* 47.5 (March 1942): 709–16.

Richter, Virginia. "Laughter and Aggression, Desire and Derision in a Postcolonial Context," in *Cheeky Fictions: Laughter and the Postcolonial*, ed. Susanne Reichl & Mark Stein (Amsterdam & New York: Rodopi, 2005): 61–72.

Taylor, Alf. *Long Time Now: Stories of the Dreamtime, the Here and Now* (Broome, WA: Magabala, 2001).

Vizenor, Gerald. *The Trickster of Liberty: Tribal Heirs to a Wild Baronage* (Minneapolis: U of Minnesota P, 1988).

Ward, Jerry W., Jr. "Two Research Notes on Richard Wright," *Southern Quarterly* 48.2 (Winter 2011): 75–86.

Watson, Sam. "Hanson: A Murri Perspective," in *The Rise and Fall on One Nation*, ed. Michael Leach, Geoffrey Stokes & Ian Ward (St Lucia: U of Queensland P, 2000): 193–205.

Willey, Keith. *You Might As Well Laugh, Mate: Australian Humour in Hard Times* (South Melbourne, Victoria: Macmillan, 1984).

"And in my dreaming I can let go of the spirits of the past"
Gothicizing the Common Law in Richard Frankland's *No Way to Forget*

KATRIN ALTHANS

O UR LIFE IS PERVADED BY LAW, which, as any introductory textbook puts it, "lies at the heart of any society."[1] It is omnipresent, ranging from our daily contractual relations when buying a hot chocolate to go – a neat chain of invitation to treat, offer, acceptance, and, finally, the exchange of considerations – to the imprisonment of convicted murderers. Being such a ubiquitous and at the same time almost indiscernible discourse, law has always also been a fundamental element in the formation of culture and identity, yet rarely without controversy. In Australia, where white law and Aboriginal Law[2] collide, intricate legal subtleties were used to make the English common law the legal tradition of Australia and to negate Indigenous forms of Law. Here, law has been used as a means to control identity, to maintain cultural supremacy, and to assert institutional power. It is therefore not surprising that concepts of law often play an important role in

---

[1] Raymond Wacks, *Law: A Very Short Introduction* (Oxford: Oxford UP, 2008): 1.

[2] In the remainder of the text, I will refer to the legal system of Australia as derived from the English common law tradition as "law," while I will use "Law" with a capital L to indicate Aboriginal customary law, as Law means "the overarching construction created over time to arbitrate [...] relationships with place and space" – Richard Frankland et al., *This is 'Forever Business': A Framework for Maintaining and Restoring Cultural Safety in Aboriginal Victoria* (East Brunswick, Victoria: Victorian Aboriginal Child Care Agency, 2010): 44 – and as such governs all aspects of life.

contemporary Aboriginal Australian cultural expressions and that legal issues have long been on the agenda of Indigenous artists.

In this essay I will discuss how Richard Frankland's award-winning short film *No Way to Forget* (1996)[3] approaches the topic of Aboriginal deaths in custody in gothic terms. As I will show, Frankland reverses gothic dichotomies, employs tropes of haunting and trauma, and ultimately exposes the fictional quality of the gothic itself in his representations of the Australian common law and its institutions. Through an appropriation and transformation of both this originally European mode and the English legal tradition, he thus creates his very own version of an Indigenous gothic. By asserting the cultural strength of that vast body of knowledge summarized as "Dreaming/Law/Lore,"[4] Frankland reclaims Aboriginal identity and subverts what he and others have described as the de-humanizing quality of the law in civic and spiritual terms.[5] I will therefore first outline the benefits that the field of law and literature offers for questioning the factual discourse of law through the study of fiction before I turn to the dangers the use of the gothic mode holds for Aboriginal appropriations. The opportunities filmmaking offers for reclaiming Koori culture and identity will conclude my theoretical outline. I will also draw on the doctrine of reception and the legal foundations of the Australian common-law tradition in order to introduce my following analysis of Frankland's *No Way to Forget*. This analysis will be supplemented by readings of Frankland's 2002 play *Conversations with the Dead*,[6] according to the author "a much heavier and harder version of 'No Way to Forget',"[7]

---

[3] All comments on *No Way to Forget* refer to Richard Frankland, dir. *From Sand to Celluloid – No Way to Forget* (Australian Film Commission, Film Australia, 1996). This edition is referred to in the text as (*NW* mins). Quotations are transcribed with the help of the author's original playscript, which is referred to in the text as (*NW* + page).

[4] Richard Frankland et al, *This is 'Forever Business'*, 15.

[5] Frankland, *This is 'Forever Business'*, 25; 29.

[6] All quotations from and comments on *Conversations with the Dead* refer to Richard Frankland, "Conversations with the Dead," in *Blak Inside: Six Indigenous Plays from Victoria*, ed. Ilbijerri Aboriginal and Torres Strait Islander Theatre Co-operative and Playbox Theatre (Sydney: Currency, 2002): 215–87. This edition is referred to in the text as (*C* + page).

[7] Richard Frankland, "Re: Script No Way to Forget," email to Katrin Althans, 13 September 2011.

and is further informed by his collection *Searching for Shadows*.⁸ I will argue that by drawing on a number of different shapes that Aboriginal gothic may take, Frankland in his work gothicizes the law while at the same time highlighting the Law by narrative, dramatic, and cinematographic means.

A discussion of legal aspects of fictional works needs to outline its scope in a law-and-literature framework and to position itself along the various strands of that field. The focus in the present essay, however, is not on the distinction of either law in literature or law as literature, as my argument draws on both aspects, but on the very purpose of using both disciplines alongside each other. As has repeatedly been pointed out by followers of the law-and-literature movement, literature often provides a persuasive critique of legal discourse, revealing the gaps and shortcomings of the law.⁹ Conversely, opponents of such a critical understanding of law-and-literature endeavours, most notably Richard Posner, have dismissed the representation of law in literature as "a dramatic necessity" rather than as comment on, or even criticism of, law.¹⁰ Despite its highly contested nature, though, the interdiscursive connection of law and literature is a fruitful approach which opens up interesting, as yet largely unexplored ways of reading Aboriginal literature and film against the legal grain. Especially law's complicity in constructing black Australian identity vis-à-vis the law's normative white self resonates in contemporary Australian literature. In her recent doctoral dissertation on the representation of law's Other in Australian literature, Naomi Sidebotham argues that "the discourse of law constructs identity and marginalizes difference," effectively silencing its Other, a practice illustrated critically in Aboriginal writing; for Sidebotham, literature "allows [...] for an interrogation of the law."¹¹

---

⁸ All quotations from and comments on *Searching for Shadows* refer to Richard Frankland, *Searching for Shadows: A Collection of Tone Poetry and Words*, ed. John G. Foss (Strawberry Hills: Australia Council, 1998). This edition is referred to in the text as (*S* + page).

⁹ See Robin West, *Narrative, Authority, and Law* (Ann Arbor: U of Michigan P, 1993): 8–12. See also Kieran Dolin, *A Critical Introduction to Law and Literature* (Cambridge: Cambridge UP, 2007): 207–209.

¹⁰ Richard Allen Posner, *Law and Literature* (1988; Cambridge MA: Harvard UP, 2009): 546.

¹¹ See Naomi Sidebotham, "'The white man never wanna hear nothin about what's different from him': Representations of Law's 'Other' in Australian Literature" (doctoral dissertation, Murdoch University, 2009): 7, 152, 230, 73.

However, she fails to take into account the fact that both subject-matter and form, law and literature, are inherently European constructs. Reworking issues of law in literature thus confronts Aboriginal artists with a twofold ideological dilemma. On the level of content, "writing back," as Byron Caminero–Santangelo claims, "severely limits the range of purposes and the transformative power of postcolonial reinscription of European literature."[12] And, on a formal level, several critics warn of Aboriginal writers' being appropriated by European aesthetic forms instead of subverting them through their own appropriations.[13] The introduction of the gothic, a genuinely European literary mode, into this already unstable ground of opinions then adds yet another shifting level of quicksand. On the one hand, much the same criticism as that which has been levelled at acts of reworking in general has been directed at the appropriation of the gothic, in postcolonial contexts in particular.[14] On the other hand, the gothic in an Aboriginal Australian context is fraught with even more colonial legacies, as it was the representation of the bloodthirsty savage that became an instant success in the evolution of colonial gothic, assuring the white 'self' of its superior position against the black Other. Yet, as I will argue with reference to Richard Frankland's work, the very nature of the gothic itself is the key to a counter-discursive transformation of its colonial offspring. Drawing on the original subversive qualities of the gothic, Frankland approaches the content level of the law and thus challenges the master-discourses of both law and the gothic tradition. His Gunditjmara cultural heritage then allows him to critically approach the formal level of literature

---

[12] Byron Caminero–Santangelo, *African Fiction and Joseph Conrad: Reading Postcolonial Intertextuality* (Albany: State U of New York P, 2005): 15.

[13] See Ivor Indyk, "Assimilation or Appropriation: Uses of European Literary Forms in Black Australian Writing," in *Australian Literary Studies* 15.4 (1992): 249, and Mudrooroo, "White Forms, Aboriginal Content," in *Aboriginal Writing Today: Papers from the First National Conference of Aboriginal Writers Held in Perth, Western Australia, in 1983*, ed. Jack Davis & Bob Hodge (Canberra: Australian Institute of Aboriginal Studies, 1985): 28. See also Mudrooroo, *Writing from the Fringe: A Study of Modern Aboriginal Literature* (South Yarra, Victoria: Hyland House, 1990): 42, and Margery Fee, "The Signifying Writer and the Ghost Reader: Mudrooroo's *Master of the Ghost Dreaming* and *Writing from the Fringe*," in *Australian and New Zealand Studies in Canada* 8 (1992): 20.

[14] See Judie Newman, "Postcolonial Gothic: Ruth Prawer Jhabvala and the Sobhraj Case," in *Modern Gothic: A Reader*, ed. Victor Sage & Allan L. Smith (Manchester: Manchester UP, 1996): 172.

through his use of film and drama. Especially in *No Way to Forget*, Frankland ventures into the field of law and film in order to explore what is variously referred to as the "strong dramatic edge which there is to law"[15] and "the relationship between law, society and culture"[16] in order to reveal the breaks and hidden gaps of the common law in gothic terms.

Film, however, is being criticized as yet another instrument of European origin, as it is still firmly located in white institutions as far as financial support and filming techniques are concerned.[17] Like literature, it is deeply rooted in colonial discourses such as ethnographic film, whose representation of Indigenous peoples is one of the challenging legacies Aboriginal filmmakers are confronted with. Accordingly, Kerstin Knopf, in her comprehensive study of North American Indigenous filmmaking, aptly entitled *Decolonizing the Lens of Power*, argues that such a

> decolonization process works in a twofold manner: first, as a political struggle, through the creation of self-fashioned images and an anti-colonialist rewriting and filming of history; and, secondly, as an aesthetic struggle, through defiance of and/or negotiation with established conventions of feature and ethnographic film.[18]

Even though Aboriginal filmmaking continues to depend on European models and standards, it also draws on its Indigenous cultural heritage of oral storytelling and performance, "a profound renaissance of Aboriginal visual arts in new media."[19] Even though it is oversimplifying to unreservedly regard modern filmmaking as the legitimate heir to oral storytelling traditions,[20] a "multifaceted medium like film can do some measure of justice to the multidimensional realities of Aboriginal philosophy."[21]

---

[15] Steve Greenfield, Guy Osborn & Peter Robson, *Film and the Law: The Cinema of Justice* (2001; Oxford: Hart, 2010): 33.

[16] Rebecca Johnson & Ruth Buchanan, "Getting the Insider's Story Out: What Popular Film Can Tell Us about Legal Method's Dirty Secrets," *Windsor Yearbook of Access to Justice* 20 (2001): 93.

[17] Katrin Althans, *Darkness Subverted*, 135–36.

[18] Kerstin Knopf, *Decolonizing the Lens of Power: Indigenous Films in North America* (Cross/Cultures 100; Amsterdam & New York: Rodopi, 2008): 63.

[19] Ian Bryson, Margaret Burns & Marcia Langton, "Painting with Light: Australian Indigenous Cinema," in *The Oxford Companion to Aboriginal Art and Culture*, ed. Sylvia Kleinert & Margo Neale (Oxford: Oxford UP, 2000): 301.

[20] *Decolonizing the Lens of Power*, 85.

[21] Bryson et al., "Painting with Light: Australian Indigenous Cinema," 304.

In *No Way to Forget*, these contradictory and, more often than not, clashing strands of European and Koori cultural traditions are brought together in a gothic critique of the law and its institutions. Frankland's Aboriginal gothic blends issues of law and Law, fiction and reality, linear narrative and the tradition of oral memory in a powerful act of transformation. To begin with, however, it is necessary to introduce the doctrine of reception and its impact on Australia in order to chart the legal boundaries which Frankland's Aboriginal gothic transgresses in its restoration of Koori identity.

Today's legal system in Australia is based on the English common law and does not include any recognition of Aboriginal Law whatsoever, owing to what is called the doctrine of reception. In the first chapter of his influential study *An Australian Legal History*, Alex Castles gives a detailed account of the principles underlying the doctrine of reception, some of which have a medieval origin and were refined by the political events of the seventeenth century.[22] As held in several cases of the late-seventeenth century, the laws of England automatically applied to territory gained by occupation.[23] This view, and with it the distinction between territory gained by conquest, inheritance, or occupation, was formally recognized by the Privy Council, the court of appeal for overseas territories of the British Empire, in a memorandum of 1722.[24] In his *Commentaries on the Laws of England*, William Blackstone sums up the legal developments following the Privy Council memorandum in what is probably the most-cited source for the doctrine of reception:

> Plantations or colonies, in distant countries, are either such where the lands are claimed by right of occupancy only, by finding them desert and uncultivated, and peopling them from the mother-country; or where, when already cultivated, they have been either gained by conquest, or ceded to us by treaties. And both these rights are founded upon the law of nature, or at least upon that of nations. But there is a difference between these two species of colonies, with respect to the laws by which they are bound. For it hath been held, that if an uninhabited country be discovered and planted by English subjects, all the English laws then in being, which are the birthright of every subject, are immediately there in force. [...] But in conquered or ceded countries, that have already laws of their own, the king may indeed

---

[22] Alex Cuthbert Castles, *An Australian Legal History* (Sydney: The Law Book, 1982): 1.

[23] See Castles, *An Australian Legal History*, 9.

[24] See *Case 15 – Anonymous* (1722) 2 P Wms 75; 24 ER 646 (Privy Council).

alter and change those laws; but, till he does actually change them, the ancient laws of the country remain [...].[25]

Codifying principles of the English law for the first time, Blackstone's commentaries reflect the point of view of eighteenth-century international law on acquiring new territory, either by means of conquest or by means of occupation. Only the acquisition of new territory by means of occupation, however, allowed for a complete reception of the English common law, as was the case in Australia. To be considered as acquired by occupation, Australia must have been regarded as "a new and uninhabited country found out by *English* subjects."[26] Therefore, it is at this point necessary to rehearse the infamous concept of '*terra nullius*'.

Among Australian historians, the very term '*terra nullius*' has been at the centre of heated debates in the 'history wars' and became most prominent through the publication of Henry Reynolds's *The Law of the Land* in 1987. In his account of British settlement of Australia, Reynolds argues: "The doctrine underlying the traditional view of settlement was that before 1788 Australia was *terra nullius*, a land belonging to no one," and he asks: "if it was legitimately applied to Australia in the late eighteenth century."[27] As Michael Connor has taken great pains to demonstrate, however, the term '*terra nullius*' only emerged in the late-nineteenth century in the form of *territorium nullius*:[28] "Terra nullius was a late nineteenth [sic] formulation within international law theory to deal with contemporary problems of sovereignty and colonisation."[29] Connor also dismisses Reynolds's references to writers such as Grotius, Wolff, or de Vattel as not constructing a doctrine amounting to *terra nullius*[30] and claims that Reynolds misinterpreted especially de Vattel's writings as supporting colonialism[31] through "using questionable analysis of classic legal

---

[25] William Blackstone, "Introduction" to *Commentaries on the Laws of England: In Four Books* (1765–69; London: T. Tegg, 1830), sec. IV: 107.

[26] *Case 15 – Anonymous* (1722) 2 P Wms 75; 24 ER 646 (Privy Council) [emphasis in the original].

[27] Henry Reynolds, *The Law of the Land* (1987; Camberwell, Victoria: Penguin, 2003): 14.

[28] See Michael Connor, *The Invention of Terra Nullius: Historical and Legal Fictions on the Foundation of Australia* (Sydney: Macleay, 2005): 11.

[29] Connor, *The Invention of Terra Nullius*, 47.

[30] *The Invention of Terra Nullius*, 62.

[31] Connor, *The Invention of Terra Nullius*, 63–69.

writers [and] selectively quoting from authorities."[32] Unfortunately, Connor goes little further than criticizing Reynolds and trivializing de Vattel when he quotes passages of de Vattel's *The Law of Nations* better suited to the Australian situation.[33] This section, of which Connor quotes only the first two sentences, reads:

> There is another celebrated question, to which the discovery of the New World has principally given rise. It is asked whether a nation may lawfully take possession of some part of a vast country, in which there are none but erratic nations whose scanty population is incapable of occupying the whole! We have already observed (§ 81), in establishing the obligation to cultivate the earth, that those nations cannot exclusively appropriate to themselves more land than they have occasion for, or more than they are able to settle and cultivate. *Their unsettled habitation in those immense regions cannot be accounted a true and legal possession*; and the people of Europe, too closely pent up at home, finding land of which the savages stood in no particular need, and of which they made no actual and constant use, were lawfully entitled to take possession of it, and settle it with colonies. [...] However, we cannot help praising the moderation of the English Puritans who first settled in New England; who, notwithstanding their being furnished with a charter from their sovereign, purchased of the Indians the land of which they intended to take possession.[34]

On the status of such colonies relative to the mother country, de Vattel states:

> when a nation takes possession of a distant country, and settles a colony there, that country, though separated from the principal establishment, or mother-country, naturally becomes a part of the state, equally with its ancient possessions.[35]

---

[32] Connor, *The Invention of Terra Nullius*, 74.

[33] *The Invention of Terra Nullius*, 68–69.

[34] Emerich de Vattel, *The Law of Nations: Or, Principles of the Law of Nature, Applied to the Conduct and Affairs of Nations and Sovereigns, with Three Early Essays on the Origin and Nature of Natural Law and on Luxury*, ed. Béla Kapossy and Richard Whatmore (1758; Indianapolis IN: Liberty Fund, 2008): Book 1, Chapter XVIII, § 209. (My emphasis.)

[35] Vattel, *The Law of Nations: Or, Principles of the Law of Nature*, Book 1, Chapter XVIII, § 210.

Here, de Vattel can be read as suggesting a rather broad version of the doctrine of reception pertaining to colonies settled subject to § 209 – of which Australia is a case in point. I here agree with Andrew Fitzmaurice, who states:

> while the term *terra nullius* was not used to justify dispossession in Australia, it was produced by the legal tradition that dominated questions of the justice of 'occupation' at the time that Australia was colonised.[36]

By the nineteenth century, the ideology it represents had become rather commonplace in jurisprudence[37] and is clearly expressed by the Lord of Appeal Lord Watson of the Privy Council in *Cooper v Stuart* of 1889:

> The extent to which English law is introduced into a British Colony, and the manner of its introduction, must necessarily vary according to circumstances. There is a great difference between the case of a Colony acquired by conquest or cession, in which there is an established system of law, and that of a Colony which consisted of a tract of territory practically unoccupied, without settled inhabitants or settled law, at the time when it was peacefully annexed to the British dominions. The Colony of New South Wales belongs to the latter class.[38]

With regard to the contested nature of *terra nullius*, however, I suggest considering it not in terms of a concept or doctrine but, rather, in terms of a legal fiction based on international law. For the purpose of this essay, I will follow the definition provided by Pierre Olivier, who understands a legal fiction as follows:

> an assumption of fact deliberately, lawfully and irrebuttably made contrary to the facts proven or probable in a particular case, with the object of bringing a particular legal rule into operation or explaining a legal rule, the assumption being permitted by law or employed in legal science.[39]

It is again Blackstone who offers the most vivid description of legal fictions when he refers to the English law, precisely because of its fictions, as being

---

[36] Andrew Fitzmaurice, "The Genealogy of 'Terra Nullius'," *Australian Historical Studies* 38/129 (2007): 2.

[37] See Merete Borch, "Rethinking the Origins of 'Terra Nullius'," *Australian Historical Studies* 34/117 (2001): 238.

[38] *Cooper v Stuart* (1889) 14 App Cas 286: 291.

[39] Pierre J.J. Olivier, *Legal Fictions in Practice and Legal Science* (Rotterdam: Rotterdam UP, 1975): 90.

"an old Gothic castle."[40] The gothic and the law, it seems, are inextricably entwined.

Leslie Moran, for example, has identified two particularly strong traditions of how the law and the gothic are connected to each other: first, the law as gothicizing instance, and, second, the law as gothic itself.[41] In his work, Richard Frankland deconstructs the first aspect through his use of the second, thus dismantling the inherent gothicity of the English common law. This powerful connection between the law and the gothic is a key issue in Frankland's *Searching for Shadows*, for instance, in which strikingly gothic poems such as "Maybe One Day" and "Listen" are gathered together with poems rather fiercely directed at the law, such as "To be sure" and "Free me." And it also already determines the opening of the stage version of *No Way to Forget*: here, the director's note before the opening scene reads "Judge in robes walks on stage and reads Terms of Reference for the Royal Commission" (*NW* 1), and the following stage directions have "light [which] slowly reveals ghosts from Shane's past" (*NW* 3). *Conversations with the Dead*, apart from its telling title, features a similar beginning in terms of law and the gothic, taken from the song "Long Tall Ships":

> Can you tell me
> Why they stole the sunlight
> Can you tell me
> How they own the land
> Can you tell me
> Why they stole the children
> Can you tell me
> Are they demons are they men. (*C* 219)

These examples vividly show both the gothicity of the law, as in *Conversations with the Dead*, in which the new law is demonized and criminalized, and the gothicizing quality of the law, as in the stage version of *No Way to Forget*, in which the judge stands metonymically for Aboriginal deaths in custody and, through the work of the Royal Commission, conjures up the ghosts they created. Both aspects, then, are visualized in the movie version of *No Way to Forget*, which brings to the screen the trauma of Aboriginal deaths in custody shot as a gothic road movie. What Gary Boire identifies in the

---

[40] Blackstone, *Commentaries on the Laws of England*, Book 3, Chapter XVII, 268.

[41] See Leslie J. Moran, "Law and the Gothic Imagination," in *The Gothic*, ed. Fred Botting (Cambridge: Brewer, 2001): 91–92, 102.

works of several African artists, an "in-depth analysis of imperialist law's in-built ambivalences, distortions, displacements and contradictions,"[42] is played out with a gothic twist in Frankland's work: on the one hand, the gothic is turned inside out through an investigation of the law; on the other, we find several instances of what I have elsewhere identified as different aspects of Aboriginal gothic: a reversal of traditional gothic binaries of victim and villain, trauma which haunts in the shape of never-to-be-exorcised ghosts, and gothic fiction which fades when compared to the gothic reality of Aboriginal life..[43]

Ranging temporally from dusk till dawn, *No Way to Forget* is, furthermore, told in spatial dimensions, "somewhere between Swan Hill and Melbourne" (*NW* 01:29-01:30 mins), and shows the on-screen battle of Shane Francis along with the memories evoked by his work for the Royal Commission into Aboriginal Deaths in Custody (RCIADIC). Shane's journey to his destination, Melbourne, where he arrives at early dawn, is interrupted by various flashbacks, each telling the story of one Aboriginal death he has investigated. Whereas the trip itself is visualized in black night, and non-diegetic commentary is added throughout, the flashbacks are shot in classic cinematographic fashion, in bright colours and with diegetic sounds. This difference in cinematography highlights a difference in storytelling which results in a difference in the use of the gothic. The spatial development of the trip, which is accompanied by the explanatory commentary from the off, is close to traditional means of Aboriginal oral storytelling and reveals the gothic reality with which the members of the RCIADIC – and, ultimately, every Australian – is faced. By means of both the images and the commentary added, *No Way to Forget* thus broaches issues of haunting, spirits, and, ultimately, trauma in Aboriginal gothic terms.

Although Shane's memories and the work of the RCIADIC itself at first sight deny a reading of gothicized trauma, *No Way to Forget* deals with what Judith Herman refers to as "the central dialectic of psychological trauma" – "the conflict between the will to deny horrible events and the will to proclaim them aloud."[44] Quite tellingly, Herman compares the denial of what happened

---

[42] Gary Boire, "'Ratione Officii': Representing Law in Postcolonial Literature," *Mosaic* 27.4 (1994): 201.

[43] See Katrin Althans, *Darkness Subverted*, 184.

[44] Judith Lewis Herman, *Trauma and Recovery: From Domestic Abuse to Political Terror* (1992; London: Pandora, 1994): 1.

to ghosts and the recovery from psychological trauma to the stories which need to be told in order to exorcize those ghosts.[45] In *No Way to Forget*, those ghosts visually come to life in the form of reflector posts, one of which turns into the figure of an Aboriginal man with traditional white painting when Shane drives past (*NW* 05:35–05:44 mins). There also is the sound of clapsticks added to the commentary: "Sometimes the white poles look like ghosts at the side of the road, standing to attention and watching me as I drive past" (*NW* 05:30-05:37 mins).

Similar to the buried secrets of conventional ghost stories, the histories of those who have died in custody are unearthed through the investigations of the RCIADIC: "when you're investigating a death in custody, you know everything about them, from when they are born, to when they die, and absolutely everything in-between" (*NW* 02:28-02:39 mins). Or, as Jack, Shane's alter ego in *Conversations with the Dead*, puts it: "It's like an imprint of him on my soul" (*C* 266). Yet, what in medical discourse means healing, in *No Way to Forget* has a double edge, as the communal trauma of Aboriginal deaths in custody is exorcized at the expense of Shane's sanity:

> I get a little scared when I feel the spirits close by. They don't want me to forget them, or what's happened. They need people to know. Sometimes I wonder what hurts more, the memories or wondering at my sanity. (*NW* 03:43-04:00 mins)

By adding his almost claustrophobic commentary to the frame narrative, Shane attempts to exorcize his own memories, much as the movie as an artform tries to exorcize the memories of communal trauma.

Richard Frankland visualizes this double road to recovery through close-ups of Shane's face and extreme close-ups of his eyes, sometimes only seen in the rear-view mirror, thus triggering a cinematographic gaze into Shane's memory in the form of flashbacks. It is these flashback episodes that talk in the most directly gothic terms but that are, eventually, overwritten by the hidden gothic agenda of the framing journey. The last flashback but one is a case in point here, as it presents the case of a young woman with "at least fifty stitches in her throat [and] another fifty or so in each arm" (*NW* 07:00-07:05 mins) and the close-ups of the sutures show a striking analogy to cinematic portrayals of Frankenstein's monster. Despite her visual likeness, however, the young woman shares much more with the literary original, the victim of his creator's whims, than with any distorted movie adaptation of Franken-

---

[45] See Herman, *Trauma and Recovery*, 1.

stein's monster: as Shane's gaze during the shot implies, the legal system of Australia and its penal institutions, embodied in the warden, is ultimately responsible for the young woman's self-harm. In *Conversations with the Dead*, the gothic nature of this reality is described in even more explicit terms:

> JACK: [to the audience] [...] This fucking suit. I held that girl in my arms and clear fluid from her neck seeped down my suit and stuck it to my body. I have to shower to get if off.
> [To WIFE] Gunna have a shower, honey, wash this woman's life fluid off me.
> (*C* 238)

No Way to Forget here visualizes a well-known kind of fictional gothic mutilation, but it tells the story of an actual victim: in their capacity as gothicizing instance, the law and its institutions thus gothicize themselves.

It is, however, not only the gothic monster who experiences a gothic twist, but also the damsel in distress: it is no longer the white maiden who is rescued from the hands of the black savage by her knight in shining white skin, but a black woman who is the victim of white rape at the hands of two white policemen – with no one coming to her rescue. The rape itself is shown in a visually and aurally multilayered double flashback, the first being the woman's narrating what happened to Shane and the second the woman's own flashback memory:

> RAPE VICTIM: They picked me up. They picked me up and raped me. Two of them.
> SHANE: When?
> RAPE VICTIM: Last week. [*shrieks and shouting is heard*] And they bashed me. Dropped me on the road.
> (*NW* 08:15–08:30 mins)

The sound of a bullroarer, an instrument of a highly sacred nature and endowed with many meanings, is added to the rape scene. Used in burials in some Aboriginal cultures, its sound serves a twofold purpose in *No Way to Forget*: on the one hand, the sound anticipates the death of the young woman, "found on the miss, bashed to death and stabbed through the eye" (*NW* 09:01–09:05 mins). On the other, it also brings the event of her death full circle into her own narrative, hence into Shane's multidimensional flashback. Both flashbacks are visually introduced by lengthy dissolves, and their sounds continually overlap, as the victim's narration is accompanied by her shrieks and cries for help during the rape, which itself is pictured quite vividly. The seemingly matter-of-fact style of the woman's narration (*NW* 08:25–08:38 mins) is thus modified by the terror of the actual event as presented on screen and by the audio track. By blending the two people's memories in both sound and pictures, Frankland not only deconstructs the classic triangle of victim, villain, and hero, but also voices in reversed terms what cannot be voiced in colonial gothic fiction: the anxiety over miscegenation. The crime which is too gothic to be committed even in fiction, the rape of a white woman by a black man, is distorted through narrative and visual means in *No Way to Forget*: the actual rape of a black woman by white policemen is, quite literally, voiced. Thus, reality has again caught up with fiction, but also voices in reversed terms what cannot be voiced in colonial gothic fiction: the anxiety over miscegenation. As Howard Malchow writes,

> The threat that white women *might* be brutalized by over-sexed black men of great strength and size became a cliché of racist writing, ready for appropriation in the creation of Gothic horror [...].[46]

Although it fuelled the imagination, the rape of a white woman by a black man mostly remained a threat in literature, too horrid to be committed even in fiction. In *No Way to Forget*, this crime is distorted through narrative and visual means: the actual rape of a black woman by white policemen is, quite literally, voiced and pictured. Here, the reality Aboriginal people are subjected to has proven much more gothic than fiction.

Apart from these rather obvious and clear-cut examples of how Richard Frankland reverses the roles of the gothic (white) victim and (black) villain, the other episodes related through Shane's flashbacks tell the very same story. There is, for instance, a young woman's father who suffered from diabetes but did not receive proper treatment in an instance of acute hypoglycaemia because the police thought he was an alcohol addict (*NW* 04:01–04:29 mins). Or the death of a young man who is, in a monotonous, grieving repetition, referred to as "a great artist" by his mother (*NW* 05:02–05:13 mins), and that of a young boy who is shown crouching next to a car tyre, shot from an aerial perspective (*NW* 02:46–02:53 mins). All these dead people, shown either through the eyes of their relatives or through that of the camera, are characterized as being not strong enough, hence victims of the gothic villain, the law and its institutions.

---

[46] Howard L. Malchow, *Gothic Images of Race in Nineteenth-Century Britain* (Stanford CA: Stanford UP, 1996): 25. Emphasis mine.

Yet it is not only the flashbacks, instances of bringing people long dead to life again in Shane's memory, that prompt a gothicized reading of the law, but also the frame to these flashbacks, Shane's journey from Swan Hill to Melbourne. The gothic of this frame stands in stark contrast to the gothic episodes the audience witnessed through the flashbacks, which seem almost classic in their loyalty to their European precursors. Both frame and flashbacks, however, are linked to each other by being bridged in a variety of ways by sound and vision; bridges which trigger Shane's memories of particular episodes. Alternating between and yet linking different time levels, *No Way to Forget* visualizes Aboriginal concepts of circularity in its trauma sequences and thus meaningfully engages in what Knopf terms the "aesthetic struggle"[47] of Indigenous filmmaking.

Four recurring shots are used in the course of the trip narrative, each stressing a different aspect of the gothicity connected to the work with Aboriginal deaths in custody. Whereas the close-ups of Shane's face open the door into his memories and thus the stories of singular deaths he investigated, medium close-ups of the car's interior are used to relate both the background to and the consequences of Shane's work. They show folders labelled "Royal Commission into Aboriginal Deaths in Custody" on which a bottle of whisky is placed (*NW* 01:43-01:47 mins). Introduced by harsh cuts rather than smooth dissolves, this take is a sudden break in the close-ups of Shane's face, This combination suggests that the experience of working for the RCIADIC needs to be drowned in alcohol in order to be borne and visualizes the seemingly inevitable consequence of Shane's work, the attempt to distance oneself by numbing the psychological pain:

> My mind is drifting between the song from the cassette player and the road. It's hard to concentrate while driving, to hold out the thoughts that keep going through my mind, to try and stave off the memories that keep plaguing me, hounding me. (*NW* 01:36-01:50 mins)

Apart from shots of the inside of the car, there are also shots of the outside, the road, and the car itself. Those shots develop their own nomadic dynamic, as there is only diegetic, but no camera movement: the camera is either in a static position on the road, showing the car driving by, or attached to the driver's position and monotonously following the centre dividing line. The audience is thus cast in the role of a nomadic viewer, who "come[s] along afterwards and

---

[47] Knopf, *Decolonizing the Lens of Power*, 63.

track[s] things up, deciphering the traces."[48] Yet it is no geographical feature that is sung into being but, rather, the stories of the deceased. As Peter in *Conversations of the Dead* puts it, "Maybe that's what you did? [...] Being a storyteller for us. Telling our stories which are now your stories as well" (*C* 272). The flashback episodes are thus framed by a spatial narrative which reflects oral storytelling in the form of Shane's commentary, and the cultural understanding of Aboriginal songlines shot as a road movie. Thus, not only does it work as a means to subvert the cultural hegemony of the law but it is itself part of the Law, and thus the Dreaming. A modern-day Dreaming narrative relating the struggle of coming to terms with Aboriginal Deaths in Custody in its various guises, *No Way to Forget* both powerfully gothicizes the law and reclaims Aboriginal cultural identity as defined by the Law. Read in terms of the possibilities performance offers for oral discourse,[49] the idea of a new songline and Dreaming is even more compelling when it comes to experiencing *No Way to Forget* alongside Frankland's play *Conversations of the Dead*, which itself contains some of the poems found in *Searching for Shadows*.[50]

This combination of the flashbacks' classic cinematography, the frame narrative's closeness to oral traditions, and the shots' visualization of contemporary songlines serves to emphasize the gothic quality of the common law. There are, on the one hand, the flashbacks and their reversal of standard gothic roles of victim and villain, an aspect of Aboriginal gothic which is further emphasized by the fact that there is no restoration of order but, inevitably, the death of the victim. On the other hand, there is the central motif of trauma, expressed in gothic terms of ghosts, nightmares, and insanity. As in traditional ghost stories, the spectres of the deceased come back to haunt Shane, but they neither can nor want to be laid to rest. Instead, they want to be remembered as epitomes of a gothic reality which lies at the heart of the trauma inflicted by the law and its penal institutions. At this point, *No Way to Forget* breaks with

---

[48] Krim Benterrak, Stephen Muecke & Paddy Roe, *Reading the Country: Introduction to Nomadology* (1984; Liverpool: Liverpool UP, 1996): 26–27. Although Muecke is concerned with ways of reading, the analogy is a very fruitful one here.

[49] See Helen Gilbert, "De-Scribing Orality: Performance and the Recuperation of Voice," in *De-Scribing Empire: Post-Colonialism and Textuality*, ed. Chris Tiffin & Alan Lawson (London: Routledge, 1994): 98–100.

[50] For a note on the differences between the published text and different performances of *Conversations with the Dead*, see Alison Lyssa, "Performing Australia's Black and White History: Acts of Danger in Four Australian Plays of the Early 21st Century" (MA thesis, Macquarie University, 2006): 16.

one of the basic rules of European gothic fiction, that of distancing itself spatially, temporally, and culturally from reality. By doing so, *No Way to Forget* unhinges, even denies, the gothic's claim to fictionality in the face of the gothic reality of Aboriginal deaths in custody. Richard Frankland thus transforms gothic fiction into a mirror of gothic realities, and his play with stock elements of the gothic and the trauma inflicted by a gothicized law works towards dragging the gothic skeleton of Aboriginal deaths in custody to the surface. Thus, the common-law tradition as a ghostly and uncanny presence in Australia, the manifestation of a legal fiction haunting the Australian psyche, is challenged in Aboriginal gothic terms and pitted against the Law in the form of a contemporary dreaming of which there is *No Way to Forget.*

WORKS CITED

Althans, Katrin. *Darkness Subverted: Aboriginal Gothic in Black Australian Literature and Film* (Representations & Reflections 2; Göttingen: V&R unipress & Bonn UP, 2010).
Benterrak, Krim, Stephen Muecke & Paddy Roe. *Reading the Country: Introduction to Nomadology* (1984. Liverpool: Liverpool UP, 1996).
Blackstone, William. *Commentaries on the Laws of England: In Four Books* (1765–69; London: T. Tegg, 17th ed. 1830).
Boire, Gary. "'Ratione Officii': Representing Law in Postcolonial Literature," *Mosaic* 27.4 (1994): 199–214.
Borch, Merete. "Rethinking the Origins of Terra Nullius," *Australian Historical Studies* 34/117 (2001): 222–39.
Bryson, Ian, Margaret Burns & Marcia Langton. "Painting with Light: Australian Indigenous Cinema," in *The Oxford Companion to Aboriginal Art and Culture*, ed. Sylvia Kleinert & Margo Neale (Oxford: Oxford UP, 2000): 297–304.
Caminero–Santangelo, Byron. *African Fiction and Joseph Conrad: Reading Postcolonial Intertextuality* (Albany: State U of New York P, 2005).
Case 15 – Anonymous (1722) 2 P Wms 75; 24 ER 646 (Privy Council).
Castles, Alex Cuthbert. *An Australian Legal History* (Sydney: The Law Book, 1982).
Connor, Michael. *The Invention of Terra Nullius: Historical and Legal Fictions on the Foundation of Australia* (Sydney: Macleay, 2005).
Cooper v Stuart (1889) 14 App Cas 286.
Dolin, Kieran. *A Critical Introduction to Law and Literature* (Cambridge: Cambridge UP, 2007).
Fee, Margery. "The Signifying Writer and the Ghost Reader: Mudrooroo's Master of the Ghost Dreaming and Writing from the Fringe," *Australian and New Zealand Studies in Canada* 8 (1992): 18–32.

Fitzmaurice, Andrew. "The Genealogy of Terra Nullius," *Australian Historical Studies* 38/129 (2007): 1–15.

Frankland, Richard J. "Conversations with the Dead," in *Blak Inside: Six Indigenous Plays from Victoria*, ed. Ilbijerri Aboriginal and Torres Strait Islander Theatre Cooperative and Playbox Theatre (Sydney: Currency, 2002): 215–87.

——, dir. *From Sand to Celluloid – No Way to Forget* (Australian Film Commission / Film Australia, Australia 1996; 11 min.).

——. *Searching for Shadows: A Collection of Tone Poetry and Words*, ed. John G. Foss (Strawberry Hills: Australia Council, 1998).

——, et al. *This is 'Forever Business': A Framework for Maintaining and Restoring Cultural Safety in Aboriginal Victoria*. East Brunswick, Victoria: Victorian Aboriginal Child Care Agency, 2010).

Gilbert, Helen. "De-Scribing Orality: Performance and the Recuperation of Voice," in *De-Scribing Empire: Post-Colonialism and Textuality*, ed. Chris Tiffin & Alan Lawson (London: Routledge, 1994): 98–111.

Greenfield, Steve, Guy Osborn & Peter Robson. *Film and the Law: The Cinema of Justice* (2001; Oxford: Hart, 2010).

Herman, Judith Lewis. *Trauma and Recovery: From Domestic Abuse to Political Terror* (1992; London: Pandora, 1994).

Indyk, Ivor. "Assimilation or Appropriation: Uses of European Literary Forms in Black Australian Writing," *Australian Literary Studies* 15.4 (1992): 249–60.

Johnson, Rebecca, & Ruth Buchanan. "Getting the Insider's Story Out: What Popular Film Can Tell Us about Legal Method's Dirty Secrets," *Windsor Yearbook of Access to Justice* 20 (2001): 87–110.

Knopf, Kerstin. *Decolonizing the Lens of Power: Indigenous Films in North America* (Cross/Cultures 100; Amsterdam & New York: Rodopi, 2008).

Lyssa, Alison. "Performing Australia's Black and White History: Acts of Danger in Four Australian Plays of the Early 21st Century" (MA thesis, Macquarie University, 2006).

Malchow, Howard L. *Gothic Images of Race in Nineteenth-Century Britain* (Stanford CA: Stanford UP, 1996).

Moran, Leslie J. "Law and the Gothic Imagination," in *The Gothic*, ed. Fred Botting (Cambridge: Brewer, 2001): 87–109.

Mudrooroo. "White Forms, Aboriginal Content," in *Aboriginal Writing Today: Papers from the First National Conference of Aboriginal Writers Held in Perth, Western Australia, in 1983*, ed. Jack Davis & Bob Hodge (Canberra: Australian Institute of Aboriginal Studies, 1985): 21–33.

——. *Writing from the Fringe: A Study of Modern Aboriginal Literature* (South Yarra, Victoria: Hyland House, 1990).

Newman, Judie. "Postcolonial Gothic: Ruth Prawer Jhabvala and the Sobhraj Case," in *Modern Gothic: A Reader*, ed. Victor Sage & Allan L. Smith (Manchester: Manchester UP, 1996): 171–87.

Olivier, Pierre J.J. *Legal Fictions in Practice and Legal Science* (Rotterdam: Rotterdam UP, 1975).

Posner, Richard Allen. *Law and Literature* (1988; Cambridge MA: Harvard UP, 2009).

Reynolds, Henry. *The Law of the Land* (1987; Camberwell, Victoria: Penguin, 2003).

Sidebotham, Naomi. "'The white man never wanna hear nothin about what's different from him': Representations of Law's 'Other' in Australian Literature" (doctoral dissertation, Murdoch University, 2009).

Vattel, Emerich de. *The Law of Nations: Or, Principles of the Law of Nature, Applied to the Conduct and Affairs of Nations and Sovereigns, with Three Early Essays on the Origin and Nature of Natural Law and on Luxury*, ed. Béla Kapossy & Richard Whatmore (1758; Indianapolis IN: Liberty Fund, 2008).

Wacks, Raymond. *Law: A Very Short Introduction* (Oxford: Oxford UP, 2008).

West, Robin. *Narrative, Authority, and Law* (Ann Arbor: U of Michigan P, 1993).

Performative Lives – Transformative Practices
Wesley Enoch and Deborah Mailman, *The 7 Stages of Grieving*, and Richard Frankland, *Conversations with the Dead*

BEATE NEUMEIER

The Performative Turn and Life Writing

THE 'PERFORMATIVE TURN' in the humanities and social sciences over the last decades is indicative of current attempts at questioning, rethinking, and redefining the role of the human in relation to the surrounding world within a Western frame of knowledge. The emphasis on identity as situated embodied performance, on intercorporality and intersubjectivity, "challenges the very foundation of the moral, social, and political relations of modernity."[1] Drawing on Levinas' constitution of "the self [...] not [as] a substance but a relation," Deborah Bird Rose has called for an "ethic of connection"[2] in terms of a rethinking of the connection between cognitive and affective response with decisive political implications. In this context, as Rosalyn Diprose has argued, difference appears not as limitation but as constitutive of the self ("the other's otherness is what makes me feel and makes me think what I feel"[3]). Consequently, "the production of knowledge, truth, and culture arises from our orientation towards [... alterity]."[4] Diprose envisions the possibility of "a politics of generosity" based on "a generosity

---

[1] Rosalyn Diprose, *Corporeal Generosity: On Giving with Nietzsche, Merleau-Ponty, and Levinas* (Albany: State U of New York P, 2002): 61.

[2] Deborah Bird Rose, *Reports from a Wild Country: Ethics for Decolonisation* (Sydney: U of New South Wales P, 2004): 13.

[3] Diprose, *Corporeal Generosity*, 137.

[4] *Corporeal Generosity*, 162.

born of an affective corporeal response to alterity that generates rather than closes off cultural difference."[5] This also necessitates a rethinking of the role of literature and the arts, as situated processes of production and reception, and of the ethics and politics involved.

The performative turn foregrounds literature and the arts as transformative practices rather than as representational products containing meaning. It thus affects established distinctions between media and genres, fiction and non-fiction, in particular with reference to life writing. One of the persistent features of Anglo-European autobiography – even if it is radically deconstructed – is the promise of an understanding, often even an invitation to identification and empathy, between author/narrator and reader, as part of "the autobiographical pact."[6] The performative turn from eurocentric definitions of autobiography towards more inclusive notions of life writing in the recent past has counteracted this tendency to reduce difference to sameness, and thus to appropriate and deny alterity.[7] At the same time it has generated productive cross-fertilizations between life writing and artforms privileging the performative mode as transformative practice, such as theatre, dance, music, and film.

The theatre in particular as performative art par excellence, which constitutes itself in the performance event, can foreground processes of production and reception of meaning, of the creation of subject-positions and its others and their implications. Theatre as site-specific and communal event can foreground the transformative aspects of being-in-process while highlighting notions of difference without subsuming difference to sameness. Theatre can foreground its relation to other forms of cultural practice, emphasizing the embodied presence of the performance event and its implications for the spectator's position and responsibility. Such a foregrounding of the performative practice of "telling lives"[8] implies an unsettling of Anglo-European approaches to archiving the past as well as an unsettling of notions of identity and identification.

---

[5] Diprose, *Corporeal Generosity*, 145, 146.

[6] See Philippe Lejeune, *On Autobiography* (Minneapolis: U of Minnesota P, 1989).

[7] See Diprose, *Corporeal Generosity*, 160–61.

[8] See Peter Snow, "Performing All Over the Place," in *Unstable Ground: Performance and the Politics of Place,* ed. Gay McAuley (Brussels & Frankfurt am Main: P.I.E. Peter Lang, 2006): 227–46.

Performative Lives as Transformative Practice

The recent interest in life writing in Anglo-European theatre, apparent in the turn to documentary and verbatim theatre[9] as well as to what has been termed "testimonial theatre,"[10] has to be contextualized within a wider shift in life writing "from a linear subject-oriented trajectory to a multi-voiced community-oriented one"[11] enabled through the increasing impact of cross-cultural performance practices which often call upon traumatic histories of oppression with radically different implications for different audiences, necessitating an ethical encounter that respects difference and resists identificatory appropriation.[12] In contrast to the often psychoanalytically informed focus on the individual in what has sometimes been termed 'post-traumatic theatre' – or (perhaps better) "precarious theater"[13] – in Anglo-European performance practice and criticism, the emphasis on notions of oral history and community in non-Western art forms, enables what Bill Ashcroft has described, with reference to the Latin American *testimonio*, as a "strategic attempt to control representation [...] install[ing] cultural difference while purporting to communicate across that difference."[14]

---

[9] See, for example, *Get Real: Documentary Theatre Past and Present*, ed. Alison Forsyth & Chris Megson (Basingstoke: Palgrave Macmillan, 2009); and Ryan Claycomb, *Lives in Play: Autobiography and Biography on the Feminist Stage* (Ann Arbor: U of Michigan P, 2012).

[10] Cf. Melissa Salz, "Theatre of Testimony: The Works of Emily Mann, Anna Deavere Smith, and Spalding Gray" (doctoral dissertation, University of Colorado, 1996).

[11] Ryan Claycomb, "(Ch)oral History: Docudrama, the Communal Subject, and Progressive Form," *Journal of Dramatic Theory and Criticism* 17.2 (2003): 98.

[12] See also Jill Bennett, *Emphatic Vision: Affect, Trauma and Contemporary Art* (Stanford CA: Stanford UP, 2005): esp. the chapter on "Global Interconnections".

[13] See Katharina Pewny's insightful distinction between post-traumatic, transformatic, and relational theatre in her discussion of precarious theatre in *Das Drama des Prekären: Über die Wiederkehr der Ethik in Theater und Performance* (Bielefeld: transcript, 2011).

[14] Bill Ashcroft, *Post-Colonial Transformation* (London & New York: Routledge, 2001): 114, 115. See also Sacha Gibbons, "Aboriginal Testimonial Life Writing" (doctoral dissertation, University of Queensland, 2005), which draws on the Latin American *testimonio* (and its focus on political resistance) *and* on Holocaust testimonies (and their focus on working through trauma) for his analysis of Aboriginal testimonial life writing.

If the repetition involved in "narrative and affective control over traumatic material"[15] in artistic cultural practices enables us to bring it into relation to the subject *and* the nation,[16] notions of a "controlled sharing"[17] across different audiences are of decisive importance on a personal as well as a political level. The performative practices I would like to focus on develop this aesthetic of controlled sharing, addressing questions of affective and cognitive response in connection with recognition and responsibility, forcing different audiences to recognize themselves differently. The use of the term 'performative lives' in this context is meant to signal the correlative turn of life writing and theatrical performance towards performative processes as cultural practice. At the same time, it functions as a reminder of my own culturally situated and thus inevitably limited spectator/reader position as well as the accompanying theoretical framework. It is this spectator/reader position that I will focus on here.

Performative lives in Australian Indigenous cultural practices are, as Larissa Behrendt has emphasized, part of a long "tradition of storytelling in our communities as a way of teaching, as a way of retaining history, and as a way of communicating across time."[18] Indigenous Australian theatre has generated performative practices focusing on a transformative process in which place, time, actors, and spectators come into being together in the performance, often integrating different artforms, dance, song, live music, painting, and/or screen-based media.[19] In recent decades, the increasing international visibility of Indigenous playwrights (such as Wesley Enoch, Richard Frankland, Leah Purcell, Tammy Anderson, Andrea James, Collen Johnson, Sam Cook, and Ernie Blackmore) and performance companies (such as Bangarra Dance Theatre) at internationally acclaimed theatre festivals on different continents testifies to the impact of Indigenous performance cultures on Australian

---

[15] Sacha Gibbons, "Aboriginal Testimonial Life-Writing and Contemporary Theory," 107; see also Kali Tal, *Worlds of Hurt: Reading the Literatures of Trauma* (Cambridge: Cambridge UP, 1996): 21.

[16] See Sacha Gibbons, "Aboriginal Testimonial Life-Writing and Contemporary Theory," 146.

[17] Kim Scott in this volume.

[18] Larissa Behrendt, "Introduction" to *Contemporary Indigenous Plays*, ed. Vivienne Cleven (Sydney: Currency, 2007): x.

[19] See Wesley Enoch, "Why Do We Applaud?" in *Contemporary Australian Plays*, ed. Russell Vandenbroucke (London: Methuen, 2001): 271–74.

society and beyond. The importance of telling lives in this context[20] has been acknowledged in groundbreaking studies by Helen Gilbert and Jacqueline Lo, Katherine Brisbane, Joanne Tompkins, and Hilary Glow.[21]

Indigenous performative lives partake in a double movement towards decolonizing history *and* decolonizing the stage.[22] The appeal of performative lives for international audiences seems to consist in precisely the cultural situatedness and experiential focus of the performance event, which resonates differently in different cultural contexts involving Indigenous and non-Indigenous, Australian and non-Australian spectator-positions with radically distinct political and ethical implications.

Performative lives radicalize the shift from an Anglo-European concept of the spectator as "judging observer" or "detached knower"[23] to the spectator as part of what is emerging in the performance event. In this context, the anthropocentrism of human action versus the environment is radically unsettled. Such a performative practice demands an 'ethic of connection' involving notions of care and responsibility. It is, thus, precisely through the collective performance event that cultural differences are respected rather than levelled out, as the different spectatorships are always located differently in the event. Such a performative practice uses strategies of resistance to the non-Indigenous spectator's desire for the self-affirming closure of identification and empathy, pity, and regret, which are based on a desire for sameness inevitably

---

[20] See. for example, Scott Rankin and Leah Purcell's *Box the Pony*, Wesley Enoch and Debra Mailman's *The 7 Stages of Grieving*, Deborah Cheetham's *White Baptist Abba Fan*, Tom E. Lewis's *Thumbul* and *Lift 'Em Up Socks*, Ningali Lawson's *Ningali*, Richard Frankland's *Conversations witht the Dead*, and Tammy Anderson's *I Don't Want to Play House*.

[21] See Helen Gilbert, *Sightlines. Race, Gender, and Nation in Contemporary Australian Theatre* (Ann Arbor: U of Michigan P, 1998); Katherine Brisbane, *Not Wrong – Just Different: Observations on the Rise of Contemporary Australian Theatre* (Sydney: Currency, 2005); Joanne Tompkins, *Unsettling Space: Contestations in Contemporary Australian Theatre* (Basingstoke: Palgrave Macmillan, 2006); Helen Gilbert & Jacqueline Lo, *Performance and Cosmopolitics: Cross-Cultural Transactions in Australasia* (Basingstoke: Palgrave Macmillan, 2007); and Hilary Glow, *Power Plays: Australian Theatre and the Public Agenda* (Sydney: Currency, 2007).

[22] Cf. Christopher Balme, *Decolonizing the Stage: Theatrical Syncretism and Post-Colonial Drama* (Oxford: Oxford UP, 1999).

[23] Cf. Michael Christie, quoting Kathryn Pyne Addelson, *Moral Passages: Toward a Collectivist Moral Theory* (New York: Routledge, 1994), in this volume, 63.

linked to a desire to *know* and control[24] and thus "just another mode of assimilation [...] a denial."[25] Instead, the non-Indigenous spectator is confronted with an affective and cognitive disturbance, an unsettlement or discomfort, which "may be different for different people, [...] but [...] reminds us that there is no such a thing as 'merely' watching."[26] This movement towards unsettlement of the non-Indigenous spectator can be a decisive motor for change despite the inevitable counter-movement towards recovering the self "through pity, regret, or memory."[27]

Bill Ashcroft has suggested transformation as a praxis of resistance "which is not so much deconstructive as dynamic, not so much ethically insoluble as practically affirmative."[28] Addressing the inevitable question of how to "transcend the trope of the boundary," he proposes horizonality, "for whereas the boundary is about cultural regulation, the horizon is about cultural possibility."[29] I would like to take this notion into my reading of Indigenous performative lives as transformative practice opening up towards the horizon. The "horizon does not dispense with boundaries altogether, but inhabits them, utilizes them, incorporates them in a different way."[30]

In the following, I would like to focus on Wesley Enoch's and Deborah Mailman's *The 7 Stages of Grieving* (1995) and Richard Frankland's *Conversations with the Dead* (2002), plays which address *and* simultaneously perform a transformative process involving actors and spectators, with specific ethical and political implications. While both plays engage in this transformative endeavour, *The 7 Stages of Grieving* explores the possibilities of connecting across boundaries towards the horizon, while *Conversations with the Dead* centres on its boundaries, foregrounding questions of difference.

---

[24] See Anne Anlin Cheng, *The Melancholy of Race* (New York: Oxford UP, 2001): 181.

[25] Diprose, *Corporeal Generosity*, 160.

[26] Cheng, *The Melancholy of Race*, 181.

[27] Diprose, *Corporeal Generosity*, 163.

[28] Ashcroft, *Post-Colonial Transformation*, 7.

[29] *Post-Colonial Transformation*, 15–16.

[30] *Post-Colonial Transformation*, 184.

Performative Lives and Transformative Horizons: Enoch and Mailman, *The 7 Stages of Grieving* (1996)

Wesley Enoch's reference to Peter Brook's *Empty Space* in his introductory essay ("Why Do We Applaud?") to the play highlights the tension in Anglo-European theatre between a desire for disembodiment and spatial abstraction, on the one hand, and for embodied emplacement, often through the appropriation of "culturally based narratives" (as in Brook's own intercultural theatre), on the other.[31] By contrast, Wesley Enoch emphasizes Indigenous cultural practices based on "an inherent connection with place and the need for everything to have a place – a story – in the greater fabric of song."[32] Consequently, the telling of the history of Indigenous Australia is necessarily an embodied and emplaced living experience. Site-specific theatrical practices in recent years have highlighted the complexity of the relation between embodiment and emplacement, indicating a "placial [sic] turn"[33] away from the Anglo-European concept of the stage as empty space to the localized, situated "reality of place."[34]

However, different performative practices can foreground the inseparability of place, time, and human experience, particularly with regard to histories, "activating and articulating the memories that circulate in relation to places of trauma."[35] The production of *The 7 Stages of Grieving* highlights how embodiment and emplacement interrelate through the performance event for wider, differently positioned audiences.[36] The play centres on Deborah Mailman performing an "Indigenous Everywoman," telling the "personal and political history of Indigenous Australia," drawing on "real events, family his-

---

[31] Enoch, "Why Do We Applaud?" 274.

[32] "Why Do We Applaud?" 272.

[33] Gay McAuley, "Introduction" to *Unstable Ground: Performance and the Politics of Place*, ed. Gay McAuley (Brussels & Frankfurt am Main: P.I.E. Peter Lang, 2006): 16.

[34] McAuley, "Introduction," 17.

[35] Gay McAuley, "Remembering and Forgetting: Place and Performance in the Memory Process," in *Unstable Ground: Performance and the Politics of Place*, ed. Gay McAuley (Brussels & Frankfurt am Main: P.I.E. Peter Lang, 2006): 171–72.

[36] See J. Lowell Lewis, "Afterword: Theoretical Reflections," in *Unstable Ground: Performance and the Politics of Place*, ed. Gay McAuley (Brussels & Frankfurt am Main: P.I.E. Peter Lang, 2006): 273–91.

tories and personal experiences of the collaborators."[37] This enactment of the inseparability of time, place, and life links the seven phases of Aboriginal history to the five stages of dying – as defined by Elisabeth Kübler–Ross in *On Death and Dying* – performing a process of grieving. The notion of grieving shifts the emphasis away from the traumatic impasse of being locked in a victim-position. Instead, in Wesley Enoch's words, "*The 7 Stages of Grieving* is a celebration of our survival, an invitation to grieve publicly, a time to exorcise our pain."[38] Accordingly, the author draws attention to the necessary distinction between audiences:

> Audiences will need to work hard to grasp the analysis of culture and place. For Murri audiences, a sense of celebration emerges from the grieving. There is a lightening of the load, an elation that comes from hearing stories that need to be told.[39]

At the same time, non-Indigenous audiences are explicitly invited to participate in the performative journey.

Given the immediate international reception of *The 7 Stages of Grieving*, moving from Brisbane (1995) on to a national tour (1996) to the London Festival of Theatre (1997), many different non-Indigenous audiences joined in bringing with them their specific experiences and histories. In Peter Snow's words: "we are never simply in one place but always in many places – we carry with us many places and therefore exist in a kind of 'in-between placedness' or 'being implaced in the in-between'."[40] The complexity of a multilayered, embodied emplacement produces different resonances for different audiences in the communal performative process, addressing the relationality between notions of collective and individual past. The trajectory of the play unfolds the multidimensional history of boundaries connected to the trauma of colonial oppression and enacts transformative strategies of resistance. This is captured powerfully through the gradual literal transformation of the set design, which consists of a large block of ice, "suspended by seven ropes above a grave of red earth," while the remaining part of "the performance area is covered in a thin layer of black powder framed by a scrape of white" (*S*

---

[37] Enoch, "Why Do We Applaud?" 273.

[38] "Why Do We Applaud?" 274.

[39] Wesley Enoch, "Murri Grief," *Dialogue* 27 (1996): 14.

[40] Snow, "Performing All Over the Place," in *Unstable Ground: Performance and the Politics of Place*, ed. Gay McAuley (Brussels & Frankfurt am Main: P.I.E. Peter Lang, 2006): 238.

277).[41] The audience witnesses the Indigenous Everywoman and the set perform together a transformative shift from an enforced colonial separation of space, time, and human identity enacting their inseparability through a process in which place and being emerge together in the material traces of time:

> The ice drips onto the grave, the performer (who arrives on stage in a clean white chemise) walks between the white fringes and the black centre smearing white into black, black into white.[42]

The Prologue addresses questions of permission and respect with regard to "Aboriginal and Torres Strait Islander people" and thus also serves as a reminder of different "members of the audience" (S 277), warning against appropriating identification. When the English semantic field of 'grief' is projected onto a screen, we hear the Woman sobbing. The words projected include 'grief', 'regret', 'misfortune', and 'guilt', as well as 'passion' and 'love', ending with the phrase "I feel nothing!" (S 278) followed by the Woman speaking in the Murri language. The spatial boundaries of the set are thus linked to boundaries between other sign systems, visual/auditive, written/oral, English/Murri,[43] foregrounding the spectators' specific, different, historically and culturally embodied emplacements. The tension between the violence of the colonizers' knowledge-system and strategies of resistance is taken up later in a powerful image when the letters of the English alphabet are projected onto the female performer's body, while her resistance is audible in Murri words.

Drawing on Rosi Braidotti, Helena Grehan has described the Woman's "nomadic wanderings through places or sites of aboriginality," her "mov[ing] in and out between scenes, shifting in emotion," in terms of "an interface, a threshold, a field of intersection of material and symbolic forces."[44] The transformative power of this performative process of embodiment and emplacement in time unfolds in terms of a complex layering that affects sign systems

---

[41] All quotations from and comments on *The 7 Stages of Grieving* refer to Wesley Enoch & Deborah Mailman, "The 7 Stages of Grieving," in *Contemporary Australian Plays,* ed. Russell Vandenbroucke (London: Methuen, 2001): 269–99. This edition is referred to in the text as (S + page).

[42] Helena Grehan, *Mapping Cultural Identity in Contemporary Australian Performance* (Brussels: P.I.E. Peter Lang, 2001): 101.

[43] See the excellent analysis of the play by Helena Grehan, *Mapping Cultural Identity in Contemporary Australian Performance,* 97–118.

[44] Grehan, *Mapping Cultural Identity in Contemporary Australian Performance,* 98–99.

on different sensorial levels. In this context, the personal, historical, and political impact of visual images is highlighted through the use of projections of historical events ("Gallery of Sorrow") and private family pictures ("Photograph Story," "Family Gallery"). The aural/oral mode is foregrounded in the stories being told ("Nana's Story" about the grandmother's death, the "Home Story" about kinship and the Stolen Generations, the "Story of the Brother" and his police record). As the boundaries between sign systems are being blurred, sound and vision are linked to evocations of smell (as in the burning of eucalypt leaves, *S* 278), and touch (as the performer embraces the block of ice, touches, and is touched by the powder covering the performance area).

The performance probes the implications of communicating in a variety of discourses, ranging from literary and performative genres, including poetry (the "Invasion poem," the "Wreck con silly nation poem"), through stand-up comedy ("Murri Gets a Dress"), to the court report ("Mugshot"), when she finally "breaks away from the written word [...] to improvise the text" (*S* 289) in a powerful enactment of resistance to the violence of a legal discourse, the supposed facticity of which deliberately leaves out the atrocity of police actions. In the scene about the march in silence in protest and grief at a young man's death in police custody, the Woman embodies the rhythm of the grieving crowd, her sentences swelling like the people joining in the march:

> I'm in a crowd. I'm in a crowd of people all walking. I'm in a crowd of people all walking along in silence. I'm in a crowd of people all walking along in silence, my dad, my brothers and sisters and my nana. (*S* 289)

This transformative process is linked to a series of stage images connecting the emplaced resting place of the burial ground as site of grieving to the non-stationary traveler's suitcase, inviting a multiplicity of assocations. The suitcase in particular calls upon different cognitive and affective associations, images, sounds, smells, and memories for different audiences connected to different experiences and histories. Its symbolic value is connected to past and future, to memory and anticipation, to the despair of separation and loss as well as to the hope for reunion, to the fear of, as well as curiosity about, the unknown. The suitcase contains what is vital to take along on the journey. It highlights the distance between voluntary and enforced migration, and the links between different histories of oppression in different geographical and historical contexts. It has to be unpacked after the return from the journey. Its contents, affected by the journey, have to be taken care of.

In the performance, the suitcase is first mentioned and visualized on the projection screen (*S* 281) as the place where "the photos of those who are dead" (*S* 281) are kept. It materializes when the Woman pulls the suitcase "out of the grave" (*S* 286) in connection with the story of Aunty Grace, who, after fifty years of married life in England, returns for Nana's funeral. In Aunty Grace's story it is her suitcase that she empties of her belongings, fills with red earth from the grave, and places on top of the grave, "crying at last" (*S* 287). Towards the end of the play it is the Woman who opens the suitcase, "throwing the red earth and family photos it contains all over the floor" (*S* 295) before leaving the stage. When she returns, "images of landscape interweave with family portraits creating a tapestry of Land and People. Music fills the space. There is a feeling of *catharsis and release*" (*S* 295).

The notion of catharsis raises questions about the non-Indigenous spectators' involvement in this transformative process as witnesses with their own specific cultural and historical embeddedness. It is precisely the foregrounding of the cathartic release embodied by the Woman returning "to the performance area cleansed, fresh" (*S* 295) that renders impossible the comforting closure of appropriating identification and makes the non-Indigenous spectator aware of the discomfort of difference created by the communal event.

Significantly, the cathartic release is followed by the playful irony of the Wreck-con-silly-nation poem and by the Woman packing the word 'reconciliation' into the now-empty suitcase, which she places at the feet of the audience, addressing them directly. Non-Indigenous spectators have to take up the suitcase differently, assuming responsibility for their own implication in the his/stories presented, as the Woman's words remind us: "Reconciliation is something that you do," and "What can I do but [...] perform" (*S* 296).

The last scene, entitled "Relief," takes up the end of the opening speech of the Woman sobbing, "Nothing – Nothing – Nothing – I feel Nothing" (*S* 297). But this time the Woman stands with her "face uplifted" in "a pool of light" (*S* 296). Rather than signalling repetition-compulsion, this ending is a 'repetition with a difference' foregrounding the transformative process that has involved and re-positioned the performer *and* the spectator differently, "which does not dispense with boundaries altogether but inhabits them, utilizes them, incorporates them in a different way."[45] The multidimensionality of the suitcase signals in-betweenness and uprootedness, a loss of and desire for belonging, but at the same time the inseparability of place, time, and human

---

[45] Ashcroft, *Post-Colonial Transformation*, 184.

lives. The transformative performative process works towards a more inclusive notion of living, with a focus on traces which may be stored or hidden away but are waiting to be unpacked by an act of mutual performing.[46]

Performative Lives and Transformative Boundaries: Richard Frankland's *Conversations with the Dead* (2002)

Notions of death, grief, pain, and despair are taken to their limits in Richard Frankland's play *Conversations with the Dead* (2002) exploring the implications of spectatorship as inhabiting boundaries in terms of radical unsettlement. The fact of Aboriginal deaths in police custody, told in one of the scenes of *The 7 Stages of Grieving*,[47] is the central theme of Frankland's *Conversations with the Dead*. The play embodies the presence of the past on stage, as the main character, Jack, who – like the playwright – is the only Indigenous member of the Royal Commission investigating the deaths, is increasingly engaged in conversations with these un-ghostly dead whom he never met during their lifetime. Jack's unique professional position situates him in-between the Indigenous communities on whose behalf he wants to act and the requirements of the non-Indigenous governmental commission. It transforms the fundamental tension between his attempt to act with care and responsibility and the accompanying sense of inadequacy into an experiential quality affecting and foregrounding the contradictions inherent in the desire for identification in the variously positioned audience members. This specific perspective radicalizes central issues of performative lives, enforcing a transformative engagement with different spectatorial positions with regard to questions of responsibility and empathy as well as guilt and despair.

Like *The 7 Stages of Grieving*, the play opens with references to the history of colonization, the voice-over of Captain Cook's orders being followed by images randomly projected onto the backdrop of the ship *Endeavour* with

---

[46] This notion of transformative energy as a strategy of resistance and survival is taken up differently in other plays, as in the family tree turned into *Cookie's Table* by Wesley Enoch or, again differently, in the "transformative influence" (172) of Crow across racialized and gendered boundaries in *Crow Fire* by Jadah Milroy, in *Blak Inside: Six Indigenous Plays from Victoria*, ed. John Harding & Tammy Anderson (Sydney: Currency, 2002).

[47] Scene 13, "Mugshot," on the life and death of Daniel Yocke (see Gilbert, *Sightlines*, and Grehan, *Mapping Cultural Identity in Contemporary Australian Performance*).

Performative Lives – Transformative Practices

accelerating speed, gradually slowing down on images of deaths in custody, ending with the onstage appearance of an actor spearing the image of the ship, which shatters like glass. Again issues of the power of sign systems are addressed, the disembodied voice and the visual image being set off against the embodied liveness of the performance event as a strategy of resistance and transformation. But the transformative process invoked is decisively different in the two plays, with *Conversations with the Dead* exploring the limits rather than the possibilities of this endeavour by foregrounding the existential boundary between life and death, challenging distinctions between inside/outside, individual/collective, personal/political.

The spectator position is thematized from the beginning, when Jack addresses the audience directly:

> Imagine that you're a Koori, that you're in your mid-twenties and that it is your job to look into the lives of the dead and the process, policy and attitude that killed them. [...] Where would you put the memories? What would keep you sane? Who do you think could understand what you carry inside you? (*C* 221–22)[48]

This explicit invitation to identify with the main character is, however, countered by the inevitable acknowledgement of the impossibility of such an identification. Moreover, this dilemma is – though differently – shared by him, inasmuch as he feels confronted with the tension between the need to tell the lives of the dead and the inevitable misrepresentation of those lives in coercive and reductive signifying systems, such as the legal report, but also – albeit less damagingly – life writing or (by implication) performative lives. Frankland foregrounds the limitations of his performative endeavour, when Jack reads "the list of those one hundred and twenty-four people who died in custody and how only ninety-nine were investigated and no one charged" (*C* 232), while only a few of the life stories of the dead can be told during the performance event. The question of how those life stories can be communicated responsibly to different audiences and their different entanglements in the traumatic histories involved is explored on multiple levels by strategically foregrounding differences while inviting participation with regard to the protagonist and the other cast members (who performed multiple roles in the

---

[48] All quotations from and comments on *Conversations with the Dead* refer to Richard Frankland, "Conversations with the Dead," in *Blak Inside: Six Indigenous plays from Victoria,* ed. John Harding & Tammy Anderson (Sydney: Currency, 2002): 216–87. This edition is referred to in the text as (*C* + page).

original production directed by the playwright),[49] as well as the different audiences. Thus, the play not only addresses but performs the central question of "how to forge an ethical (that is, non-appropriative and not self-serving) relation to the other."[50]

The notion of death as absolute otherness, as "the limit of our understanding,"[51] is evoked but at the same time questioned by the insistence on the presence of the dead in the lives of the living. This presence cannot be adequately conceptualized intellectually, but has to be addressed on an experiential level. The protagonist, Jack, explicitly thematizes the necessity of notions of empathy and identification – "What do you say to someone you knew but never met. [...] I feel for him. I stretch out my feelings to see what he feels like" (*C* 224/225) – while at the same time acknowledging the limits of this attempt to get to know and do justice to the lives of the dead. He feels distant from ("an intruder," *C* 235) *and* similar to them ("we were the same in so many ways," *C* 237). He feels "always alone" (*C* 230) and never alone at the same time ("our lives become so intertwined that I don't know where one begins and one ends," *C* 231). He increasingly feels caught between his professional role as a detached observer, objectifying and judging the lives of the victims, and his growing emotional involvement, which separates him from the living. The course of the play follows Jack turning his job from investigating to desperately trying to prevent deaths in custody (*C* 239) as a movement of radical unsettlement, tracing the protagonist's experience of a radical rift between closeness and distance to those who died, between feeling "a fraud" gaining public recognition through his job, and "a warrior" attempting to set things right (*C* 253), between imminent self-loss ("I don't know how I feel. I don't know who I am. Or even what I am," *C* 237) and defiant self-assertion ("I know who I am!," *C* 253, but: "How long will that feeling last?," *C* 254).

The play foregrounds in disturbing images the inability of the living to distance themselves from the lives of the dead, when, after having cleansed the body of David on the morgue table in order to "pay respect," Jack's at-

---

[49] According to the play text, "*Conversations with the Dead* can be played by 5 actors and 1 musician." (*C* 217).

[50] Cheng, "Psychoanalysis without Symptoms," *Differences: A Journal of Feminist Cultural Studies* 20.1 (2009): 95.

[51] Cathy Caruth on trauma in *Trauma: Explorations in Memory* (Baltimore MD & London: Johns Hopkins UP, 1995): 4.

tempts to clean himself only increase the "traces of blood all over him" (*C* 259). Dressed in a white tuxedo, he attends a dinner party, where the non-Indigenous guests' ignorant and appropriating attitude pointed up in the dialogue is juxtaposed with a rain of blood turning into a storm, as a party guest's question, "why do they kill themselves in jail?" (*C* 262), is answered by Jack's aside to the audience: "We know, don't we?" (*C* 264). The performative process avoids moving Jack into a victim-position allowing for undifferentiated redemptive audience identification, as the tensions described take Jack to the brink of suicide as well as to murderous fantasies and to seemingly futile acts of violence against others, as in a bar scene, when he beats up the publican, forcing him to "a headjob" (*C* 265).

Towards the end, Jack's suicidal despair is increasingly countered *and* emphasized by attempts at healing with reference to professional therapy (visualized by the psychiatrist's couch), but also by appeals to love and trust. In this context, the play evokes Shakespeare's *King Lear* as one of the central texts challenging notions of empathy and cathartic closure in Anglo-European theatre history, when Jack retreats to a place of his youth "to challenge the spirits" (*C* 283), eventually "launching off the cliff" (*C* 285) in a storm. Thrown back into a tree by strong winds, he asks the question of meaning ("Is it all mapped out?," *C* 286), but still denies a comforting belief in a higher plan ("I just ended up somewhere? [...] Who gives a fuck anyway?," *C* 286). In the final scene of the play, Jack is sleeping with his head resting on a woman's lap, when the whole cast starts singing about hope for the future ("Maybe one day"), while the photo and headline of another death in custody "flashes on the screen behind them" (*C* 287).

This ending evokes Lear challenging the spirits in the storm, Gloucester's suicide-attempt at Dover cliff, and the dying Lear holding his dead daughter in his arms. However, Shakespeare's play reinscribes the boundaries between life and death, self and other in terms of a tragedy of the individual, whose learning process in empathy and responsibility cannot be translated into the future, as the personal guilt of both, Lear and Gloucester, has to be recognized and atoned for by death from a broken heart. By contrast, Frankland's play describes the unbearable but necessarily ongoing burden of bearing witness, of testifying, and of communicating the terror and trauma of injustice and death across cultural and historical boundaries. *Conversations with the Dead* leaves the boundaries between life and death, past and present, hope and despair decisively unsettled in Frankland's telling of the pain of his people's suffering. The focus is not on healing as closure, but on the experiential processual transformative aspect of the theatrical experience addressing different audiences in different ways, linked to what Anne Cheng has called "the gift of discomfort," because it is "in those very moments when the boundaries of the subject and object of power are most jeopardized and most undetermined we can truly begin to ask ethical questions."[52]

Frankland's *Conversations with the Dead* and Enoch and Mailman's *The Seven Stages of Grieving* powerfully partake in the creative process of a decolonization of history and the stage, and, by the same token, of a transcultural transformation of notions of life writing and theatre as performative practices. Both can be seen as performative life writing engaging in an impossible transformative practice, addressing and communicating aspects of a traumatic history for widely different audiences. As indicated above, this necessitates strategies of resistance against the appropriation of otherness by postcolonial audiences, an insistence on difference, as well as strategies of communication across that difference (cf. Ashcroft). *Conversations with the Dead* and *The Seven Stages of Grieving* enact this double strategy, turning the performance event into a process crossing boundaries and opening towards the possibilities of a new horizon, towards "transforming the 'intellectual concept' of reconciliation into an 'emotional' reality,"[53] while at the same time enjoining non-Indigenous audiences to see themselves differently and to act upon this knowledge. As Rosalyn Diprose has argued, "The politics of generosity begins with all of us, it begins and remains in trouble, and it begins within the act."[54]

Works Cited

Addelson, Kathryn Pyne. *Moral Passages: Toward a Collectivist Moral Theory* (New York: Routledge, 1994).

Ashcroft, Bill. *Post-Colonial Transformation* (New York: Routledge, 2001).

Balme, Christopher. *Decolonizing the Stage: Theatrical Syncretism and Post-Colonial Drama* (Oxford: Oxford UP, 1999).

---

[52] Cheng, "Psychoanalysis without Symptoms," 93.

[53] Wesley Enoch, quoted in Helen Gilbert & Jacqueline Lo, *Performance and Cosmopolitics. Cross-Cultural Transactions in Australasia* (Basingstoke: Palgrave Macmillan, 2007): 65–66.

[54] Diprose, *Corporeal Generosity*, 188.

Behrendt, Larissa. "Introduction" to *Contemporary Indigenous Plays*, ed. Vivienne Cleven (Sydney: Currency, 2007): vii–x.
Bennett, Jill. *Emphatic Vision: Affect, Trauma and Contemporary Art* (Stanford CA: Stanford UP, 2005).
Brisbane, Katherine. *Not Wrong – Just Different: Observations on the Rise of Contemporary Australian Theatre* (Sydney: Currency, 2005).
Caruth, Cathy, ed. *Trauma: Explorations in Memory* (Baltimore MD & London: Johns Hopkins UP, 1995).
Cheng, Anne Anlin. *The Melancholy of Race* (New York: Oxford UP, 2001).
——. "Psychoanalysis without Symptoms," *Differences: A Journal of Feminist Cultural Studies* 20.1 (2009): 87–102.
Claycomb, Ryan. "(Ch)oral History: Docudrama, the Communal Subject, and Progressive Form," *Journal of Dramatic Theory and Criticism* 17.2 (2003): 95–121.
——. *Lives in Play: Autobiography and Biography on the Feminist Stage* (Ann Arbor: U of Michigan P, 2012).
Diprose, Rosalyn. *Corporeal Generosity: On Giving with Nietzsche, Merleau-Ponty, and Levinas* (Albany: State U of New York P, 2002).
Enoch, Wesley. "Murri Grief," *Dialogue* 27 (1996): 10 &14.
——. *The Story of the Miracles at Cookie's Table* (Sydney: Currency, 2007).
——. "Why Do We Applaud?" in *Contemporary Australian Plays*, ed. Russell Vandenbroucke (London: Methuen, 2001): 271–74.
——, & Deborah Mailman. "The 7 Stages of Grieving," in *Contemporary Australian Plays*, ed. Russell Vandenbroucke (London: Methuen, 2001): 269–99.
Forsyth, Alison, & Chris Megson, ed. *Get Real: Documentary Theatre Past and Present* (Basingstoke: Palgrave Macmillan, 2009).
Frankland, Richard. "Conversations with the Dead," in *Blak Inside: Six Indigenous plays from Victoria*, ed. John Harding & Tammy Anderson (Sydney: Currency, 2002): 216–87.
Gibbons, Sacha. "Aboriginal Testimonial Life-Writing and Contemporary Theory" (doctoral dissertation, University of Queensland, 2005).
Gilbert, Helen. *Sightlines: Race, Gender, and Nation in Contemporary Australian Theatre* (Ann Arbor: U of Michigan P, 1998).
——, & Jacqueline Lo. *Performance and Cosmopolitics: Cross-Cultural Transactions in Australasia* (Basingstoke: Palgrave Macmillan, 2007).
Glow, Hilary. *Power Plays: Australian Theatre and the Public Agenda* (Sydney: Currency, 2007).
Grehan, Helena. *Mapping Cultural Identity in Contemporary Australian Performance* (Brussels: P.I.E. Peter Lang, 2001).
Kübler–Ross, Elisabeth. *On Death and Dying* (New York: Macmillan, 1969).
Lejeune, Philippe. *On Autobiography* (Minneapolis: U of Minnesota P, 1989).

Lewis, J. Lowell. "Afterword: Theoretical Reflections," in *Unstable Ground* (2006), ed. McAuley, 273–91.

McAuley, Gay, ed. *Unstable Ground: Performance and the Politics of Place* (Brussels & Frankfurt am Main: P.I.E. Peter Lang, 2006).

——. "Introduction" to *Unstable Ground* (2006), ed. McAuley, 15–23.

——. "Remembering and Forgetting: Place and Performance in the Memory Process" to *Unstable Ground* (2006), ed. McAuley, 149–75.

Milroy, Jadah. "Crow Fire," in *Blak Inside: Six Indigenous Plays from Victoria*, ed. John Harding & Tammy Anderson (Sydney: Currency, 2002): 169–213.

Pewny, Katharina. *Das Drama des Prekären: Über die Wiederkehr der Ethik in Theater und Performance* (Bielefeld: Transcript, 2011).

Rose, Deborah Bird. *Reports from a Wild Country: Ethics for Decolonisation* (Sydney: U of New South Wales P, 2004).

Salz, Melissa. "Theatre of Testimony: The Works of Emily Mann, Anna Deavere Smith, and Spalding Gray" (doctoral dissertation, University of Colorado, 1996).

Snow, Peter. "Performing All Over the Place," in *Unstable Ground* (2006), ed. McAuley, 227–46.

Tal, Kalí. *Worlds of Hurt: Reading the Literatures of Trauma* (Cambridge: Cambridge UP, 1996).

Tompkins, Joanne. *Unsettling Space: Contestations in Contemporary Australian Theatre* (Basingstoke: Palgrave Macmillan, 2006).

⌘

Notes on Contributors

KATRIN ALTHANS teaches at the University of Osnabrück, Germany and is currently working on a postdoctoral project in the field of law and literature. Her book *Darkness Subverted: Aboriginal Gothic in Black Australian Literature and Film* (2010) was nominated for the Walter McRae Russell Award. Her research focuses on Australian Indigenous writing, the Gothic, and Victorian literature and legal theory. She is the author of essays on Aboriginal gothic as well as on gender, the Gothic, and new media.

HEINZ ANTOR is Professor of English Literatures at the University of Cologne. He is editor of the journal *Anglistik*. Among his books are *The Bloomsbury Group* (1986); *Die Narrativik der Angry Young Men* (1989); *Text – Culture – Reception: Cross-Cultural Aspects of English Studies* (1992); *Der englische Universitätsroman* (1996); *Intercultural Encounters – Studies in English Literatures* (1999); *English Literatures in International Contexts* (2000); *Refractions of Germany in Canadian Literature and Culture* (2003); *Refractions of Canada in European Literature and Culture* (2005); *Inter- und Transkulturelle Studien* (2006); *Fremde Kulturen verstehen – fremde Kulturen lehren: Theorie und Praxis der Vermittlung interkultureller Kompetenz* (2007); and *From Interculturalism to Transculturalism: Mediating Encounters in Cosmopolitan Contexts* (2010).

BILL ASHCROFT is a renowned critic and theorist, founding exponent of postcolonial theory, and co-author of *The Empire Writes Back*, the first text to examine systematically the field of postcolonial studies. He is author and co-author of sixteen books and over 160 articles and chapters, variously translated into six languages. He was Dr R. Marika Guest Chair in Australian Studies at the University of Cologne (2011). Currently he holds an Australian Professorial Fellowship at the University of New South Wales, working on the project 'Future Thinking: Utopianism in Postcolonial Literatures'.

ANNE BREWSTER is an Associate Professor at the University of New South Wales. Her books include *Literary Formations: Postcoloniality, Nationalism, Globalism* (1996), *Aboriginal Women's Autobiography* (1995), *Towards a Semiotic of Post-Colonial Discourse: University Writing in Singapore and Malaysia 1949–1964* (1988), and *Notes on Catherine Lim's Little Ironies: Stories of Singapore* (with Kirpal Singh 1987). She has co-edited, with Angeline O'Neill and Rosemary van den Berg, an anthology of Australian Indigenous writing, *Those Who Remain Will Always Remember* (2000).

MICHAEL CHRISTIE worked as a teacher linguist in Yolŋu communities in Arnhem Land, Northern Territory, Australia, for over twenty years before moving to Darwin to set up the Yolŋu Studies programme at Charles Darwin University in 1994. He is currently Professor in the Northern Institute, working on collaborative transdisciplinary research and consultancies in a number of areas including health communication, 'both-ways' education, water management, Yolŋu epistemology and philosophy, and research methodologies in the decolonization of the academy.

ANNA HAEBICH is a Distinguished Professor at Curtin University in Western Australia. She is known for her leadership in interdisciplinary and cross-cultural research. Her multi-award-winning publications include *Broken Circles: Fragmenting Indigenous Families 1820–2000* (2000), *Spinning the Dream: Assimilation in Australia* (2008), and *For Their Own Good: Aborigines and Government in the South West of Western Australia* (1992). Her current research focuses on cultural histories of Aboriginal Australians in the performing and visual arts. She is a Vice-President of the Australian Academy of Humanities.

IAN HENDERSON is Menzies Lecturer in Australian Studies in the Department of English Language and Literature at King's College London. He has published widely on nineteenth- and twentieth-century Australian literature and on Australian cinema, with a particular interest in the representation of Australia's Indigenous peoples. Between 2007 and 2010 he was founding editor of *Studies in Australasian Cinema*.

SUE KOSSEW is Professor of English and Head of the School of English, Communications and Performance Studies at Monash University. She has published numerous journal articles and book chapters on postcolonial, Australian, and South African literature. She is author of the monographs *Writing Woman, Writing Place: Contemporary Australian and South African Fiction*

(2004, 2006) and *Pen and Power: A Post-Colonial Reading of J.M. Coetzee and André Brink* (1996). Her edited books include *Lighting Dark Places: Essays on Kate Grenville* (2010), *Strong Opinions: J.M. Coetzee and the Authority of Contemporary Fiction* (with Chris Danta and Julian Murphet, 2011), and *Critical Essays in World Literature: J.M. Coetzee* (1998). She has held the positions of Distinguished Visiting Chair in Australian Studies at Copenhagen University (2009) and Dr R. Marika Guest Chair in Australian Studies at the University of Cologne (2013).

PHILIP MEAD is Winthrop Professor and inaugural Chair of Australian Literature at the University of Western Australia. He is the author of *Networked Language: History & Culture in Australian Poetry*, which won the New South Wales Premier's Prize for Literary Scholarship in 2010. His publications include studies of literary education in Australia, Shakespeare memorialization, poetry and inauthenticity, and Australian literature in the world.

STEPHEN MUECKE is Professor of Writing at the University of New South Wales, Australia. Recent publications include, with Max Pam, photographer, *Contingency in Madagascar* (2012) and *Butcher Joe, Documenta 13: 100 Notizen – 100 Gedanken, English/German* (2011).

BEATE NEUMEIER is Professor of English at the University of Cologne. She is the editor of the e-journal *GenderForum* and the database GenderInn. Her research is in gender, performance, and postcolonial studies. She has published on English Renaissance drama as well as contemporary anglophone drama, contemporary British-Jewish literature, and women's writing. Her books include *Jüdische Erfahrung in den Kulturen Großbritanniens und Nordamerikas nach 1945* (1998); *Engendering Realism and Postmodernism: Contemporary Women Writers in Britain* (2001); *Dichotonies: Gender and Music* (2009); and *Gothic Renaissance* (with Elisabeth Bronfen, 2014).

KAY SCHAFFER is an Adjunct Professor in Gender Studies and Social Analysis, School of Social Studies at the University of Adelaide and at the Hawke Research Centre for Sustainable Environment, University of South Australia. Working in the areas of gender studies, cultural studies, and literary studies, she has most recently published *Women Writers in Postsocialist China* (with Xianlin Song 2013), *The Bush, Gender and History: Australian Feminist Perspectives* (2010), and *Human Rights and Narrated Lives: The Ethics of Recognition* (with Sidonie Smith, 2004). She was Dr R. Marika Guest Chair in Australian and Indigenous Studies at the University of Cologne (2010).

KIM SCOTT is Professor of Writing at Curtin University, Western Australia. He is a novelist whose most recent novel, *That Deadman Dance*, has won numerous Australian literary awards. He is also the leader of a community-based project to revitalize his ancestral Australian Aboriginal (Nyungar) language and which has resulted in a number of publications, including *Noongar Mambara Bakitj*, and the website www.wirlomin.com.au.

LISA SLATER is a Lecturer in Cultural Studies at the University of Wollongong, Australia. Her research seeks to understand and critique the processes of neo-colonialism, settler-colonial belonging, and contemporary Indigenous cultural practices, with a particular focus on the ways in which cultural production – most recently cultural festivals – constitutes innovative sites for the expression of Indigenous sovereignty and ethical inter-cultural engagement. She is currently writing a monograph, 'Close to Home: Anxieties of Settler Belonging'.

ELEONORE WILDBURGER is affiliated with the Department of English and American Studies at Klagenfurt University, Austria. She is the author of *Politics, Power and Poetry: An Intercultural Perspective on Aboriginal Identity in Black Australian Poetry* (2003) and *The 'cultural design' of Indigenous Australian art: A cross-cultural perspective* (2010). Her research focuses on Indigenous Australian art and cultures, cross-cultural methodology, cross-cultural communication and competence, and cross-cultural curatorial practices.